ASTRO BOY®

by
Osamu Tezuka

translation
Frederik L. Schodt

lettering and retouch
Sno Cone Studios

Dark Horse Comics®

publisher
MIKE RICHARDSON

editor
CHRIS WARNER

consulting editor
TOREN SMITH for **STUDIO PROTEUS**

collection designers
DAVID NESTELLE and **LANI SCHREIBSTEIN**

English-language version produced by **DARK HORSE COMICS** and **STUDIO PROTEUS**

ASTRO BOY® VOLUME 15

The artwork of this volume has been produced as a mirror-image of the
original Japanese edition to conform to English-language standards.

Published by
Dark Horse Comics, Inc.
10956 SE Main Street
Milwaukie, OR 97222

WWW.DARKHORSE.COM

To find a comics shop in your area, call the Comic Shop Locator Service toll-free
at 1-888-266-4226.

First edition: May 2003
ISBN: 1-56971-896-2

10 9 8 7 6 5 4 3 2 1
Printed in Canada

Table of Contents

A NOTE TO READERS

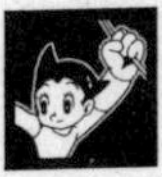

Many non-Japanese, including people from Africa and Southeast Asia, appear in Osamu Tezuka's works. Sometimes these people are depicted very differently from the way they actually are today, in a manner that exaggerates a time long past or shows them to be from extremely undeveloped lands. Some feel that such images contribute to racial discrimination, especially against people of African descent. This was never Osamu Tezuka's intent, but we believe that as long as there are people who feel insulted or demeaned by these depictions, we must not ignore their feelings.

We are against discrimination, in all its forms, and intend to continue to work for its elimination. Nonetheless, we do not believe it would be proper to revise these works. Tezuka is no longer with us, and we cannot erase what he has done, and to alter his work would only violate his rights as a creator. More importantly, stopping publication or changing the content of his work would do little to solve the problems of discrimination that exist in the world.

We are presenting Osamu Tezuka's work as it was originally created, without changes. We do this because we believe it is also important to promote the underlying themes in his work, such as love for mankind and the sanctity of life. We hope that when you, the reader, encounter this work, you will keep in mind the differences in attitudes, then and now, toward discrimination, and that this will contribute to an even greater awareness of such problems.

— Tezuka Productions and Dark Horse Comics

ELECTRO

First appeared in the supplement to the
January 1955 edition of *Shonen* magazine.

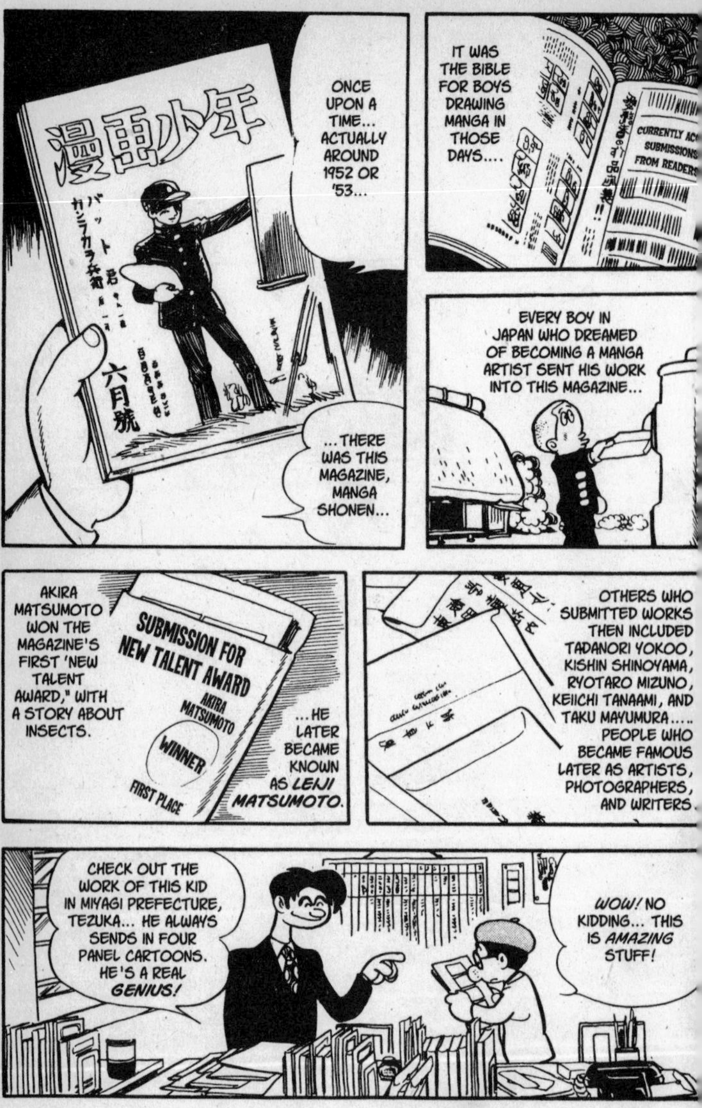
漫画少年
六月號
ONCE UPON A TIME... ACTUALLY AROUND 1952 OR '53...
...THERE WAS THIS MAGAZINE, MANGA SHONEN...
IT WAS THE BIBLE FOR BOYS DRAWING MANGA IN THOSE DAYS....
CURRENTLY AC
SUBMISSIONS
FROM READERS
EVERY BOY IN JAPAN WHO DREAMED OF BECOMING A MANGA ARTIST SENT HIS WORK INTO THIS MAGAZINE...
AKIRA MATSUMOTO WON THE MAGAZINE'S FIRST 'NEW TALENT AWARD," WITH A STORY ABOUT INSECTS.
SUBMISSION FOR NEW TALENT AWARD
AKIRA MATSUMOTO
WINNER
FIRST PLACE
...HE LATER BECAME KNOWN AS *LEIJI MATSUMOTO*.
OTHERS WHO SUBMITTED WORKS THEN INCLUDED TADANORI YOKOO, KISHIN SHINOYAMA, RYOTARO MIZUNO, KEIICHI TANAAMI, AND TAKU MAYUMURA..... PEOPLE WHO BECAME FAMOUS LATER AS ARTISTS, PHOTOGRAPHERS, AND WRITERS.
CHECK OUT THE WORK OF THIS KID IN MIYAGI PREFECTURE, TEZUKA... HE ALWAYS SENDS IN FOUR PANEL CARTOONS. HE'S A REAL *GENIUS!*
WOW! NO KIDDING... THIS IS *AMAZING* STUFF!

WISH I COULD GET HIM TO HELP ME OUT WITH *MY* MANGA...

HIS NAME'S *ONODERA*...

HE'S APPARENTLY THE PRESIDENT OF A BIG MANGA STUDY GROUP IN EASTERN JAPAN...

I'LL SEND HIM A TELEGRAM...

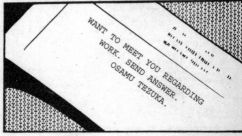

WANT TO MEET YOU REGARDING WORK. SEND ANSWER. OSAMU TEZUKA.

HI. I'M *ONODERA*...

SO *YOU'RE* ONODERA!

LOOKS A BIT LIKE A POTATO..."

I'VE GOTTA TELL YOU.... YOUR DRAWINGS ARE *FANTASTIC!*

JAPANESE INN

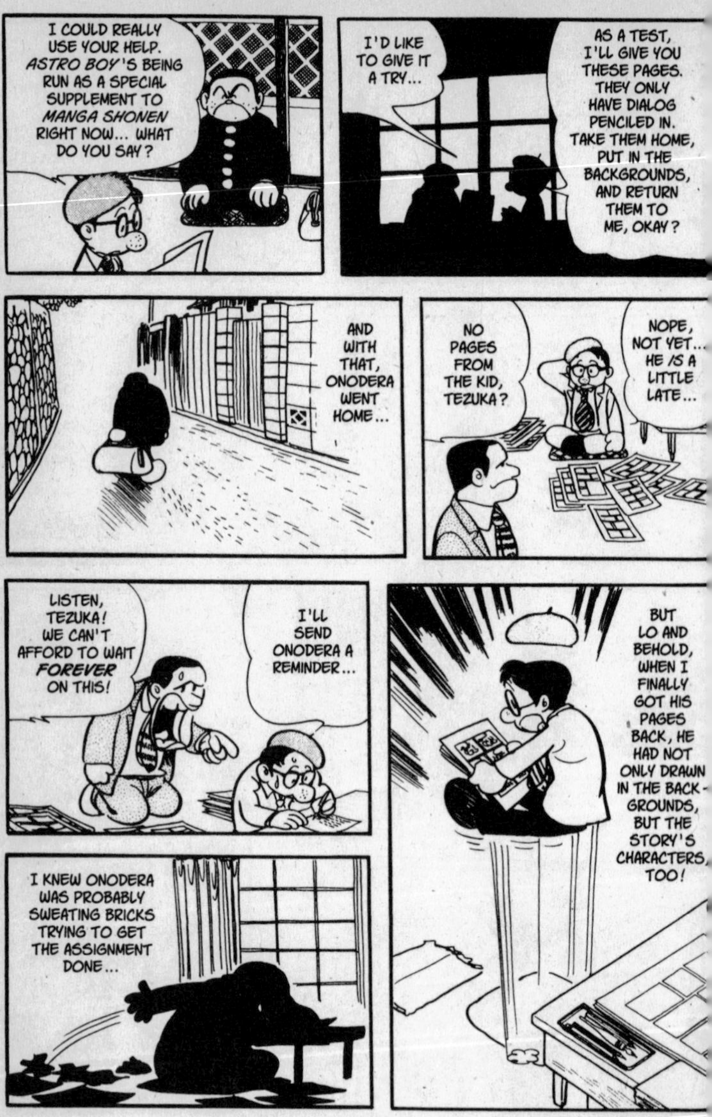
I COULD REALLY USE YOUR HELP. *ASTRO BOY*'S BEING RUN AS A SPECIAL SUPPLEMENT TO *MANGA SHONEN* RIGHT NOW... WHAT DO YOU SAY?
I'D LIKE TO GIVE IT A TRY...
AS A TEST, I'LL GIVE YOU THESE PAGES. THEY ONLY HAVE DIALOG PENCILED IN. TAKE THEM HOME, PUT IN THE BACKGROUNDS, AND RETURN THEM TO ME, OKAY?
AND WITH THAT, ONODERA WENT HOME...
NO PAGES FROM THE KID, TEZUKA?
NOPE, NOT YET... HE *IS* A LITTLE LATE...
LISTEN, TEZUKA! WE CAN'T AFFORD TO WAIT **FOREVER** ON THIS!
I'LL SEND ONODERA A REMINDER...
I KNEW ONODERA WAS PROBABLY SWEATING BRICKS TRYING TO GET THE ASSIGNMENT DONE...
BUT LO AND BEHOLD, WHEN I FINALLY GOT HIS PAGES BACK, HE HAD NOT ONLY DRAWN IN THE BACKGROUNDS, BUT THE STORY'S CHARACTERS, TOO!

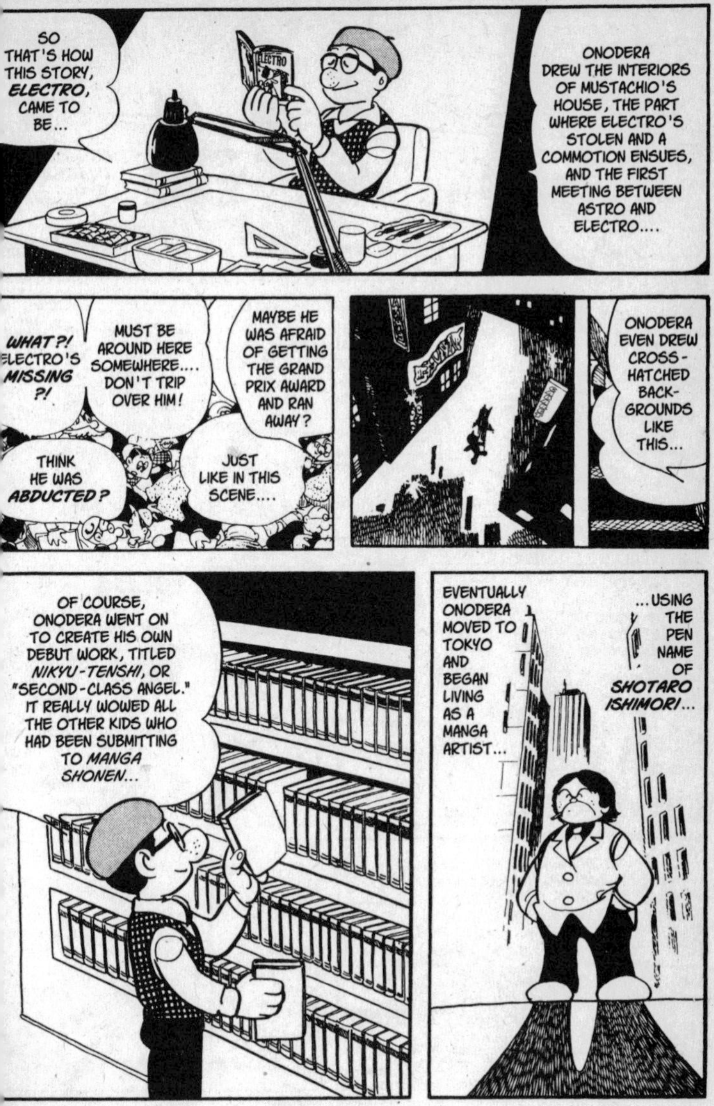
SO THAT'S HOW THIS STORY, ELECTRO, CAME TO BE...
ELECTRO
ONODERA DREW THE INTERIORS OF MUSTACHIO'S HOUSE, THE PART WHERE ELECTRO'S STOLEN AND A COMMOTION ENSUES, AND THE FIRST MEETING BETWEEN ASTRO AND ELECTRO....
WHAT?! ELECTRO'S MISSING?!
MUST BE AROUND HERE SOMEWHERE.... DON'T TRIP OVER HIM!
MAYBE HE WAS AFRAID OF GETTING THE GRAND PRIX AWARD AND RAN AWAY?
THINK HE WAS ABDUCTED?
JUST LIKE IN THIS SCENE....
ONODERA EVEN DREW CROSS-HATCHED BACK-GROUNDS LIKE THIS...
OF COURSE, ONODERA WENT ON TO CREATE HIS OWN DEBUT WORK, TITLED NIKYU-TENSHI, OR "SECOND-CLASS ANGEL." IT REALLY WOWED ALL THE OTHER KIDS WHO HAD BEEN SUBMITTING TO MANGA SHONEN...
EVENTUALLY ONODERA MOVED TO TOKYO AND BEGAN LIVING AS A MANGA ARTIST...
...USING THE PEN NAME OF SHOTARO ISHIMORI...

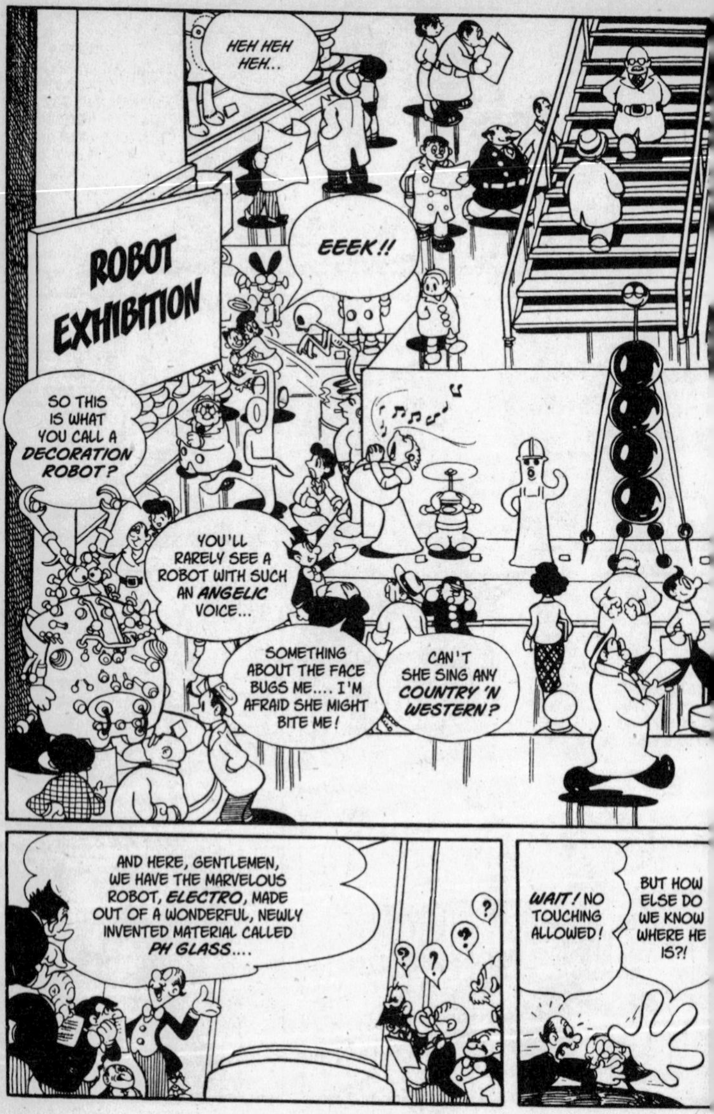
HEH HEH HEH...
EEEK!!
ROBOT EXHIBITION
SO THIS IS WHAT YOU CALL A DECORATION ROBOT?
YOU'LL RARELY SEE A ROBOT WITH SUCH AN ANGELIC VOICE...
SOMETHING ABOUT THE FACE BUGS ME.... I'M AFRAID SHE MIGHT BITE ME!
CAN'T SHE SING ANY COUNTRY 'N WESTERN?
AND HERE, GENTLEMEN, WE HAVE THE MARVELOUS ROBOT, ELECTRO, MADE OUT OF A WONDERFUL, NEWLY INVENTED MATERIAL CALLED PH GLASS....
?
?
?
?
WAIT! NO TOUCHING ALLOWED!
BUT HOW ELSE DO WE KNOW WHERE HE IS?!

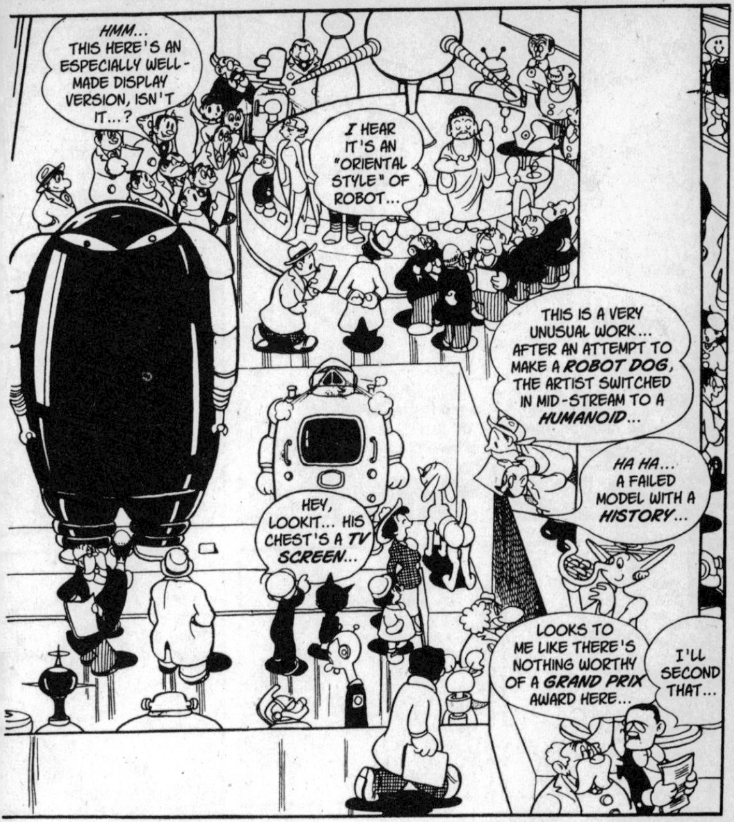
HMM... THIS HERE'S AN ESPECIALLY WELL-MADE DISPLAY VERSION, ISN'T IT...?
I HEAR IT'S AN "ORIENTAL STYLE" OF ROBOT...
THIS IS A VERY UNUSUAL WORK... AFTER AN ATTEMPT TO MAKE A ROBOT DOG, THE ARTIST SWITCHED IN MID-STREAM TO A HUMANOID...
HA HA... A FAILED MODEL WITH A HISTORY...
HEY, LOOKIT... HIS CHEST'S A TV SCREEN...
LOOKS TO ME LIKE THERE'S NOTHING WORTHY OF A GRAND PRIX AWARD HERE...
I'LL SECOND THAT...
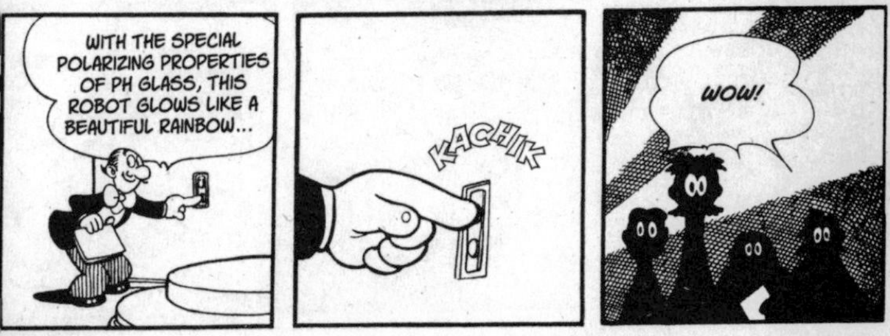
WITH THE SPECIAL POLARIZING PROPERTIES OF PH GLASS, THIS ROBOT GLOWS LIKE A BEAUTIFUL RAINBOW...
KACHIK
WOW!

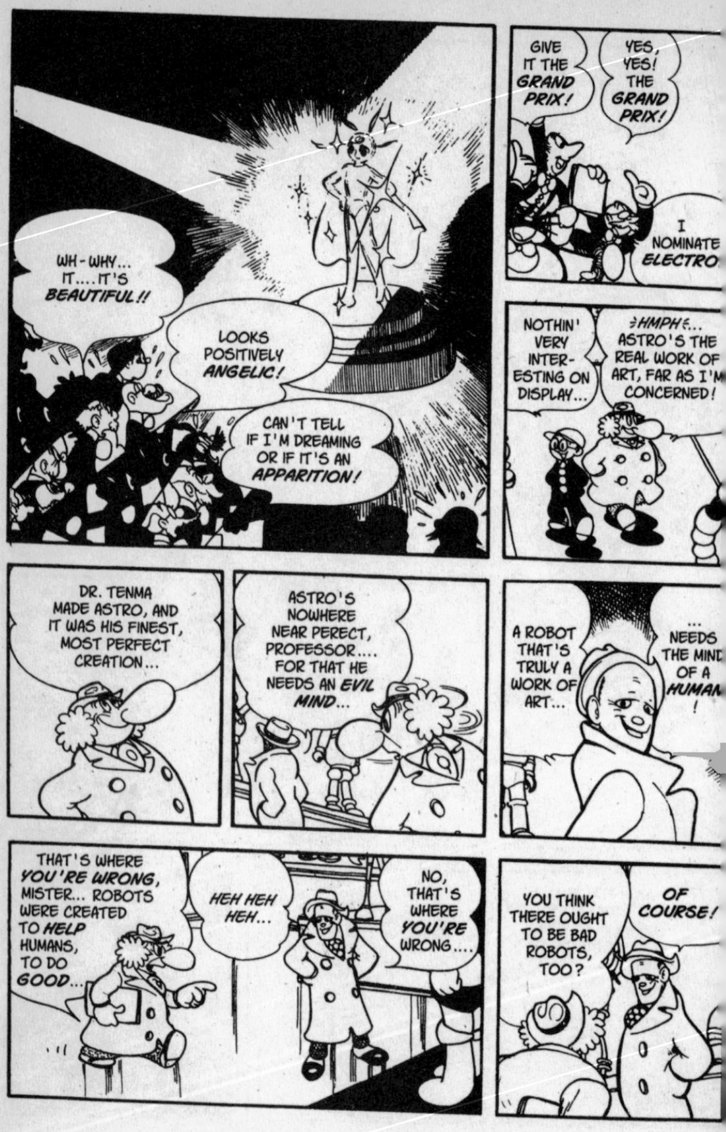

WH-WHY... IT.... IT'S BEAUTIFUL!!
LOOKS POSITIVELY ANGELIC!
CAN'T TELL IF I'M DREAMING OR IF IT'S AN APPARITION!
GIVE IT THE GRAND PRIX!
YES, YES! THE GRAND PRIX!
I NOMINATE ELECTRO
NOTHIN' VERY INTER-ESTING ON DISPLAY...
HMPH... ASTRO'S THE REAL WORK OF ART, FAR AS I'M CONCERNED!
DR. TENMA MADE ASTRO, AND IT WAS HIS FINEST, MOST PERFECT CREATION...
ASTRO'S NOWHERE NEAR PERECT, PROFESSOR.... FOR THAT HE NEEDS AN EVIL MIND...
A ROBOT THAT'S TRULY A WORK OF ART...
... NEEDS THE MIND OF A HUMAN !
THAT'S WHERE YOU'RE WRONG, MISTER... ROBOTS WERE CREATED TO HELP HUMANS, TO DO GOOD...
HEH HEH HEH...
NO, THAT'S WHERE YOU'RE WRONG....
YOU THINK THERE OUGHT TO BE BAD ROBOTS, TOO?
OF COURSE!

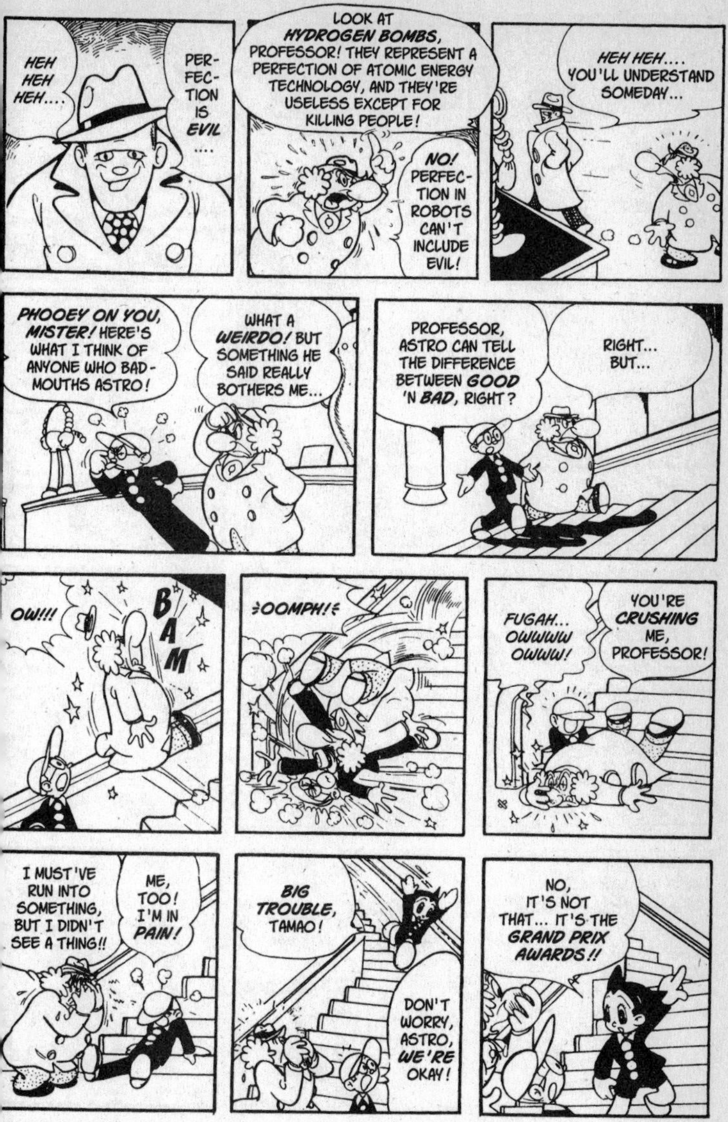
HEH HEH HEH....
PER-FEC-TION IS EVIL ....
LOOK AT HYDROGEN BOMBS, PROFESSOR! THEY REPRESENT A PERFECTION OF ATOMIC ENERGY TECHNOLOGY, AND THEY'RE USELESS EXCEPT FOR KILLING PEOPLE!
NO! PERFEC-TION IN ROBOTS CAN'T INCLUDE EVIL!
HEH HEH.... YOU'LL UNDERSTAND SOMEDAY...
PHOOEY ON YOU, MISTER! HERE'S WHAT I THINK OF ANYONE WHO BAD-MOUTHS ASTRO!
WHAT A WEIRDO! BUT SOMETHING HE SAID REALLY BOTHERS ME...
PROFESSOR, ASTRO CAN TELL THE DIFFERENCE BETWEEN GOOD 'N BAD, RIGHT?
RIGHT... BUT...
OW!!!
BAM
OOMPH!
FUGAH... OWWWW OWWW!
YOU'RE CRUSHING ME, PROFESSOR!
I MUST'VE RUN INTO SOMETHING, BUT I DIDN'T SEE A THING!!
ME, TOO! I'M IN PAIN!
BIG TROUBLE, TAMAO!
DON'T WORRY, ASTRO, WE'RE OKAY!
NO, IT'S NOT THAT... IT'S THE GRAND PRIX AWARDS!!

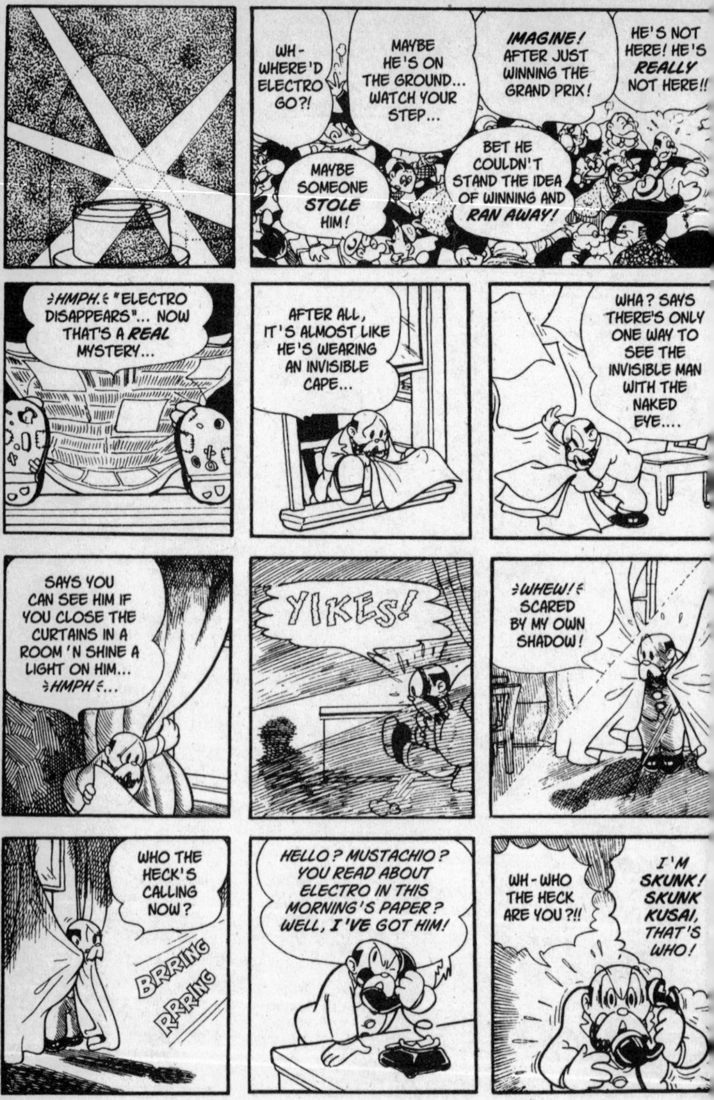
WH- WHERE'D ELECTRO GO?!
MAYBE HE'S ON THE GROUND... WATCH YOUR STEP...
MAYBE SOMEONE STOLE HIM!
IMAGINE! AFTER JUST WINNING THE GRAND PRIX!
BET HE COULDN'T STAND THE IDEA OF WINNING AND RAN AWAY!
HE'S NOT HERE! HE'S REALLY NOT HERE!!
HMPH. "ELECTRO DISAPPEARS"... NOW THAT'S A REAL MYSTERY...
AFTER ALL, IT'S ALMOST LIKE HE'S WEARING AN INVISIBLE CAPE...
WHA? SAYS THERE'S ONLY ONE WAY TO SEE THE INVISIBLE MAN WITH THE NAKED EYE....
SAYS YOU CAN SEE HIM IF YOU CLOSE THE CURTAINS IN A ROOM 'N SHINE A LIGHT ON HIM... HMPH...
YIKES!
WHEW! SCARED BY MY OWN SHADOW!
WHO THE HECK'S CALLING NOW?
BRRING
RRRING
HELLO? MUSTACHIO? YOU READ ABOUT ELECTRO IN THIS MORNING'S PAPER? WELL, I'VE GOT HIM!
WH-WHO THE HECK ARE YOU?!!
I'M SKUNK! SKUNK KUSAI, THAT'S WHO!

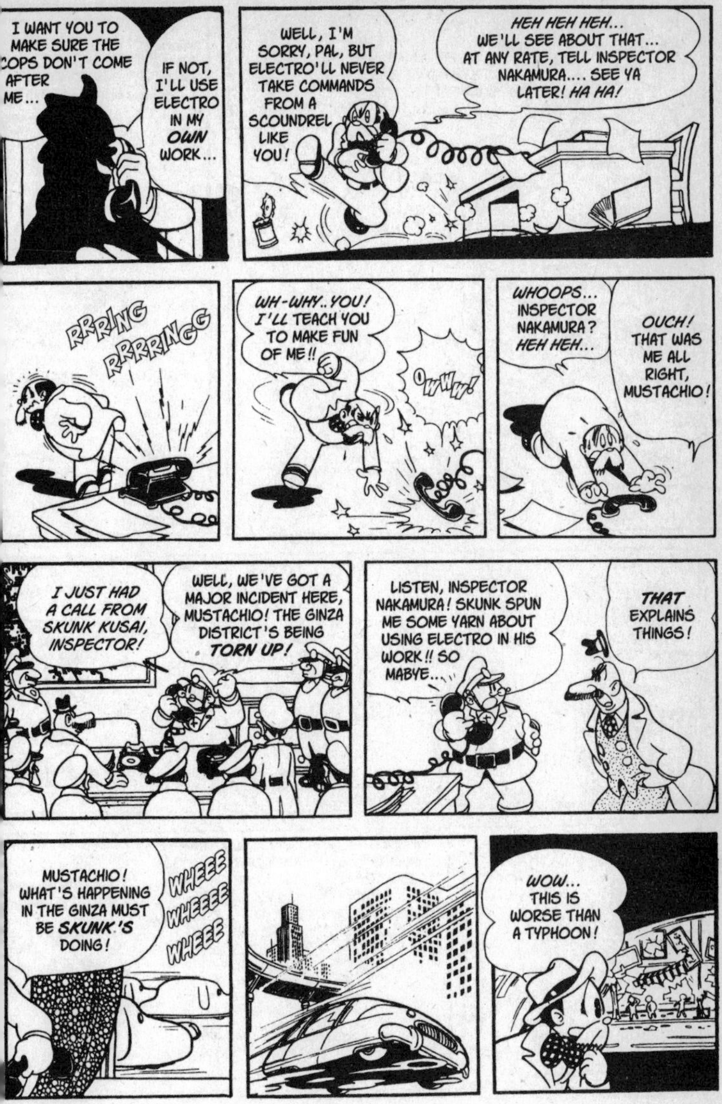
I WANT YOU TO MAKE SURE THE COPS DON'T COME AFTER ME...
IF NOT, I'LL USE ELECTRO IN MY *OWN* WORK...
WELL, I'M SORRY, PAL, BUT ELECTRO'LL NEVER TAKE COMMANDS FROM A SCOUNDREL LIKE YOU!
HEH HEH HEH... WE'LL SEE ABOUT THAT... AT ANY RATE, TELL INSPECTOR NAKAMURA.... SEE YA LATER! *HA HA!*
RRRING
RRRRINGG
WH-WHY..YOU! I'LL TEACH YOU TO MAKE FUN OF ME!!
OWWW!
WHOOPS... INSPECTOR NAKAMURA? *HEH HEH...*
OUCH! THAT WAS ME ALL RIGHT, MUSTACHIO!
I JUST HAD A CALL FROM SKUNK KUSAI, INSPECTOR!
WELL, WE'VE GOT A MAJOR INCIDENT HERE, MUSTACHIO! THE GINZA DISTRICT'S BEING *TORN UP!*
LISTEN, INSPECTOR NAKAMURA! SKUNK SPUN ME SOME YARN ABOUT USING ELECTRO IN HIS WORK!! SO MABYE...
THAT EXPLAINS THINGS!
MUSTACHIO! WHAT'S HAPPENING IN THE GINZA MUST BE *SKUNK'S* DOING!
WHEEE
WHEEEE
WHEEE
WOW... THIS IS WORSE THAN A TYPHOON!

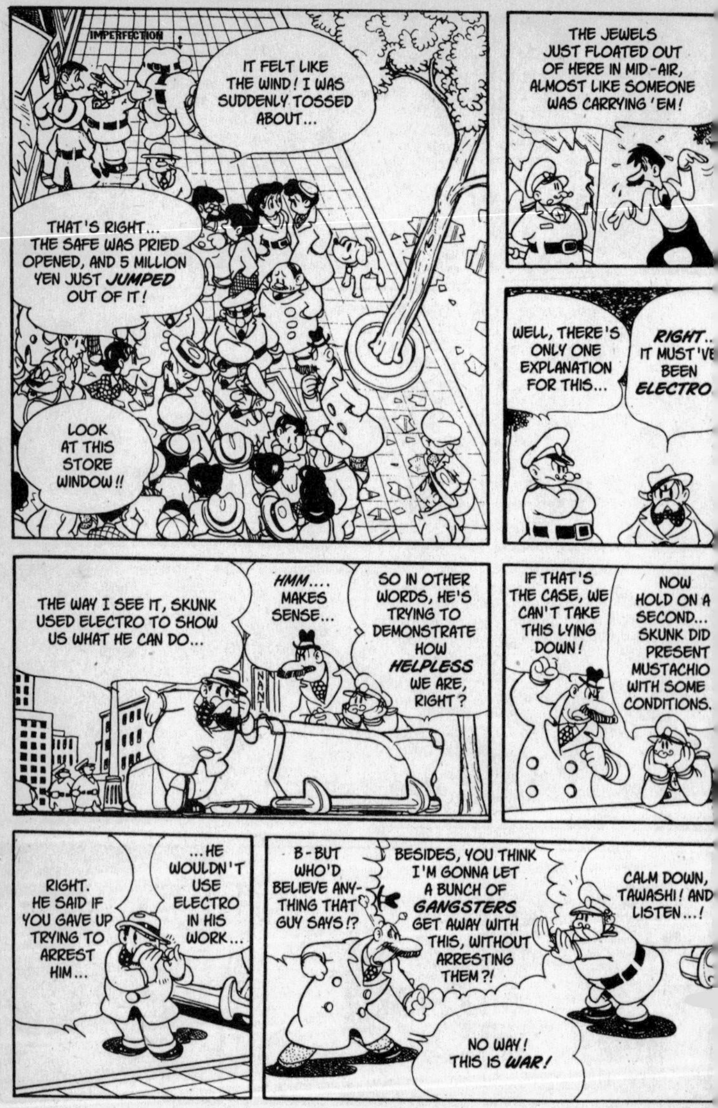
IMPERFECTION
IT FELT LIKE THE WIND! I WAS SUDDENLY TOSSED ABOUT...
THAT'S RIGHT... THE SAFE WAS PRIED OPENED, AND 5 MILLION YEN JUST *JUMPED* OUT OF IT!
LOOK AT THIS STORE WINDOW!!
THE JEWELS JUST FLOATED OUT OF HERE IN MID-AIR, ALMOST LIKE SOMEONE WAS CARRYING 'EM!
WELL, THERE'S ONLY ONE EXPLANATION FOR THIS...
RIGHT... IT MUST'VE BEEN *ELECTRO*.
THE WAY I SEE IT, SKUNK USED ELECTRO TO SHOW US WHAT HE CAN DO...
HMM.... MAKES SENSE...
SO IN OTHER WORDS, HE'S TRYING TO DEMONSTRATE HOW *HELPLESS* WE ARE, RIGHT?
IF THAT'S THE CASE, WE CAN'T TAKE THIS LYING DOWN!
NOW HOLD ON A SECOND... SKUNK DID PRESENT MUSTACHIO WITH SOME CONDITIONS.
RIGHT. HE SAID IF YOU GAVE UP TRYING TO ARREST HIM...
...HE WOULDN'T USE ELECTRO IN HIS WORK...
B-BUT WHO'D BELIEVE ANY-THING THAT GUY SAYS!?
BESIDES, YOU THINK I'M GONNA LET A BUNCH OF *GANGSTERS* GET AWAY WITH THIS, WITHOUT ARRESTING THEM?!
CALM DOWN, TAWASHI! AND LISTEN...!
NO WAY! THIS IS *WAR*!

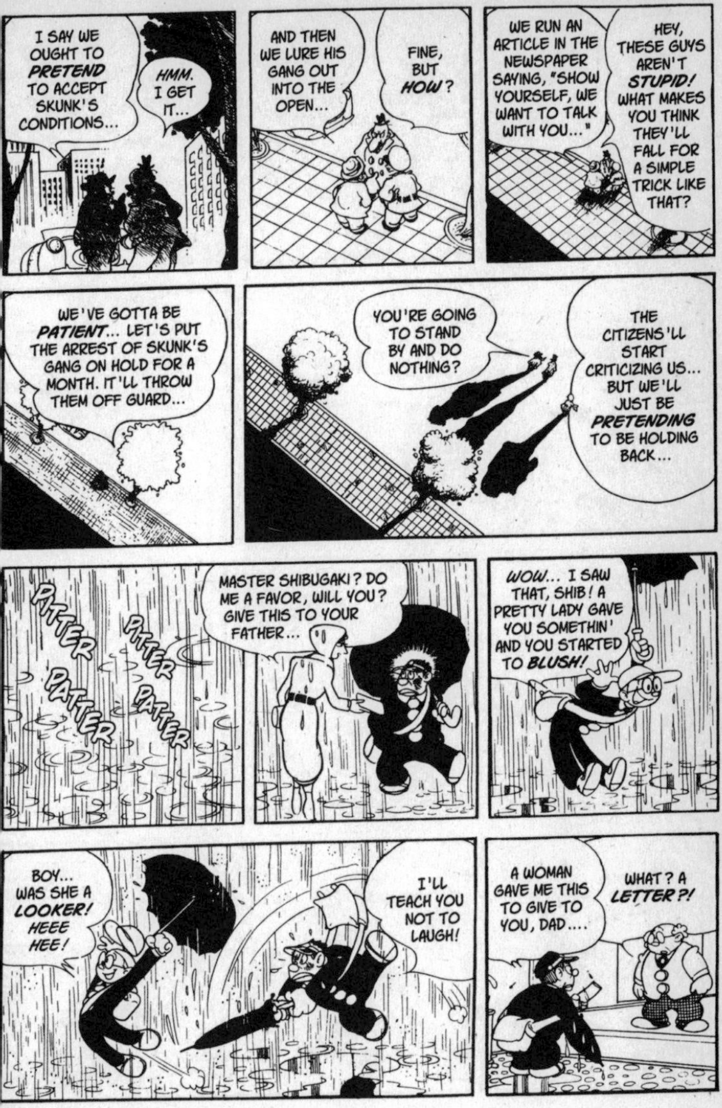
I SAY WE OUGHT TO *PRETEND* TO ACCEPT SKUNK'S CONDITIONS...
HMM. I GET IT...
AND THEN WE LURE HIS GANG OUT INTO THE OPEN...
FINE, BUT *HOW*?
WE RUN AN ARTICLE IN THE NEWSPAPER SAYING, "SHOW YOURSELF, WE WANT TO TALK WITH YOU..."
HEY, THESE GUYS AREN'T *STUPID!* WHAT MAKES YOU THINK THEY'LL FALL FOR A SIMPLE TRICK LIKE THAT?
WE'VE GOTTA BE *PATIENT*... LET'S PUT THE ARREST OF SKUNK'S GANG ON HOLD FOR A MONTH. IT'LL THROW THEM OFF GUARD...
YOU'RE GOING TO STAND BY AND DO NOTHING?
THE CITIZENS'LL START CRITICIZING US... BUT WE'LL JUST BE *PRETENDING* TO BE HOLDING BACK...
PITTER PATTER
PITTER PATTER
MASTER SHIBUGAKI? DO ME A FAVOR, WILL YOU? GIVE THIS TO YOUR FATHER...
WOW... I SAW THAT, SHIB! A PRETTY LADY GAVE YOU SOMETHIN' AND YOU STARTED TO *BLUSH!*
BOY... WAS SHE A *LOOKER! HEEE HEE!*
I'LL TEACH YOU NOT TO LAUGH!
A WOMAN GAVE ME THIS TO GIVE TO YOU, DAD....
WHAT? A *LETTER?!*

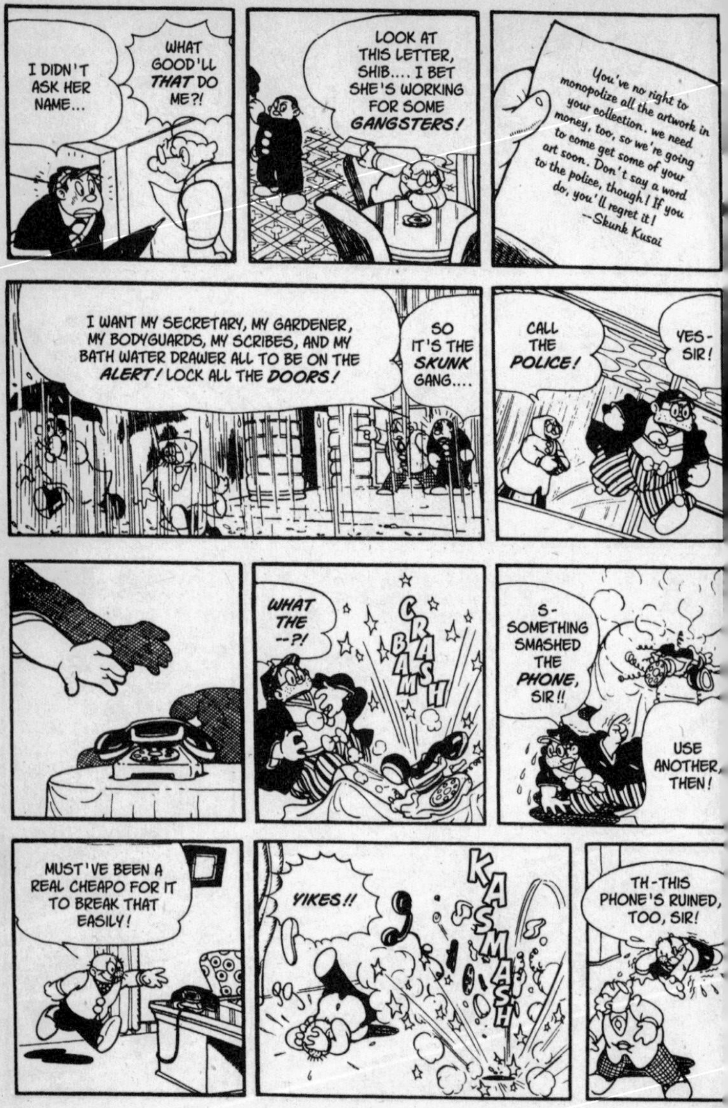
I DIDN'T ASK HER NAME...
WHAT GOOD'LL THAT DO ME?!
LOOK AT THIS LETTER, SHIB.... I BET SHE'S WORKING FOR SOME GANGSTERS!
You've no right to monopolize all the artwork in your collection. we need money, too, so we're going to come get some of your art soon. Don't say a word to the police, though! If you do, you'll regret it!
--Skunk Kusai
I WANT MY SECRETARY, MY GARDENER, MY BODYGUARDS, MY SCRIBES, AND MY BATH WATER DRAWER ALL TO BE ON THE ALERT! LOCK ALL THE DOORS!
SO IT'S THE SKUNK GANG....
CALL THE POLICE!
YES-SIR!
WHAT THE --?!
CRASH
BAM
S-SOMETHING SMASHED THE PHONE, SIR!!
USE ANOTHER, THEN!
MUST'VE BEEN A REAL CHEAPO FOR IT TO BREAK THAT EASILY!
YIKES!!
KASMASH
TH-THIS PHONE'S RUINED, TOO, SIR!

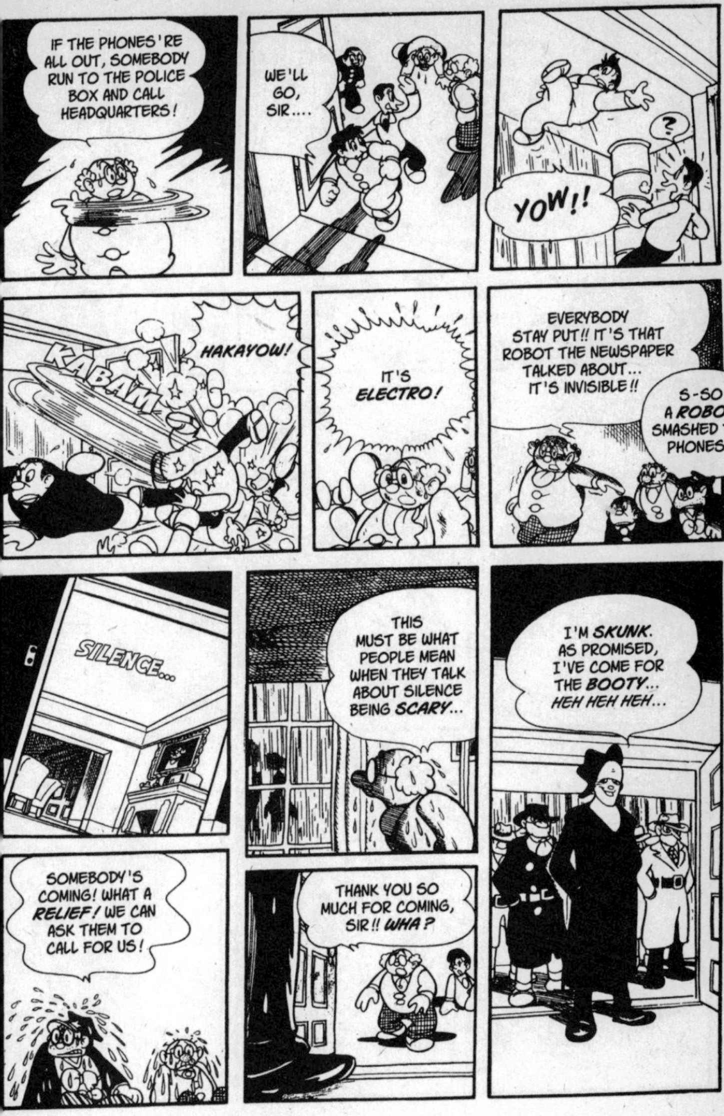
IF THE PHONES'RE ALL OUT, SOMEBODY RUN TO THE POLICE BOX AND CALL HEADQUARTERS!
WE'LL GO, SIR....
?
YOW!!
KABAM
HAKAYOW!
IT'S ELECTRO!
EVERYBODY STAY PUT!! IT'S THAT ROBOT THE NEWSPAPER TALKED ABOUT... IT'S INVISIBLE!!
S-SO A ROBOT SMASHED THE PHONES?!!
SILENCE...
THIS MUST BE WHAT PEOPLE MEAN WHEN THEY TALK ABOUT SILENCE BEING SCARY...
I'M SKUNK. AS PROMISED, I'VE COME FOR THE BOOTY... HEH HEH HEH...
SOMEBODY'S COMING! WHAT A RELIEF! WE CAN ASK THEM TO CALL FOR US!
THANK YOU SO MUCH FOR COMING, SIR!! WHA?

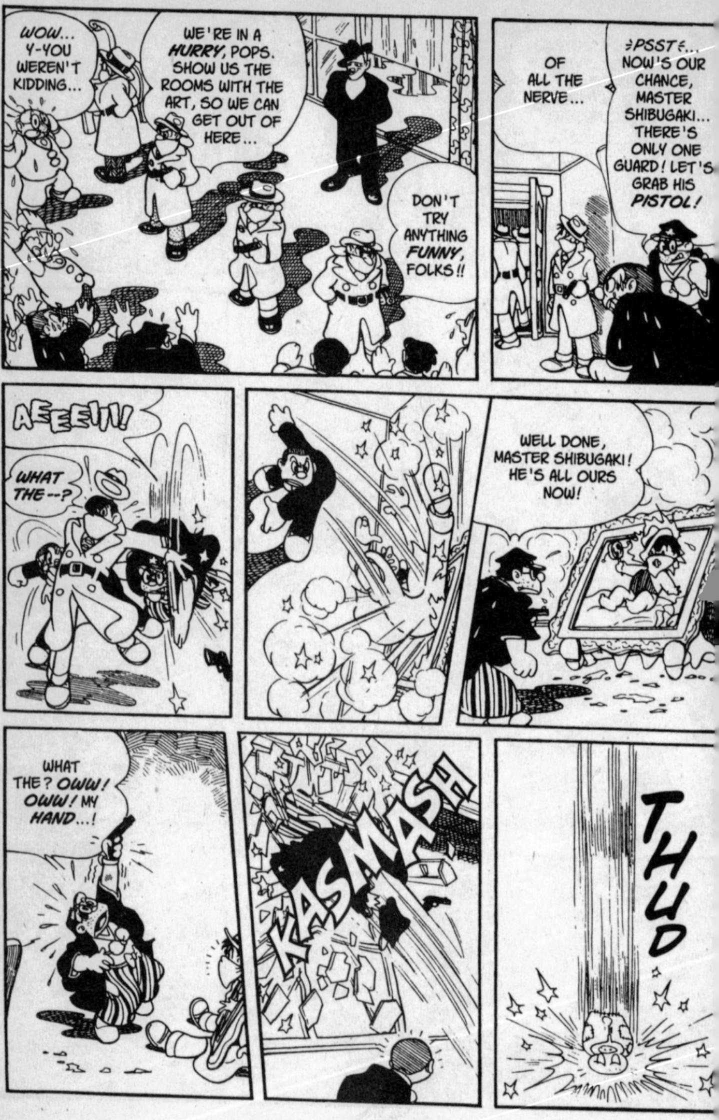

WOW... Y-YOU WEREN'T KIDDING...
WE'RE IN A HURRY, POPS. SHOW US THE ROOMS WITH THE ART, SO WE CAN GET OUT OF HERE...
DON'T TRY ANYTHING FUNNY, FOLKS!!
OF ALL THE NERVE...
PSST... NOW'S OUR CHANCE, MASTER SHIBUGAKI... THERE'S ONLY ONE GUARD! LET'S GRAB HIS PISTOL!
AEEEIII!
WHAT THE--?
WELL DONE, MASTER SHIBUGAKI! HE'S ALL OURS NOW!
WHAT THE? OWW! OWW! MY HAND...!
KASMASH
THUD

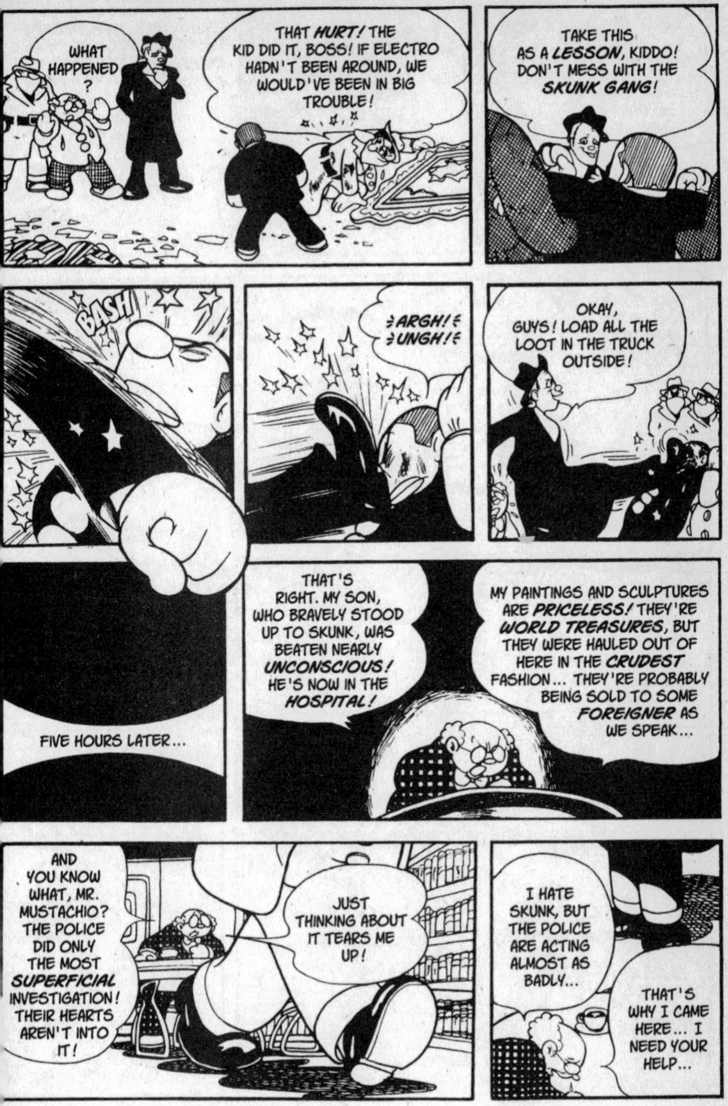
WHAT HAPPENED ?
THAT HURT! THE KID DID IT, BOSS! IF ELECTRO HADN'T BEEN AROUND, WE WOULD'VE BEEN IN BIG TROUBLE!
TAKE THIS AS A LESSON, KIDDO! DON'T MESS WITH THE SKUNK GANG!
BASH
ARGH! UNGH!
OKAY, GUYS! LOAD ALL THE LOOT IN THE TRUCK OUTSIDE!
FIVE HOURS LATER...
THAT'S RIGHT. MY SON, WHO BRAVELY STOOD UP TO SKUNK, WAS BEATEN NEARLY UNCONSCIOUS! HE'S NOW IN THE HOSPITAL!
MY PAINTINGS AND SCULPTURES ARE PRICELESS! THEY'RE WORLD TREASURES, BUT THEY WERE HAULED OUT OF HERE IN THE CRUDEST FASHION... THEY'RE PROBABLY BEING SOLD TO SOME FOREIGNER AS WE SPEAK...
AND YOU KNOW WHAT, MR. MUSTACHIO? THE POLICE DID ONLY THE MOST SUPERFICIAL INVESTIGATION! THEIR HEARTS AREN'T INTO IT!
JUST THINKING ABOUT IT TEARS ME UP!
I HATE SKUNK, BUT THE POLICE ARE ACTING ALMOST AS BADLY...
THAT'S WHY I CAME HERE... I NEED YOUR HELP...

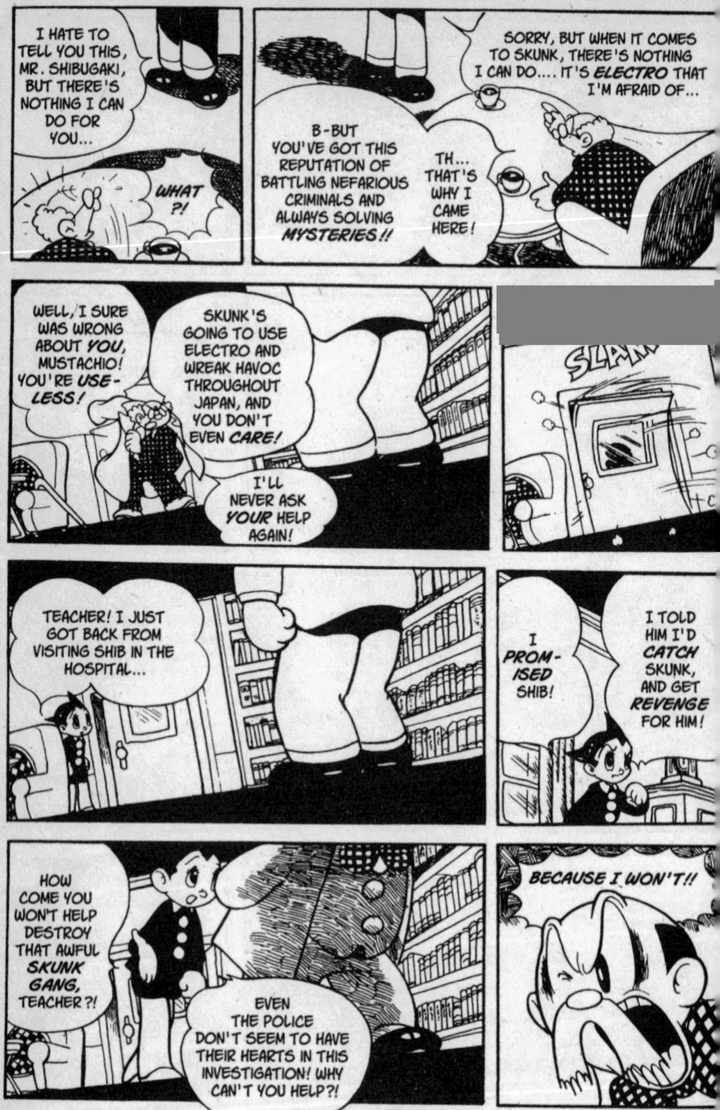
I HATE TO TELL YOU THIS, MR. SHIBUGAKI, BUT THERE'S NOTHING I CAN DO FOR YOU...
WHAT ?!
SORRY, BUT WHEN IT COMES TO SKUNK, THERE'S NOTHING I CAN DO.... IT'S ELECTRO THAT I'M AFRAID OF...
B-BUT YOU'VE GOT THIS REPUTATION OF BATTLING NEFARIOUS CRIMINALS AND ALWAYS SOLVING MYSTERIES!!
TH... THAT'S WHY I CAME HERE!
WELL, I SURE WAS WRONG ABOUT YOU, MUSTACHIO! YOU'RE USE-LESS!
SKUNK'S GOING TO USE ELECTRO AND WREAK HAVOC THROUGHOUT JAPAN, AND YOU DON'T EVEN CARE!
I'LL NEVER ASK YOUR HELP AGAIN!
TEACHER! I JUST GOT BACK FROM VISITING SHIB IN THE HOSPITAL...
I PROM-ISED SHIB!
I TOLD HIM I'D CATCH SKUNK, AND GET REVENGE FOR HIM!
HOW COME YOU WON'T HELP DESTROY THAT AWFUL SKUNK GANG, TEACHER?!
EVEN THE POLICE DON'T SEEM TO HAVE THEIR HEARTS IN THIS INVESTIGATION! WHY CAN'T YOU HELP?!
BECAUSE I WON'T!!

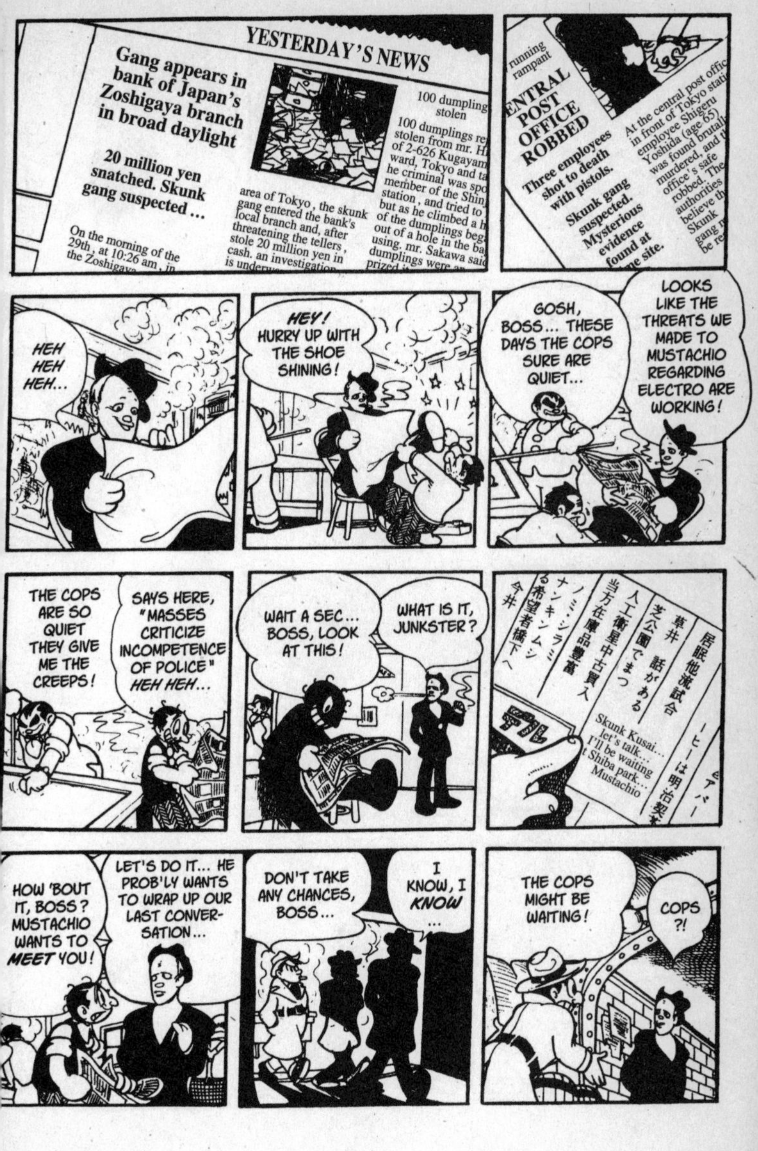

YESTERDAY'S NEWS
Gang appears in bank of Japan's Zoshigaya branch in broad daylight
20 million yen snatched. Skunk gang suspected ...
On the morning of the 29th, at 10:26 am, in the Zoshigaya
area of Tokyo, the skunk gang entered the bank's local branch and, after threatening the tellers, stole 20 million yen in cash. an investigation is underw
100 dumpling stolen
100 dumplings re stolen from mr. H of 2-626 Kugayam ward, Tokyo and ta he criminal was spo member of the Shin station, and tried to but as he climbed a h of the dumplings beg out of a hole in the ba using. mr. Sakawa said dumplings were an prized it
running rampant
ENTRAL POST OFFICE ROBBED
Three employees shot to death with pistols.
Skunk gang suspected. Mysterious evidence found at ne site.
At the central post offic in front of Tokyo stati employee Shigeru Yoshida (age 65) was found brutall murdered, and th office's safe robbed. The authorities believe th Skunk gang m be re
HEH HEH HEH...
HEY! HURRY UP WITH THE SHOE SHINING!
GOSH, BOSS... THESE DAYS THE COPS SURE ARE QUIET...
LOOKS LIKE THE THREATS WE MADE TO MUSTACHIO REGARDING ELECTRO ARE WORKING!
THE COPS ARE SO QUIET THEY GIVE ME THE CREEPS!
SAYS HERE, "MASSES CRITICIZE INCOMPETENCE OF POLICE" HEH HEH...
WAIT A SEC... BOSS, LOOK AT THIS!
WHAT IS IT, JUNKSTER?
居眠他流試合
草井 話がある
芝公園でまつ
人工衛星中古買入
当方在庫品豊富
ノミ・シラミ
ナンキンムシ
る希望者橋下へ
今井
ーヒーは明治製
Skunk Kusai... let's talk... I'll be waiting t Shiba park... Mustachio
HOW 'BOUT IT, BOSS? MUSTACHIO WANTS TO MEET YOU!
LET'S DO IT... HE PROB'LY WANTS TO WRAP UP OUR LAST CONVERSATION...
DON'T TAKE ANY CHANCES, BOSS...
I KNOW, I KNOW ...
THE COPS MIGHT BE WAITING!
COPS ?!

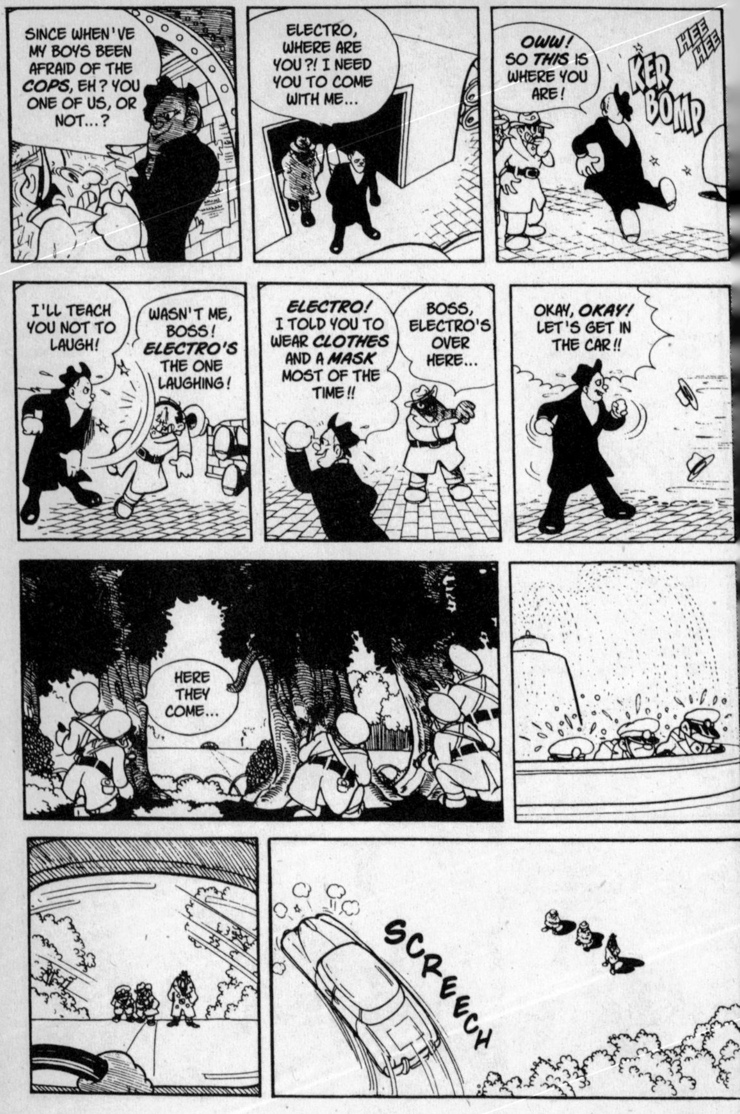
SINCE WHEN'VE MY BOYS BEEN AFRAID OF THE COPS, EH? YOU ONE OF US, OR NOT...?
ELECTRO, WHERE ARE YOU?! I NEED YOU TO COME WITH ME...
OWW! SO THIS IS WHERE YOU ARE!
HEE HEE
KER BOMP
I'LL TEACH YOU NOT TO LAUGH!
WASN'T ME, BOSS! ELECTRO'S THE ONE LAUGHING!
ELECTRO! I TOLD YOU TO WEAR CLOTHES AND A MASK MOST OF THE TIME!!
BOSS, ELECTRO'S OVER HERE...
OKAY, OKAY! LET'S GET IN THE CAR!!
HERE THEY COME...
SCREECH

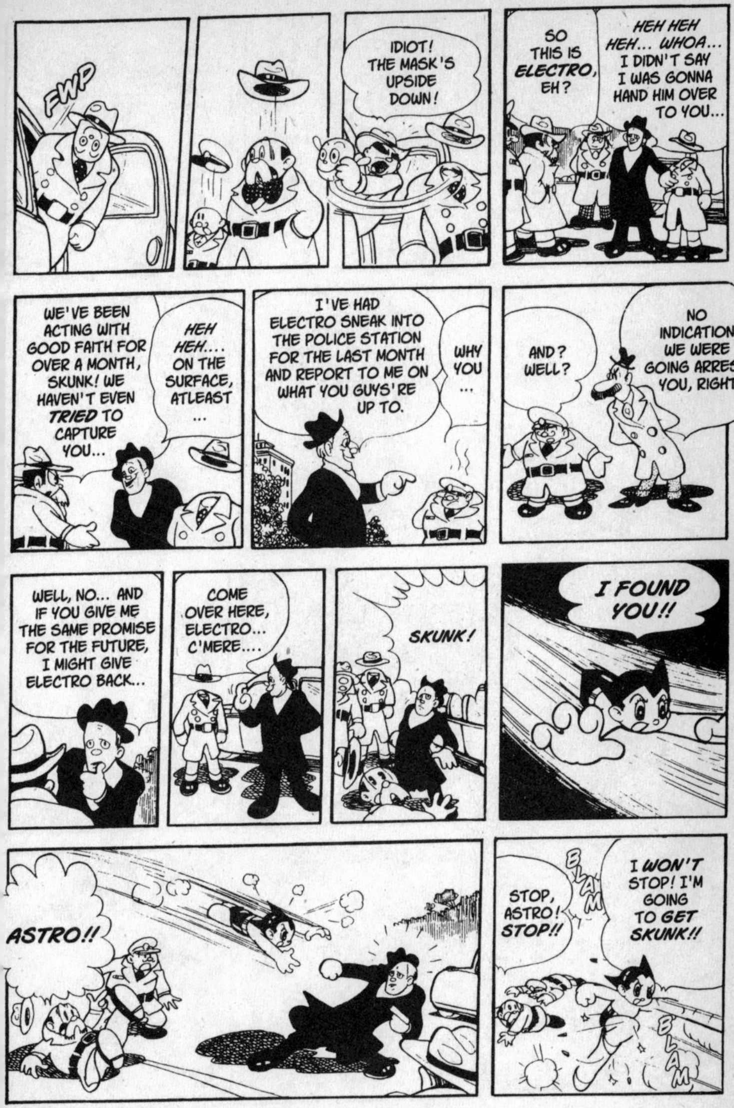
FWP
IDIOT! THE MASK'S UPSIDE DOWN!
SO THIS IS ELECTRO, EH?
HEH HEH HEH... WHOA... I DIDN'T SAY I WAS GONNA HAND HIM OVER TO YOU...
WE'VE BEEN ACTING WITH GOOD FAITH FOR OVER A MONTH, SKUNK! WE HAVEN'T EVEN TRIED TO CAPTURE YOU...
HEH HEH.... ON THE SURFACE, ATLEAST ...
I'VE HAD ELECTRO SNEAK INTO THE POLICE STATION FOR THE LAST MONTH AND REPORT TO ME ON WHAT YOU GUYS'RE UP TO.
WHY YOU ...
AND? WELL?
NO INDICATION WE WERE GOING ARREST YOU, RIGHT?
WELL, NO... AND IF YOU GIVE ME THE SAME PROMISE FOR THE FUTURE, I MIGHT GIVE ELECTRO BACK...
COME OVER HERE, ELECTRO... C'MERE....
SKUNK!
I FOUND YOU!!
ASTRO!!
BLAM
STOP, ASTRO! STOP!!
I WON'T STOP! I'M GOING TO GET SKUNK!!
BLAM

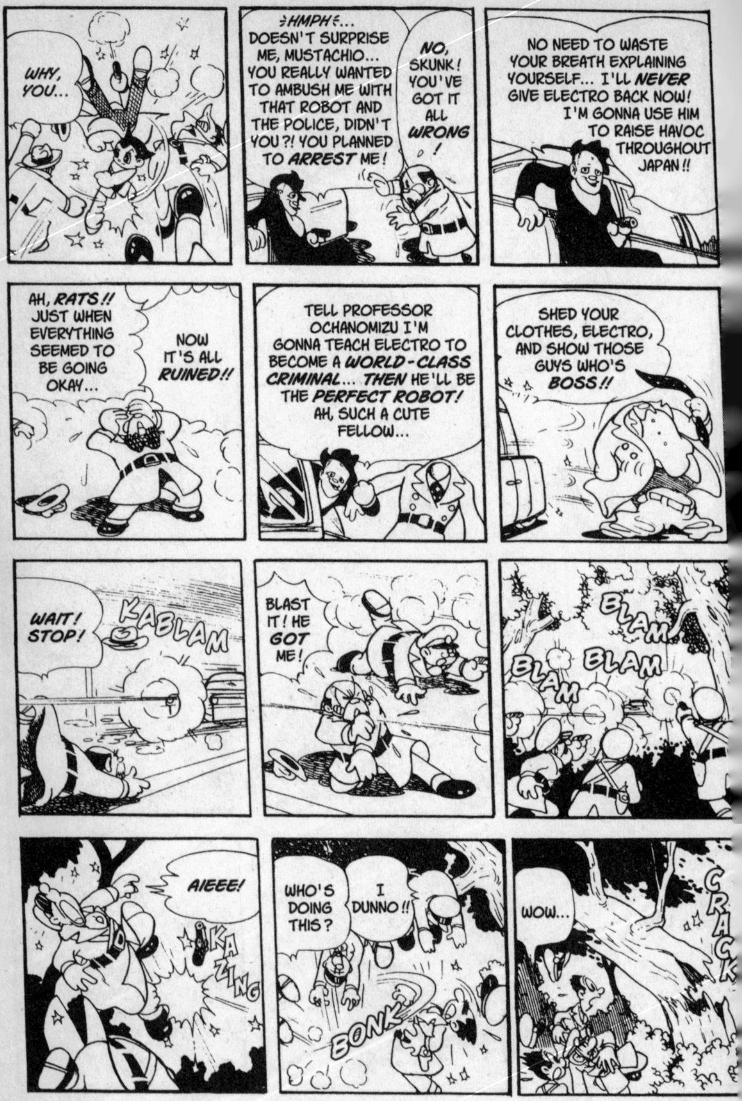
WHY, YOU...
HMPH... DOESN'T SURPRISE ME, MUSTACHIO... YOU REALLY WANTED TO AMBUSH ME WITH THAT ROBOT AND THE POLICE, DIDN'T YOU?! YOU PLANNED TO ARREST ME!
NO, SKUNK! YOU'VE GOT IT ALL WRONG!
NO NEED TO WASTE YOUR BREATH EXPLAINING YOURSELF... I'LL NEVER GIVE ELECTRO BACK NOW! I'M GONNA USE HIM TO RAISE HAVOC THROUGHOUT JAPAN!!
AH, RATS!! JUST WHEN EVERYTHING SEEMED TO BE GOING OKAY...
NOW IT'S ALL RUINED!!
TELL PROFESSOR OCHANOMIZU I'M GONNA TEACH ELECTRO TO BECOME A WORLD-CLASS CRIMINAL... THEN HE'LL BE THE PERFECT ROBOT! AH, SUCH A CUTE FELLOW...
SHED YOUR CLOTHES, ELECTRO, AND SHOW THOSE GUYS WHO'S BOSS!!
WAIT! STOP!
KABLAM
BLAST IT! HE GOT ME!
BLAM
BLAM
BLAM
AIEEE!
KAZING
WHO'S DOING THIS?
I DUNNO!!
BONK
WOW...
CRACK

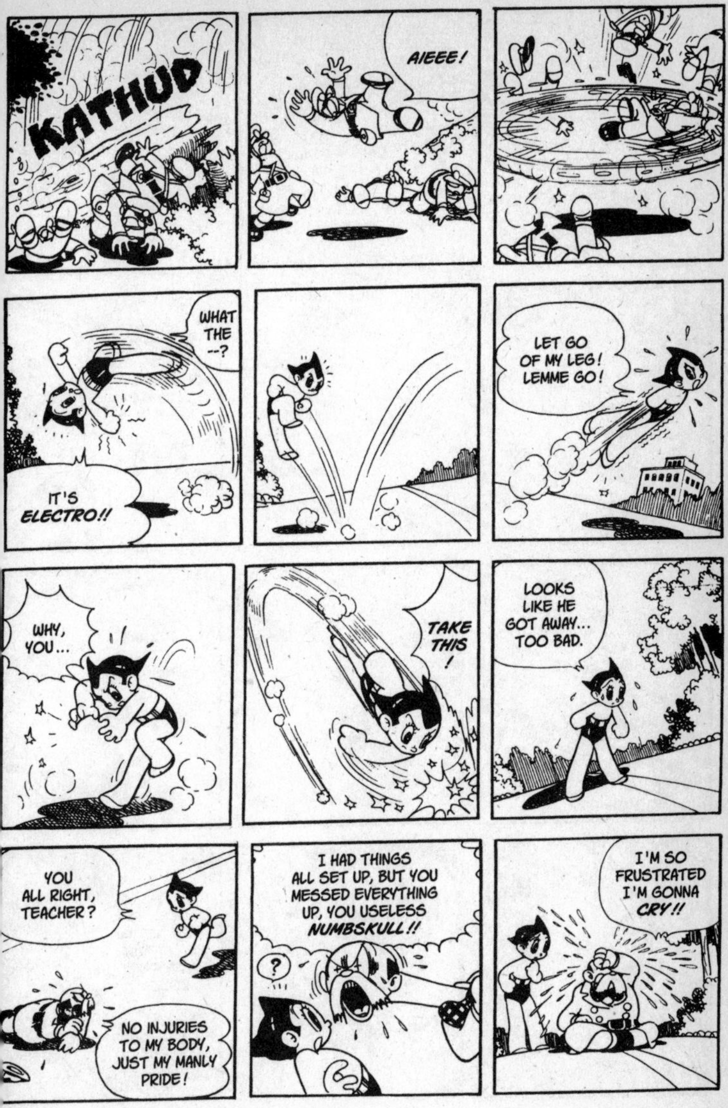
KATHUD
AIEEE!
WHAT THE --?
IT'S ELECTRO!!
LET GO OF MY LEG! LEMME GO!
WHY, YOU...
TAKE THIS!
LOOKS LIKE HE GOT AWAY... TOO BAD.
YOU ALL RIGHT, TEACHER?
NO INJURIES TO MY BODY, JUST MY MANLY PRIDE!
I HAD THINGS ALL SET UP, BUT YOU MESSED EVERYTHING UP, YOU USELESS NUMBSKULL!!
?
I'M SO FRUSTRATED I'M GONNA CRY!!

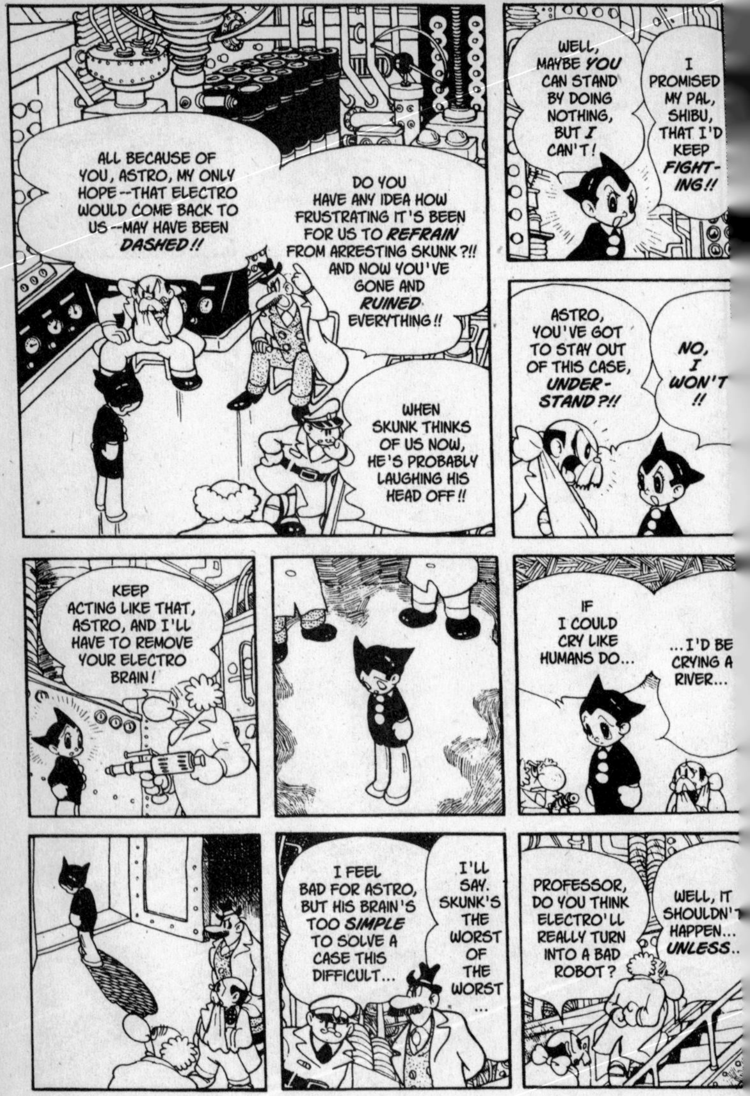
ALL BECAUSE OF YOU, ASTRO, MY ONLY HOPE --THAT ELECTRO WOULD COME BACK TO US --MAY HAVE BEEN DASHED!!
DO YOU HAVE ANY IDEA HOW FRUSTRATING IT'S BEEN FOR US TO REFRAIN FROM ARRESTING SKUNK?!! AND NOW YOU'VE GONE AND RUINED EVERYTHING!!
WHEN SKUNK THINKS OF US NOW, HE'S PROBABLY LAUGHING HIS HEAD OFF!!
WELL, MAYBE YOU CAN STAND BY DOING NOTHING, BUT I CAN'T!
I PROMISED MY PAL, SHIBU, THAT I'D KEEP FIGHT-ING!!
ASTRO, YOU'VE GOT TO STAY OUT OF THIS CASE, UNDER-STAND?!!
NO, I WON'T!!
KEEP ACTING LIKE THAT, ASTRO, AND I'LL HAVE TO REMOVE YOUR ELECTRO BRAIN!
IF I COULD CRY LIKE HUMANS DO...
...I'D BE CRYING A RIVER...
I FEEL BAD FOR ASTRO, BUT HIS BRAIN'S TOO SIMPLE TO SOLVE A CASE THIS DIFFICULT...
I'LL SAY. SKUNK'S THE WORST OF THE WORST...
PROFESSOR, DO YOU THINK ELECTRO'LL REALLY TURN INTO A BAD ROBOT?
WELL, IT SHOULDN'T HAPPEN... UNLESS...

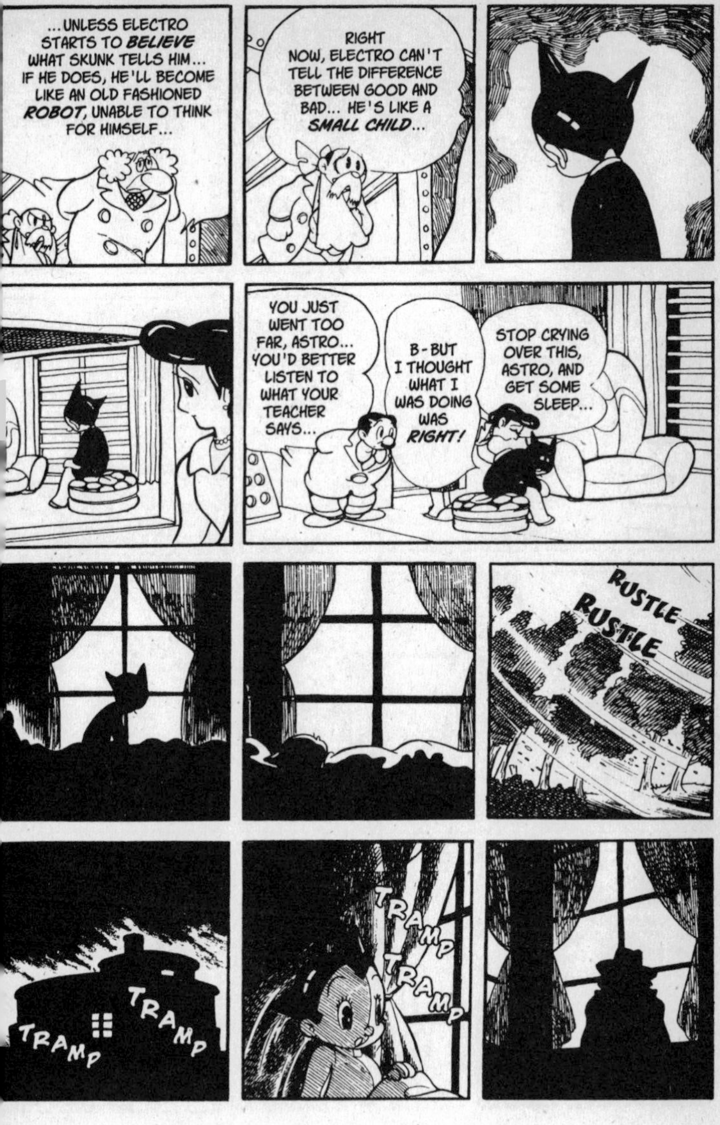
...UNLESS ELECTRO STARTS TO *BELIEVE* WHAT SKUNK TELLS HIM... IF HE DOES, HE'LL BECOME LIKE AN OLD FASHIONED *ROBOT*, UNABLE TO THINK FOR HIMSELF...
RIGHT NOW, ELECTRO CAN'T TELL THE DIFFERENCE BETWEEN GOOD AND BAD... HE'S LIKE A *SMALL CHILD*...
YOU JUST WENT TOO FAR, ASTRO... YOU'D BETTER LISTEN TO WHAT YOUR TEACHER SAYS...
B-BUT I THOUGHT WHAT I WAS DOING WAS *RIGHT!*
STOP CRYING OVER THIS, ASTRO, AND GET SOME SLEEP...
RUSTLE RUSTLE
TRAMP TRAMP
TRAMP TRAMP

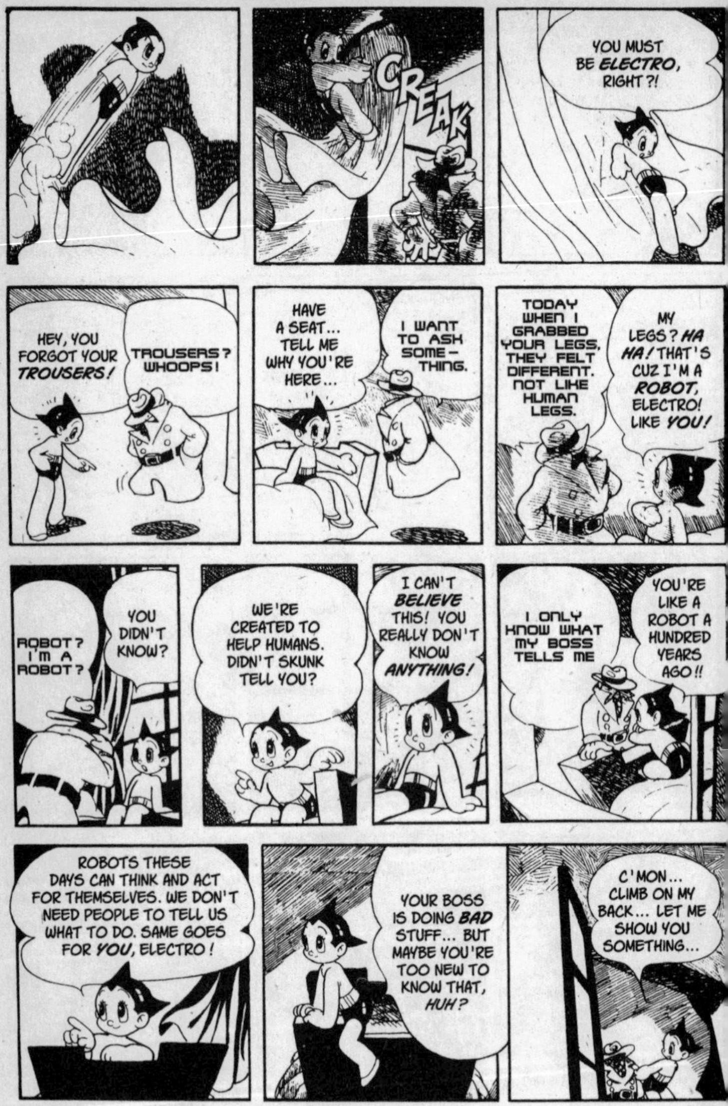
CREAK
YOU MUST BE ELECTRO, RIGHT?!
HEY, YOU FORGOT YOUR TROUSERS!
TROUSERS? WHOOPS!
HAVE A SEAT... TELL ME WHY YOU'RE HERE...
I WANT TO ASK SOME-THING.
TODAY WHEN I GRABBED YOUR LEGS, THEY FELT DIFFERENT. NOT LIKE HUMAN LEGS.
MY LEGS? HA HA! THAT'S CUZ I'M A ROBOT, ELECTRO! LIKE YOU!
ROBOT? I'M A ROBOT?
YOU DIDN'T KNOW?
WE'RE CREATED TO HELP HUMANS. DIDN'T SKUNK TELL YOU?
I CAN'T BELIEVE THIS! YOU REALLY DON'T KNOW ANYTHING!
I ONLY KNOW WHAT MY BOSS TELLS ME
YOU'RE LIKE A ROBOT A HUNDRED YEARS AGO!!
ROBOTS THESE DAYS CAN THINK AND ACT FOR THEMSELVES. WE DON'T NEED PEOPLE TO TELL US WHAT TO DO. SAME GOES FOR YOU, ELECTRO!
YOUR BOSS IS DOING BAD STUFF... BUT MAYBE YOU'RE TOO NEW TO KNOW THAT, HUH?
C'MON... CLIMB ON MY BACK... LET ME SHOW YOU SOMETHING...

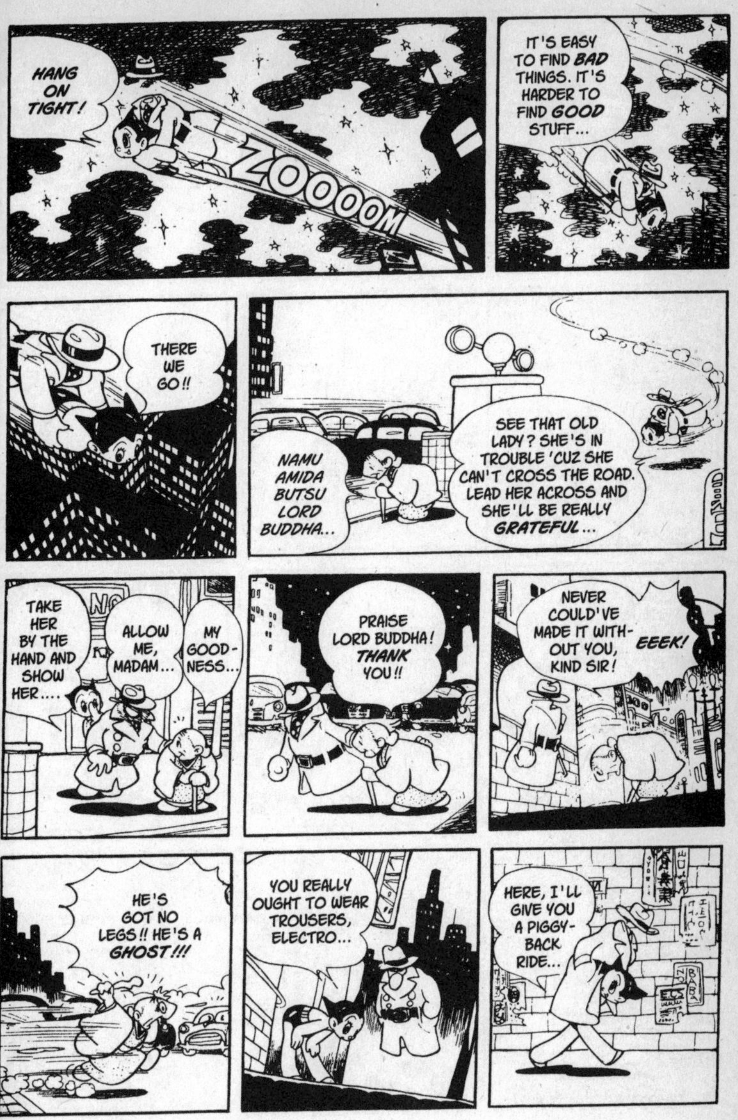

HANG ON TIGHT!
ZOOOOM
IT'S EASY TO FIND BAD THINGS. IT'S HARDER TO FIND GOOD STUFF...
THERE WE GO!!
NAMU AMIDA BUTSU LORD BUDDHA...
SEE THAT OLD LADY? SHE'S IN TROUBLE 'CUZ SHE CAN'T CROSS THE ROAD. LEAD HER ACROSS AND SHE'LL BE REALLY GRATEFUL...
TAKE HER BY THE HAND AND SHOW HER....
ALLOW ME, MADAM...
MY GOODNESS...
PRAISE LORD BUDDHA! THANK YOU!!
NEVER COULD'VE MADE IT WITHOUT YOU, KIND SIR!
EEEK!
HE'S GOT NO LEGS!! HE'S A GHOST!!!
YOU REALLY OUGHT TO WEAR TROUSERS, ELECTRO...
HERE, I'LL GIVE YOU A PIGGY-BACK RIDE...

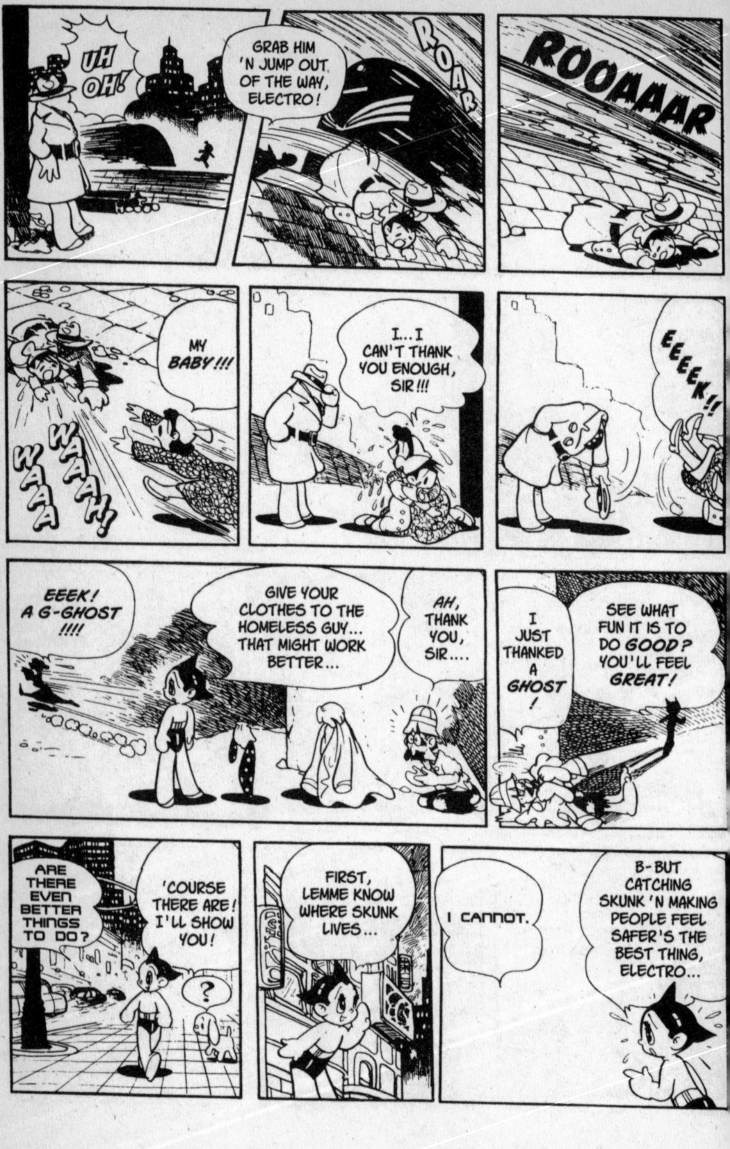

UH OH!
GRAB HIM 'N JUMP OUT OF THE WAY, ELECTRO!
ROAR
ROOAAAR
MY BABY!!!
WAAAA WAAAAH!
I...I CAN'T THANK YOU ENOUGH, SIR!!!
EEEEK!!
EEEK! A G-GHOST !!!!
GIVE YOUR CLOTHES TO THE HOMELESS GUY... THAT MIGHT WORK BETTER...
AH, THANK YOU, SIR....
I JUST THANKED A GHOST!
SEE WHAT FUN IT IS TO DO GOOD? YOU'LL FEEL GREAT!
ARE THERE EVEN BETTER THINGS TO DO?
'COURSE THERE ARE! I'LL SHOW YOU!
?
FIRST, LEMME KNOW WHERE SKUNK LIVES...
I CANNOT.
B-BUT CATCHING SKUNK 'N MAKING PEOPLE FEEL SAFER'S THE BEST THING, ELECTRO...

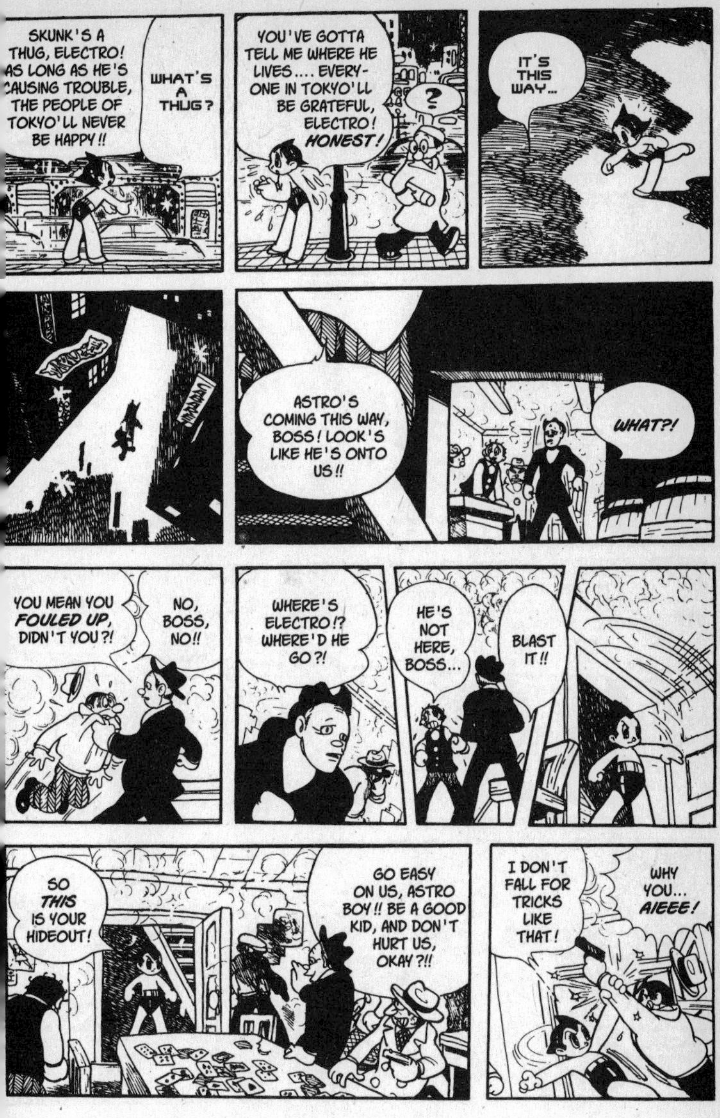

SKUNK'S A THUG, ELECTRO! AS LONG AS HE'S CAUSING TROUBLE, THE PEOPLE OF TOKYO'LL NEVER BE HAPPY!!
WHAT'S A THUG?
YOU'VE GOTTA TELL ME WHERE HE LIVES.... EVERY-ONE IN TOKYO'LL BE GRATEFUL, ELECTRO! HONEST!
?
IT'S THIS WAY...
ASTRO'S COMING THIS WAY, BOSS! LOOK'S LIKE HE'S ONTO US!!
WHAT?!
YOU MEAN YOU FOULED UP, DIDN'T YOU?!
NO, BOSS, NO!!
WHERE'S ELECTRO!? WHERE'D HE GO?!
HE'S NOT HERE, BOSS...
BLAST IT!!
SO THIS IS YOUR HIDEOUT!
GO EASY ON US, ASTRO BOY!! BE A GOOD KID, AND DON'T HURT US, OKAY?!!
I DON'T FALL FOR TRICKS LIKE THAT!
WHY YOU... AIEEE!

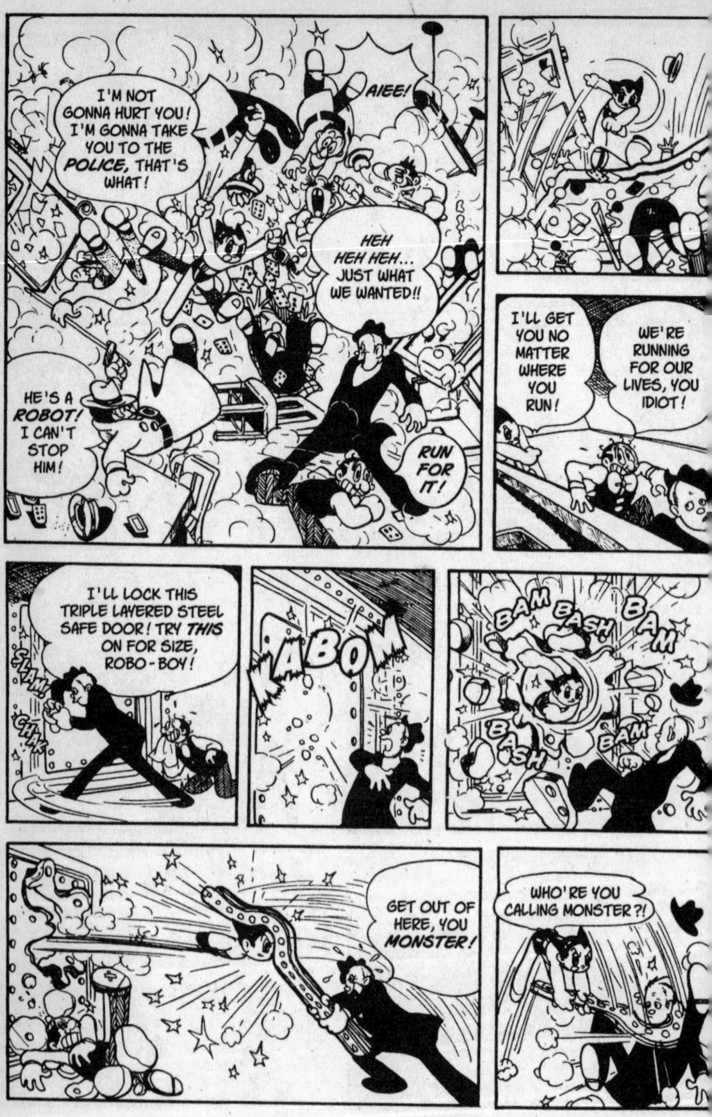
I'M NOT GONNA HURT YOU! I'M GONNA TAKE YOU TO THE POLICE, THAT'S WHAT!
AIEE!
HEH HEH HEH... JUST WHAT WE WANTED!!
HE'S A ROBOT! I CAN'T STOP HIM!
RUN FOR IT!
I'LL GET YOU NO MATTER WHERE YOU RUN!
WE'RE RUNNING FOR OUR LIVES, YOU IDIOT!
I'LL LOCK THIS TRIPLE LAYERED STEEL SAFE DOOR! TRY THIS ON FOR SIZE, ROBO-BOY!
SLAM!!
CHAK
KABOOM
BAM BASH BAM
BASH BAM
GET OUT OF HERE, YOU MONSTER!
WHO'RE YOU CALLING MONSTER?!

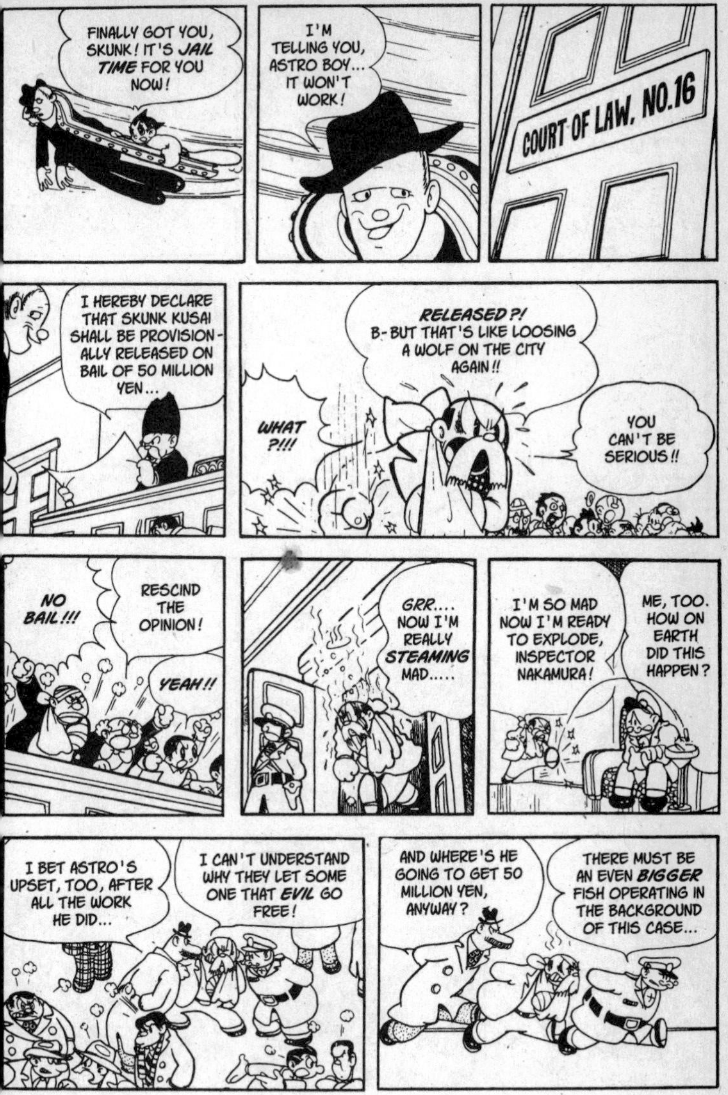
FINALLY GOT YOU, SKUNK! IT'S *JAIL TIME* FOR YOU NOW!
I'M TELLING YOU, ASTRO BOY... IT WON'T WORK!
COURT OF LAW. NO.16
I HEREBY DECLARE THAT SKUNK KUSAI SHALL BE PROVISION-ALLY RELEASED ON BAIL OF 50 MILLION YEN...
WHAT ?!!!
RELEASED ?! B- BUT THAT'S LIKE LOOSING A WOLF ON THE CITY AGAIN !!
YOU CAN'T BE SERIOUS !!
NO BAIL !!!
RESCIND THE OPINION!
YEAH !!
GRR.... NOW I'M REALLY *STEAMING* MAD.....
I'M SO MAD NOW I'M READY TO EXPLODE, INSPECTOR NAKAMURA!
ME, TOO. HOW ON EARTH DID THIS HAPPEN?
I BET ASTRO'S UPSET, TOO, AFTER ALL THE WORK HE DID...
I CAN'T UNDERSTAND WHY THEY LET SOME ONE THAT *EVIL* GO FREE!
AND WHERE'S HE GOING TO GET 50 MILLION YEN, ANYWAY?
THERE MUST BE AN EVEN *BIGGER* FISH OPERATING IN THE BACKGROUND OF THIS CASE...

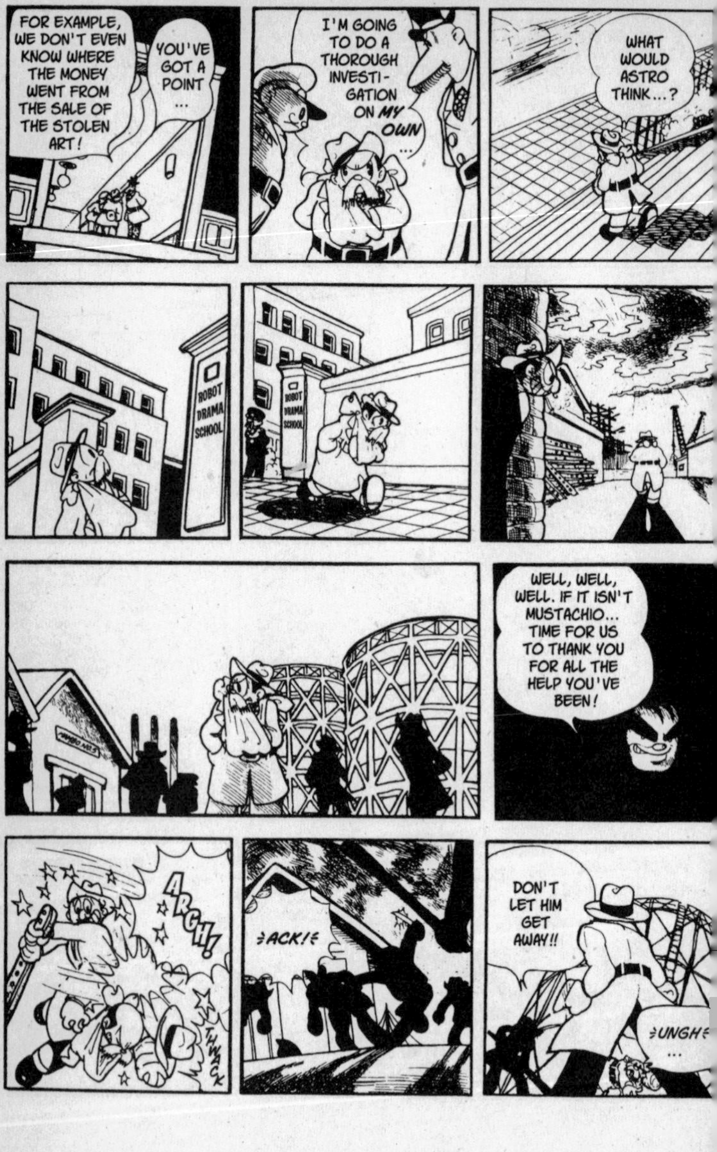

FOR EXAMPLE, WE DON'T EVEN KNOW WHERE THE MONEY WENT FROM THE SALE OF THE STOLEN ART!
YOU'VE GOT A POINT ...
I'M GOING TO DO A THOROUGH INVESTI-GATION ON MY OWN ...
WHAT WOULD ASTRO THINK...?
ROBOT DRAMA SCHOOL
ROBOT DRAMA SCHOOL
WELL, WELL, WELL. IF IT ISN'T MUSTACHIO... TIME FOR US TO THANK YOU FOR ALL THE HELP YOU'VE BEEN!
ARGH!
THWACK
ACK!
DON'T LET HIM GET AWAY!!
UNGH ...

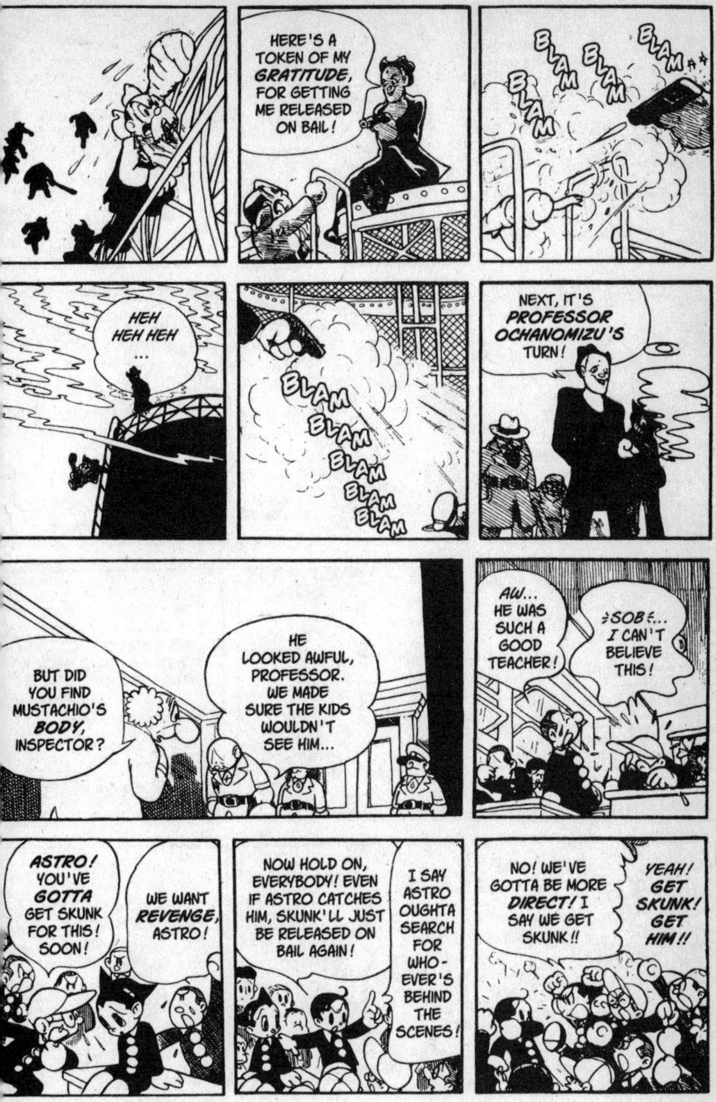
HERE'S A TOKEN OF MY GRATITUDE, FOR GETTING ME RELEASED ON BAIL!
BLAM BLAM BLAM BLAM
HEH HEH HEH ...
BLAM BLAM BLAM BLAM BLAM
NEXT, IT'S PROFESSOR OCHANOMIZU'S TURN!
BUT DID YOU FIND MUSTACHIO'S BODY, INSPECTOR?
HE LOOKED AWFUL, PROFESSOR. WE MADE SURE THE KIDS WOULDN'T SEE HIM...
AW... HE WAS SUCH A GOOD TEACHER!
SOB... I CAN'T BELIEVE THIS!
ASTRO! YOU'VE GOTTA GET SKUNK FOR THIS! SOON!
WE WANT REVENGE, ASTRO!
NOW HOLD ON, EVERYBODY! EVEN IF ASTRO CATCHES HIM, SKUNK'LL JUST BE RELEASED ON BAIL AGAIN!
I SAY ASTRO OUGHTA SEARCH FOR WHO-EVER'S BEHIND THE SCENES!
NO! WE'VE GOTTA BE MORE DIRECT! I SAY WE GET SKUNK!!
YEAH! GET SKUNK! GET HIM!!

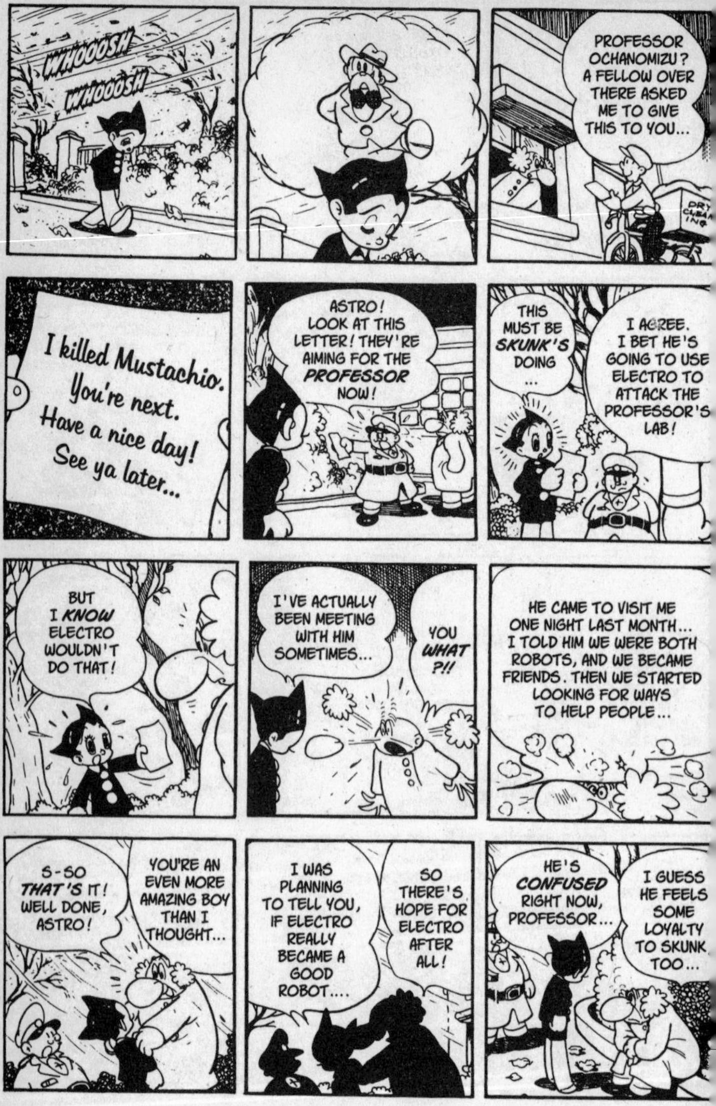
WHOOOSH
WHOOOSH
PROFESSOR OCHANOMIZU? A FELLOW OVER THERE ASKED ME TO GIVE THIS TO YOU...
DRY CLEANING
I killed Mustachio. You're next. Have a nice day! See ya later...
ASTRO! LOOK AT THIS LETTER! THEY'RE AIMING FOR THE PROFESSOR NOW!
THIS MUST BE SKUNK'S DOING ...
I AGREE. I BET HE'S GOING TO USE ELECTRO TO ATTACK THE PROFESSOR'S LAB!
BUT I KNOW ELECTRO WOULDN'T DO THAT!
I'VE ACTUALLY BEEN MEETING WITH HIM SOMETIMES...
YOU WHAT?!!
HE CAME TO VISIT ME ONE NIGHT LAST MONTH... I TOLD HIM WE WERE BOTH ROBOTS, AND WE BECAME FRIENDS. THEN WE STARTED LOOKING FOR WAYS TO HELP PEOPLE...
S-SO THAT'S IT! WELL DONE, ASTRO!
YOU'RE AN EVEN MORE AMAZING BOY THAN I THOUGHT...
I WAS PLANNING TO TELL YOU, IF ELECTRO REALLY BECAME A GOOD ROBOT....
SO THERE'S HOPE FOR ELECTRO AFTER ALL!
HE'S CONFUSED RIGHT NOW, PROFESSOR...
I GUESS HE FEELS SOME LOYALTY TO SKUNK TOO...

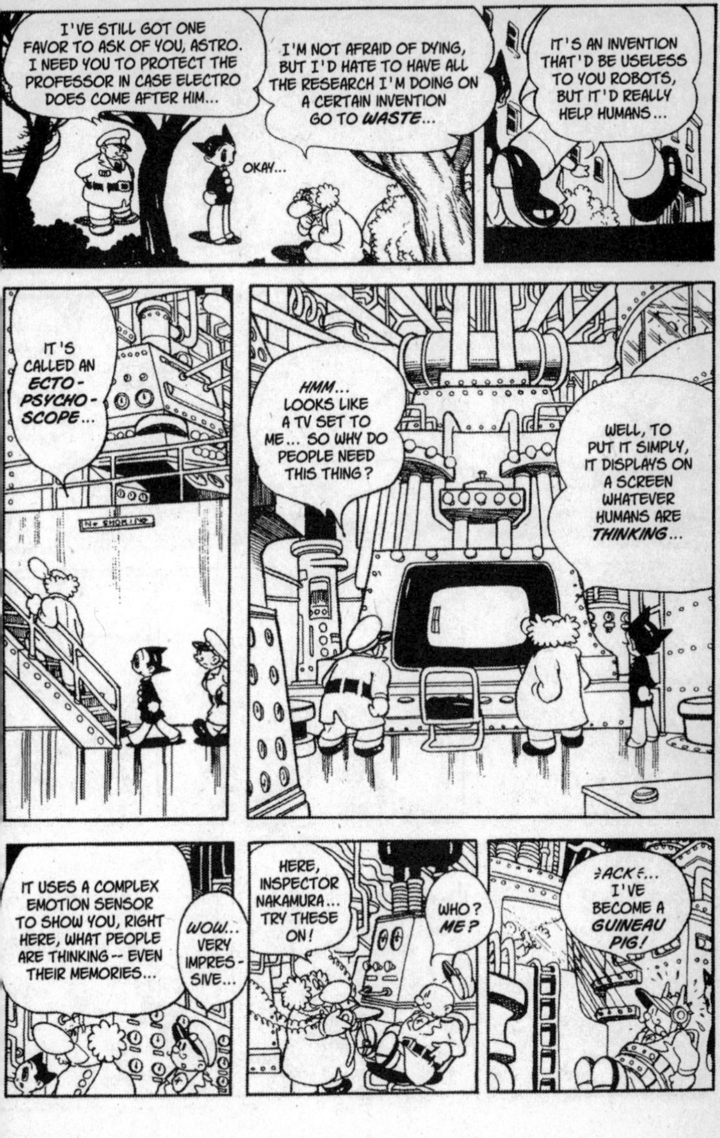
I'VE STILL GOT ONE FAVOR TO ASK OF YOU, ASTRO. I NEED YOU TO PROTECT THE PROFESSOR IN CASE ELECTRO DOES COME AFTER HIM...
OKAY...
I'M NOT AFRAID OF DYING, BUT I'D HATE TO HAVE ALL THE RESEARCH I'M DOING ON A CERTAIN INVENTION GO TO *WASTE*...
IT'S AN INVENTION THAT'D BE USELESS TO YOU ROBOTS, BUT IT'D REALLY HELP HUMANS...
IT'S CALLED AN *ECTO-PSYCHO-SCOPE*...
HMM... LOOKS LIKE A TV SET TO ME... SO WHY DO PEOPLE NEED THIS THING?
WELL, TO PUT IT SIMPLY, IT DISPLAYS ON A SCREEN WHATEVER HUMANS ARE *THINKING*...
IT USES A COMPLEX EMOTION SENSOR TO SHOW YOU, RIGHT HERE, WHAT PEOPLE ARE THINKING -- EVEN THEIR MEMORIES...
WOW... VERY IMPRES-SIVE...
HERE, INSPECTOR NAKAMURA... TRY THESE ON!
WHO? *ME?*
ACK... I'VE BECOME A *GUINEAU PIG!*

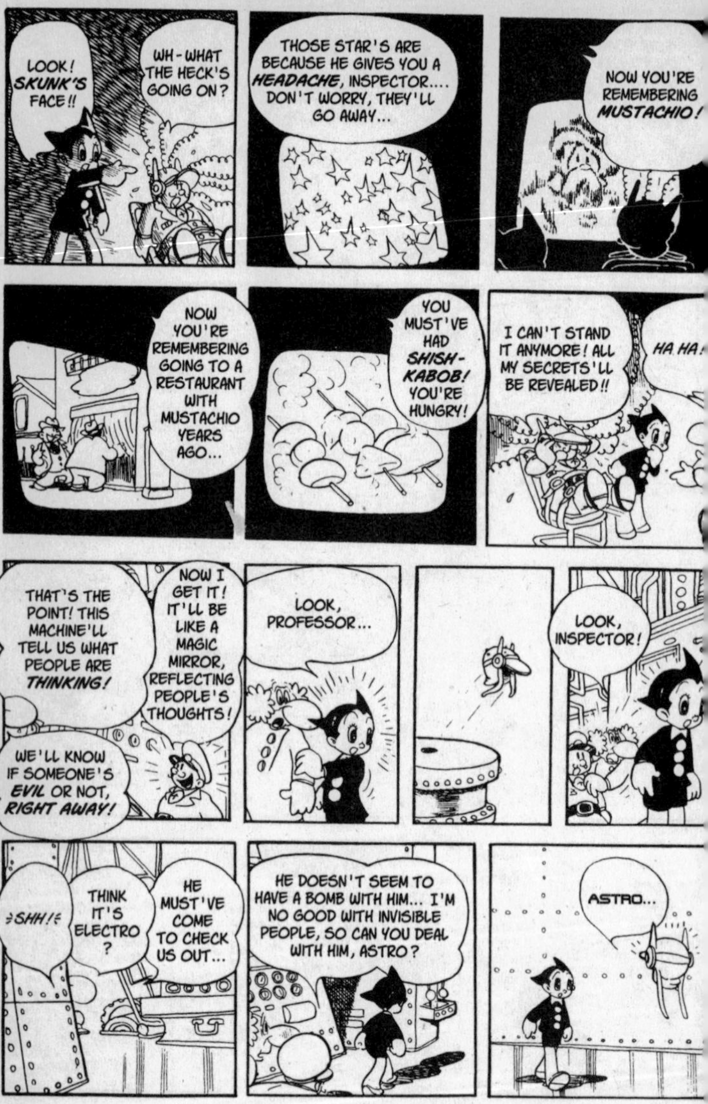
LOOK! SKUNK'S FACE!!
WH-WHAT THE HECK'S GOING ON?
THOSE STAR'S ARE BECAUSE HE GIVES YOU A HEADACHE, INSPECTOR.... DON'T WORRY, THEY'LL GO AWAY...
NOW YOU'RE REMEMBERING MUSTACHIO!
NOW YOU'RE REMEMBERING GOING TO A RESTAURANT WITH MUSTACHIO YEARS AGO...
YOU MUST'VE HAD SHISH-KABOB! YOU'RE HUNGRY!
I CAN'T STAND IT ANYMORE! ALL MY SECRETS'LL BE REVEALED!!
HA HA!
THAT'S THE POINT! THIS MACHINE'LL TELL US WHAT PEOPLE ARE THINKING!
NOW I GET IT! IT'LL BE LIKE A MAGIC MIRROR, REFLECTING PEOPLE'S THOUGHTS!
WE'LL KNOW IF SOMEONE'S EVIL OR NOT, RIGHT AWAY!
LOOK, PROFESSOR...
LOOK, INSPECTOR!
SHH!
THINK IT'S ELECTRO?
HE MUST'VE COME TO CHECK US OUT...
HE DOESN'T SEEM TO HAVE A BOMB WITH HIM... I'M NO GOOD WITH INVISIBLE PEOPLE, SO CAN YOU DEAL WITH HIM, ASTRO?
ASTRO...

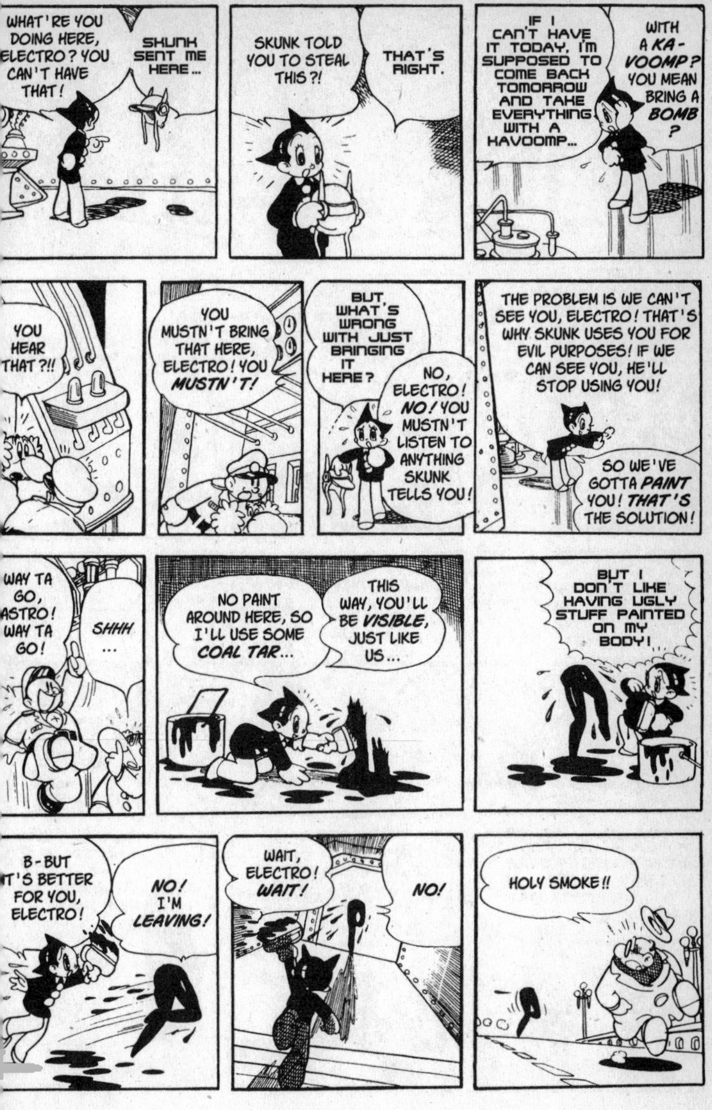

WHAT'RE YOU DOING HERE, ELECTRO? YOU CAN'T HAVE THAT!
SKUNK SENT ME HERE...
SKUNK TOLD YOU TO STEAL THIS?!
THAT'S RIGHT.
IF I CAN'T HAVE IT TODAY, I'M SUPPOSED TO COME BACK TOMORROW AND TAKE EVERYTHING WITH A KAVOOMP...
WITH A KA-VOOMP? YOU MEAN BRING A BOMB?
YOU HEAR THAT?!!
YOU MUSTN'T BRING THAT HERE, ELECTRO! YOU MUSTN'T!
BUT, WHAT'S WRONG WITH JUST BRINGING IT HERE?
NO, ELECTRO! NO! YOU MUSTN'T LISTEN TO ANYTHING SKUNK TELLS YOU!
THE PROBLEM IS WE CAN'T SEE YOU, ELECTRO! THAT'S WHY SKUNK USES YOU FOR EVIL PURPOSES! IF WE CAN SEE YOU, HE'LL STOP USING YOU!
SO WE'VE GOTTA PAINT YOU! THAT'S THE SOLUTION!
WAY TA GO, ASTRO! WAY TA GO!
SHHH...
NO PAINT AROUND HERE, SO I'LL USE SOME COAL TAR...
THIS WAY, YOU'LL BE VISIBLE, JUST LIKE US...
BUT I DON'T LIKE HAVING UGLY STUFF PAINTED ON MY BODY!
B-BUT IT'S BETTER FOR YOU, ELECTRO!
NO! I'M LEAVING!
WAIT, ELECTRO! WAIT!
NO!
HOLY SMOKE!!

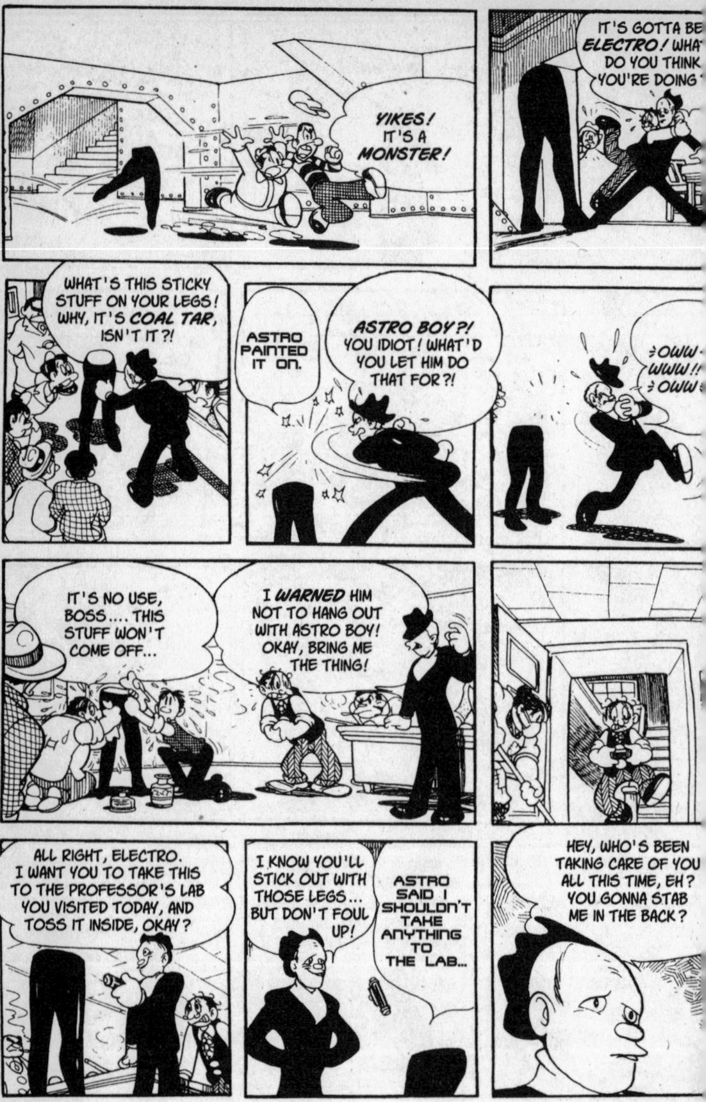
YIKES! IT'S A MONSTER!
IT'S GOTTA BE ELECTRO! WHA DO YOU THINK YOU'RE DOING
WHAT'S THIS STICKY STUFF ON YOUR LEGS! WHY, IT'S COAL TAR, ISN'T IT?!
ASTRO PAINTED IT ON.
ASTRO BOY?! YOU IDIOT! WHAT'D YOU LET HIM DO THAT FOR?!
OWW- WWW!! OWW
IT'S NO USE, BOSS.... THIS STUFF WON'T COME OFF...
I WARNED HIM NOT TO HANG OUT WITH ASTRO BOY! OKAY, BRING ME THE THING!
ALL RIGHT, ELECTRO. I WANT YOU TO TAKE THIS TO THE PROFESSOR'S LAB YOU VISITED TODAY, AND TOSS IT INSIDE, OKAY?
I KNOW YOU'LL STICK OUT WITH THOSE LEGS... BUT DON'T FOUL UP!
ASTRO SAID I SHOULDN'T TAKE ANYTHING TO THE LAB...
HEY, WHO'S BEEN TAKING CARE OF YOU ALL THIS TIME, EH? YOU GONNA STAB ME IN THE BACK?

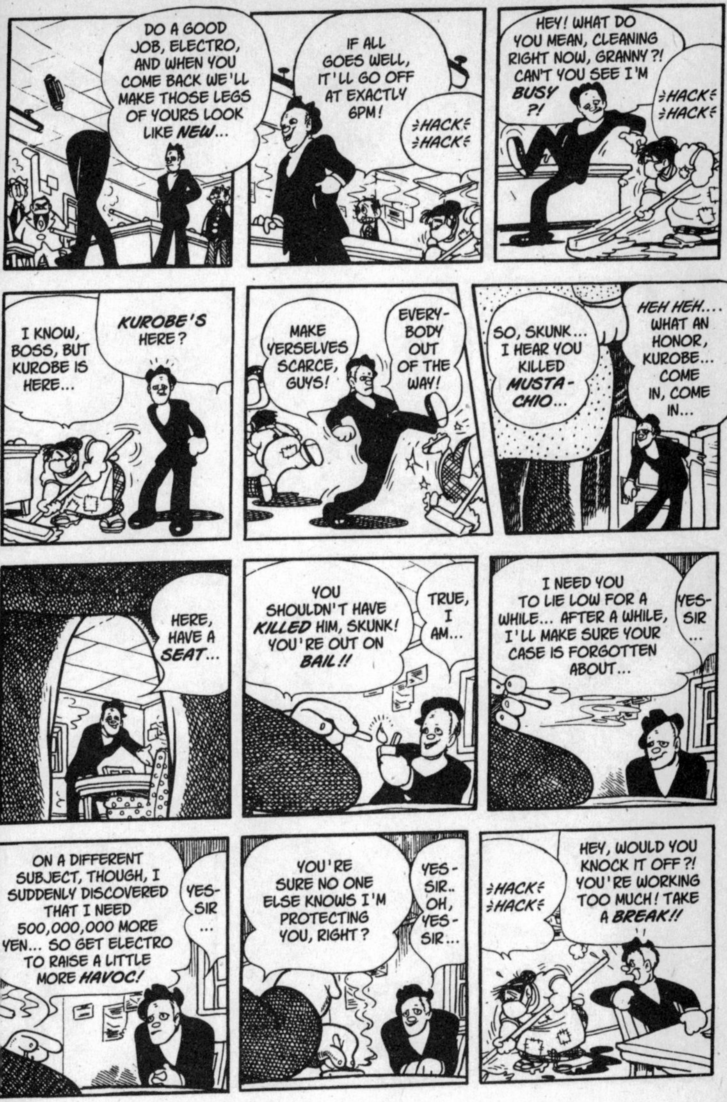
DO A GOOD JOB, ELECTRO, AND WHEN YOU COME BACK WE'LL MAKE THOSE LEGS OF YOURS LOOK LIKE NEW...
IF ALL GOES WELL, IT'LL GO OFF AT EXACTLY 6PM!
HACK HACK
HEY! WHAT DO YOU MEAN, CLEANING RIGHT NOW, GRANNY?! CAN'T YOU SEE I'M BUSY?!
HACK HACK
I KNOW, BOSS, BUT KUROBE IS HERE...
KUROBE'S HERE?
MAKE YERSELVES SCARCE, GUYS!
EVERY-BODY OUT OF THE WAY!
SO, SKUNK... I HEAR YOU KILLED MUSTA-CHIO...
HEH HEH.... WHAT AN HONOR, KUROBE... COME IN, COME IN...
HERE, HAVE A SEAT...
YOU SHOULDN'T HAVE KILLED HIM, SKUNK! YOU'RE OUT ON BAIL!!
TRUE, I AM...
I NEED YOU TO LIE LOW FOR A WHILE... AFTER A WHILE, I'LL MAKE SURE YOUR CASE IS FORGOTTEN ABOUT...
YES-SIR...
ON A DIFFERENT SUBJECT, THOUGH, I SUDDENLY DISCOVERED THAT I NEED 500,000,000 MORE YEN... SO GET ELECTRO TO RAISE A LITTLE MORE HAVOC!
YES-SIR...
YOU'RE SURE NO ONE ELSE KNOWS I'M PROTECTING YOU, RIGHT?
YES-SIR.. OH, YES-SIR...
HACK HACK
HEY, WOULD YOU KNOCK IT OFF?! YOU'RE WORKING TOO MUCH! TAKE A BREAK!!

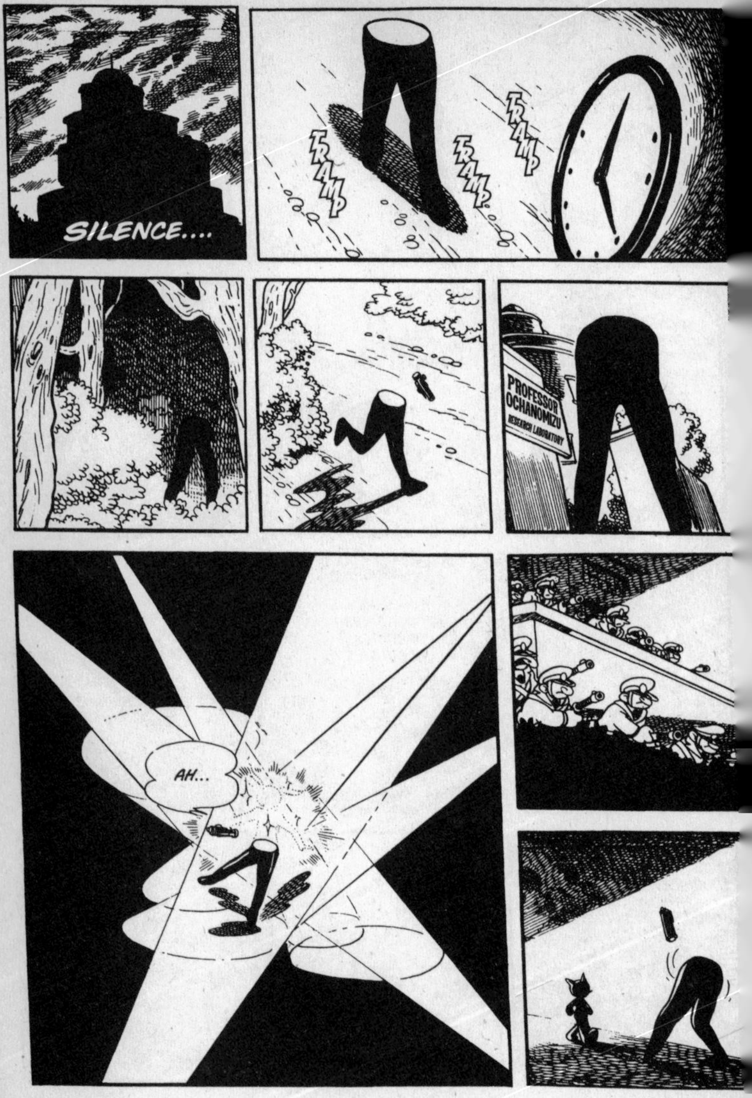
SILENCE....
TRAMP
TRAMP
TRAMP
PROFESSOR OCHANOMIZU RESEARCH LABORATORY
AH...

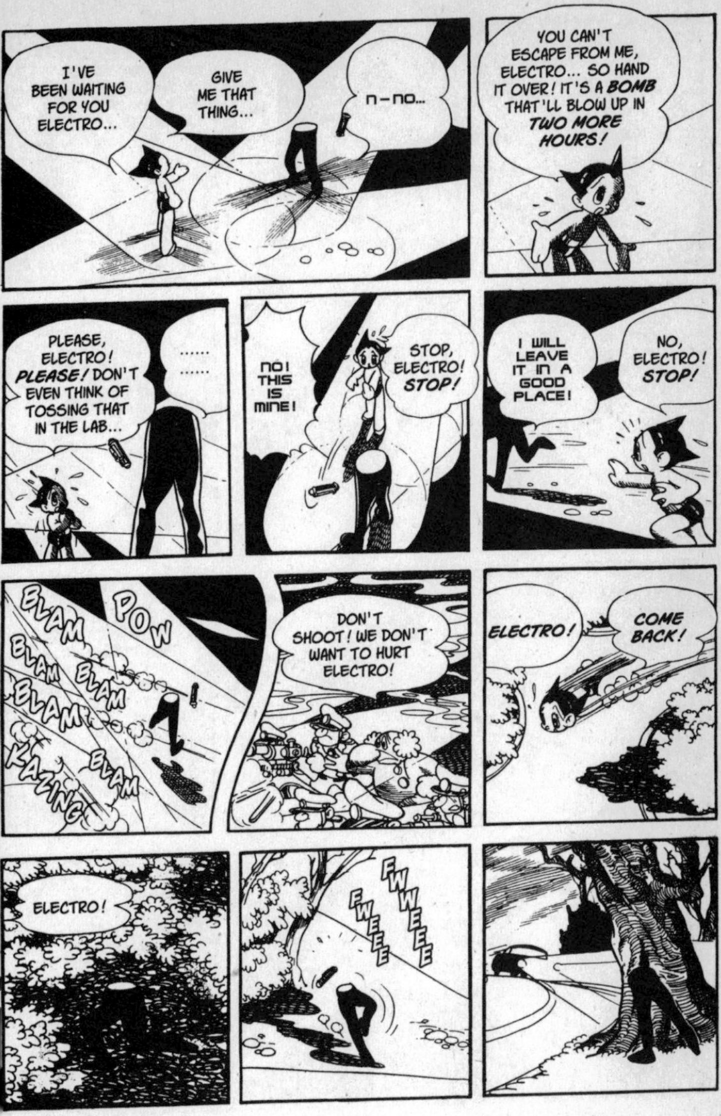
I'VE BEEN WAITING FOR YOU ELECTRO...
GIVE ME THAT THING...
n-no...
YOU CAN'T ESCAPE FROM ME, ELECTRO... SO HAND IT OVER! IT'S A ***BOMB*** THAT'LL BLOW UP IN ***TWO MORE HOURS!***
PLEASE, ELECTRO! ***PLEASE!*** DON'T EVEN THINK OF TOSSING THAT IN THE LAB...
......
......
NO! THIS IS MINE!
STOP, ELECTRO! ***STOP!***
I WILL LEAVE IT IN A GOOD PLACE!
NO, ELECTRO! ***STOP!***
BLAM
POW
BLAM
BLAM
BLAM
BLAM
KAZING
DON'T SHOOT! WE DON'T WANT TO HURT ELECTRO!
ELECTRO!
COME BACK!
ELECTRO!
FWEEE
FWWEEE

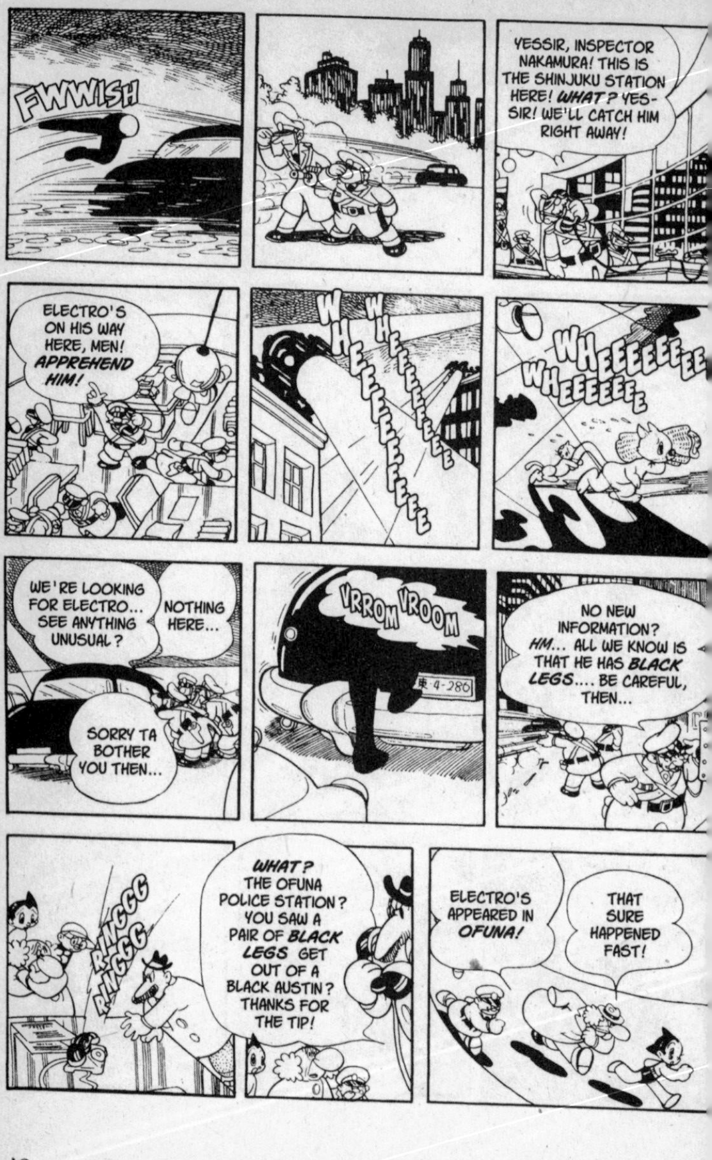
FWWISH
YESSIR, INSPECTOR NAKAMURA! THIS IS THE SHINJUKU STATION HERE! WHAT? YES-SIR! WE'LL CATCH HIM RIGHT AWAY!
ELECTRO'S ON HIS WAY HERE, MEN! APPREHEND HIM!
WHEEEEEEEEEE
WHEEEEEEEEE
WHEEEEEEEEE
WHEEEEEEE
WE'RE LOOKING FOR ELECTRO... SEE ANYTHING UNUSUAL?
NOTHING HERE...
SORRY TA BOTHER YOU THEN...
VRROM VROOM
東 4-280
NO NEW INFORMATION? HM... ALL WE KNOW IS THAT HE HAS BLACK LEGS.... BE CAREFUL, THEN...
RINGGG
RINGGG
WHAT? THE OFUNA POLICE STATION? YOU SAW A PAIR OF BLACK LEGS GET OUT OF A BLACK AUSTIN? THANKS FOR THE TIP!
ELECTRO'S APPEARED IN OFUNA!
THAT SURE HAPPENED FAST!

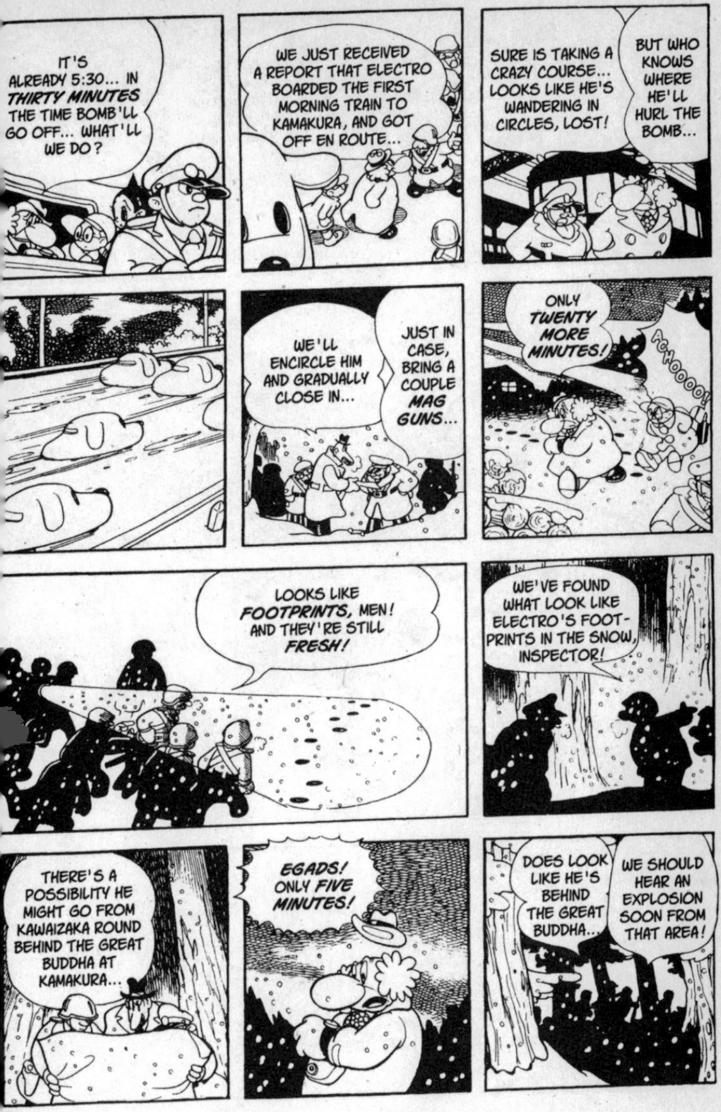
IT'S ALREADY 5:30... IN *THIRTY MINUTES* THE TIME BOMB'LL GO OFF... WHAT'LL WE DO?
WE JUST RECEIVED A REPORT THAT ELECTRO BOARDED THE FIRST MORNING TRAIN TO KAMAKURA, AND GOT OFF EN ROUTE...
SURE IS TAKING A CRAZY COURSE... LOOKS LIKE HE'S WANDERING IN CIRCLES, LOST!
BUT WHO KNOWS WHERE HE'LL HURL THE BOMB...
WE'LL ENCIRCLE HIM AND GRADUALLY CLOSE IN...
JUST IN CASE, BRING A COUPLE *MAG GUNS*...
ONLY *TWENTY MORE MINUTES!*
ACHOOOO!
LOOKS LIKE *FOOTPRINTS,* MEN! AND THEY'RE STILL *FRESH!*
WE'VE FOUND WHAT LOOK LIKE ELECTRO'S FOOT-PRINTS IN THE SNOW, INSPECTOR!
THERE'S A POSSIBILITY HE MIGHT GO FROM KAWAIZAKA ROUND BEHIND THE GREAT BUDDHA AT KAMAKURA...
EGADS! ONLY *FIVE MINUTES!*
DOES LOOK LIKE HE'S BEHIND THE GREAT BUDDHA...
WE SHOULD HEAR AN EXPLOSION SOON FROM THAT AREA!

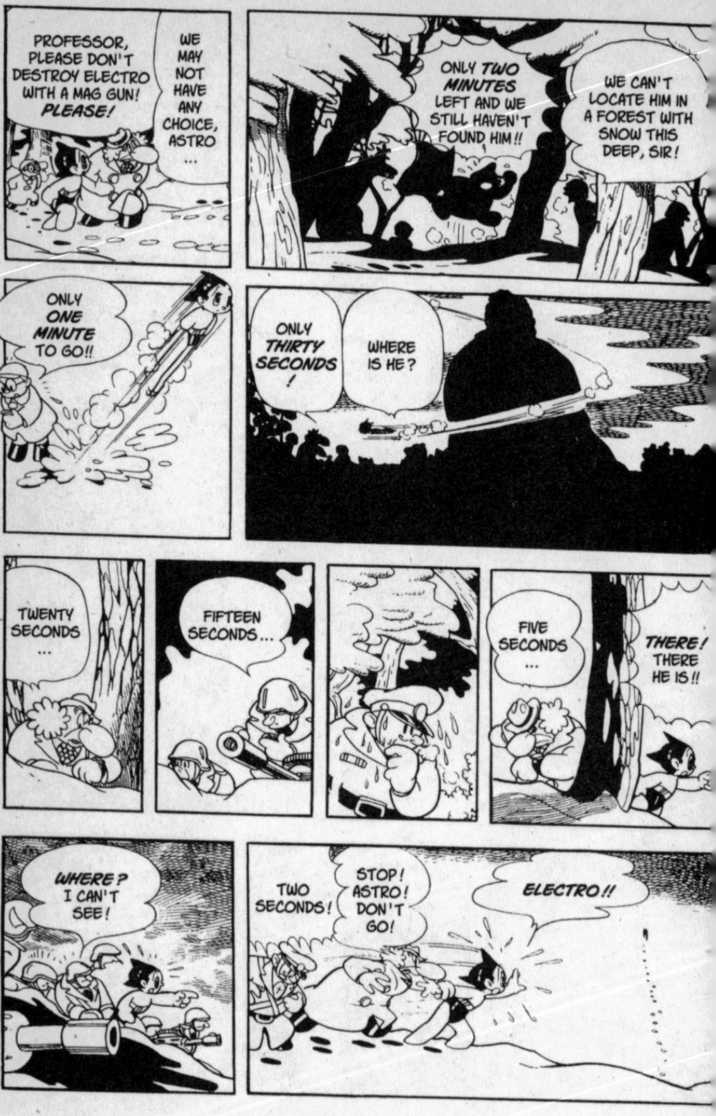
PROFESSOR, PLEASE DON'T DESTROY ELECTRO WITH A MAG GUN! PLEASE!
WE MAY NOT HAVE ANY CHOICE, ASTRO ...
ONLY TWO MINUTES LEFT AND WE STILL HAVEN'T FOUND HIM!!
WE CAN'T LOCATE HIM IN A FOREST WITH SNOW THIS DEEP, SIR!
ONLY ONE MINUTE TO GO!!
ONLY THIRTY SECONDS!
WHERE IS HE?
TWENTY SECONDS ...
FIFTEEN SECONDS ...
FIVE SECONDS ...
THERE! THERE HE IS!!
WHERE? I CAN'T SEE!
TWO SECONDS!
STOP! ASTRO! DON'T GO!
ELECTRO!!

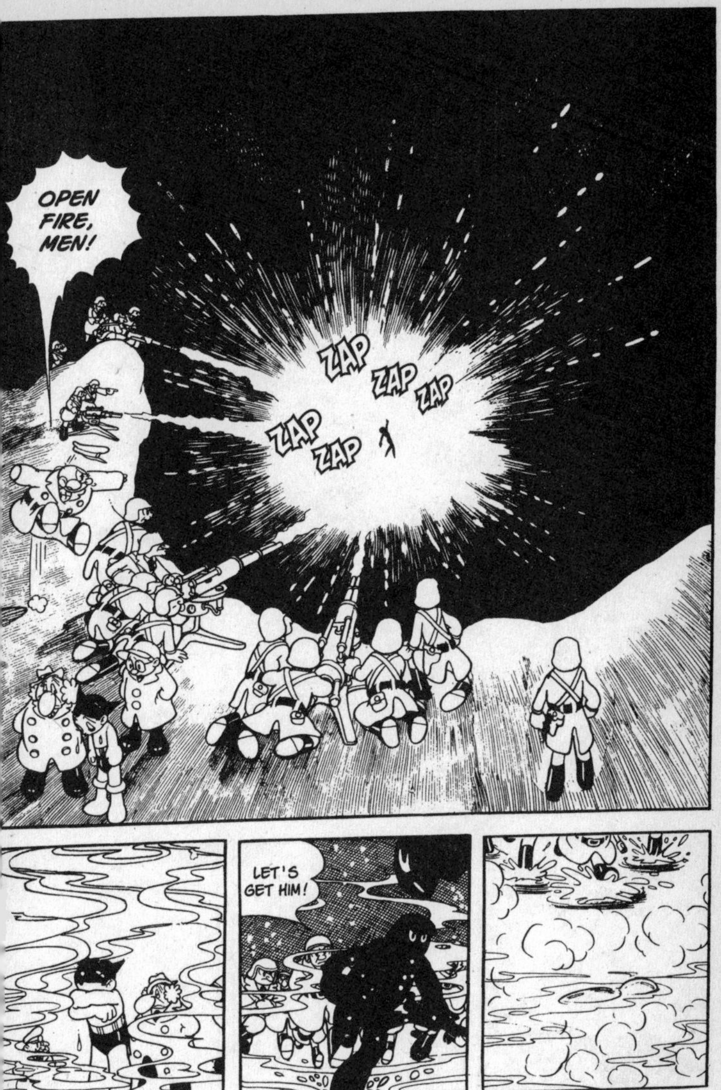
OPEN FIRE, MEN!
ZAP
ZAP
ZAP
ZAP
ZAP
LET'S GET HIM!

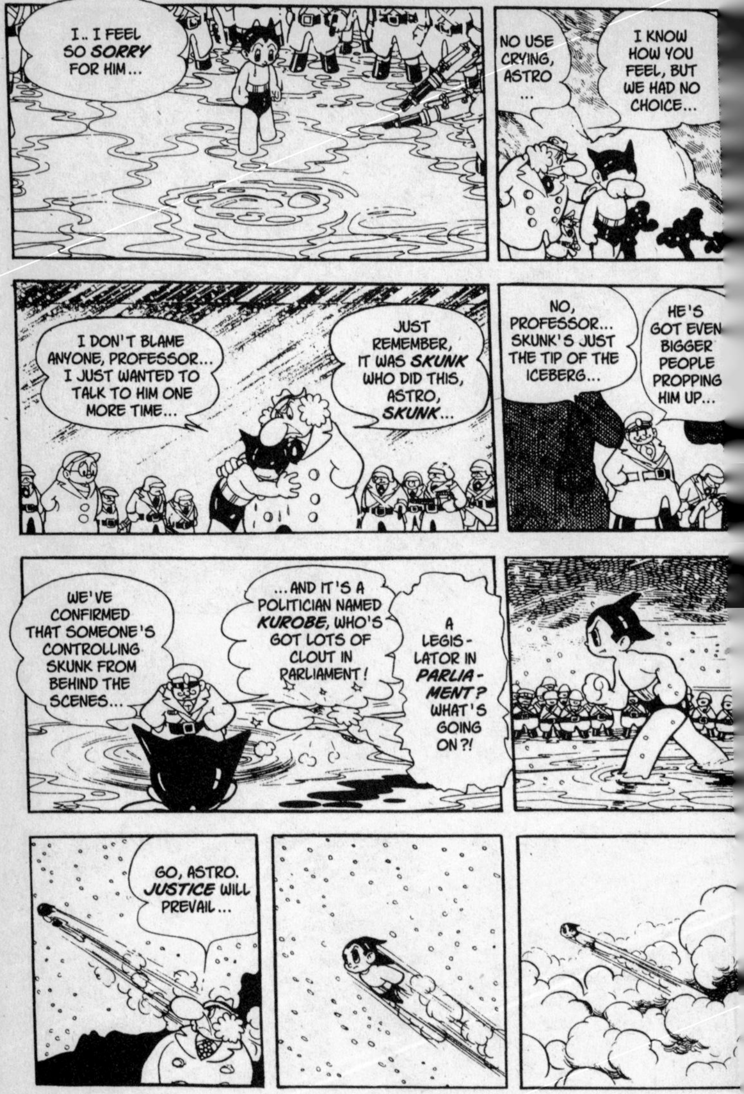
I.. I FEEL SO SORRY FOR HIM...
NO USE CRYING, ASTRO ...
I KNOW HOW YOU FEEL, BUT WE HAD NO CHOICE...
I DON'T BLAME ANYONE, PROFESSOR... I JUST WANTED TO TALK TO HIM ONE MORE TIME...
JUST REMEMBER, IT WAS SKUNK WHO DID THIS, ASTRO, SKUNK...
NO, PROFESSOR... SKUNK'S JUST THE TIP OF THE ICEBERG...
HE'S GOT EVEN BIGGER PEOPLE PROPPING HIM UP...
WE'VE CONFIRMED THAT SOMEONE'S CONTROLLING SKUNK FROM BEHIND THE SCENES...
...AND IT'S A POLITICIAN NAMED KUROBE, WHO'S GOT LOTS OF CLOUT IN PARLIAMENT!
A LEGIS-LATOR IN PARLIA-MENT? WHAT'S GOING ON?!
GO, ASTRO. JUSTICE WILL PREVAIL...

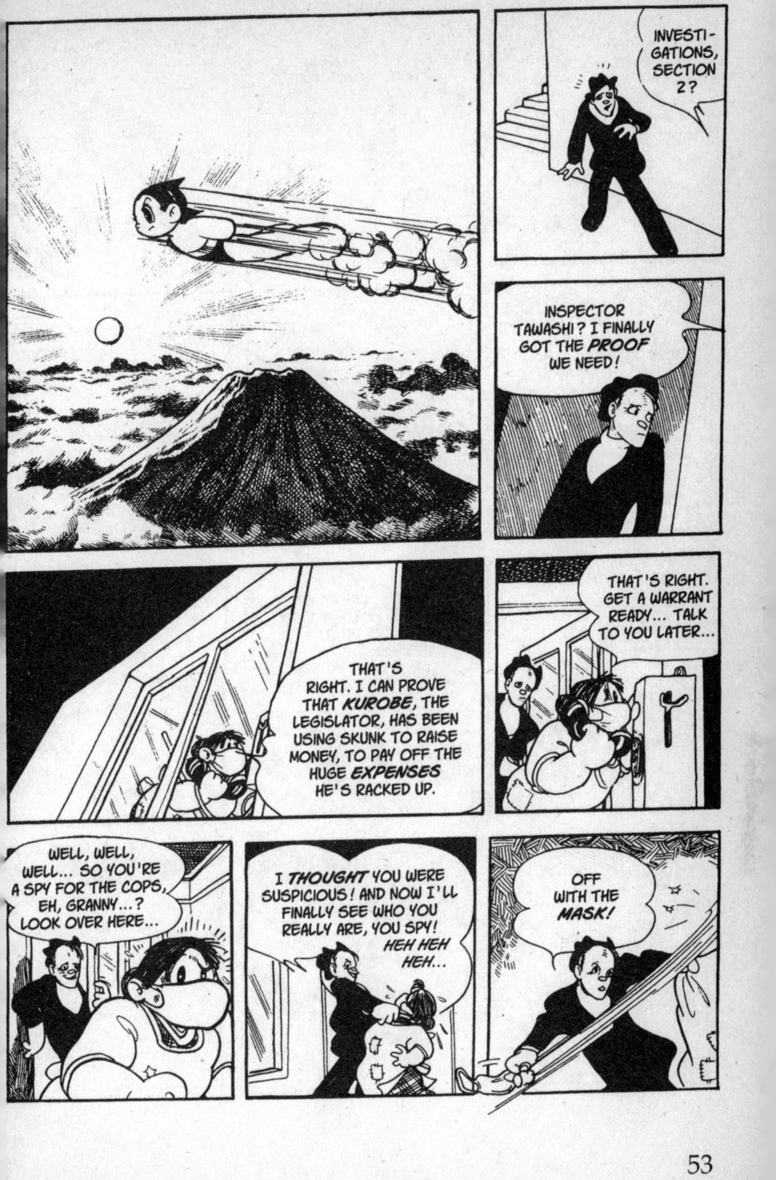
INVESTI-GATIONS, SECTION 2?
INSPECTOR TAWASHI? I FINALLY GOT THE *PROOF* WE NEED!
THAT'S RIGHT. I CAN PROVE THAT *KUROBE*, THE LEGISLATOR, HAS BEEN USING SKUNK TO RAISE MONEY, TO PAY OFF THE HUGE *EXPENSES* HE'S RACKED UP.
THAT'S RIGHT. GET A WARRANT READY... TALK TO YOU LATER...
WELL, WELL, WELL... SO YOU'RE A SPY FOR THE COPS, EH, GRANNY...? LOOK OVER HERE...
I *THOUGHT* YOU WERE SUSPICIOUS! AND NOW I'LL FINALLY SEE WHO YOU REALLY ARE, YOU SPY!
HEH HEH HEH...
OFF WITH THE *MASK!*

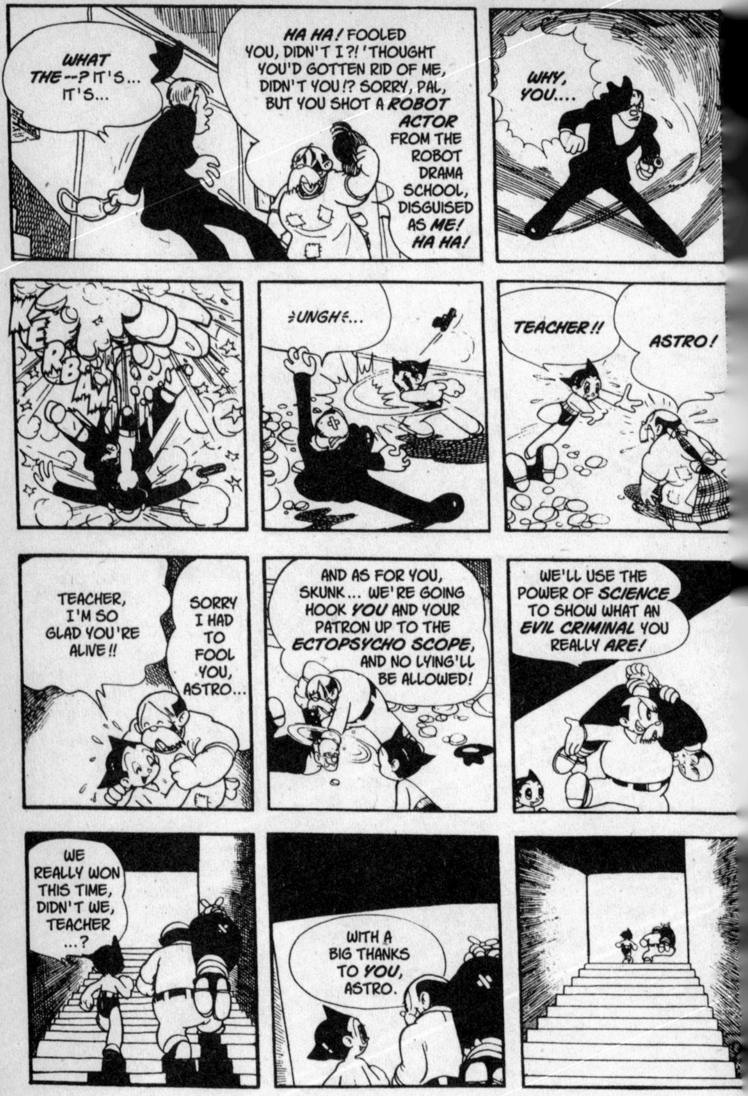
WHAT THE--? IT'S... IT'S...
HA HA! FOOLED YOU, DIDN'T I?! 'THOUGHT YOU'D GOTTEN RID OF ME, DIDN'T YOU!? SORRY, PAL, BUT YOU SHOT A ROBOT ACTOR FROM THE ROBOT DRAMA SCHOOL, DISGUISED AS ME! HA HA!
WHY, YOU....
KERBAM
UNGH...
TEACHER!!
ASTRO!
TEACHER, I'M SO GLAD YOU'RE ALIVE!!
SORRY I HAD TO FOOL YOU, ASTRO...
AND AS FOR YOU, SKUNK... WE'RE GOING HOOK YOU AND YOUR PATRON UP TO THE ECTOPSYCHO SCOPE, AND NO LYING'LL BE ALLOWED!
WE'LL USE THE POWER OF SCIENCE TO SHOW WHAT AN EVIL CRIMINAL YOU REALLY ARE!
WE REALLY WON THIS TIME, DIDN'T WE, TEACHER ...?
WITH A BIG THANKS TO YOU, ASTRO.

BLACK LUX

First appeared in the supplement to the
September 1957 edition of *Shonen* magazine.

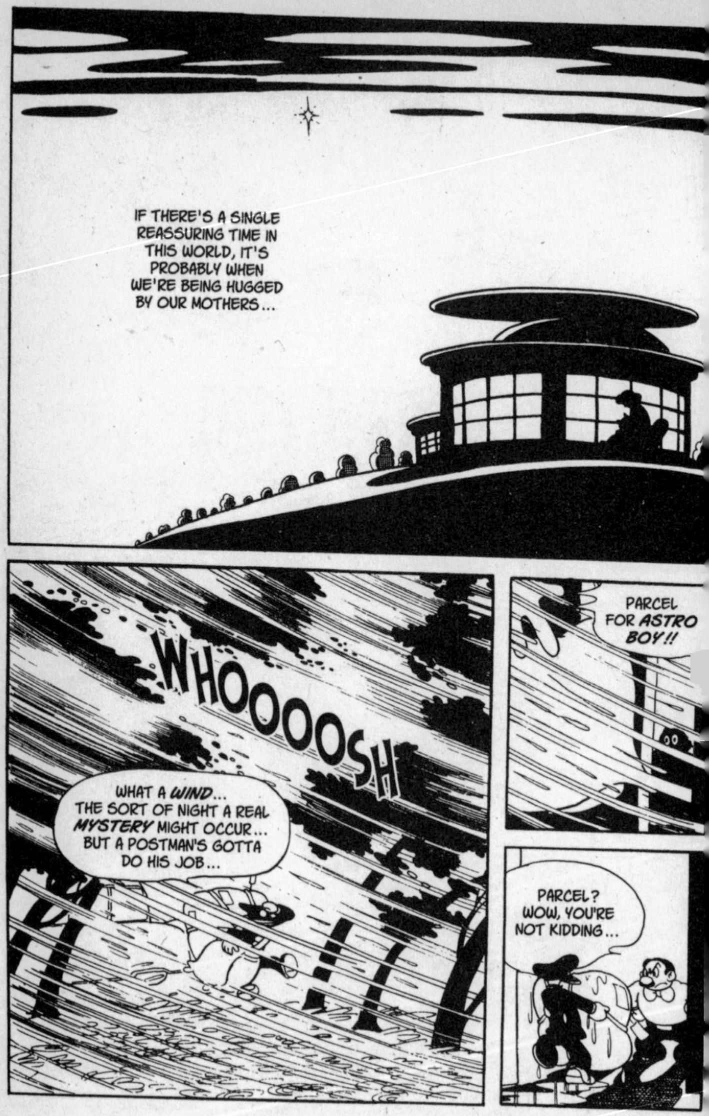
IF THERE'S A SINGLE REASSURING TIME IN THIS WORLD, IT'S PROBABLY WHEN WE'RE BEING HUGGED BY OUR MOTHERS...
WHOOOOOSH
WHAT A *WIND*... THE SORT OF NIGHT A REAL *MYSTERY* MIGHT OCCUR... BUT A POSTMAN'S GOTTA DO HIS JOB...
PARCEL FOR *ASTRO BOY!!*
PARCEL? WOW, YOU'RE NOT KIDDING...

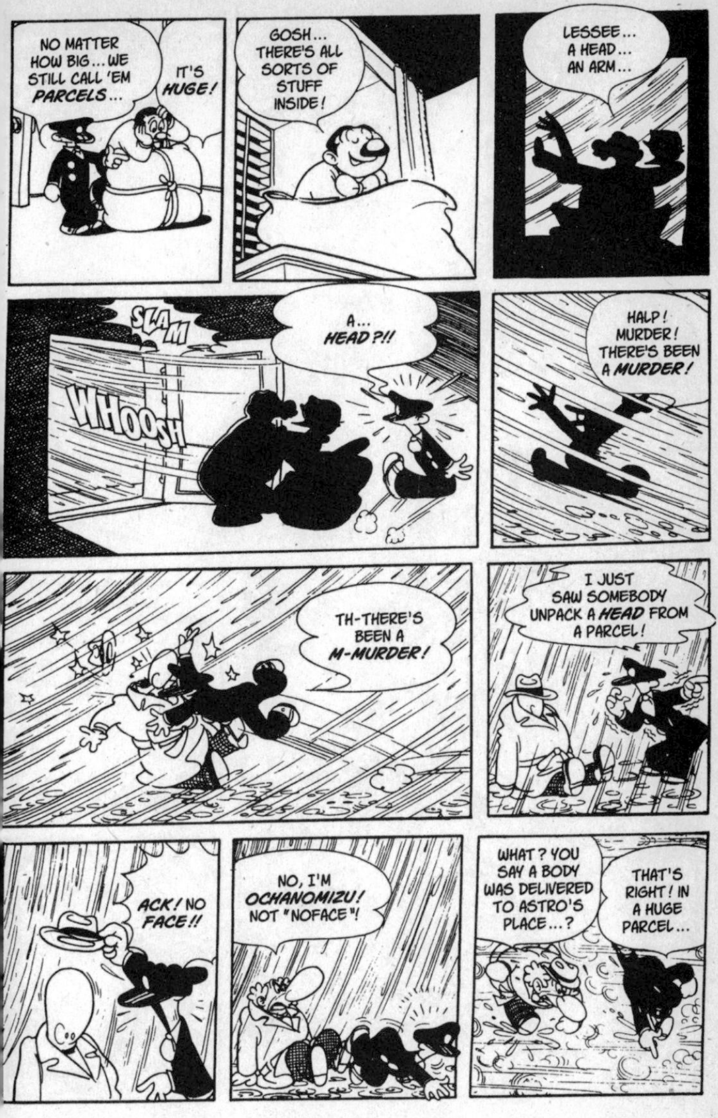
NO MATTER HOW BIG... WE STILL CALL 'EM PARCELS...
IT'S HUGE!
GOSH... THERE'S ALL SORTS OF STUFF INSIDE!
LESSEE... A HEAD... AN ARM...
SLAM
A... HEAD?!!
WHOOSH
HALP! MURDER! THERE'S BEEN A MURDER!
TH-THERE'S BEEN A M-MURDER!
I JUST SAW SOMEBODY UNPACK A HEAD FROM A PARCEL!
ACK! NO FACE!!
NO, I'M OCHANOMIZU! NOT "NOFACE"!
WHAT? YOU SAY A BODY WAS DELIVERED TO ASTRO'S PLACE...?
THAT'S RIGHT! IN A HUGE PARCEL...

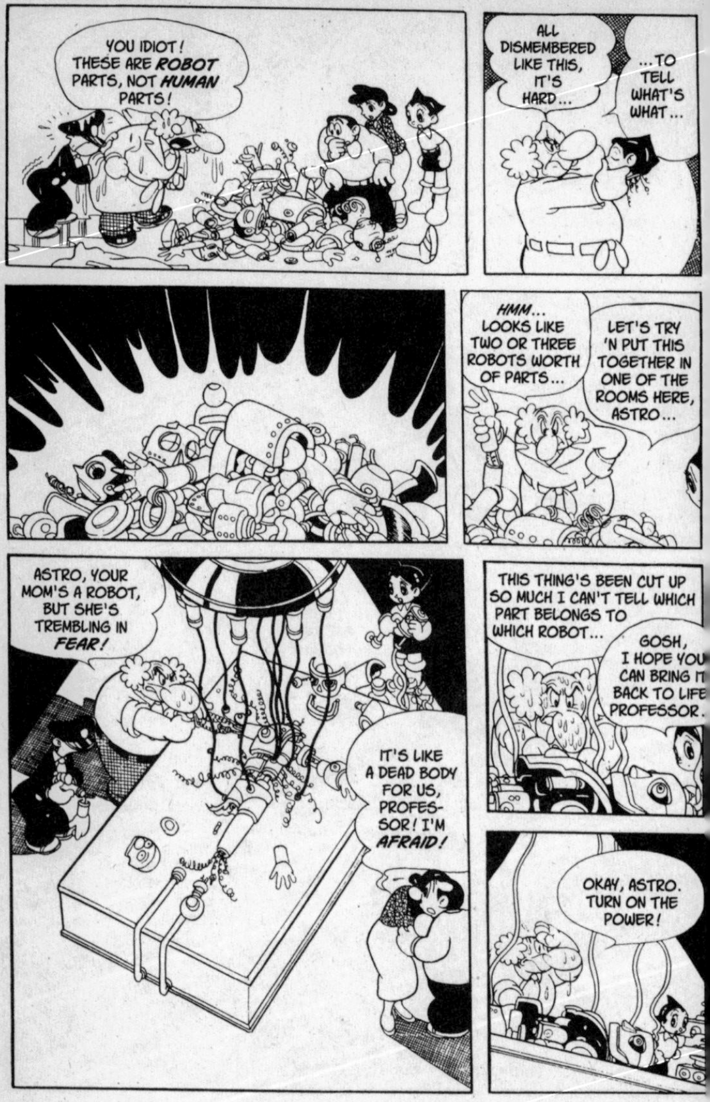
YOU IDIOT! THESE ARE ROBOT PARTS, NOT HUMAN PARTS!
ALL DISMEMBERED LIKE THIS, IT'S HARD...
...TO TELL WHAT'S WHAT...
HMM... LOOKS LIKE TWO OR THREE ROBOTS WORTH OF PARTS...
LET'S TRY 'N PUT THIS TOGETHER IN ONE OF THE ROOMS HERE, ASTRO...
ASTRO, YOUR MOM'S A ROBOT, BUT SHE'S TREMBLING IN FEAR!
IT'S LIKE A DEAD BODY FOR US, PROFES-SOR! I'M AFRAID!
THIS THING'S BEEN CUT UP SO MUCH I CAN'T TELL WHICH PART BELONGS TO WHICH ROBOT...
GOSH, I HOPE YOU CAN BRING IT BACK TO LIFE PROFESSOR.
OKAY, ASTRO. TURN ON THE POWER!

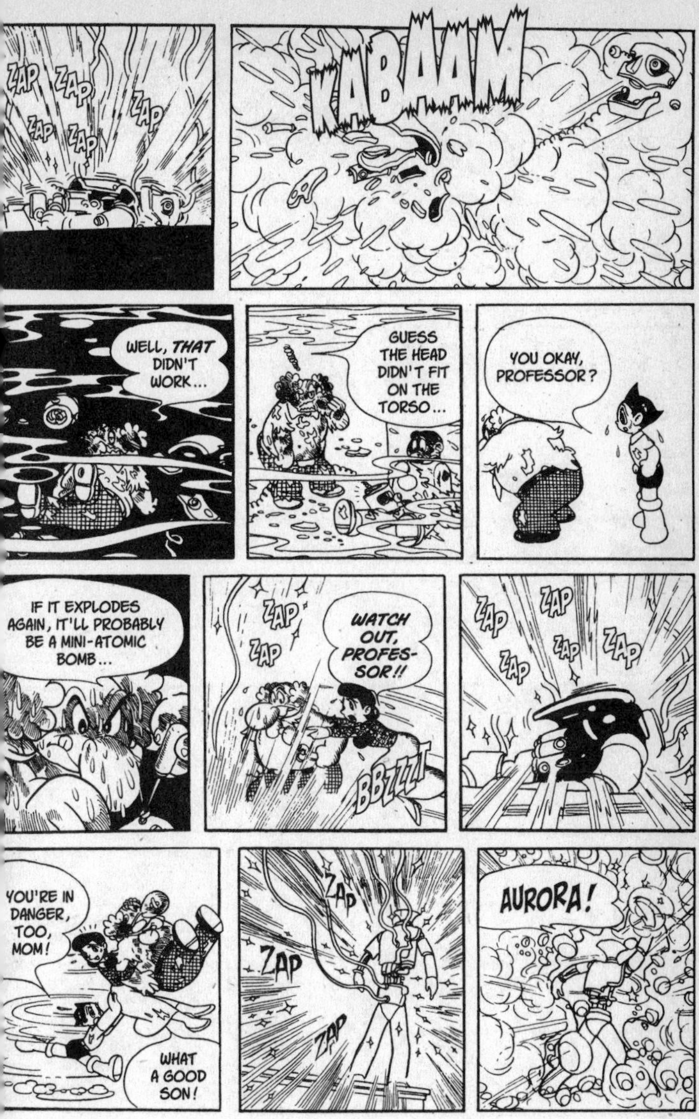

ZAP ZAP ZAP ZAP ZAP
KABAAM
WELL, *THAT* DIDN'T WORK...
GUESS THE HEAD DIDN'T FIT ON THE TORSO...
YOU OKAY, PROFESSOR?
IF IT EXPLODES AGAIN, IT'LL PROBABLY BE A MINI-ATOMIC BOMB...
ZAP ZAP
WATCH OUT, PROFES-SOR!!
BBZZZT
ZAP ZAP ZAP ZAP ZAP ZAP
YOU'RE IN DANGER, TOO, MOM!
WHAT A GOOD SON!
ZAP ZAP ZAP
AURORA!

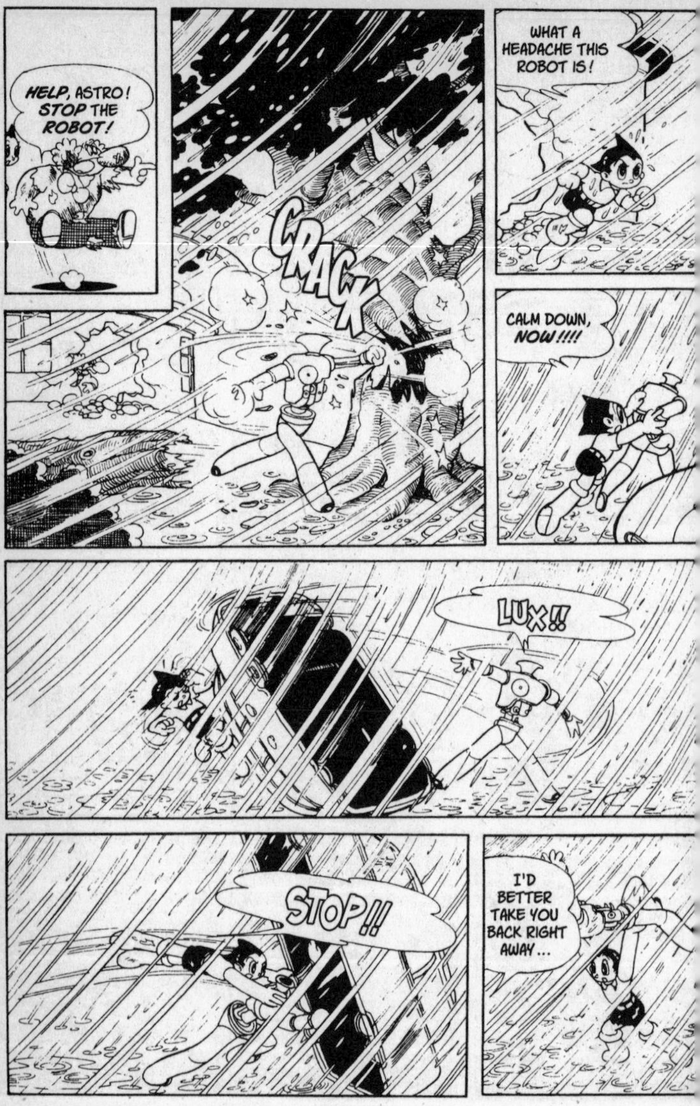
HELP, ASTRO! STOP THE ROBOT!
CRACK
WHAT A HEADACHE THIS ROBOT IS!
CALM DOWN, NOW!!!!
LUX!!
STOP!!
I'D BETTER TAKE YOU BACK RIGHT AWAY...

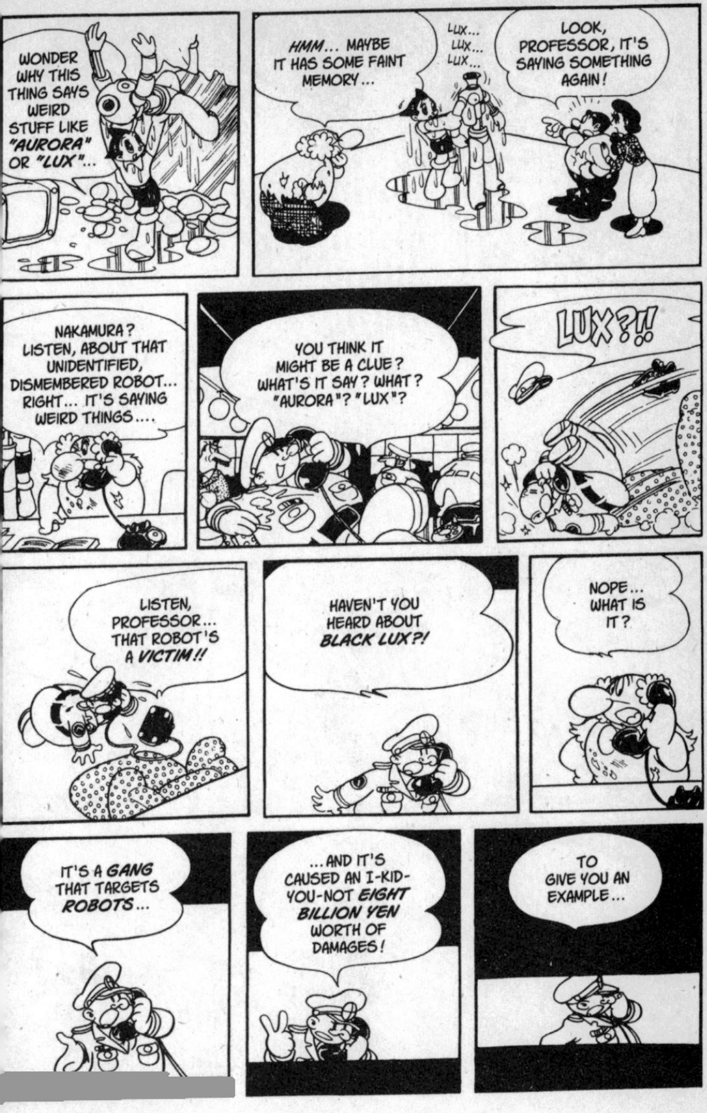
WONDER WHY THIS THING SAYS WEIRD STUFF LIKE "AURORA" OR "LUX"...
HMM... MAYBE IT HAS SOME FAINT MEMORY...
LUX... LUX... LUX...
LOOK, PROFESSOR, IT'S SAYING SOMETHING AGAIN!
NAKAMURA? LISTEN, ABOUT THAT UNIDENTIFIED, DISMEMBERED ROBOT... RIGHT... IT'S SAYING WEIRD THINGS....
YOU THINK IT MIGHT BE A CLUE? WHAT'S IT SAY? WHAT? "AURORA"? "LUX"?
LUX?!!
LISTEN, PROFESSOR... THAT ROBOT'S A VICTIM!!
HAVEN'T YOU HEARD ABOUT BLACK LUX?!
NOPE... WHAT IS IT?
IT'S A GANG THAT TARGETS ROBOTS...
...AND IT'S CAUSED AN I-KID-YOU-NOT EIGHT BILLION YEN WORTH OF DAMAGES!
TO GIVE YOU AN EXAMPLE...

...AMONG THE NEFARIOUS CRIMES THEY'VE COMMITTED ARE...

HALT!

WHO GOES THERE? MAN OR MACHINE?

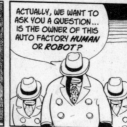

ACTUALLY, WE WANT TO ASK YOU A QUESTION... IS THE OWNER OF THIS AUTO FACTORY *HUMAN* OR *ROBOT*?

EVERYONE'S A ROBOT HERE!!

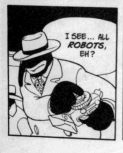

I SEE... ALL *ROBOTS*, EH?

IN THAT CASE, THERE'S NO REASON TO HESITATE...

VOOOSH VOOOSH VOOSH

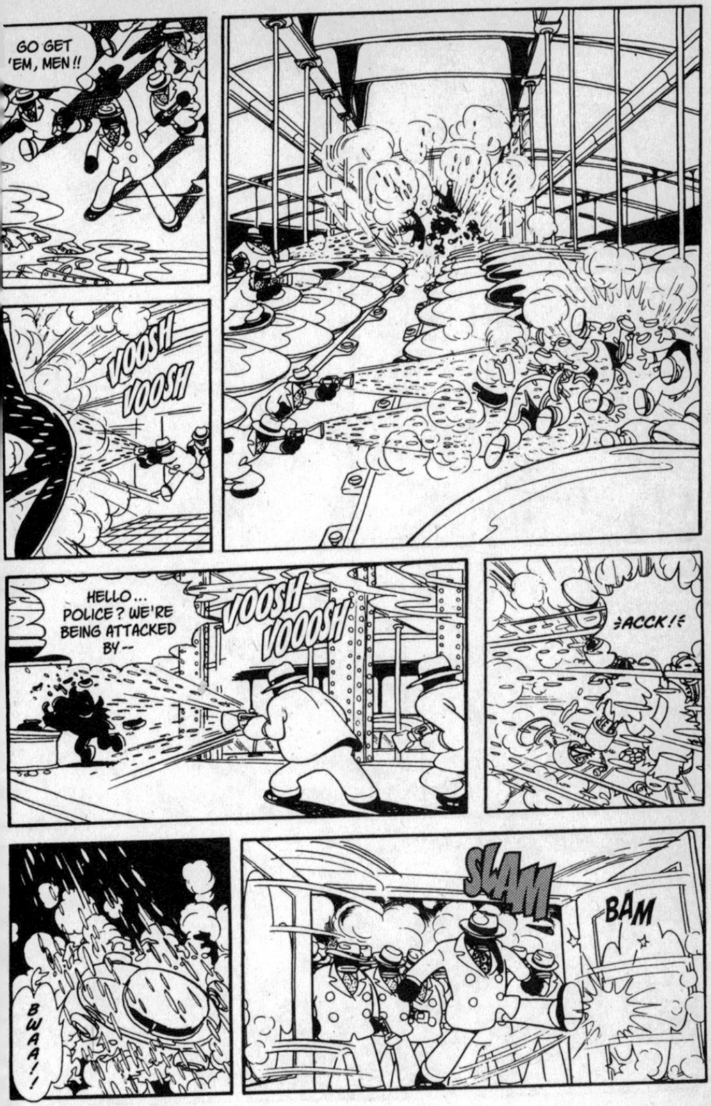

GO GET 'EM, MEN!!
VOOSH
VOOSH
HELLO... POLICE? WE'RE BEING ATTACKED BY--
VOOSH
VOOOSH
ACCK!
BWAAA!!
SLAM
BAM

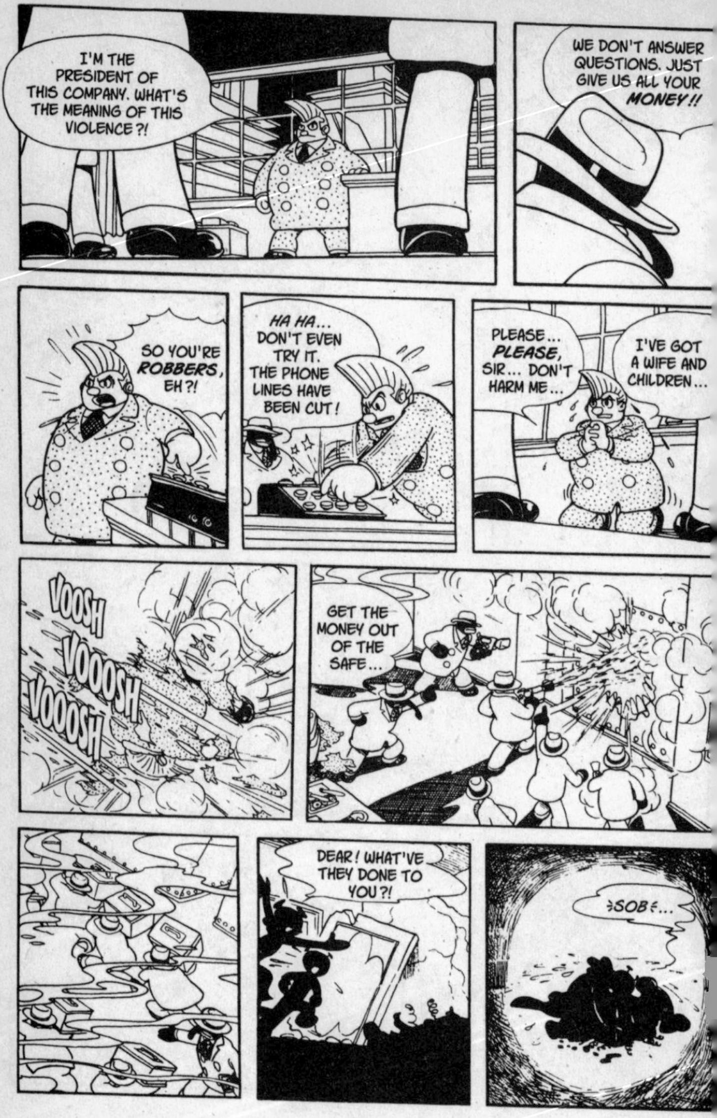
I'M THE PRESIDENT OF THIS COMPANY. WHAT'S THE MEANING OF THIS VIOLENCE?!
WE DON'T ANSWER QUESTIONS. JUST GIVE US ALL YOUR *MONEY!!*
SO YOU'RE *ROBBERS*, EH?!
HA HA... DON'T EVEN TRY IT. THE PHONE LINES HAVE BEEN CUT!
PLEASE... *PLEASE*, SIR... DON'T HARM ME...
I'VE GOT A WIFE AND CHILDREN...
VOOSH
VOOOSH
VOOOSH
GET THE MONEY OUT OF THE SAFE...
DEAR! WHAT'VE THEY DONE TO YOU?!
SOB...

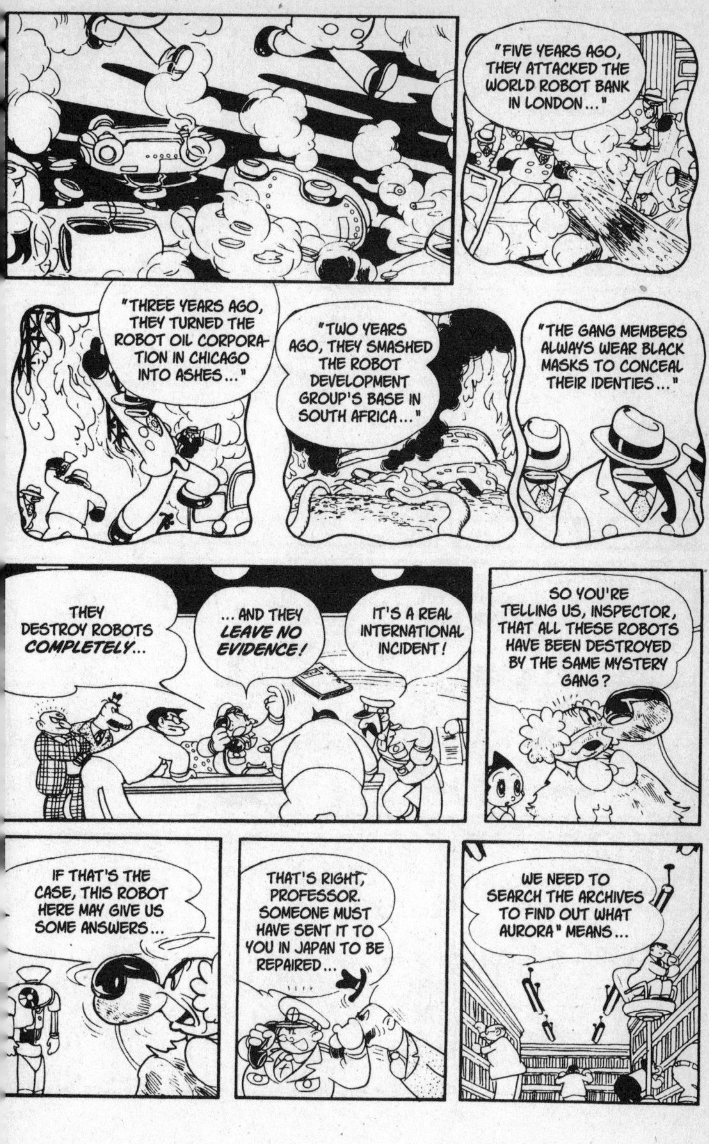
"FIVE YEARS AGO, THEY ATTACKED THE WORLD ROBOT BANK IN LONDON..."
"THREE YEARS AGO, THEY TURNED THE ROBOT OIL CORPORATION IN CHICAGO INTO ASHES..."
"TWO YEARS AGO, THEY SMASHED THE ROBOT DEVELOPMENT GROUP'S BASE IN SOUTH AFRICA..."
"THE GANG MEMBERS ALWAYS WEAR BLACK MASKS TO CONCEAL THEIR IDENTIES..."
THEY DESTROY ROBOTS COMPLETELY...
... AND THEY LEAVE NO EVIDENCE!
IT'S A REAL INTERNATIONAL INCIDENT!
SO YOU'RE TELLING US, INSPECTOR, THAT ALL THESE ROBOTS HAVE BEEN DESTROYED BY THE SAME MYSTERY GANG?
IF THAT'S THE CASE, THIS ROBOT HERE MAY GIVE US SOME ANSWERS...
THAT'S RIGHT, PROFESSOR. SOMEONE MUST HAVE SENT IT TO YOU IN JAPAN TO BE REPAIRED...
WE NEED TO SEARCH THE ARCHIVES TO FIND OUT WHAT AURORA" MEANS...

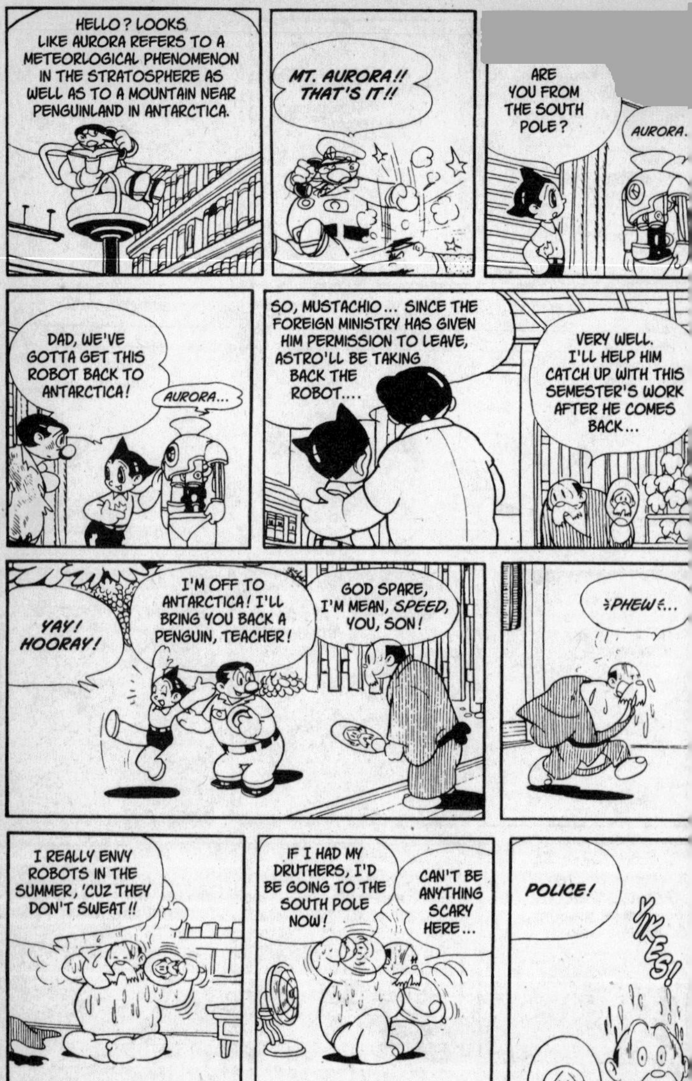
HELLO? LOOKS LIKE AURORA REFERS TO A METEORLOGICAL PHENOMENON IN THE STRATOSPHERE AS WELL AS TO A MOUNTAIN NEAR PENGUINLAND IN ANTARCTICA.
MT. AURORA!! THAT'S IT!!
ARE YOU FROM THE SOUTH POLE?
AURORA.
DAD, WE'VE GOTTA GET THIS ROBOT BACK TO ANTARCTICA!
AURORA...
SO, MUSTACHIO... SINCE THE FOREIGN MINISTRY HAS GIVEN HIM PERMISSION TO LEAVE, ASTRO'LL BE TAKING BACK THE ROBOT....
VERY WELL. I'LL HELP HIM CATCH UP WITH THIS SEMESTER'S WORK AFTER HE COMES BACK...
YAY! HOORAY!
I'M OFF TO ANTARCTICA! I'LL BRING YOU BACK A PENGUIN, TEACHER!
GOD SPARE, I'M MEAN, SPEED, YOU, SON!
PHEW...
I REALLY ENVY ROBOTS IN THE SUMMER, 'CUZ THEY DON'T SWEAT!!
IF I HAD MY DRUTHERS, I'D BE GOING TO THE SOUTH POLE NOW!
CAN'T BE ANYTHING SCARY HERE...
POLICE!
YIKES!

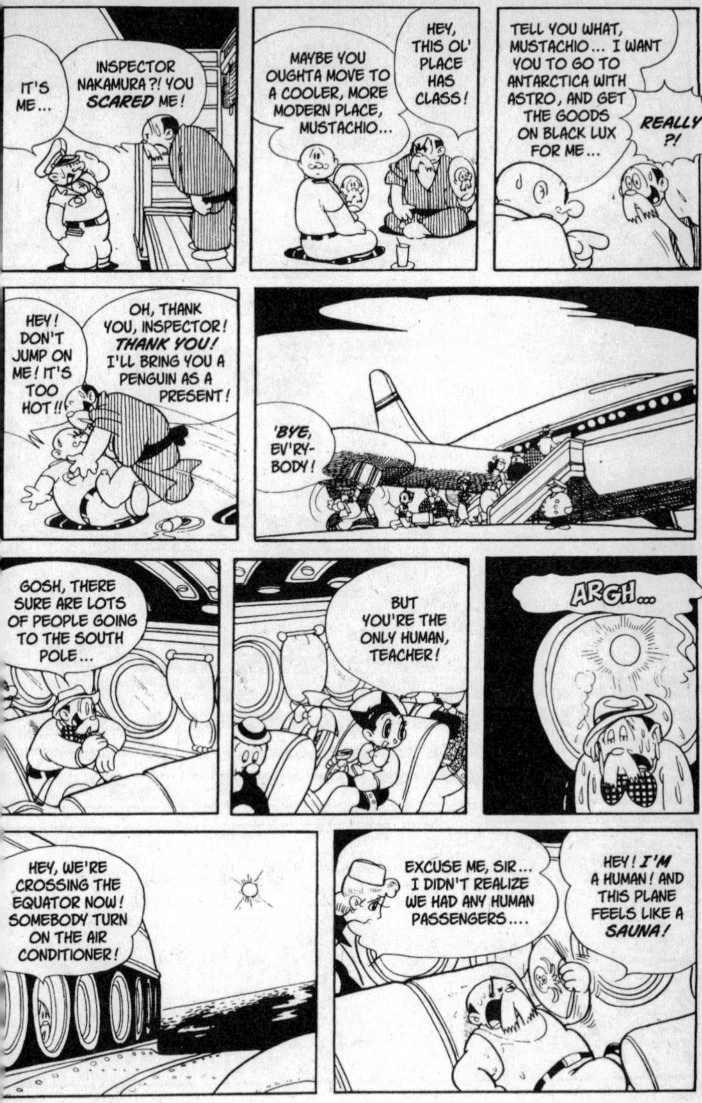
IT'S ME...
INSPECTOR NAKAMURA?! YOU *SCARED* ME!
MAYBE YOU OUGHTA MOVE TO A COOLER, MORE MODERN PLACE, MUSTACHIO...
HEY, THIS OL' PLACE HAS CLASS!
TELL YOU WHAT, MUSTACHIO... I WANT YOU TO GO TO ANTARCTICA WITH ASTRO, AND GET THE GOODS ON BLACK LUX FOR ME...
REALLY?!
HEY! DON'T JUMP ON ME! IT'S TOO HOT!!
OH, THANK YOU, INSPECTOR! *THANK YOU!* I'LL BRING YOU A PENGUIN AS A PRESENT!
'BYE, EV'RY-BODY!
GOSH, THERE SURE ARE LOTS OF PEOPLE GOING TO THE SOUTH POLE...
BUT YOU'RE THE ONLY HUMAN, TEACHER!
ARGH...
HEY, WE'RE CROSSING THE EQUATOR NOW! SOMEBODY TURN ON THE AIR CONDITIONER!
EXCUSE ME, SIR... I DIDN'T REALIZE WE HAD ANY HUMAN PASSENGERS....
HEY! *I'M* A HUMAN! AND THIS PLANE FEELS LIKE A *SAUNA*!

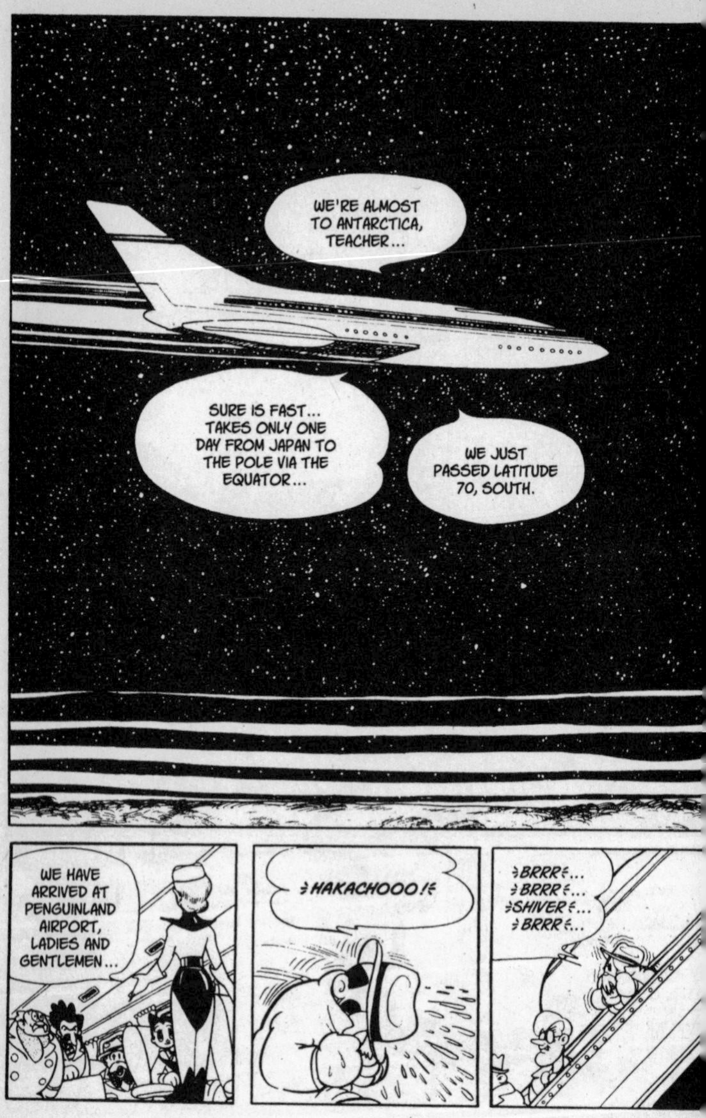
WE'RE ALMOST TO ANTARCTICA, TEACHER...
SURE IS FAST... TAKES ONLY ONE DAY FROM JAPAN TO THE POLE VIA THE EQUATOR...
WE JUST PASSED LATITUDE 70, SOUTH.
WE HAVE ARRIVED AT PENGUINLAND AIRPORT, LADIES AND GENTLEMEN...
HAKACHOOO!
BRRR... BRRR... SHIVER... BRRR...

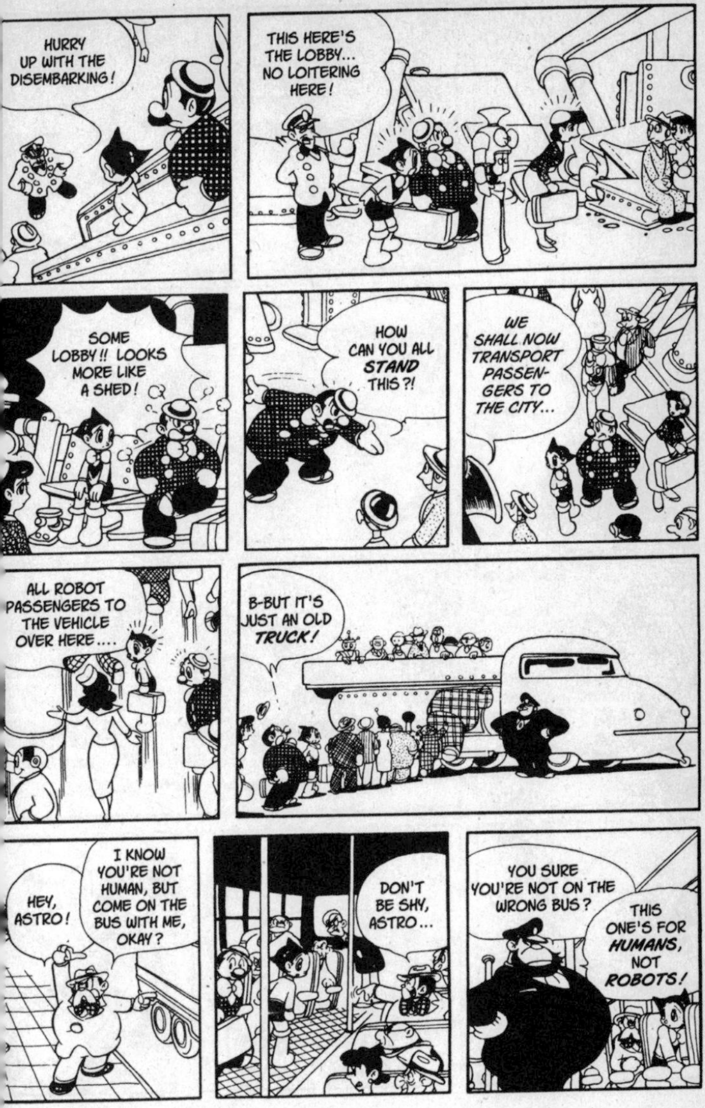

HURRY UP WITH THE DISEMBARKING!
THIS HERE'S THE LOBBY... NO LOITERING HERE!
SOME LOBBY!! LOOKS MORE LIKE A SHED!
HOW CAN YOU ALL *STAND* THIS?!
WE SHALL NOW TRANSPORT PASSENGERS TO THE CITY...
ALL ROBOT PASSENGERS TO THE VEHICLE OVER HERE....
B-BUT IT'S JUST AN OLD *TRUCK*!
HEY, ASTRO!
I KNOW YOU'RE NOT HUMAN, BUT COME ON THE BUS WITH ME, OKAY?
DON'T BE SHY, ASTRO...
YOU SURE YOU'RE NOT ON THE WRONG BUS?
THIS ONE'S FOR *HUMANS*, NOT *ROBOTS*!

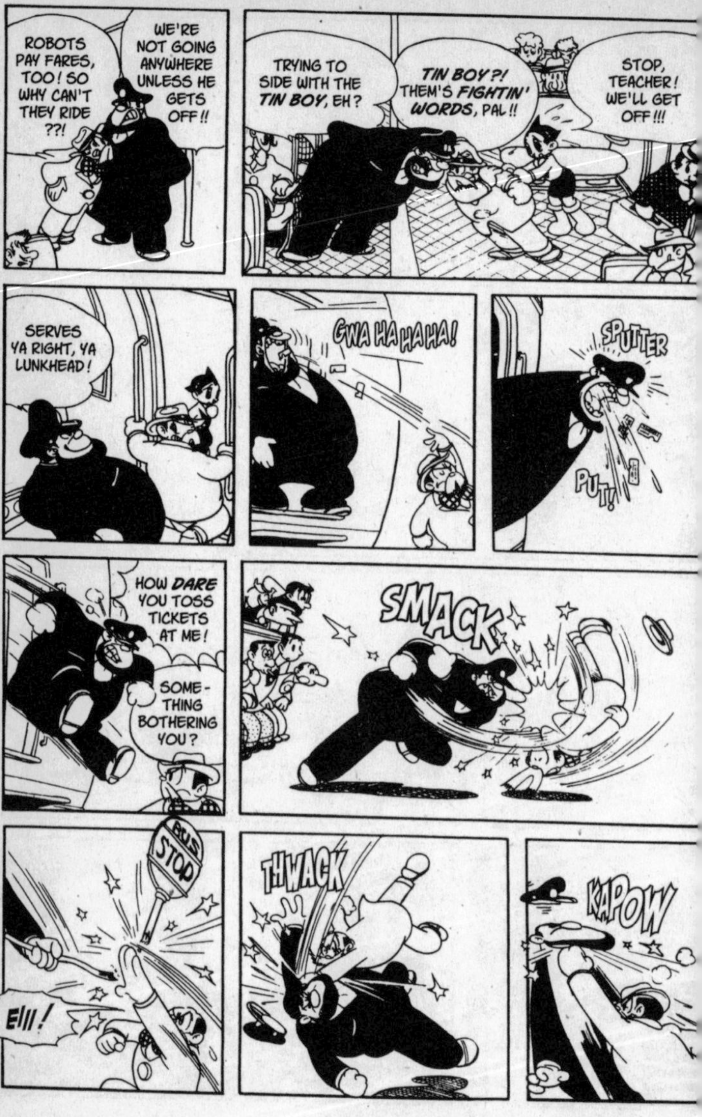
ROBOTS PAY FARES, TOO! SO WHY CAN'T THEY RIDE ??!
WE'RE NOT GOING ANYWHERE UNLESS HE GETS OFF!!
TRYING TO SIDE WITH THE *TIN BOY*, EH?
TIN BOY?! THEM'S *FIGHTIN' WORDS*, PAL!!
STOP, TEACHER! WE'LL GET OFF!!!
SERVES YA RIGHT, YA LUNKHEAD!
GWA HA HA HA!
SPUTTER
PUT!
HOW *DARE* YOU TOSS TICKETS AT ME!
SOME-THING BOTHERING YOU?
SMACK
BUS STOP
EII!
THWACK
KAPOW

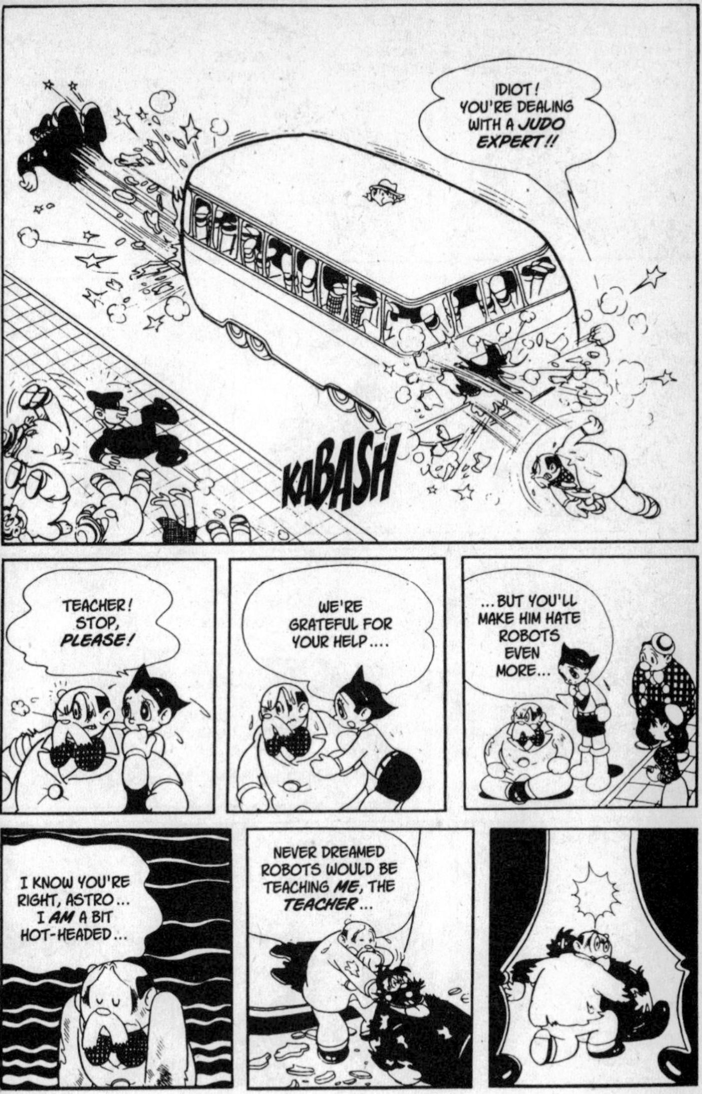
IDIOT! YOU'RE DEALING WITH A JUDO EXPERT!!
KABASH
TEACHER! STOP, PLEASE!
WE'RE GRATEFUL FOR YOUR HELP....
...BUT YOU'LL MAKE HIM HATE ROBOTS EVEN MORE...
I KNOW YOU'RE RIGHT, ASTRO... I AM A BIT HOT-HEADED...
NEVER DREAMED ROBOTS WOULD BE TEACHING ME, THE TEACHER...

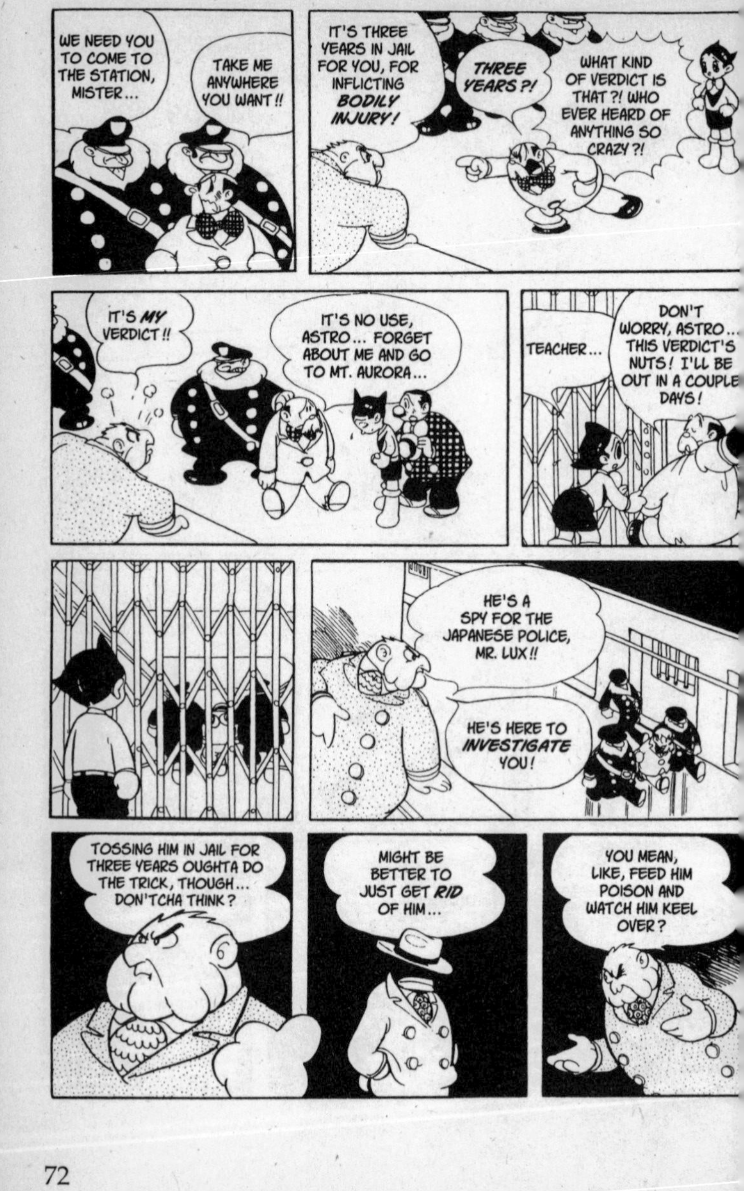
WE NEED YOU TO COME TO THE STATION, MISTER...
TAKE ME ANYWHERE YOU WANT!!
IT'S THREE YEARS IN JAIL FOR YOU, FOR INFLICTING BODILY INJURY!
THREE YEARS?!
WHAT KIND OF VERDICT IS THAT?! WHO EVER HEARD OF ANYTHING SO CRAZY?!
IT'S MY VERDICT!!
IT'S NO USE, ASTRO... FORGET ABOUT ME AND GO TO MT. AURORA...
TEACHER...
DON'T WORRY, ASTRO... THIS VERDICT'S NUTS! I'LL BE OUT IN A COUPLE DAYS!
HE'S A SPY FOR THE JAPANESE POLICE, MR. LUX!!
HE'S HERE TO INVESTIGATE YOU!
TOSSING HIM IN JAIL FOR THREE YEARS OUGHTA DO THE TRICK, THOUGH... DON'TCHA THINK?
MIGHT BE BETTER TO JUST GET RID OF HIM...
YOU MEAN, LIKE, FEED HIM POISON AND WATCH HIM KEEL OVER?

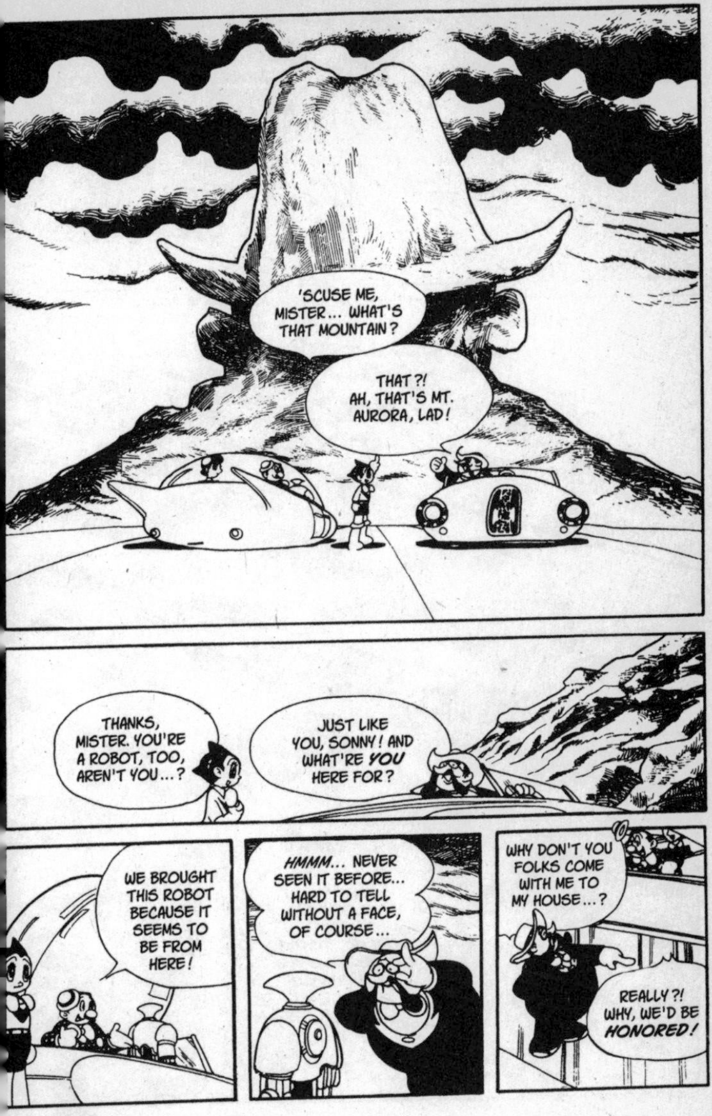
'SCUSE ME, MISTER... WHAT'S THAT MOUNTAIN?
THAT?! AH, THAT'S MT. AURORA, LAD!
THANKS, MISTER. YOU'RE A ROBOT, TOO, AREN'T YOU...?
JUST LIKE YOU, SONNY! AND WHAT'RE *YOU* HERE FOR?
WE BROUGHT THIS ROBOT BECAUSE IT SEEMS TO BE FROM HERE!
HMMM... NEVER SEEN IT BEFORE... HARD TO TELL WITHOUT A FACE, OF COURSE...
WHY DON'T YOU FOLKS COME WITH ME TO MY HOUSE...?
REALLY?! WHY, WE'D BE ***HONORED!***

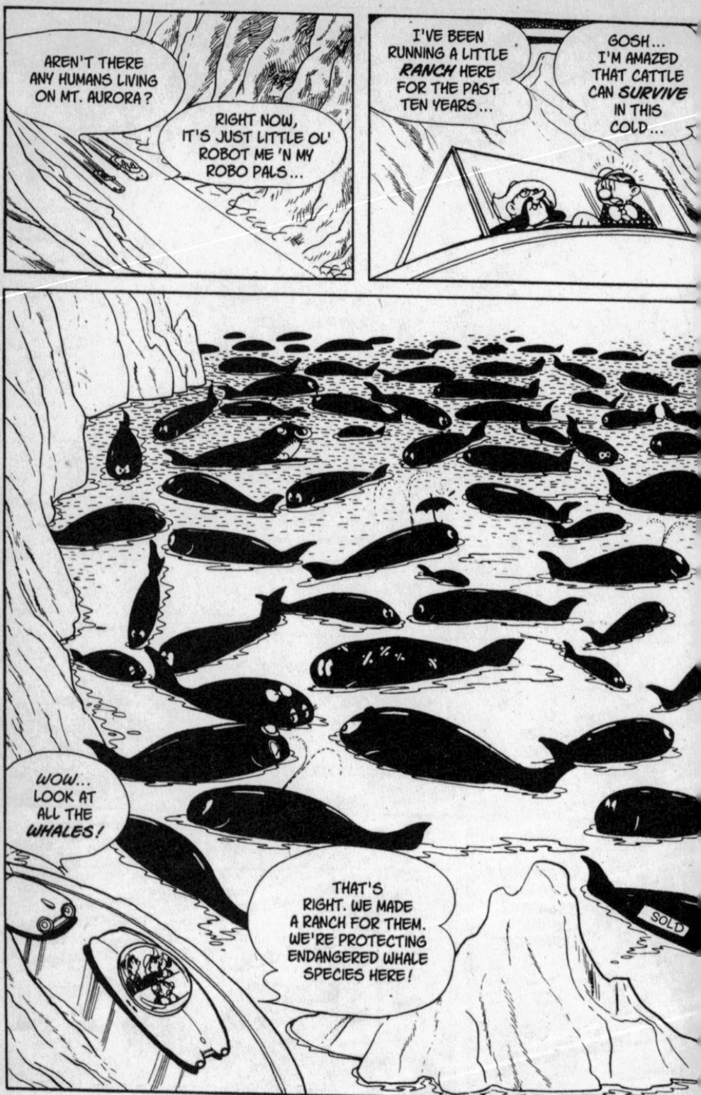
AREN'T THERE ANY HUMANS LIVING ON MT. AURORA?
RIGHT NOW, IT'S JUST LITTLE OL' ROBOT ME 'N MY ROBO PALS...
I'VE BEEN RUNNING A LITTLE RANCH HERE FOR THE PAST TEN YEARS...
GOSH... I'M AMAZED THAT CATTLE CAN SURVIVE IN THIS COLD...
WOW... LOOK AT ALL THE WHALES!
THAT'S RIGHT. WE MADE A RANCH FOR THEM. WE'RE PROTECTING ENDANGERED WHALE SPECIES HERE!
SOLD

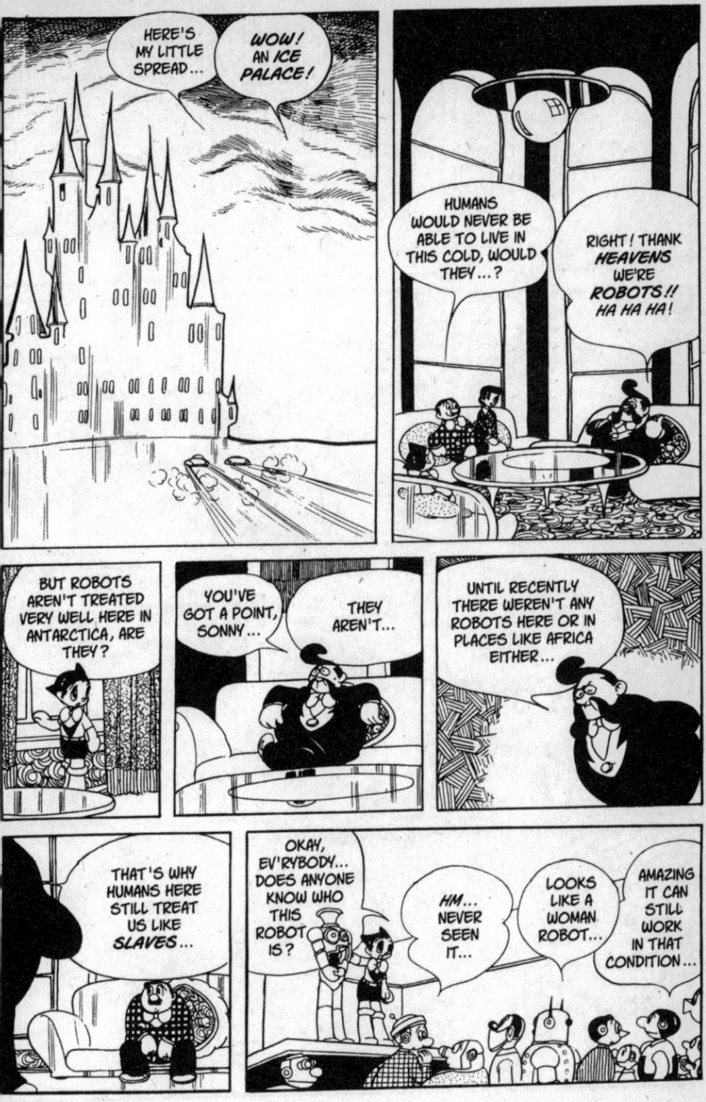

HERE'S MY LITTLE SPREAD...
WOW! AN ICE PALACE!
HUMANS WOULD NEVER BE ABLE TO LIVE IN THIS COLD, WOULD THEY...?
RIGHT! THANK HEAVENS WE'RE ROBOTS!! HA HA HA!
BUT ROBOTS AREN'T TREATED VERY WELL HERE IN ANTARCTICA, ARE THEY?
YOU'VE GOT A POINT, SONNY...
THEY AREN'T...
UNTIL RECENTLY THERE WEREN'T ANY ROBOTS HERE OR IN PLACES LIKE AFRICA EITHER...
THAT'S WHY HUMANS HERE STILL TREAT US LIKE SLAVES...
OKAY, EV'RYBODY... DOES ANYONE KNOW WHO THIS ROBOT IS?
HM... NEVER SEEN IT...
LOOKS LIKE A WOMAN ROBOT...
AMAZING IT CAN STILL WORK IN THAT CONDITION...

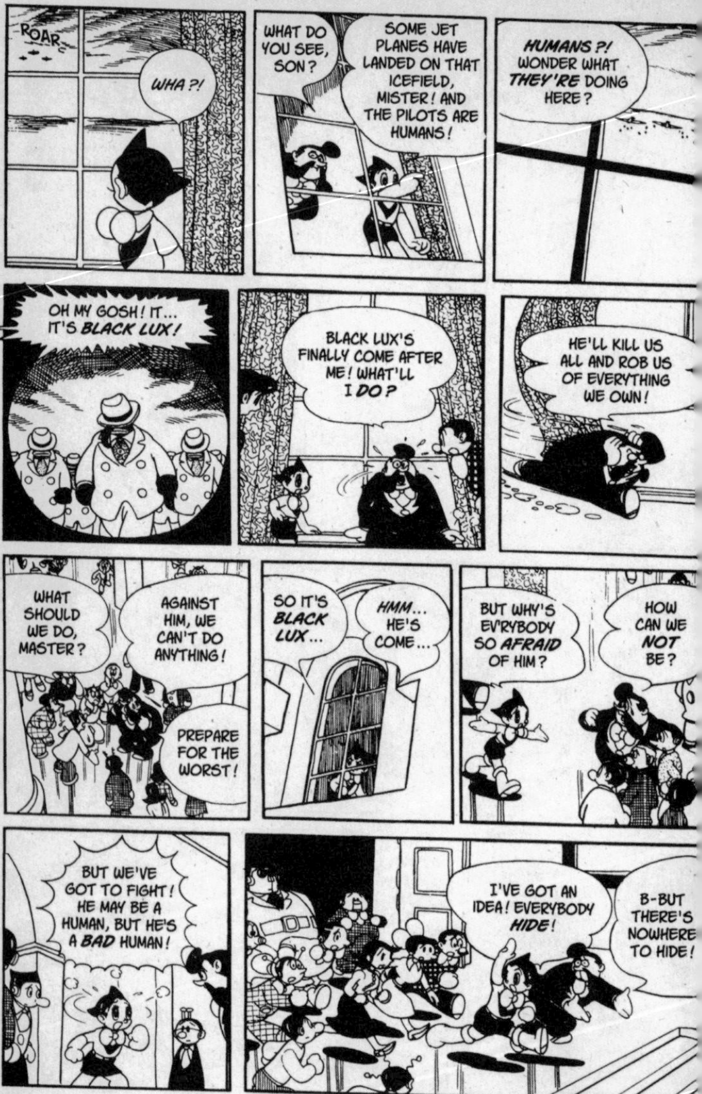
ROAR
WHA?!
WHAT DO YOU SEE, SON?
SOME JET PLANES HAVE LANDED ON THAT ICEFIELD, MISTER! AND THE PILOTS ARE HUMANS!
HUMANS?! WONDER WHAT THEY'RE DOING HERE?
OH MY GOSH! IT... IT'S BLACK LUX!
BLACK LUX'S FINALLY COME AFTER ME! WHAT'LL I DO?
HE'LL KILL US ALL AND ROB US OF EVERYTHING WE OWN!
WHAT SHOULD WE DO, MASTER?
AGAINST HIM, WE CAN'T DO ANYTHING!
PREPARE FOR THE WORST!
SO IT'S BLACK LUX...
HMM... HE'S COME...
BUT WHY'S EV'RYBODY SO AFRAID OF HIM?
HOW CAN WE NOT BE?
BUT WE'VE GOT TO FIGHT! HE MAY BE A HUMAN, BUT HE'S A BAD HUMAN!
I'VE GOT AN IDEA! EVERYBODY HIDE!
B-BUT THERE'S NOWHERE TO HIDE!

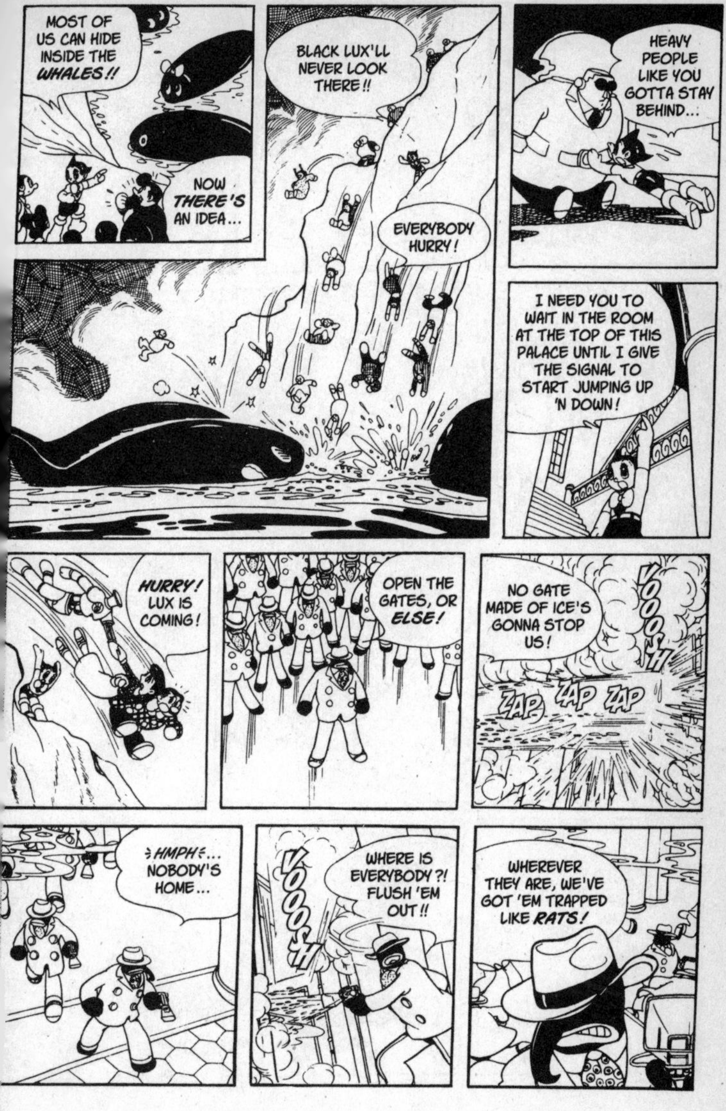
MOST OF US CAN HIDE INSIDE THE WHALES!!
NOW THERE'S AN IDEA...
BLACK LUX'LL NEVER LOOK THERE!!
EVERYBODY HURRY!
HEAVY PEOPLE LIKE YOU GOTTA STAY BEHIND...
I NEED YOU TO WAIT IN THE ROOM AT THE TOP OF THIS PALACE UNTIL I GIVE THE SIGNAL TO START JUMPING UP 'N DOWN!
HURRY! LUX IS COMING!
OPEN THE GATES, OR ELSE!
NO GATE MADE OF ICE'S GONNA STOP US!
VOOOSH
ZAP ZAP ZAP
HMPH... NOBODY'S HOME...
VOOOSH
WHERE IS EVERYBODY?! FLUSH 'EM OUT!!
WHEREVER THEY ARE, WE'VE GOT 'EM TRAPPED LIKE RATS!

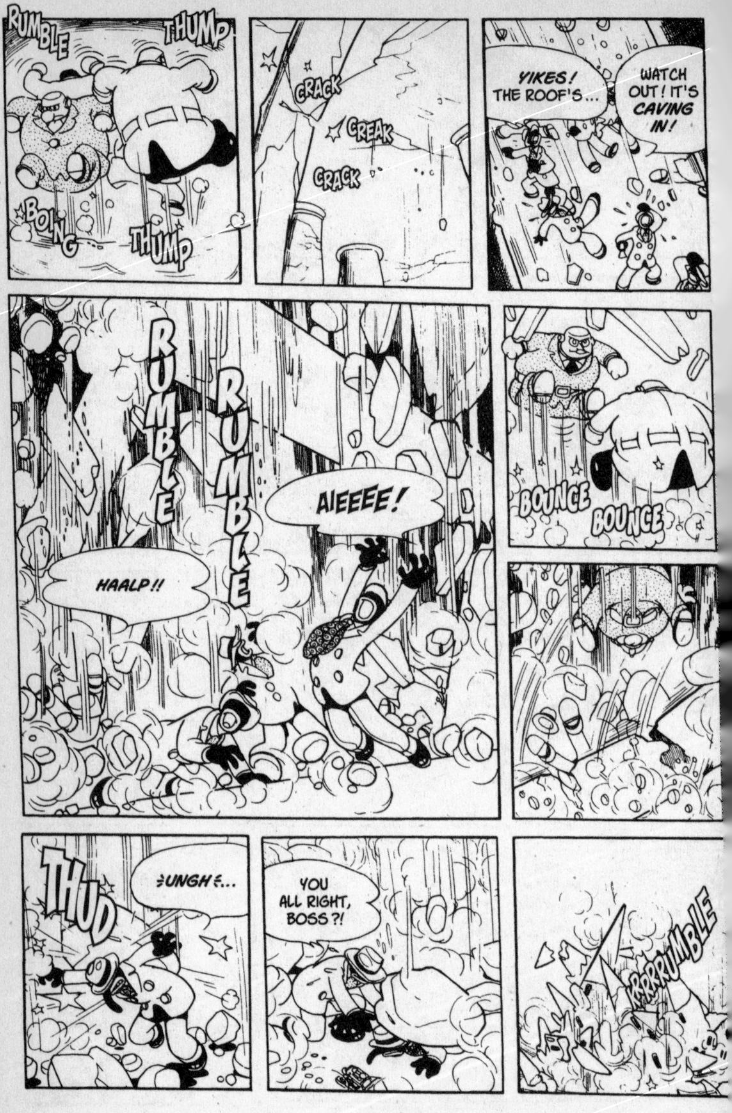
RUMBLE
THUMP
BOING
THUMP
CRACK
CREAK
CRACK
YIKES! THE ROOF'S...
WATCH OUT! IT'S CAVING IN!
RUMBLE
RUMBLE
AIEEEE!
HAALP!!
BOUNCE
BOUNCE
THUD
UNGH...
YOU ALL RIGHT, BOSS?!
KRRRUMBLE

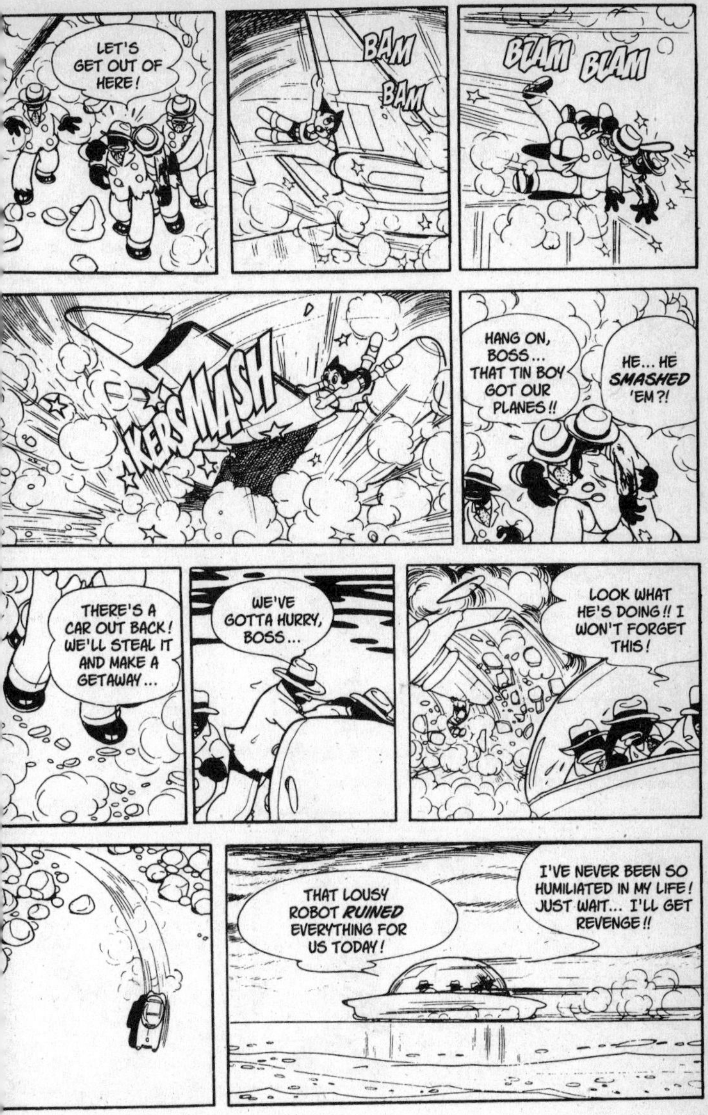
LET'S GET OUT OF HERE!
BAM
BAM
BLAM
BLAM
KERSMASH
HANG ON, BOSS... THAT TIN BOY GOT OUR PLANES!!
HE... HE SMASHED 'EM?!
THERE'S A CAR OUT BACK! WE'LL STEAL IT AND MAKE A GETAWAY...
WE'VE GOTTA HURRY, BOSS...
LOOK WHAT HE'S DOING!! I WON'T FORGET THIS!
THAT LOUSY ROBOT RUINED EVERYTHING FOR US TODAY!
I'VE NEVER BEEN SO HUMILIATED IN MY LIFE! JUST WAIT... I'LL GET REVENGE!!

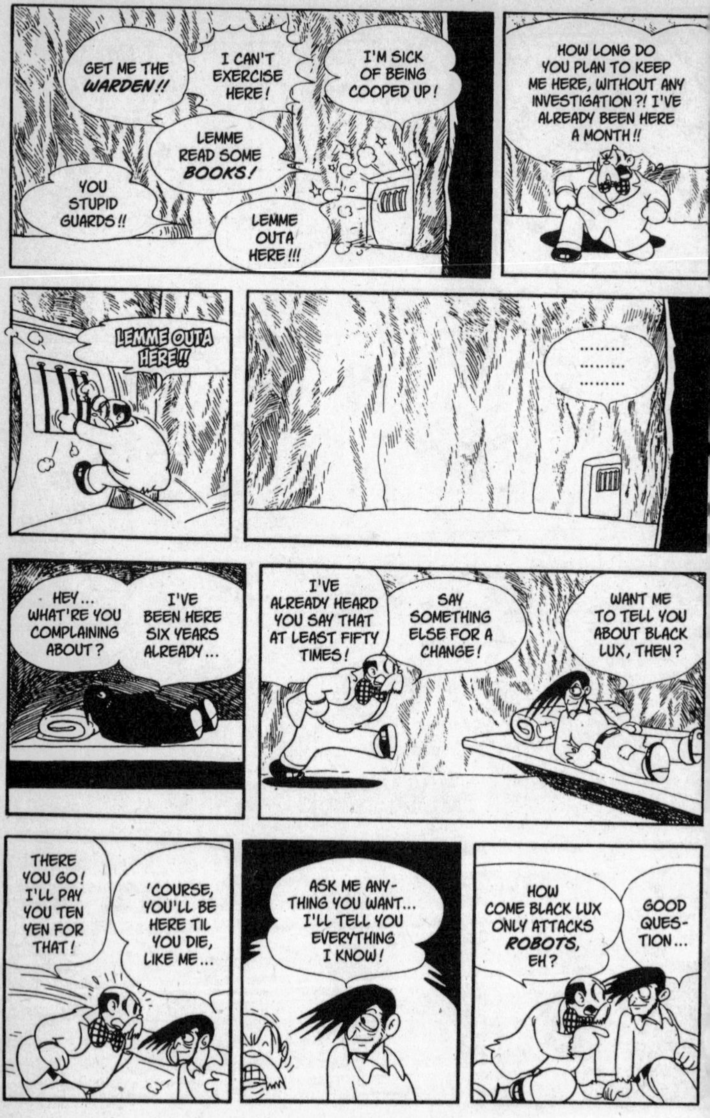
GET ME THE WARDEN!!
I CAN'T EXERCISE HERE!
I'M SICK OF BEING COOPED UP!
LEMME READ SOME BOOKS!
YOU STUPID GUARDS!!
LEMME OUTA HERE!!!
HOW LONG DO YOU PLAN TO KEEP ME HERE, WITHOUT ANY INVESTIGATION?! I'VE ALREADY BEEN HERE A MONTH!!
LEMME OUTA HERE!!
....
....
....
HEY... WHAT'RE YOU COMPLAINING ABOUT?
I'VE BEEN HERE SIX YEARS ALREADY...
I'VE ALREADY HEARD YOU SAY THAT AT LEAST FIFTY TIMES!
SAY SOMETHING ELSE FOR A CHANGE!
WANT ME TO TELL YOU ABOUT BLACK LUX, THEN?
THERE YOU GO! I'LL PAY YOU TEN YEN FOR THAT!
'COURSE, YOU'LL BE HERE TIL YOU DIE, LIKE ME...
ASK ME ANY-THING YOU WANT... I'LL TELL YOU EVERYTHING I KNOW!
HOW COME BLACK LUX ONLY ATTACKS ROBOTS, EH?
GOOD QUES-TION...

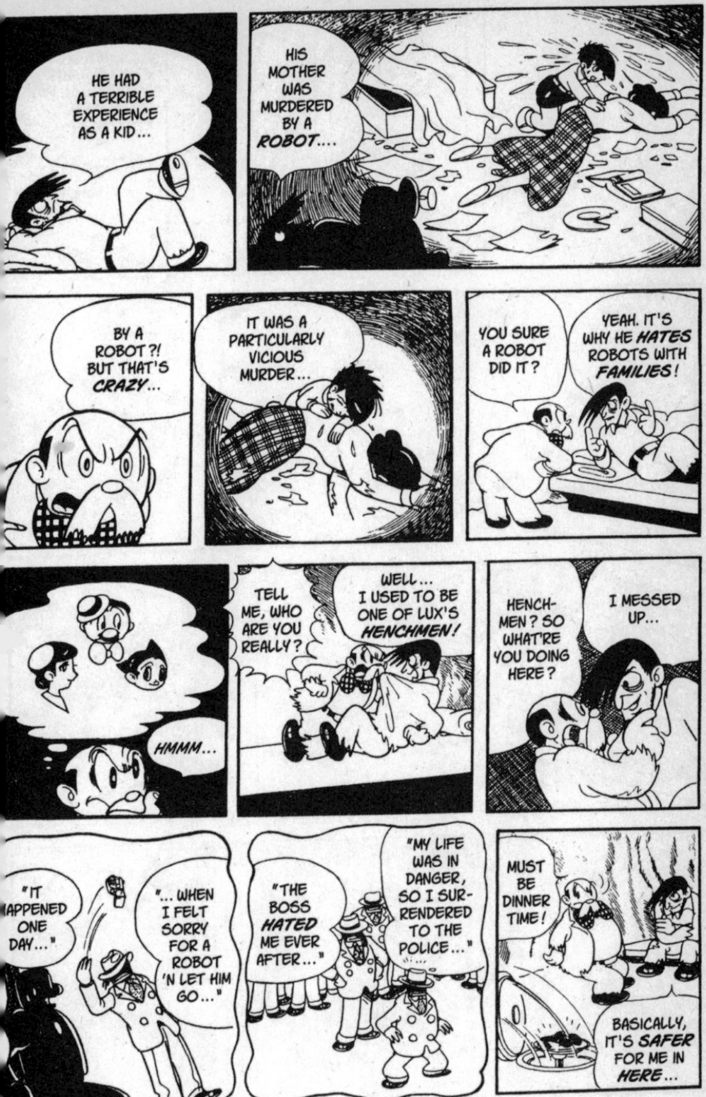
HE HAD A TERRIBLE EXPERIENCE AS A KID...
HIS MOTHER WAS MURDERED BY A ROBOT....
BY A ROBOT?! BUT THAT'S CRAZY...
IT WAS A PARTICULARLY VICIOUS MURDER...
YOU SURE A ROBOT DID IT?
YEAH. IT'S WHY HE HATES ROBOTS WITH FAMILIES!
HMMM...
TELL ME, WHO ARE YOU REALLY?
WELL... I USED TO BE ONE OF LUX'S HENCHMEN!
HENCH-MEN? SO WHAT'RE YOU DOING HERE?
I MESSED UP...
"IT HAPPENED ONE DAY..."
"... WHEN I FELT SORRY FOR A ROBOT 'N LET HIM GO..."
"THE BOSS HATED ME EVER AFTER..."
"MY LIFE WAS IN DANGER, SO I SUR-RENDERED TO THE POLICE..."
MUST BE DINNER TIME!
BASICALLY, IT'S SAFER FOR ME IN HERE...

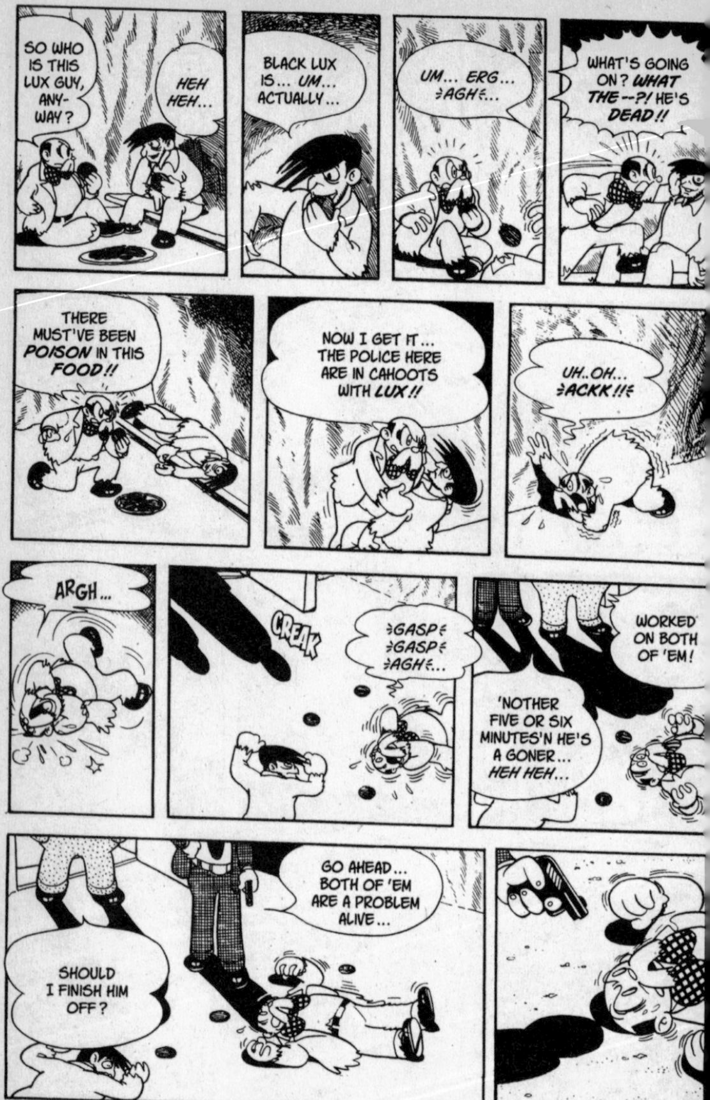
SO WHO IS THIS LUX GUY, ANYWAY?
HEH HEH...
BLACK LUX IS... UM... ACTUALLY...
UM... ERG... AGH...
WHAT'S GOING ON? WHAT THE--?! HE'S DEAD!!
THERE MUST'VE BEEN POISON IN THIS FOOD!!
NOW I GET IT... THE POLICE HERE ARE IN CAHOOTS WITH LUX!!
UH..OH... ACKK!!!
ARGH...
CREAK
GASP GASP AGH...
WORKED ON BOTH OF 'EM!
'NOTHER FIVE OR SIX MINUTES'N HE'S A GONER... HEH HEH...
SHOULD I FINISH HIM OFF?
GO AHEAD... BOTH OF 'EM ARE A PROBLEM ALIVE...

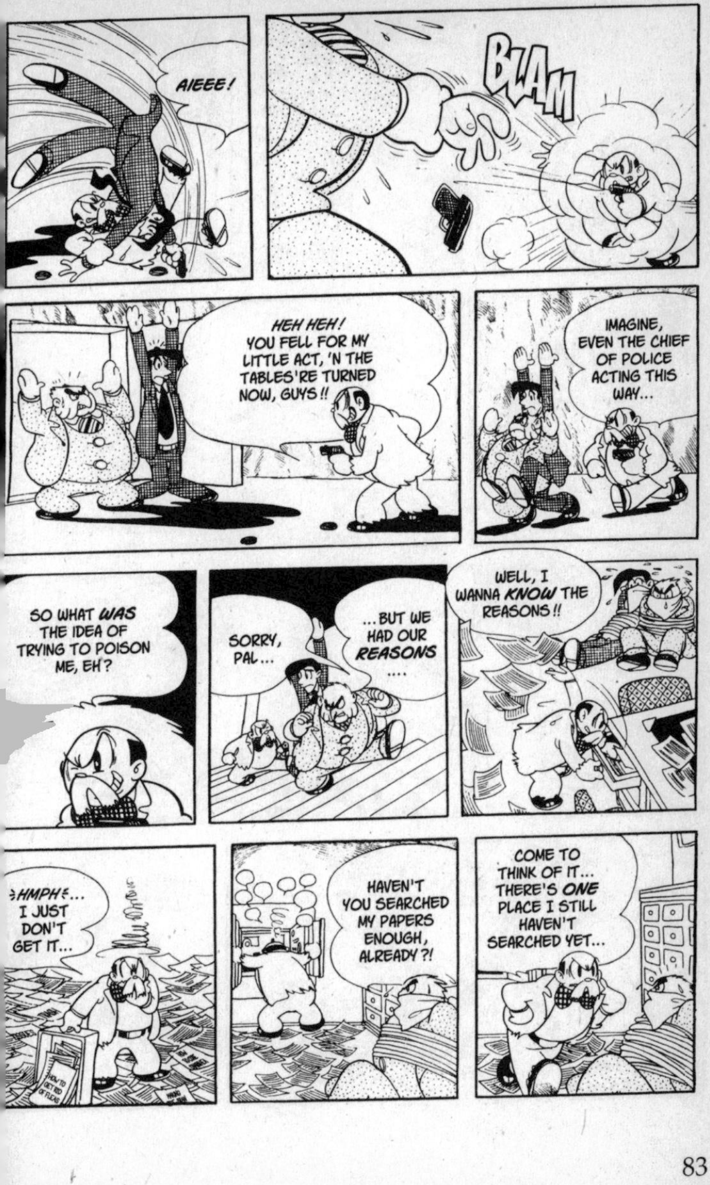
AIEEE!
BLAM
HEH HEH! YOU FELL FOR MY LITTLE ACT, 'N THE TABLES'RE TURNED NOW, GUYS!!
IMAGINE, EVEN THE CHIEF OF POLICE ACTING THIS WAY...
SO WHAT *WAS* THE IDEA OF TRYING TO POISON ME, EH?
SORRY, PAL...
...BUT WE HAD OUR *REASONS* ....
WELL, I WANNA *KNOW* THE REASONS!!
≑HMPH≑... I JUST DON'T GET IT...
HOW TO GET RID OF FLEAS
HAVEN'T YOU SEARCHED MY PAPERS ENOUGH, ALREADY?!
COME TO THINK OF IT... THERE'S *ONE* PLACE I STILL HAVEN'T SEARCHED YET...

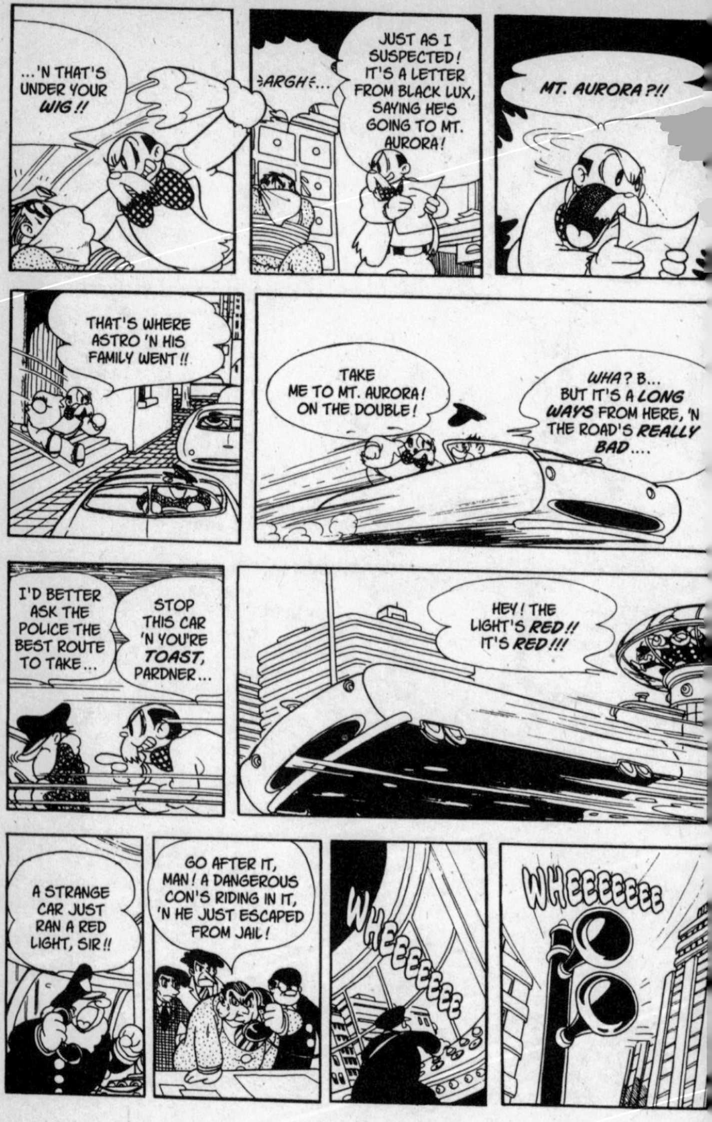
...'N THAT'S UNDER YOUR WIG!!
ARGH...
JUST AS I SUSPECTED! IT'S A LETTER FROM BLACK LUX, SAYING HE'S GOING TO MT. AURORA!
MT. AURORA?!!
THAT'S WHERE ASTRO 'N HIS FAMILY WENT!!
TAKE ME TO MT. AURORA! ON THE DOUBLE!
WHA? B... BUT IT'S A LONG WAYS FROM HERE, 'N THE ROAD'S REALLY BAD....
I'D BETTER ASK THE POLICE THE BEST ROUTE TO TAKE...
STOP THIS CAR 'N YOU'RE TOAST, PARDNER...
HEY! THE LIGHT'S RED!! IT'S RED!!!
A STRANGE CAR JUST RAN A RED LIGHT, SIR!!
GO AFTER IT, MAN! A DANGEROUS CON'S RIDING IN IT, 'N HE JUST ESCAPED FROM JAIL!
WHEEEEEEE
WHEEEEEEEE

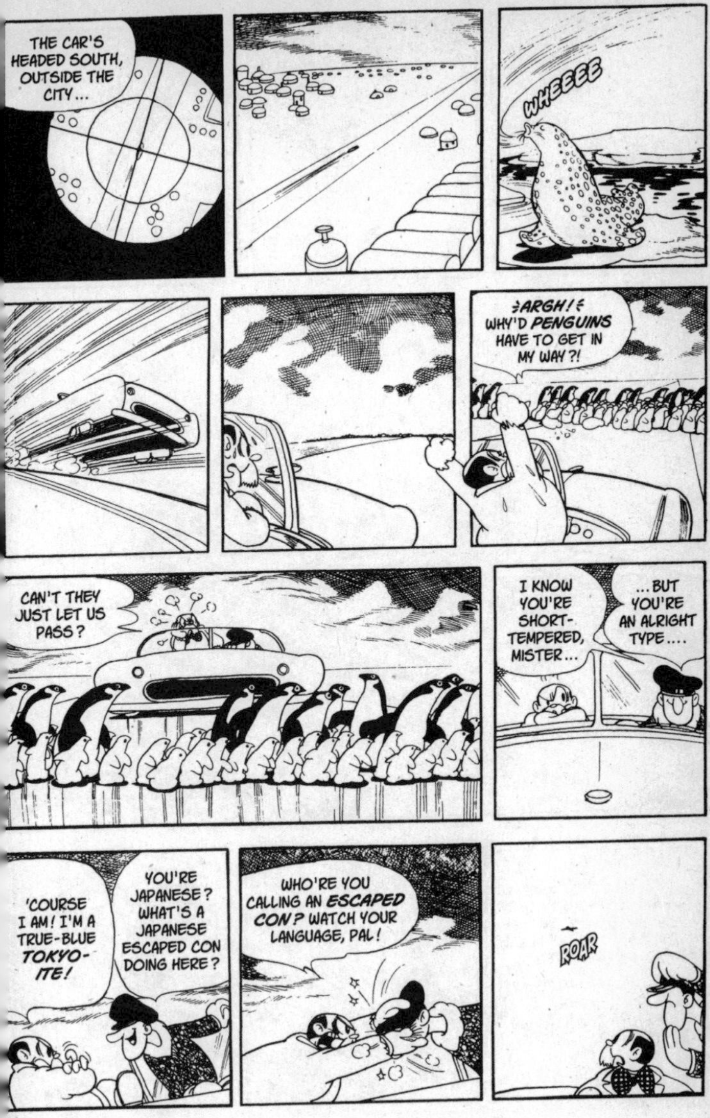
THE CAR'S HEADED SOUTH, OUTSIDE THE CITY...
WHEEEE
ARGH! WHY'D PENGUINS HAVE TO GET IN MY WAY?!
CAN'T THEY JUST LET US PASS?
I KNOW YOU'RE SHORT-TEMPERED, MISTER...
...BUT YOU'RE AN ALRIGHT TYPE....
YOU'RE JAPANESE? WHAT'S A JAPANESE ESCAPED CON DOING HERE?
'COURSE I AM! I'M A TRUE-BLUE TOKYO-ITE!
WHO'RE YOU CALLING AN ESCAPED CON? WATCH YOUR LANGUAGE, PAL!
ROAR

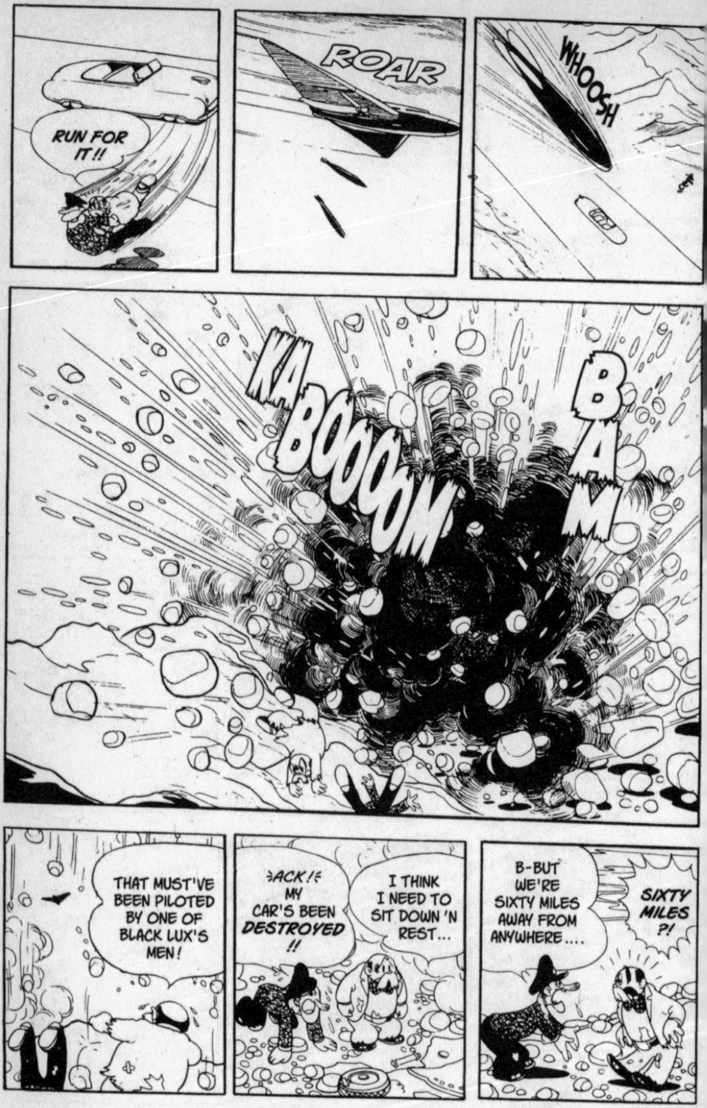
RUN FOR IT!!
ROAR
WHOOSH
KA BOOOOOM
BAM
THAT MUST'VE BEEN PILOTED BY ONE OF BLACK LUX'S MEN!
ACK! MY CAR'S BEEN DESTROYED !!
I THINK I NEED TO SIT DOWN 'N REST...
B-BUT WE'RE SIXTY MILES AWAY FROM ANYWHERE....
SIXTY MILES ?!

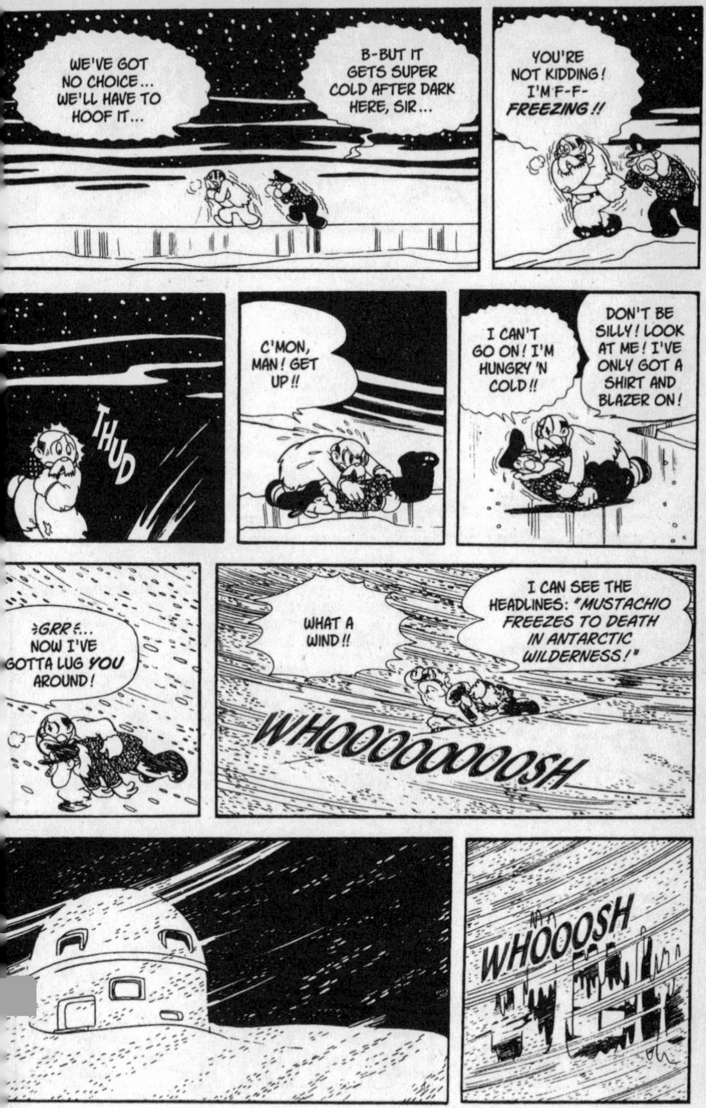
WE'VE GOT NO CHOICE... WE'LL HAVE TO HOOF IT...
B-BUT IT GETS SUPER COLD AFTER DARK HERE, SIR...
YOU'RE NOT KIDDING! I'M F-F-FREEZING!!
THUD
C'MON, MAN! GET UP!!
I CAN'T GO ON! I'M HUNGRY 'N COLD!!
DON'T BE SILLY! LOOK AT ME! I'VE ONLY GOT A SHIRT AND BLAZER ON!
GRR... NOW I'VE GOTTA LUG YOU AROUND!
WHAT A WIND!!
I CAN SEE THE HEADLINES: "MUSTACHIO FREEZES TO DEATH IN ANTARCTIC WILDERNESS!"
WHOOOOOOOOOSH
WHOOOSH

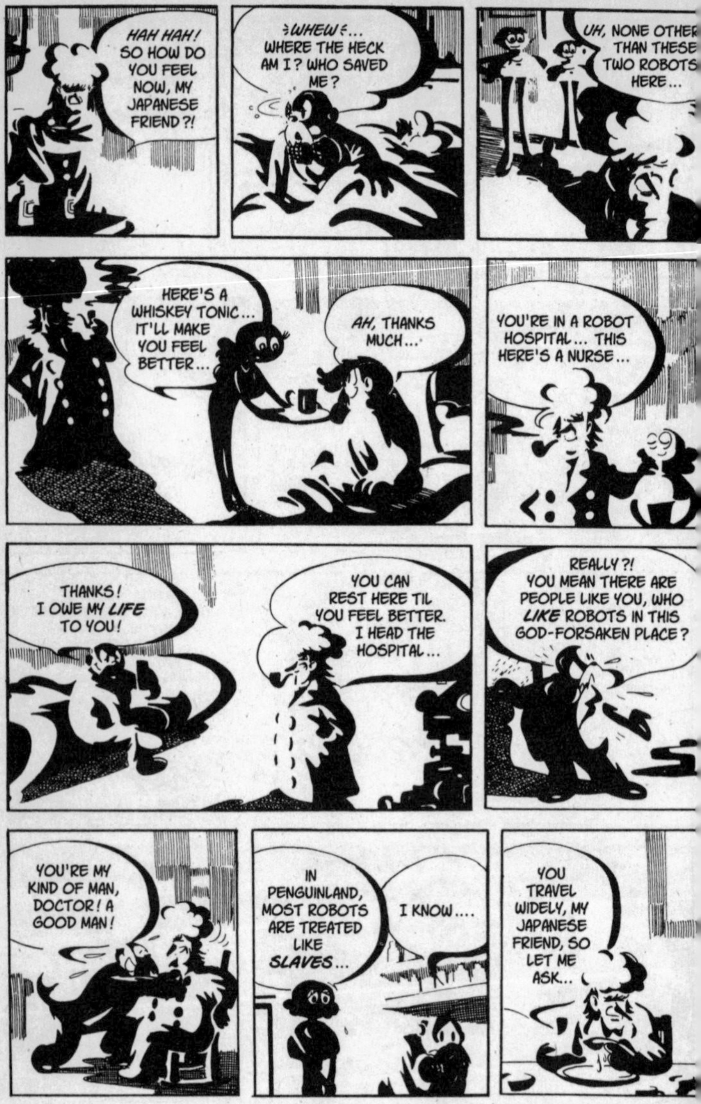
HAH HAH! SO HOW DO YOU FEEL NOW, MY JAPANESE FRIEND?!
WHEW... WHERE THE HECK AM I? WHO SAVED ME?
UH, NONE OTHER THAN THESE TWO ROBOTS HERE...
HERE'S A WHISKEY TONIC... IT'LL MAKE YOU FEEL BETTER...
AH, THANKS MUCH...
YOU'RE IN A ROBOT HOSPITAL... THIS HERE'S A NURSE...
THANKS! I OWE MY LIFE TO YOU!
YOU CAN REST HERE TIL YOU FEEL BETTER. I HEAD THE HOSPITAL...
REALLY?! YOU MEAN THERE ARE PEOPLE LIKE YOU, WHO LIKE ROBOTS IN THIS GOD-FORSAKEN PLACE?
YOU'RE MY KIND OF MAN, DOCTOR! A GOOD MAN!
IN PENGUINLAND, MOST ROBOTS ARE TREATED LIKE SLAVES...
I KNOW....
YOU TRAVEL WIDELY, MY JAPANESE FRIEND, SO LET ME ASK...

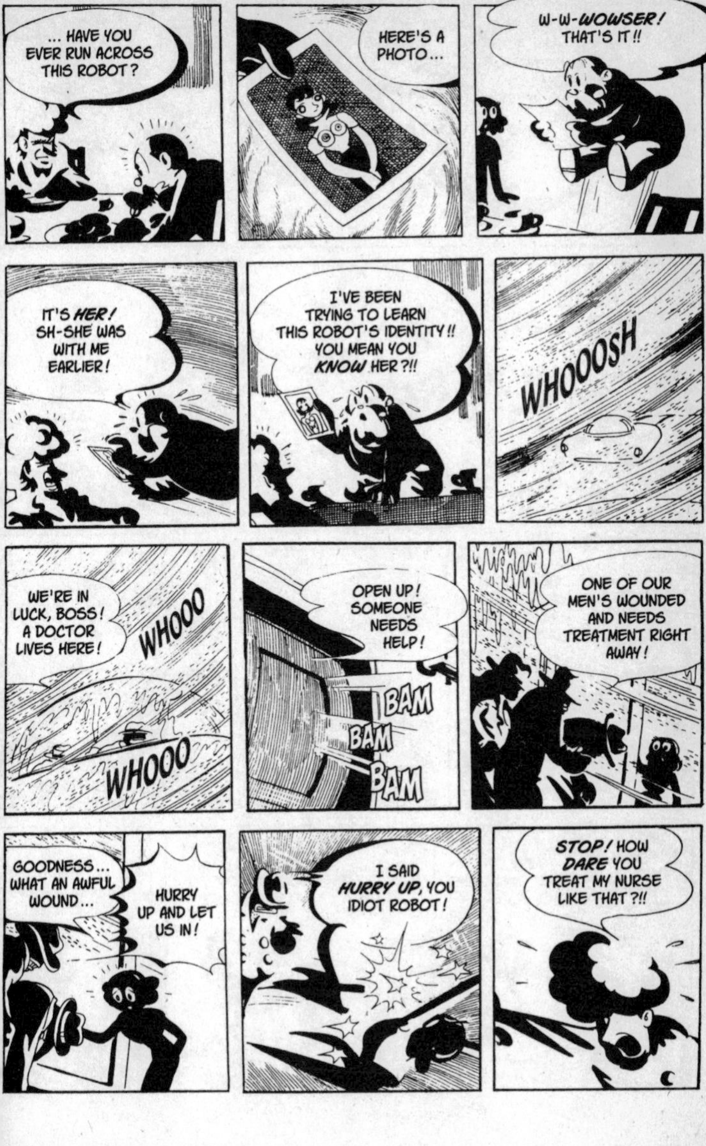
... HAVE YOU EVER RUN ACROSS THIS ROBOT?
HERE'S A PHOTO...
W-W-*WOWSER!* THAT'S IT!!
IT'S *HER!* SH-SHE WAS WITH ME EARLIER!
I'VE BEEN TRYING TO LEARN THIS ROBOT'S IDENTITY!! YOU MEAN YOU *KNOW* HER?!!
WHOOOSH
WE'RE IN LUCK, BOSS! A DOCTOR LIVES HERE!
WHOOO
WHOOO
OPEN UP! SOMEONE NEEDS HELP!
BAM
BAM
BAM
ONE OF OUR MEN'S WOUNDED AND NEEDS TREATMENT RIGHT AWAY!
GOODNESS... WHAT AN AWFUL WOUND...
HURRY UP AND LET US IN!
I SAID *HURRY UP,* YOU IDIOT ROBOT!
STOP! HOW *DARE* YOU TREAT MY NURSE LIKE THAT?!!

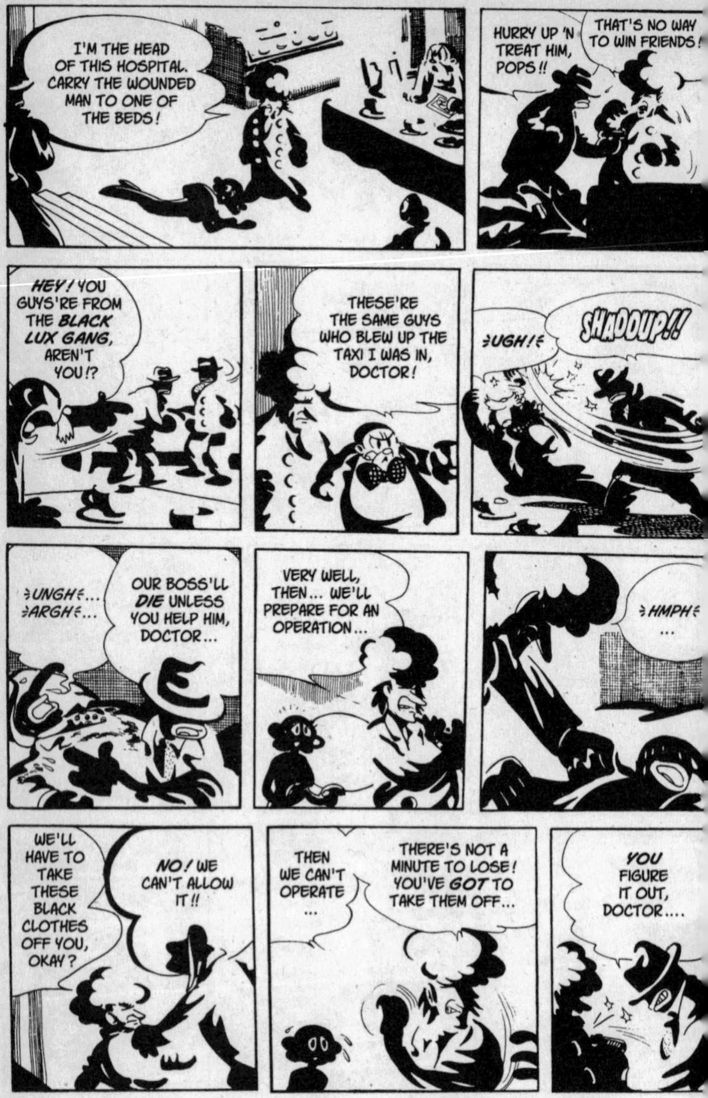
I'M THE HEAD OF THIS HOSPITAL. CARRY THE WOUNDED MAN TO ONE OF THE BEDS!
HURRY UP 'N TREAT HIM, POPS!!
THAT'S NO WAY TO WIN FRIENDS!
HEY! YOU GUYS'RE FROM THE BLACK LUX GANG, AREN'T YOU!?
THESE'RE THE SAME GUYS WHO BLEW UP THE TAXI I WAS IN, DOCTOR!
UGH!
SHADDUP!!
UNGH... ARGH...
OUR BOSS'LL DIE UNLESS YOU HELP HIM, DOCTOR...
VERY WELL, THEN... WE'LL PREPARE FOR AN OPERATION...
HMPH...
WE'LL HAVE TO TAKE THESE BLACK CLOTHES OFF YOU, OKAY?
NO! WE CAN'T ALLOW IT!!
THEN WE CAN'T OPERATE...
THERE'S NOT A MINUTE TO LOSE! YOU'VE GOT TO TAKE THEM OFF...
YOU FIGURE IT OUT, DOCTOR....

WE'LL TAKE OFF HIS CLOTHES 'N WORK IN THE *DARK!!*

TURN OFF THE ROOM LIGHTS, NURSE...

EVERYONE, *QUIET!* I'M STARTING THE *OPERATION!*

TWEEZERS...

GAUZE...

THAT'S IT...

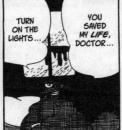

TURN ON THE LIGHTS...

YOU SAVED *MY LIFE,* DOCTOR...

BUT YOU SAW MY *FACE,* DIDN'T YOU!?

WAIT, YOU MUSTN'T MOVE YET!

NO ONE IS ALLOWED TO SEE MY FACE!!

WH-WHAT DO YOU MEAN?

KEEP YOUR HANDS OFF THE DOCTOR!

VOOSH VOOSH

91

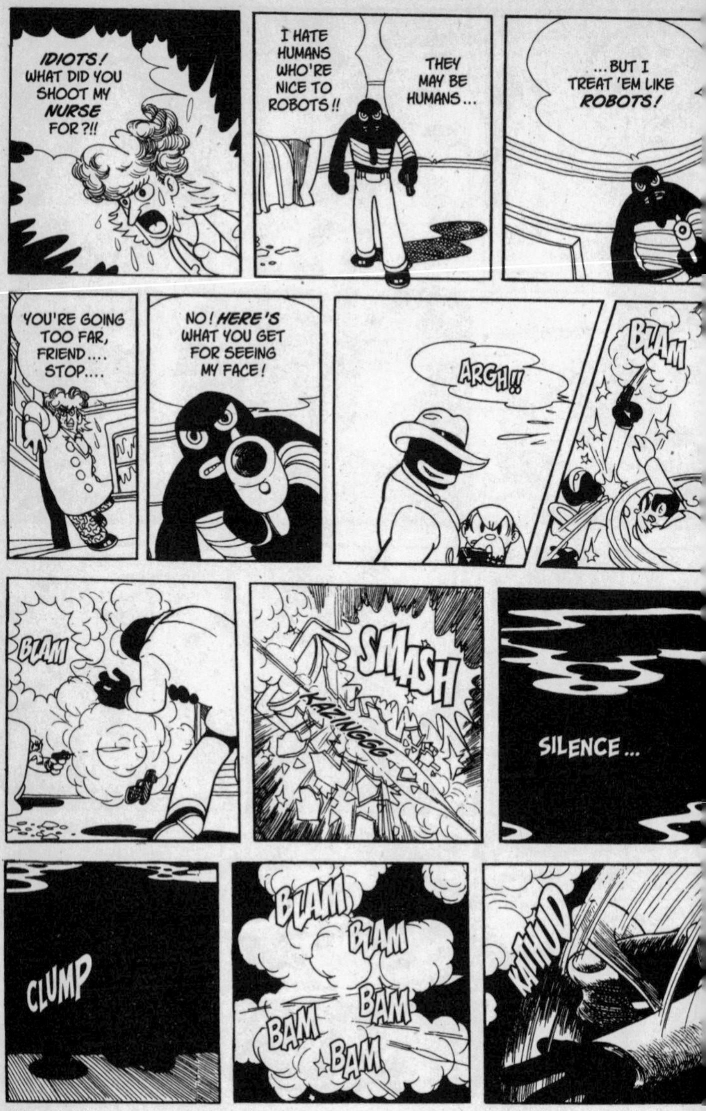
IDIOTS! WHAT DID YOU SHOOT MY NURSE FOR?!!
I HATE HUMANS WHO'RE NICE TO ROBOTS!!
THEY MAY BE HUMANS...
...BUT I TREAT 'EM LIKE ROBOTS!
YOU'RE GOING TOO FAR, FRIEND.... STOP....
NO! HERE'S WHAT YOU GET FOR SEEING MY FACE!
ARGH!!
BLAM
BLAM
SMASH
KAZINGGG
SILENCE...
CLUMP
BLAM
BLAM
BAM
BAM
BAM
KATHUD

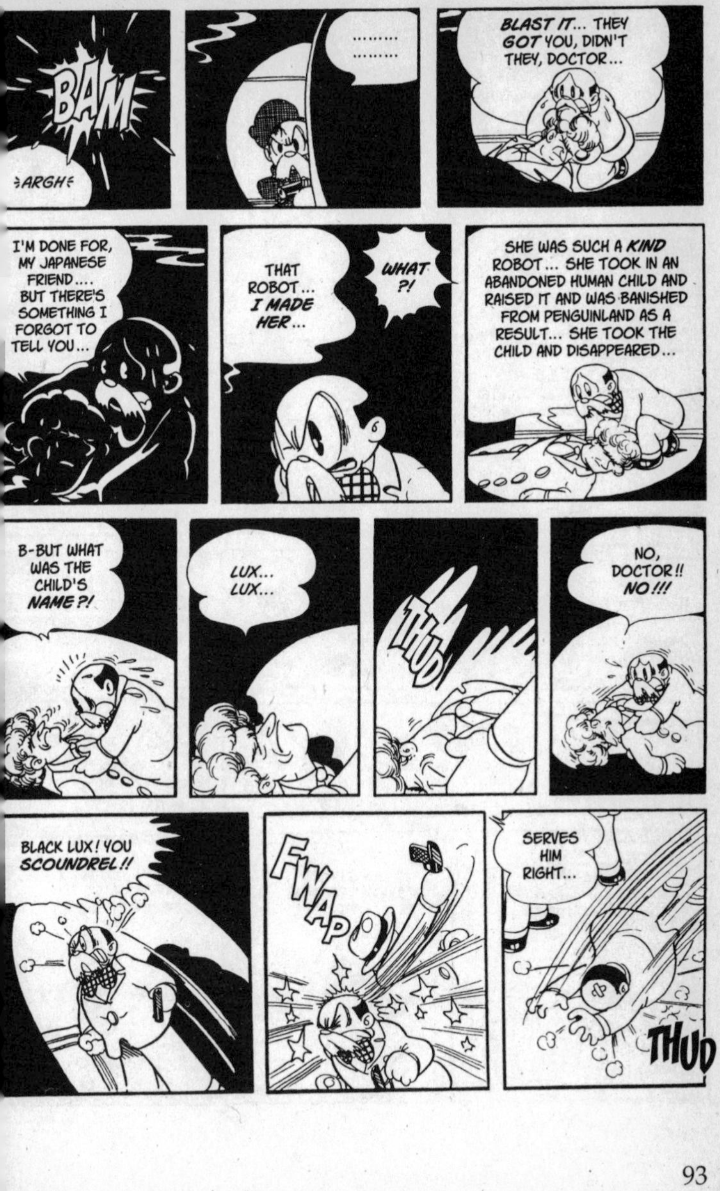
BAM
≡ARGH≡
....
....
BLAST IT... THEY GOT YOU, DIDN'T THEY, DOCTOR...
I'M DONE FOR, MY JAPANESE FRIEND.... BUT THERE'S SOMETHING I FORGOT TO TELL YOU...
THAT ROBOT... I MADE HER...
WHAT ?!
SHE WAS SUCH A KIND ROBOT... SHE TOOK IN AN ABANDONED HUMAN CHILD AND RAISED IT AND WAS BANISHED FROM PENGUINLAND AS A RESULT... SHE TOOK THE CHILD AND DISAPPEARED...
B-BUT WHAT WAS THE CHILD'S NAME ?!
LUX... LUX...
THUD
NO, DOCTOR!! NO!!!
BLACK LUX! YOU SCOUNDREL!!
FWAP
SERVES HIM RIGHT...
THUD

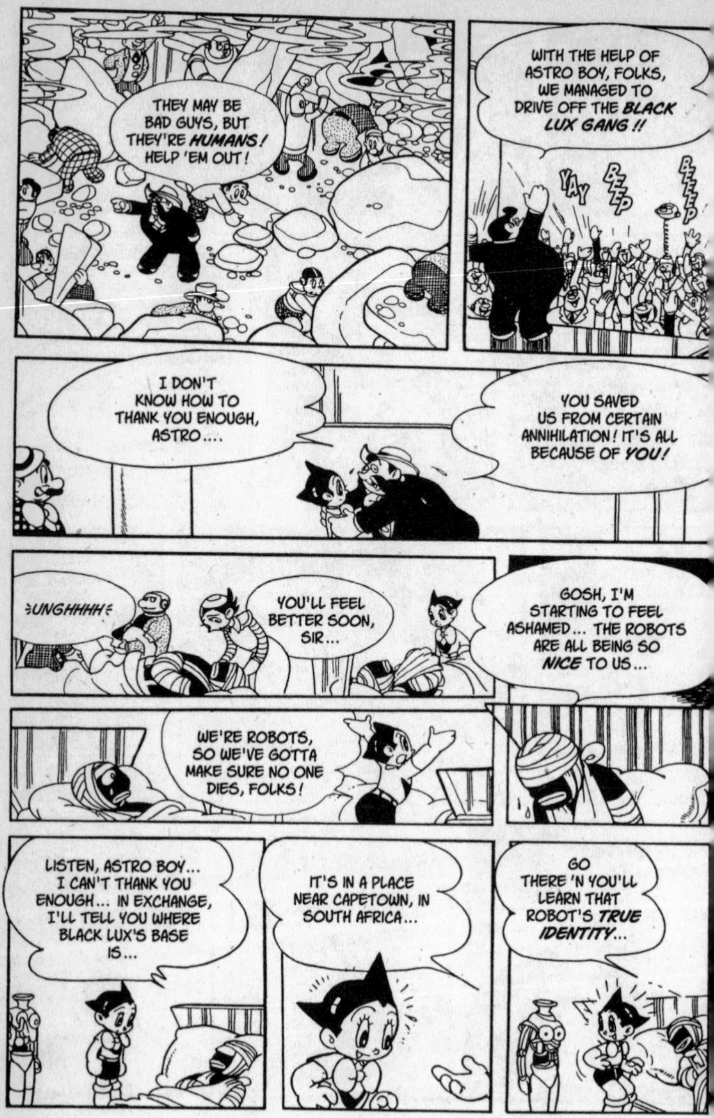
THEY MAY BE BAD GUYS, BUT THEY'RE *HUMANS!* HELP 'EM OUT!
WITH THE HELP OF ASTRO BOY, FOLKS, WE MANAGED TO DRIVE OFF THE *BLACK LUX GANG!!*
YAY
BEEP
BEEEP
I DON'T KNOW HOW TO THANK YOU ENOUGH, ASTRO....
YOU SAVED US FROM CERTAIN ANNIHILATION! IT'S ALL BECAUSE OF *YOU!*
UNGHHHH
YOU'LL FEEL BETTER SOON, SIR...
GOSH, I'M STARTING TO FEEL ASHAMED... THE ROBOTS ARE ALL BEING SO *NICE* TO US...
WE'RE ROBOTS, SO WE'VE GOTTA MAKE SURE NO ONE DIES, FOLKS!
LISTEN, ASTRO BOY... I CAN'T THANK YOU ENOUGH... IN EXCHANGE, I'LL TELL YOU WHERE BLACK LUX'S BASE IS...
IT'S IN A PLACE NEAR CAPETOWN, IN SOUTH AFRICA...
GO THERE 'N YOU'LL LEARN THAT ROBOT'S *TRUE IDENTITY*...

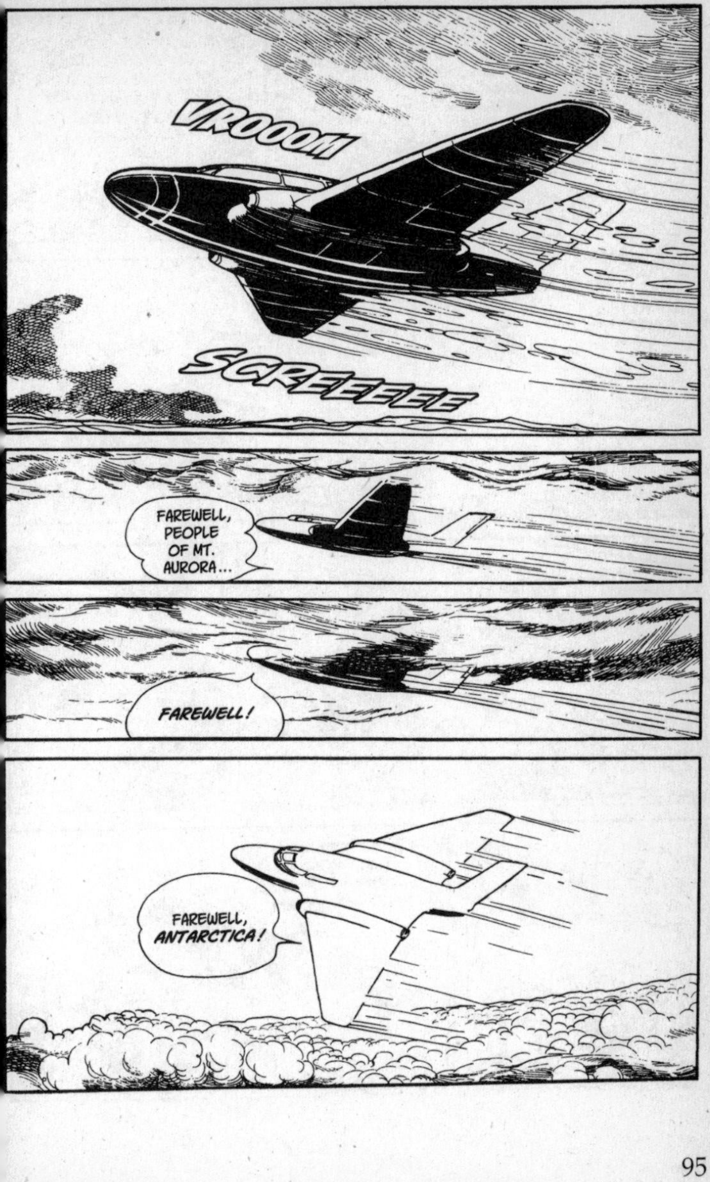
VROOOM
SCREEEEEE
FAREWELL, PEOPLE OF MT. AURORA...
FAREWELL!
FAREWELL, ANTARCTICA!

WE'LL HEAD FOR AFRICA AND *BLACK LUX'S BASE*, DAD!

I SURE WONDER WHERE *MUSTACHIO* WENT...

LOOK! THAT'S *CAPETOWN*, THERE!

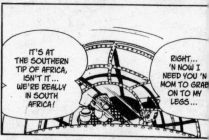

IT'S AT THE SOUTHERN TIP OF AFRICA, ISN'T IT ... WE'RE REALLY IN SOUTH AFRICA!

RIGHT... 'N NOW I NEED YOU 'N MOM TO GRAB ON TO MY LEGS...

COMING IN FOR A LANDING...

THIS IS A SUSPICIOUS LOOKING PLACE...

LOOK AT ALL THESE ROBOTS THAT'VE BEEN THROWN AWAY!

GARBAGE DUMP

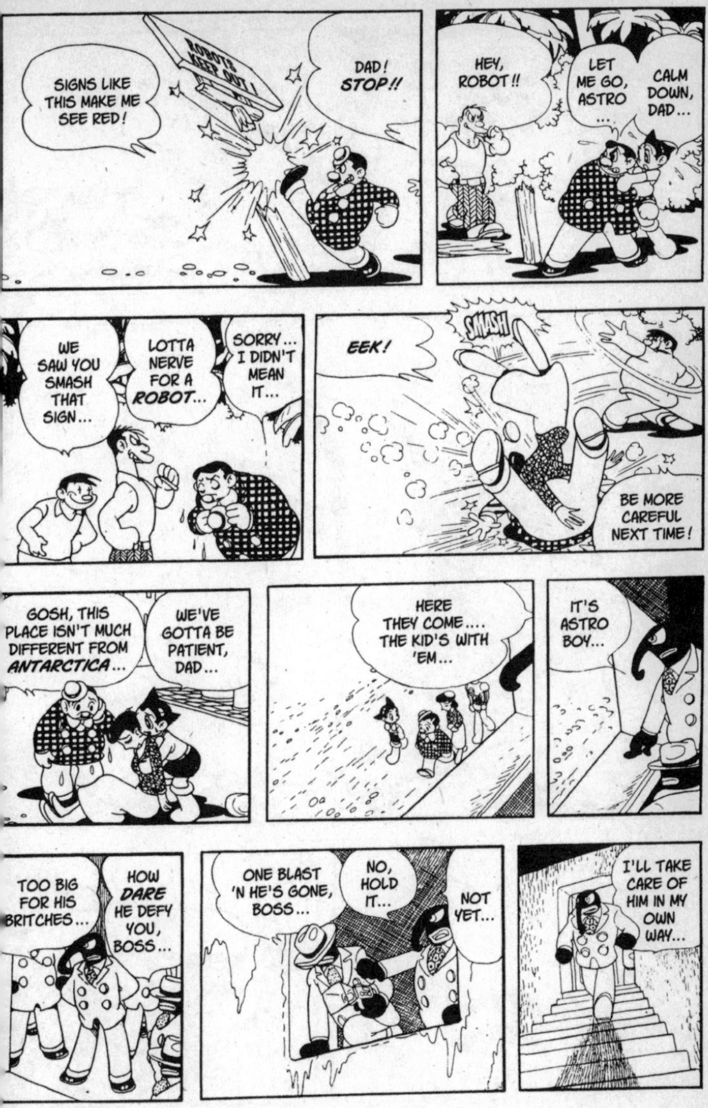
SIGNS LIKE THIS MAKE ME SEE RED!
ROBOTS KEEP OUT!
DAD! STOP!!
HEY, ROBOT!!
LET ME GO, ASTRO ...
CALM DOWN, DAD...
WE SAW YOU SMASH THAT SIGN...
LOTTA NERVE FOR A ROBOT...
SORRY... I DIDN'T MEAN IT...
EEK!
SMASH
BE MORE CAREFUL NEXT TIME!
GOSH, THIS PLACE ISN'T MUCH DIFFERENT FROM ANTARCTICA...
WE'VE GOTTA BE PATIENT, DAD...
HERE THEY COME.... THE KID'S WITH 'EM...
IT'S ASTRO BOY...
TOO BIG FOR HIS BRITCHES...
HOW DARE HE DEFY YOU, BOSS...
ONE BLAST 'N HE'S GONE, BOSS...
NO, HOLD IT...
NOT YET...
I'LL TAKE CARE OF HIM IN MY OWN WAY...

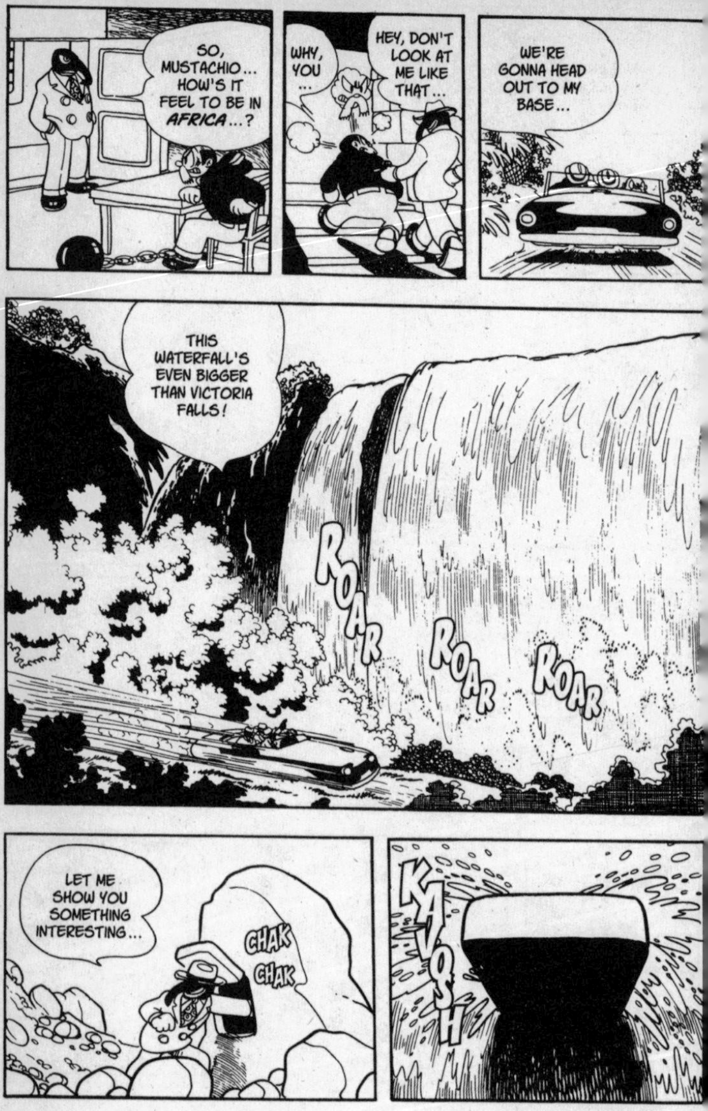
SO, MUSTACHIO... HOW'S IT FEEL TO BE IN AFRICA...?
WHY, YOU ...
HEY, DON'T LOOK AT ME LIKE THAT...
WE'RE GONNA HEAD OUT TO MY BASE...
THIS WATERFALL'S EVEN BIGGER THAN VICTORIA FALLS!
ROAR
ROAR
ROAR
LET ME SHOW YOU SOMETHING INTERESTING...
CHAK
CHAK
KAVOOSH

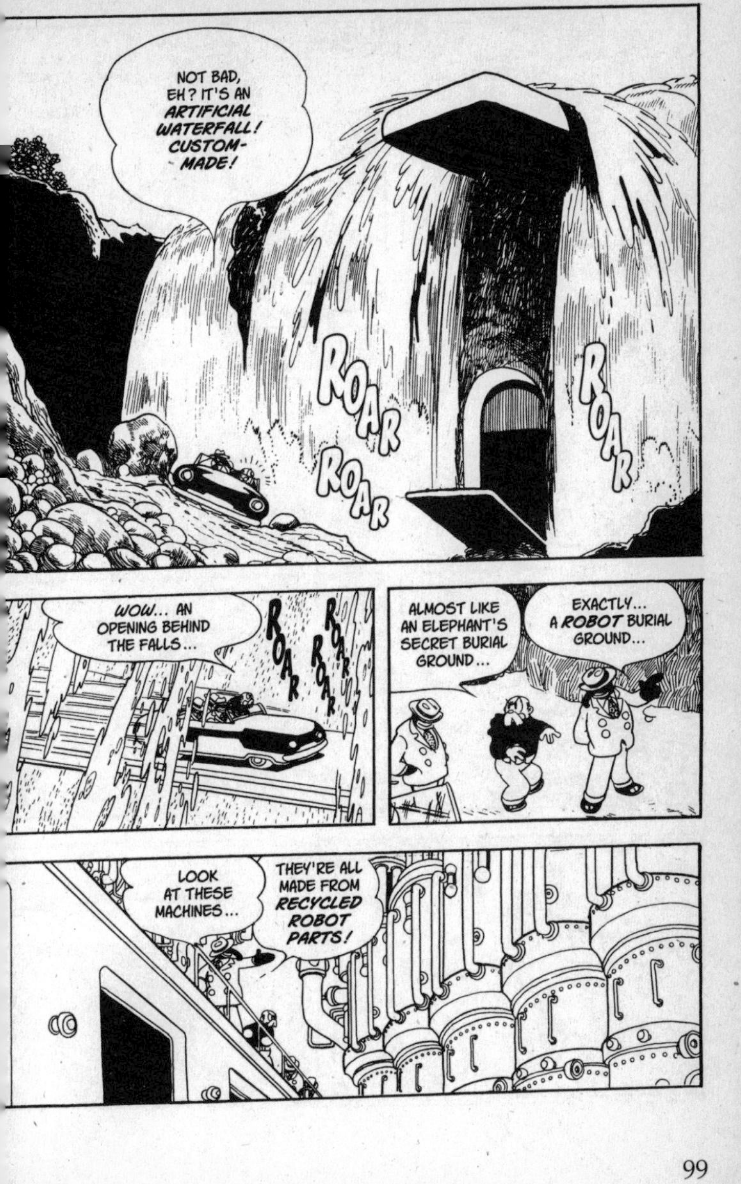

NOT BAD, EH? IT'S AN *ARTIFICIAL WATERFALL! CUSTOM-MADE!*
ROAR
ROAR
ROAR
WOW... AN OPENING BEHIND THE FALLS...
ROAR
ROAR
ROAR
ALMOST LIKE AN ELEPHANT'S SECRET BURIAL GROUND...
EXACTLY... A *ROBOT* BURIAL GROUND...
LOOK AT THESE MACHINES...
THEY'RE ALL MADE FROM *RECYCLED ROBOT PARTS!*

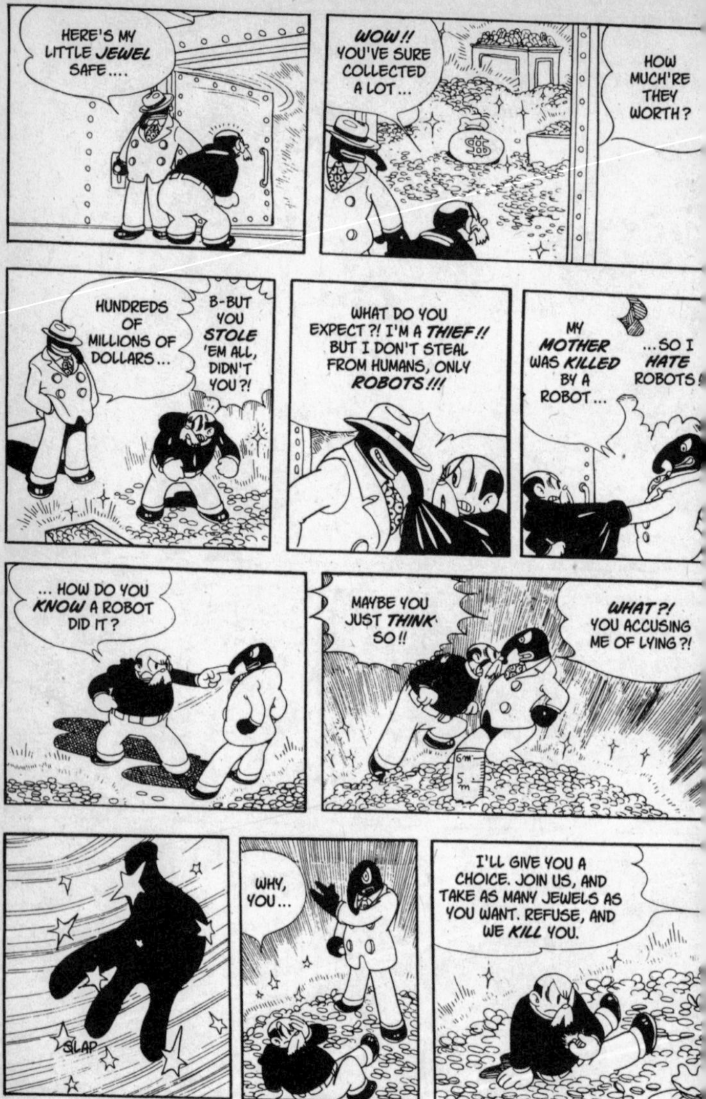
HERE'S MY LITTLE JEWEL SAFE....
WOW!! YOU'VE SURE COLLECTED A LOT...
HOW MUCH'RE THEY WORTH?
HUNDREDS OF MILLIONS OF DOLLARS...
B-BUT YOU STOLE 'EM ALL, DIDN'T YOU?!
WHAT DO YOU EXPECT?! I'M A THIEF!! BUT I DON'T STEAL FROM HUMANS, ONLY ROBOTS!!!
MY MOTHER WAS KILLED BY A ROBOT...
...SO I HATE ROBOTS!
... HOW DO YOU KNOW A ROBOT DID IT?
MAYBE YOU JUST THINK SO!!
WHAT?! YOU ACCUSING ME OF LYING?!
SLAP
WHY, YOU...
I'LL GIVE YOU A CHOICE. JOIN US, AND TAKE AS MANY JEWELS AS YOU WANT. REFUSE, AND WE KILL YOU.

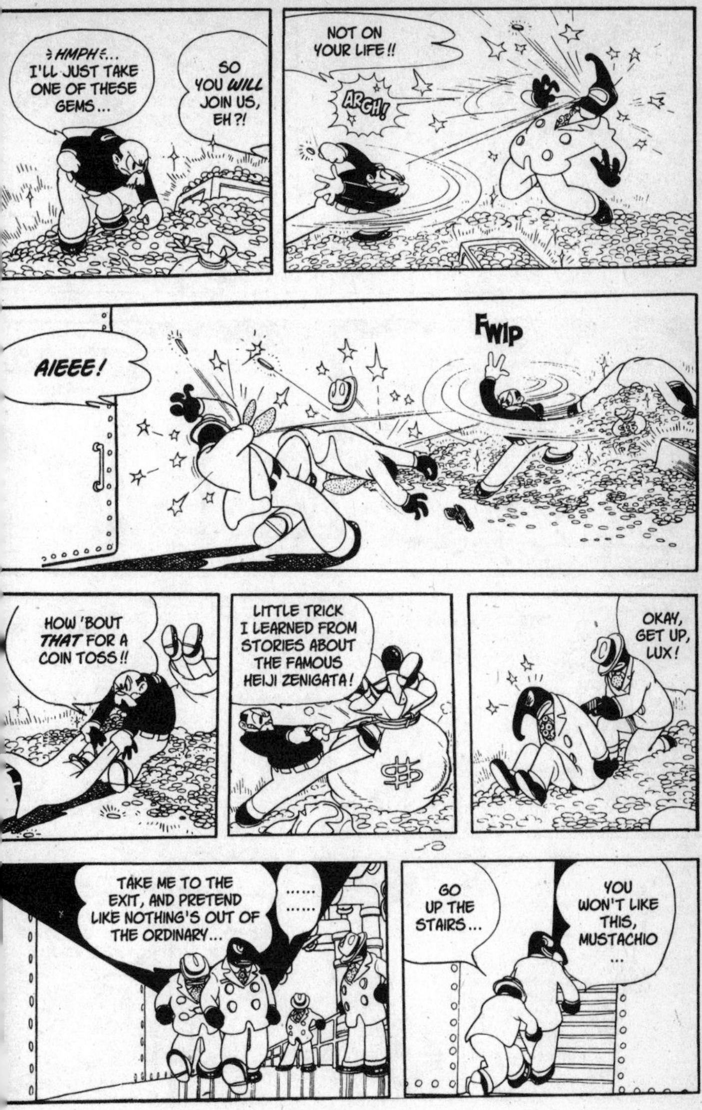
HMPH...
I'LL JUST TAKE ONE OF THESE GEMS...
SO YOU WILL JOIN US, EH?!
NOT ON YOUR LIFE!!
ARGH!
AIEEE!
FWIP
HOW 'BOUT THAT FOR A COIN TOSS!!
LITTLE TRICK I LEARNED FROM STORIES ABOUT THE FAMOUS HEIJI ZENIGATA!
OKAY, GET UP, LUX!
TAKE ME TO THE EXIT, AND PRETEND LIKE NOTHING'S OUT OF THE ORDINARY...
......
......
GO UP THE STAIRS...
YOU WON'T LIKE THIS, MUSTACHIO
...

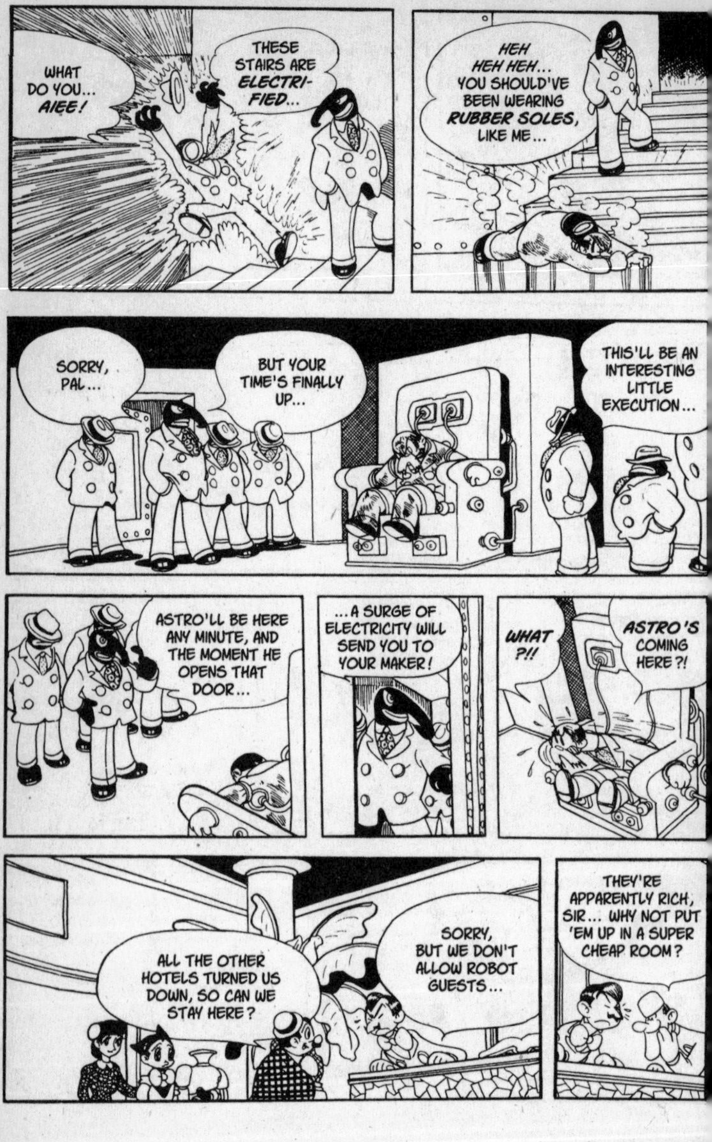
WHAT DO YOU... AIEE!
THESE STAIRS ARE ELECTRIFIED...
HEH HEH HEH... YOU SHOULD'VE BEEN WEARING RUBBER SOLES, LIKE ME...
SORRY, PAL...
BUT YOUR TIME'S FINALLY UP...
THIS'LL BE AN INTERESTING LITTLE EXECUTION...
ASTRO'LL BE HERE ANY MINUTE, AND THE MOMENT HE OPENS THAT DOOR...
...A SURGE OF ELECTRICITY WILL SEND YOU TO YOUR MAKER!
WHAT ?!!
ASTRO'S COMING HERE ?!
ALL THE OTHER HOTELS TURNED US DOWN, SO CAN WE STAY HERE ?
SORRY, BUT WE DON'T ALLOW ROBOT GUESTS...
THEY'RE APPARENTLY RICH, SIR... WHY NOT PUT 'EM UP IN A SUPER CHEAP ROOM ?

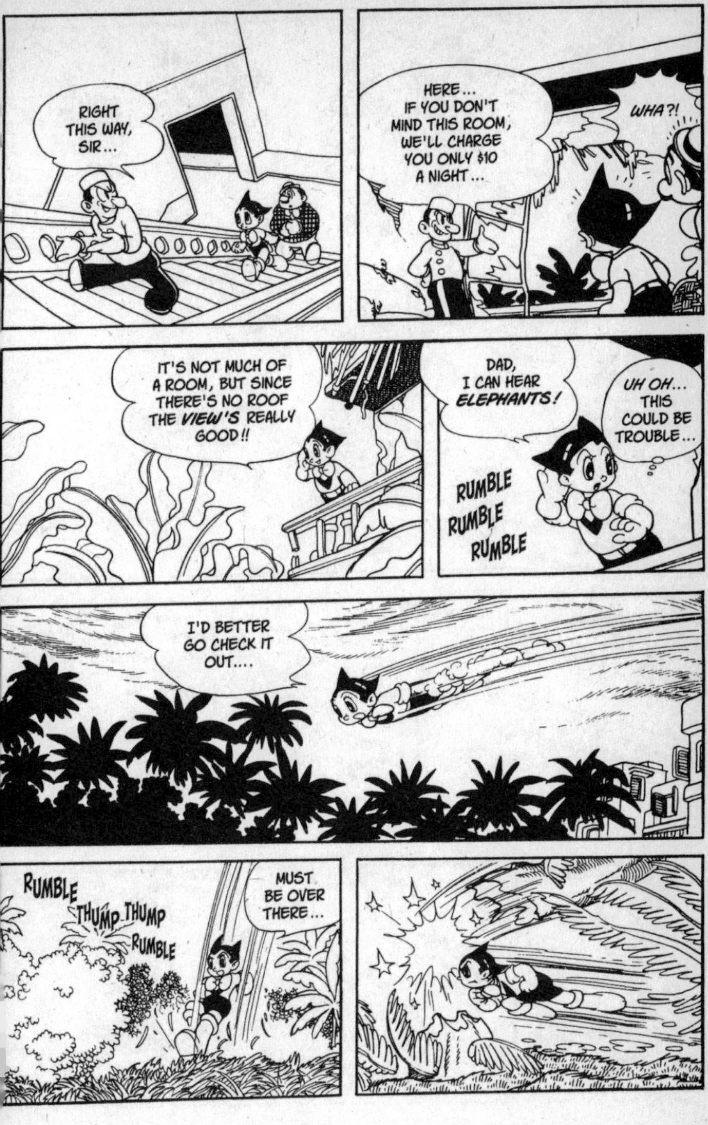
RIGHT THIS WAY, SIR...
HERE... IF YOU DON'T MIND THIS ROOM, WE'LL CHARGE YOU ONLY $10 A NIGHT...
WHA?!
IT'S NOT MUCH OF A ROOM, BUT SINCE THERE'S NO ROOF THE VIEW'S REALLY GOOD!!
DAD, I CAN HEAR ELEPHANTS!
UH OH... THIS COULD BE TROUBLE...
RUMBLE RUMBLE RUMBLE
I'D BETTER GO CHECK IT OUT....
RUMBLE THUMP THUMP RUMBLE
MUST BE OVER THERE...

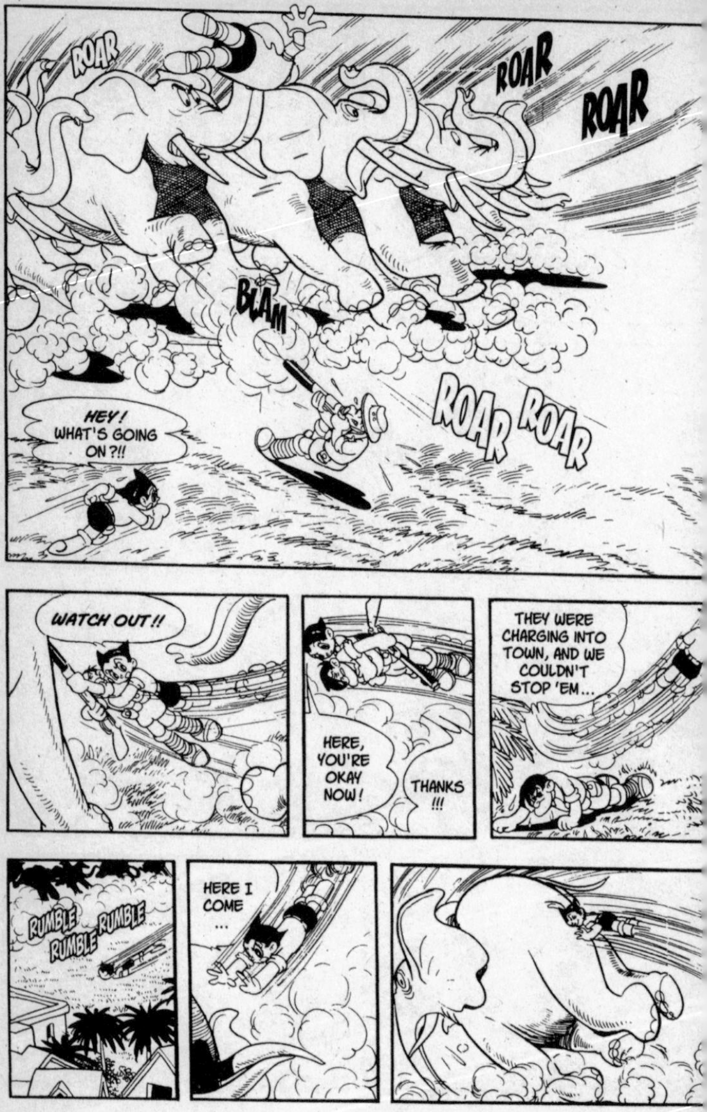

ROAR
ROAR
ROAR
BLAM
HEY! WHAT'S GOING ON?!!
ROAR ROAR
WATCH OUT!!
HERE, YOU'RE OKAY NOW!
THANKS !!!
THEY WERE CHARGING INTO TOWN, AND WE COULDN'T STOP 'EM...
RUMBLE RUMBLE RUMBLE
HERE I COME ...

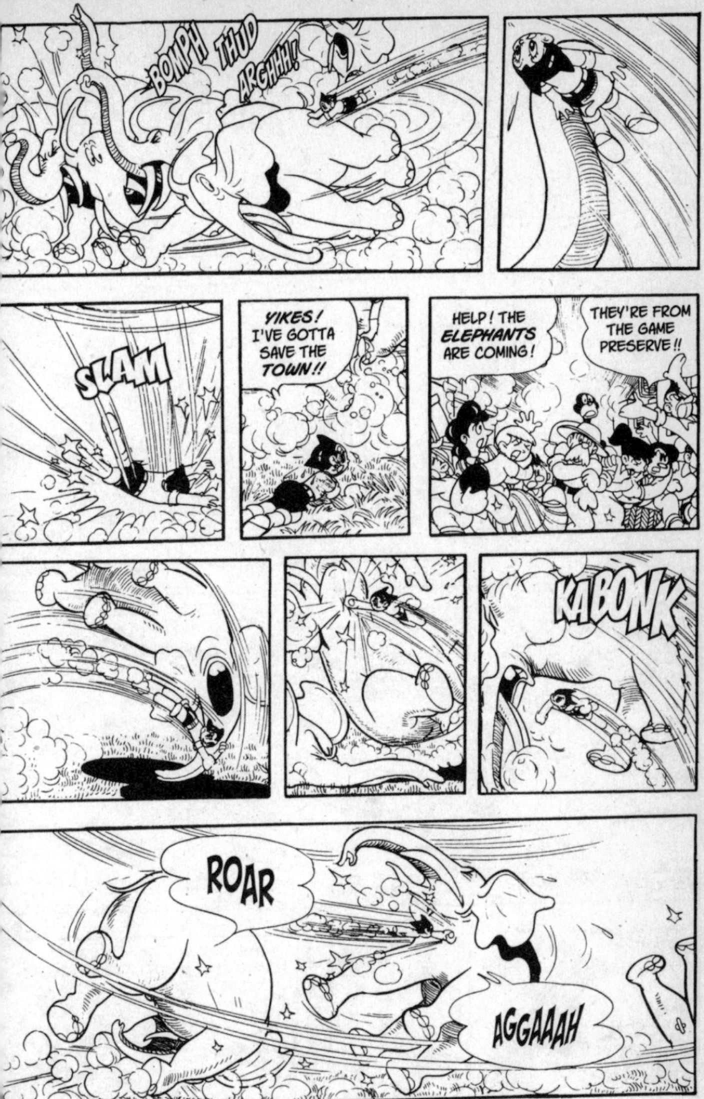
BOMPH
THUD
ARGHHH!
SLAM
YIKES! I'VE GOTTA SAVE THE TOWN!!
HELP! THE ELEPHANTS ARE COMING!
THEY'RE FROM THE GAME PRESERVE!!
KABONK
ROAR
AGGAAAH

WOW! YOU SEE THAT? A SINGLE *ROBOT* SAVED US!

SPUTTER SPUT

SPUT

ARROOO!

GET 'EM, MR. ROBOT! GET 'EM!

EEEK!

BASH

HELP THE ROBOT! *OPEN FIRE*, MEN!

BLAM

BLAM

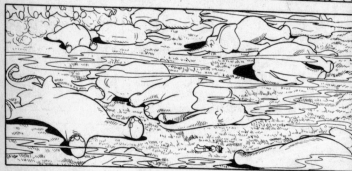

ASTRO...

HI, MOM....

IT'S THE TOWNSPEOPLE, ASTRO...

WE JUST WANT TO *THANK* YOU, SON...

106

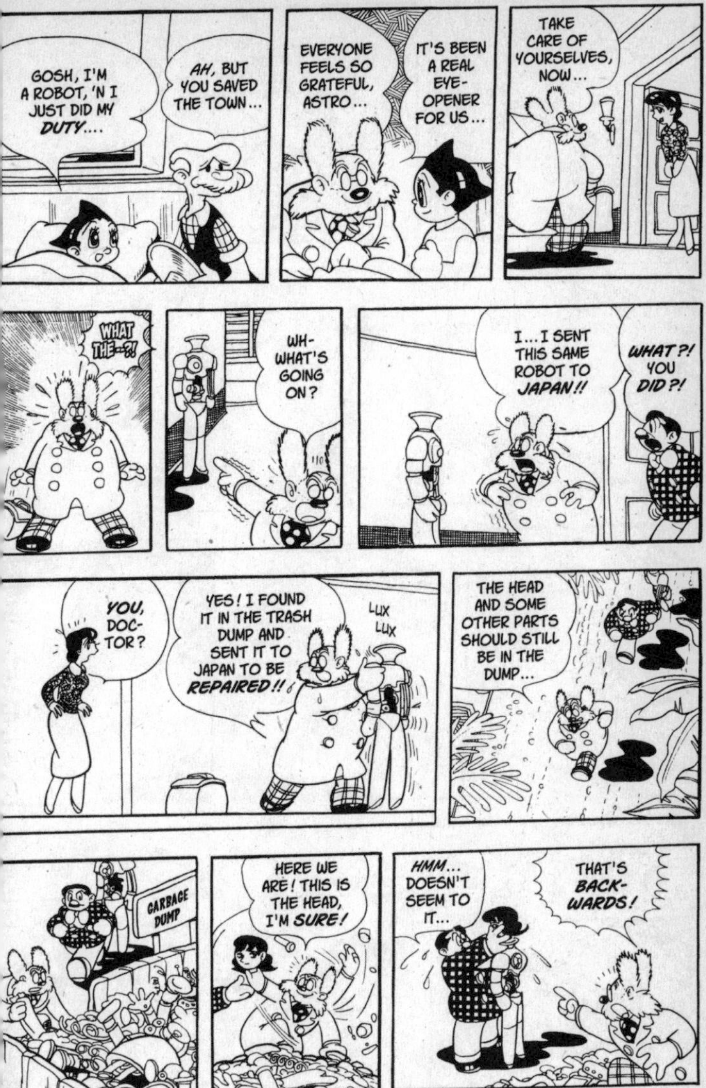
GOSH, I'M A ROBOT, 'N I JUST DID MY DUTY....
AH, BUT YOU SAVED THE TOWN...
EVERYONE FEELS SO GRATEFUL, ASTRO...
IT'S BEEN A REAL EYE-OPENER FOR US...
TAKE CARE OF YOURSELVES, NOW...
WHAT THE--?!
WH-WHAT'S GOING ON?
I...I SENT THIS SAME ROBOT TO JAPAN!!
WHAT?! YOU DID?!
YOU, DOC-TOR?
YES! I FOUND IT IN THE TRASH DUMP AND SENT IT TO JAPAN TO BE REPAIRED!!
LUX LUX
THE HEAD AND SOME OTHER PARTS SHOULD STILL BE IN THE DUMP...
GARBAGE DUMP
HERE WE ARE! THIS IS THE HEAD, I'M SURE!
HMM... DOESN'T SEEM TO IT...
THAT'S BACK-WARDS!

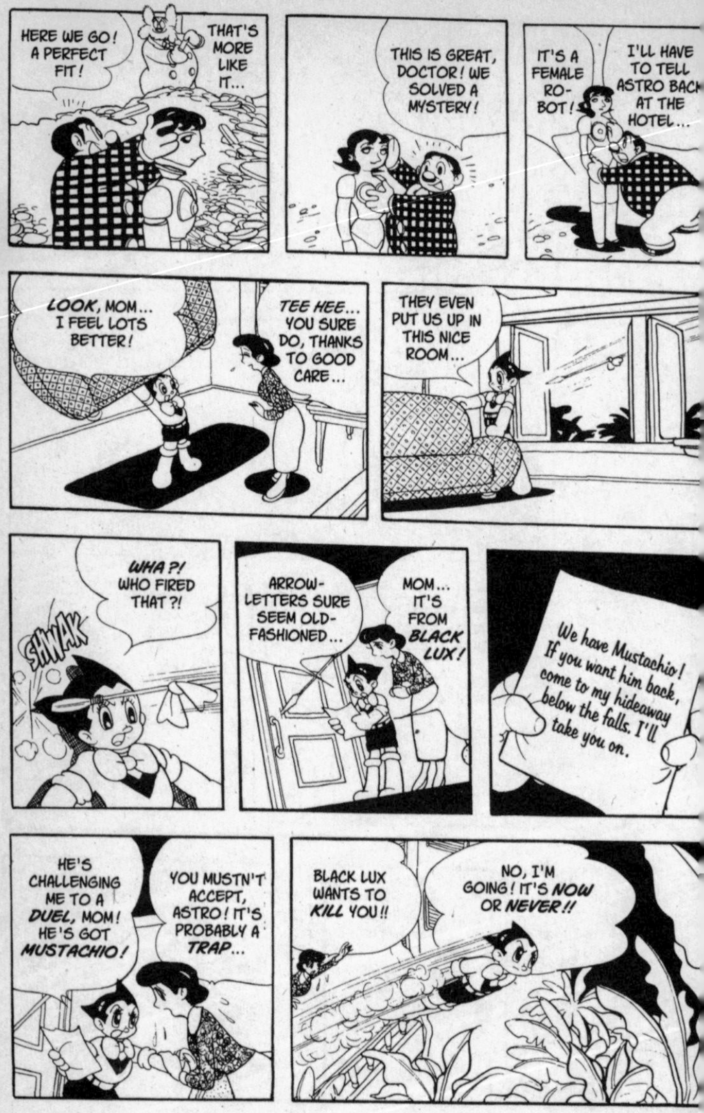
HERE WE GO! A PERFECT FIT!
THAT'S MORE LIKE IT...
THIS IS GREAT, DOCTOR! WE SOLVED A MYSTERY!
IT'S A FEMALE RO-BOT!
I'LL HAVE TO TELL ASTRO BACK AT THE HOTEL...
LOOK, MOM... I FEEL LOTS BETTER!
TEE HEE... YOU SURE DO, THANKS TO GOOD CARE...
THEY EVEN PUT US UP IN THIS NICE ROOM...
WHA?! WHO FIRED THAT?!
SHWAK
ARROW-LETTERS SURE SEEM OLD-FASHIONED...
MOM... IT'S FROM BLACK LUX!
We have Mustachio! If you want him back, come to my hideaway below the falls. I'll take you on.
HE'S CHALLENGING ME TO A DUEL, MOM! HE'S GOT MUSTACHIO!
YOU MUSTN'T ACCEPT, ASTRO! IT'S PROBABLY A TRAP...
BLACK LUX WANTS TO KILL YOU!!
NO, I'M GOING! IT'S NOW OR NEVER!!

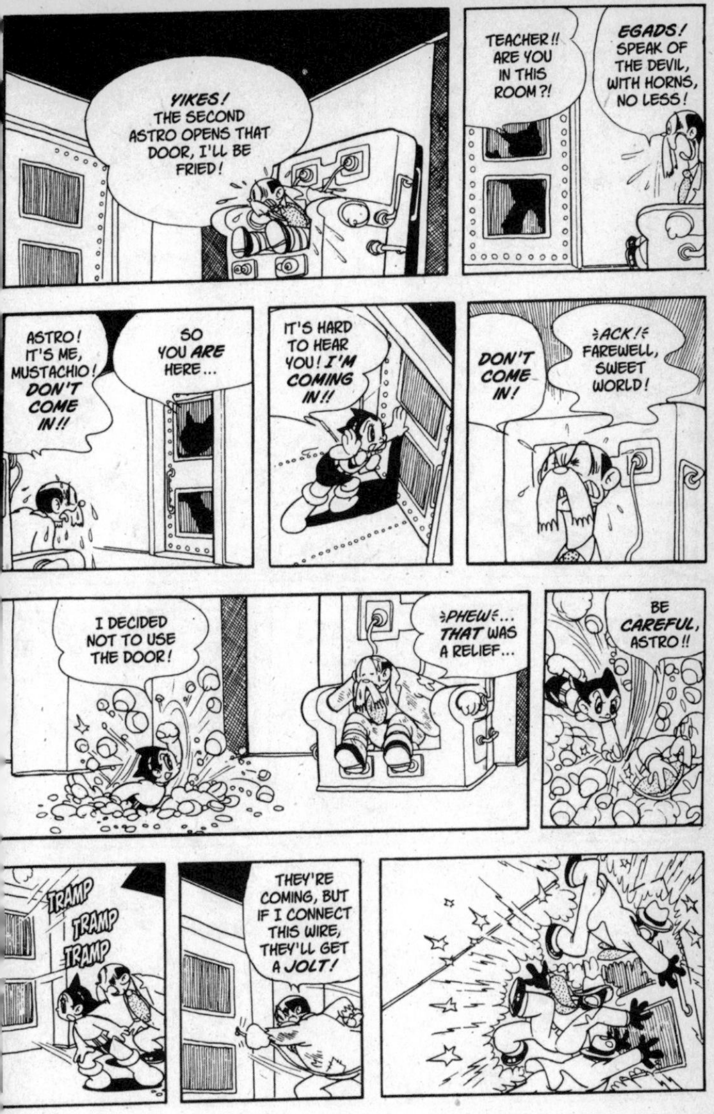
YIKES! THE SECOND ASTRO OPENS THAT DOOR, I'LL BE FRIED!
TEACHER!! ARE YOU IN THIS ROOM?!
EGADS! SPEAK OF THE DEVIL, WITH HORNS, NO LESS!
ASTRO! IT'S ME, MUSTACHIO! DON'T COME IN!!
SO YOU ARE HERE...
IT'S HARD TO HEAR YOU! I'M COMING IN!!
DON'T COME IN!
ACK! FAREWELL, SWEET WORLD!
I DECIDED NOT TO USE THE DOOR!
PHEW... THAT WAS A RELIEF...
BE CAREFUL, ASTRO!!
TRAMP
TRAMP
TRAMP
THEY'RE COMING, BUT IF I CONNECT THIS WIRE, THEY'LL GET A JOLT!

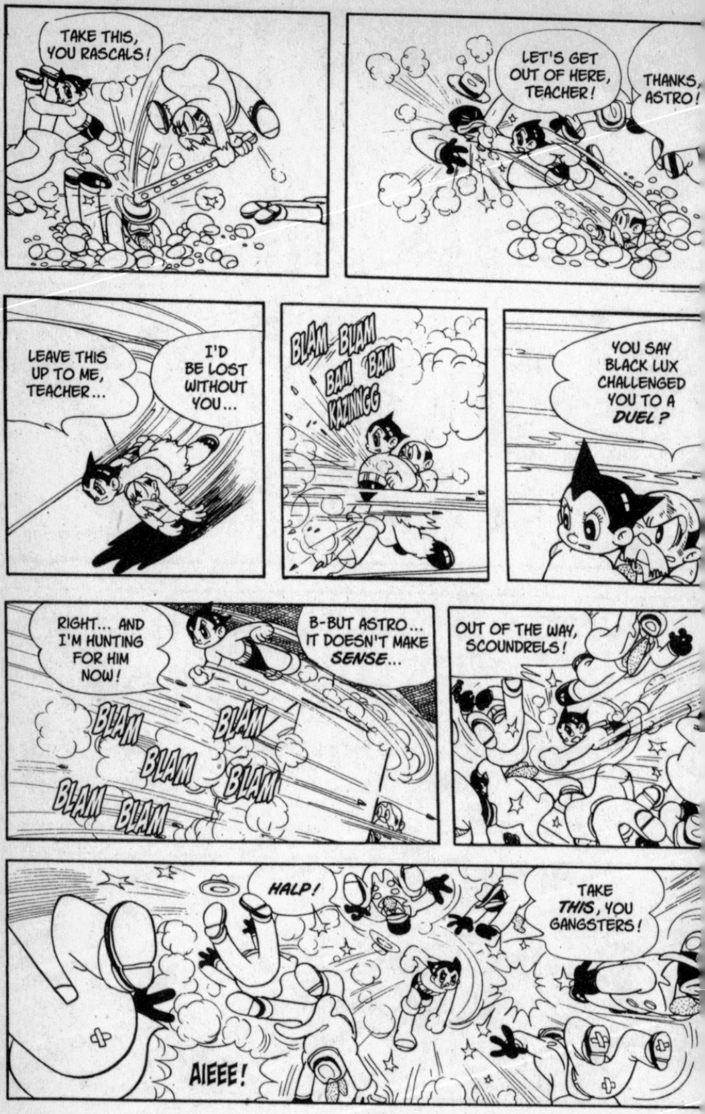
TAKE THIS, YOU RASCALS!
LET'S GET OUT OF HERE, TEACHER!
THANKS, ASTRO!
LEAVE THIS UP TO ME, TEACHER...
I'D BE LOST WITHOUT YOU...
BLAM BLAM BAM BAM KAZINNGG
YOU SAY BLACK LUX CHALLENGED YOU TO A *DUEL?*
RIGHT... AND I'M HUNTING FOR HIM NOW!
B-BUT ASTRO... IT DOESN'T MAKE *SENSE*...
BLAM BLAM BLAM BLAM BLAM BLAM
OUT OF THE WAY, SCOUNDRELS!
HALP!
TAKE *THIS*, YOU GANGSTERS!
AIEEE!

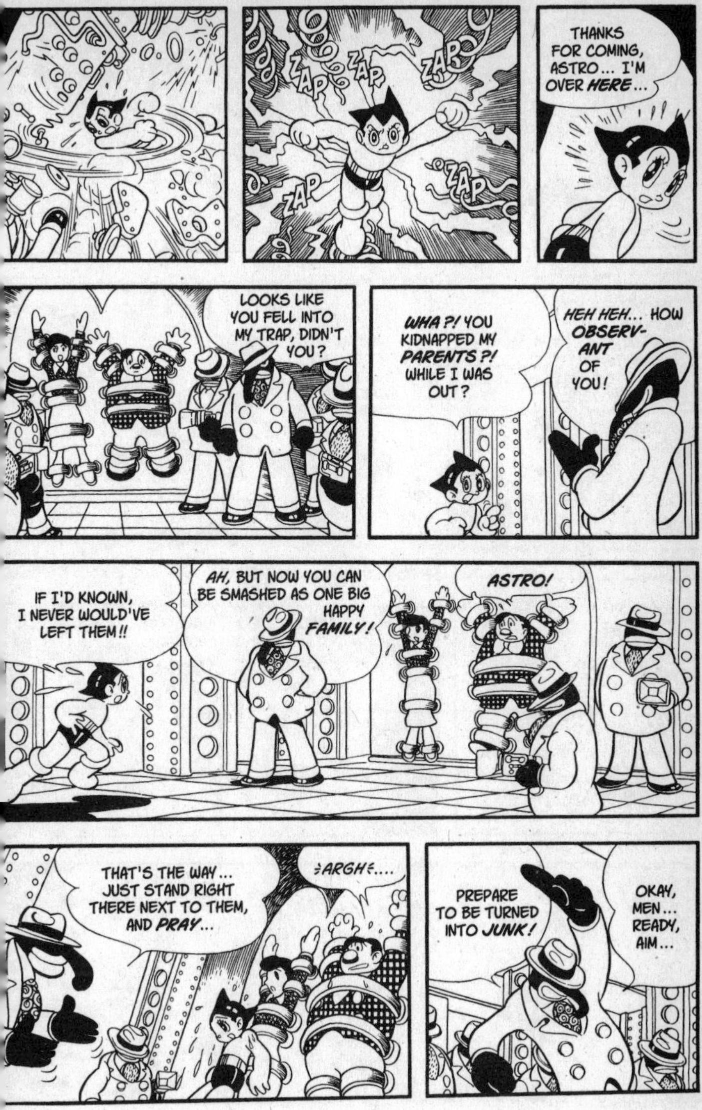
ZAP
ZAP
ZAP
ZAP
ZAP
THANKS FOR COMING, ASTRO... I'M OVER HERE...
LOOKS LIKE YOU FELL INTO MY TRAP, DIDN'T YOU?
WHA?! YOU KIDNAPPED MY PARENTS?! WHILE I WAS OUT?
HEH HEH... HOW OBSERV-ANT OF YOU!
IF I'D KNOWN, I NEVER WOULD'VE LEFT THEM!!
AH, BUT NOW YOU CAN BE SMASHED AS ONE BIG HAPPY FAMILY!
ASTRO!
THAT'S THE WAY... JUST STAND RIGHT THERE NEXT TO THEM, AND PRAY...
ARGH....
PREPARE TO BE TURNED INTO JUNK!
OKAY, MEN... READY, AIM...

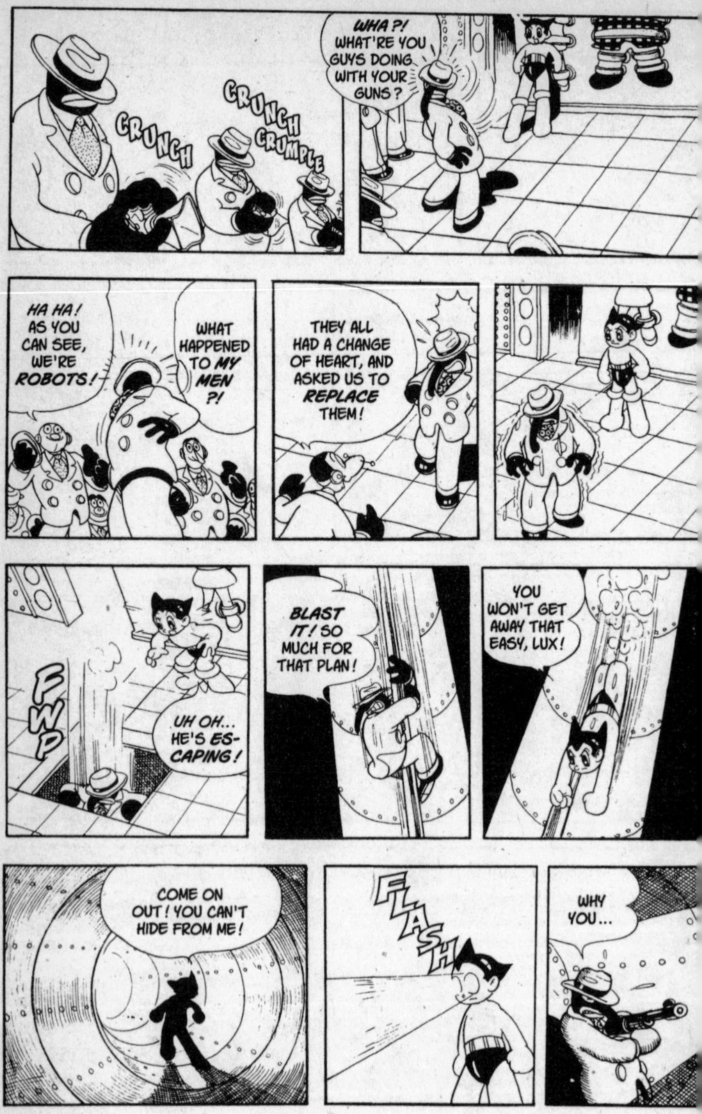
CRUNCH
CRUNCH CRUMPLE
WHA?! WHAT'RE YOU GUYS DOING WITH YOUR GUNS?
HA HA! AS YOU CAN SEE, WE'RE ROBOTS!
WHAT HAPPENED TO MY MEN ?!
THEY ALL HAD A CHANGE OF HEART, AND ASKED US TO REPLACE THEM!
FWP
UH OH... HE'S ES-CAPING!
BLAST IT! SO MUCH FOR THAT PLAN!
YOU WON'T GET AWAY THAT EASY, LUX!
COME ON OUT! YOU CAN'T HIDE FROM ME!
FLASH
WHY YOU...

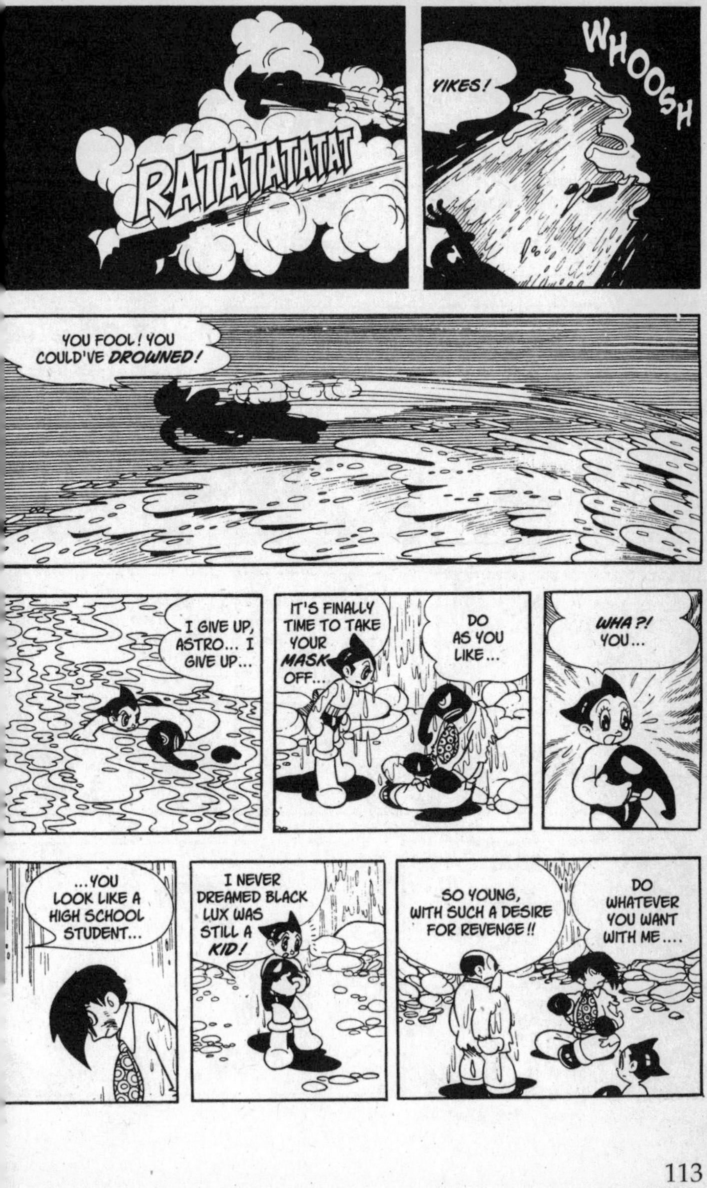
RATATATATAT
YIKES!
WHOOSH
YOU FOOL! YOU COULD'VE DROWNED!
I GIVE UP, ASTRO... I GIVE UP...
IT'S FINALLY TIME TO TAKE YOUR MASK OFF...
DO AS YOU LIKE...
WHA?! YOU...
...YOU LOOK LIKE A HIGH SCHOOL STUDENT...
I NEVER DREAMED BLACK LUX WAS STILL A KID!
SO YOUNG, WITH SUCH A DESIRE FOR REVENGE!!
DO WHATEVER YOU WANT WITH ME....

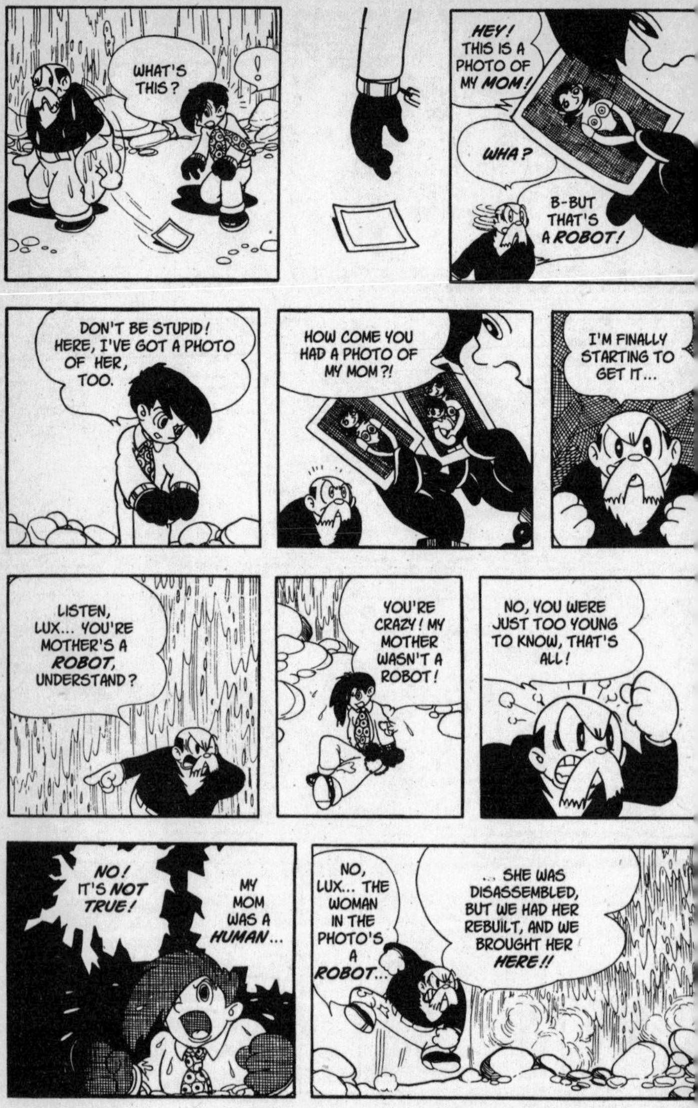
WHAT'S THIS?
!
HEY! THIS IS A PHOTO OF MY MOM!
WHA?
B-BUT THAT'S A ROBOT!
DON'T BE STUPID! HERE, I'VE GOT A PHOTO OF HER, TOO.
HOW COME YOU HAD A PHOTO OF MY MOM?!
I'M FINALLY STARTING TO GET IT...
LISTEN, LUX... YOU'RE MOTHER'S A ROBOT, UNDERSTAND?
YOU'RE CRAZY! MY MOTHER WASN'T A ROBOT!
NO, YOU WERE JUST TOO YOUNG TO KNOW, THAT'S ALL!
NO! IT'S NOT TRUE!
MY MOM WAS A HUMAN...
NO, LUX... THE WOMAN IN THE PHOTO'S A ROBOT...
... SHE WAS DISASSEMBLED, BUT WE HAD HER REBUILT, AND WE BROUGHT HER HERE!!

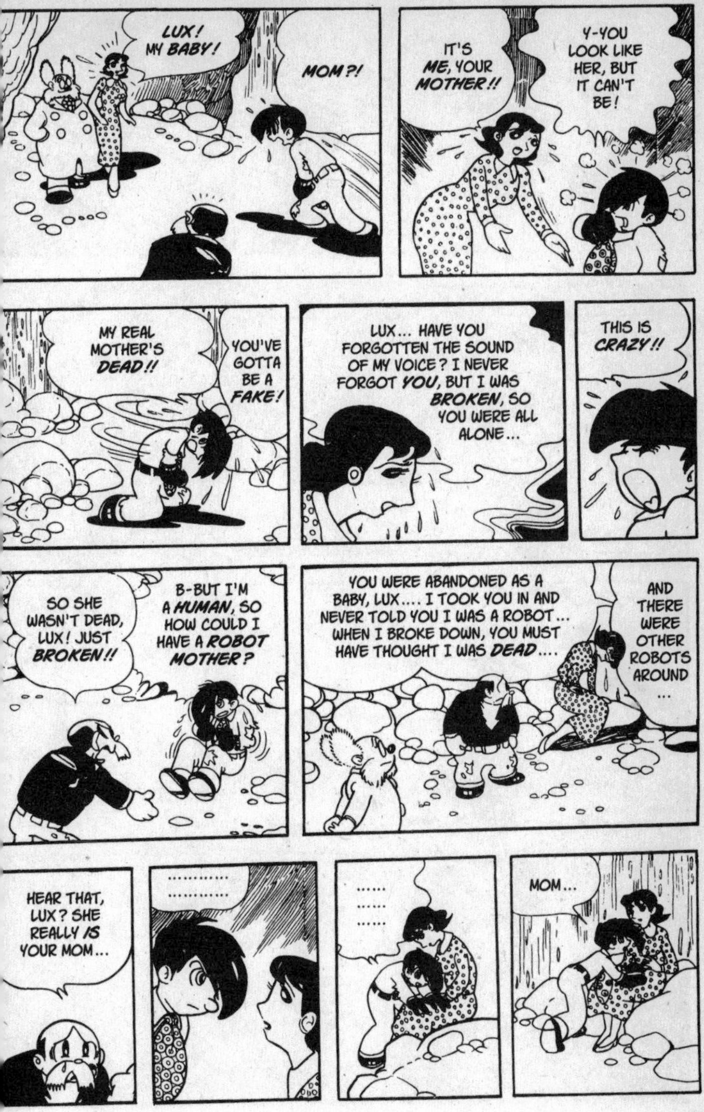
LUX! MY BABY!
MOM?!
IT'S ME, YOUR MOTHER!!
Y-YOU LOOK LIKE HER, BUT IT CAN'T BE!
MY REAL MOTHER'S DEAD!!
YOU'VE GOTTA BE A FAKE!
LUX... HAVE YOU FORGOTTEN THE SOUND OF MY VOICE? I NEVER FORGOT YOU, BUT I WAS BROKEN, SO YOU WERE ALL ALONE...
THIS IS CRAZY!!
SO SHE WASN'T DEAD, LUX! JUST BROKEN!!
B-BUT I'M A HUMAN, SO HOW COULD I HAVE A ROBOT MOTHER?
YOU WERE ABANDONED AS A BABY, LUX.... I TOOK YOU IN AND NEVER TOLD YOU I WAS A ROBOT... WHEN I BROKE DOWN, YOU MUST HAVE THOUGHT I WAS DEAD....
AND THERE WERE OTHER ROBOTS AROUND ...
HEAR THAT, LUX? SHE REALLY IS YOUR MOM...
....
....
MOM...

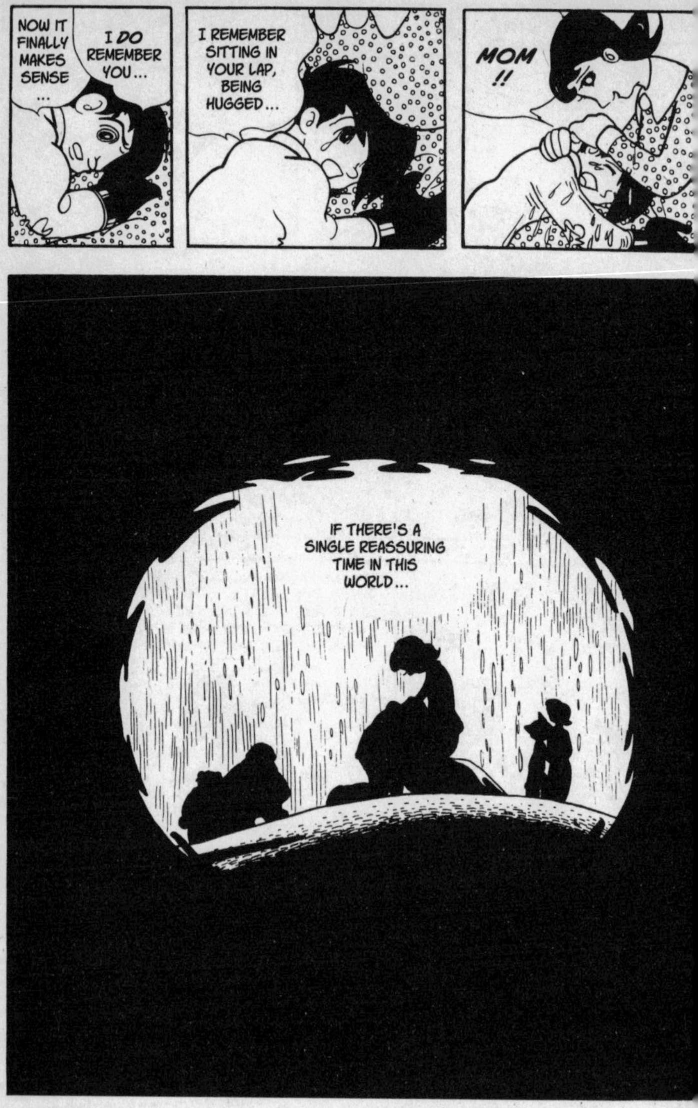
NOW IT FINALLY MAKES SENSE ...
I DO REMEMBER YOU...
I REMEMBER SITTING IN YOUR LAP, BEING HUGGED...
MOM !!
IF THERE'S A SINGLE REASSURING TIME IN THIS WORLD...

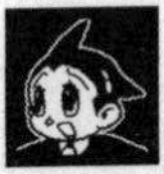

AMBASSADOR ATOM

First serialized from April 1951 to March 1952
in *Shonen* magazine.

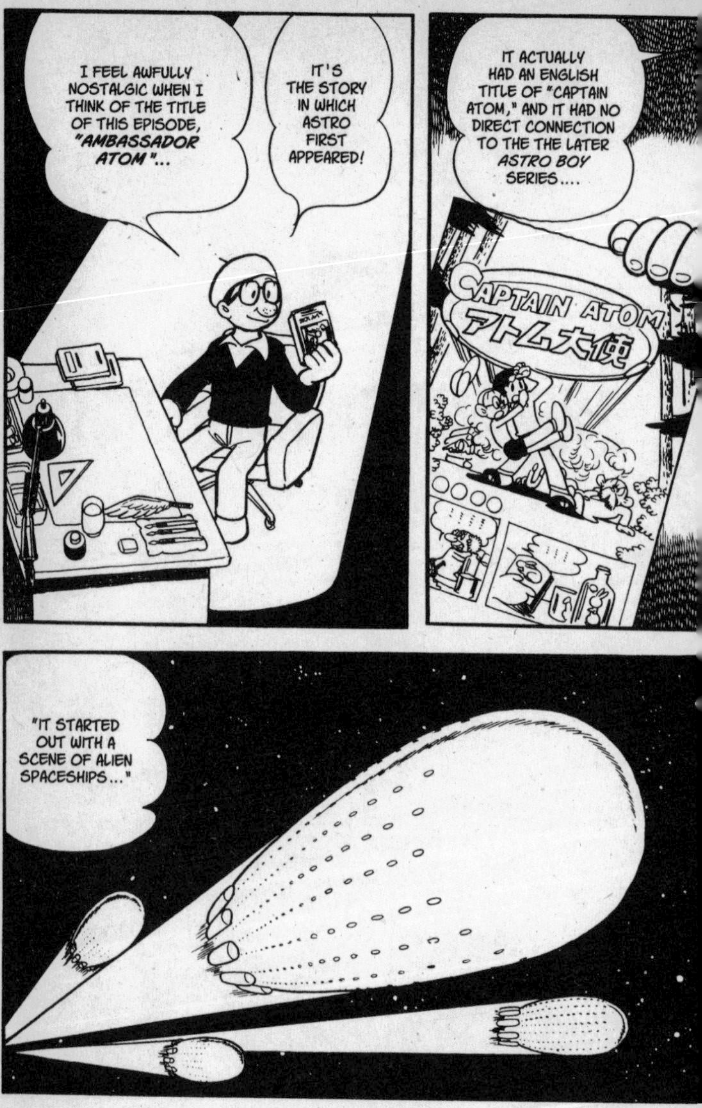
I FEEL AWFULLY NOSTALGIC WHEN I THINK OF THE TITLE OF THIS EPISODE, *"AMBASSADOR ATOM"*...
IT'S THE STORY IN WHICH ASTRO FIRST APPEARED!
IT ACTUALLY HAD AN ENGLISH TITLE OF "CAPTAIN ATOM," AND IT HAD NO DIRECT CONNECTION TO THE THE LATER *ASTRO BOY* SERIES....
CAPTAIN ATOM
アトム大使
"IT STARTED OUT WITH A SCENE OF ALIEN SPACESHIPS..."

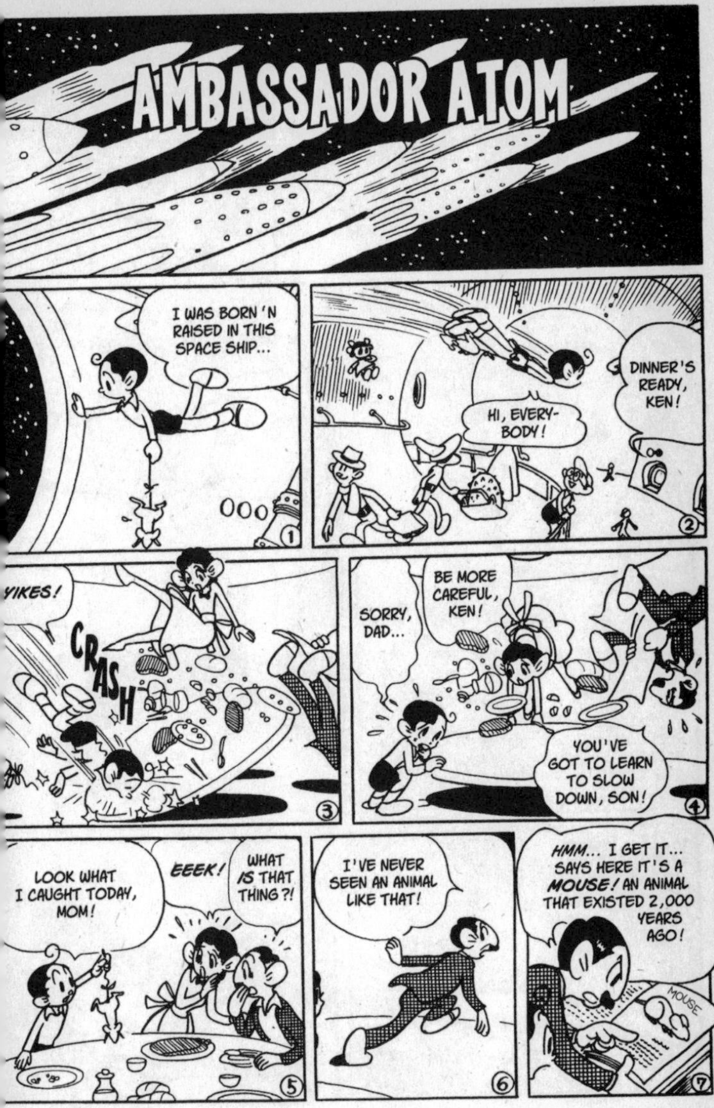
AMBASSADOR ATOM
I WAS BORN 'N RAISED IN THIS SPACE SHIP...
HI, EVERY-BODY!
DINNER'S READY, KEN!
YIKES!
CRASH
SORRY, DAD...
BE MORE CAREFUL, KEN!
YOU'VE GOT TO LEARN TO SLOW DOWN, SON!
LOOK WHAT I CAUGHT TODAY, MOM!
EEEK!
WHAT IS THAT THING?!
I'VE NEVER SEEN AN ANIMAL LIKE THAT!
HMM... I GET IT... SAYS HERE IT'S A MOUSE! AN ANIMAL THAT EXISTED 2,000 YEARS AGO!
MOUSE

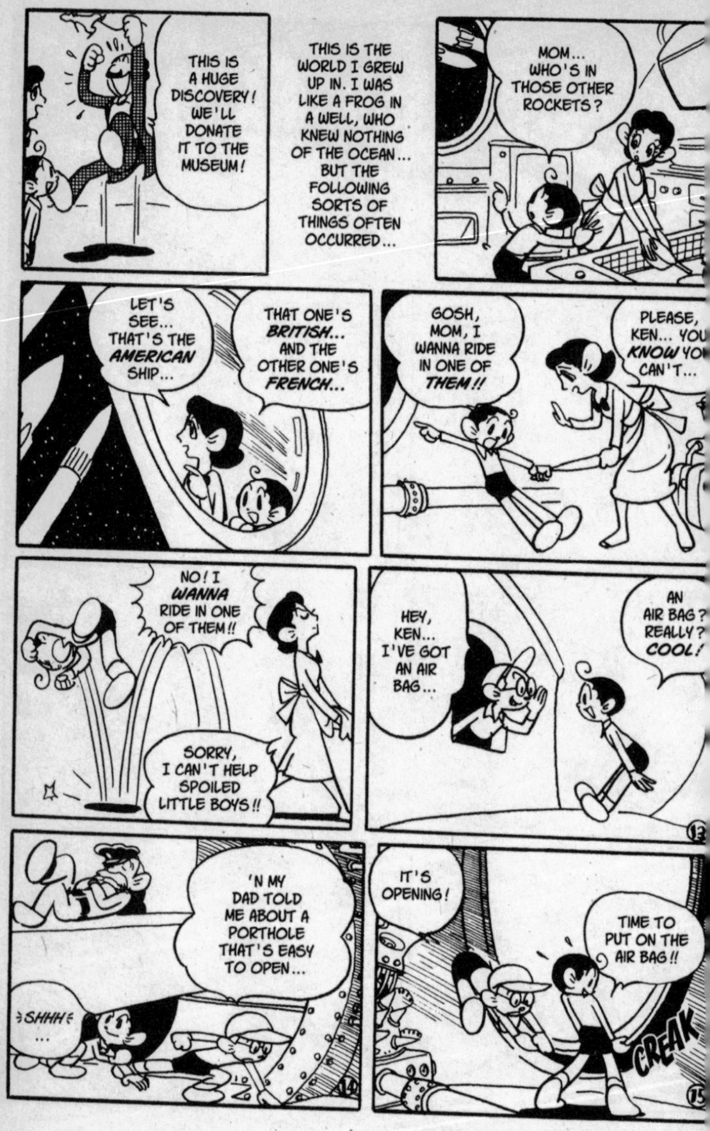
THIS IS A HUGE DISCOVERY! WE'LL DONATE IT TO THE MUSEUM!
THIS IS THE WORLD I GREW UP IN. I WAS LIKE A FROG IN A WELL, WHO KNEW NOTHING OF THE OCEAN... BUT THE FOLLOWING SORTS OF THINGS OFTEN OCCURRED...
MOM... WHO'S IN THOSE OTHER ROCKETS?
LET'S SEE... THAT'S THE *AMERICAN* SHIP...
THAT ONE'S *BRITISH...* AND THE OTHER ONE'S *FRENCH...*
GOSH, MOM, I WANNA RIDE IN ONE OF *THEM!!*
PLEASE, KEN... YOU *KNOW* YO CAN'T...
NO! I *WANNA* RIDE IN ONE OF THEM!!
SORRY, I CAN'T HELP SPOILED LITTLE BOYS!!
HEY, KEN... I'VE GOT AN AIR BAG...
AN AIR BAG? REALLY? *COOL!*
'N MY DAD TOLD ME ABOUT A PORTHOLE THAT'S EASY TO OPEN...
SHHH ...
IT'S OPENING!
TIME TO PUT ON THE AIR BAG!!
CREAK

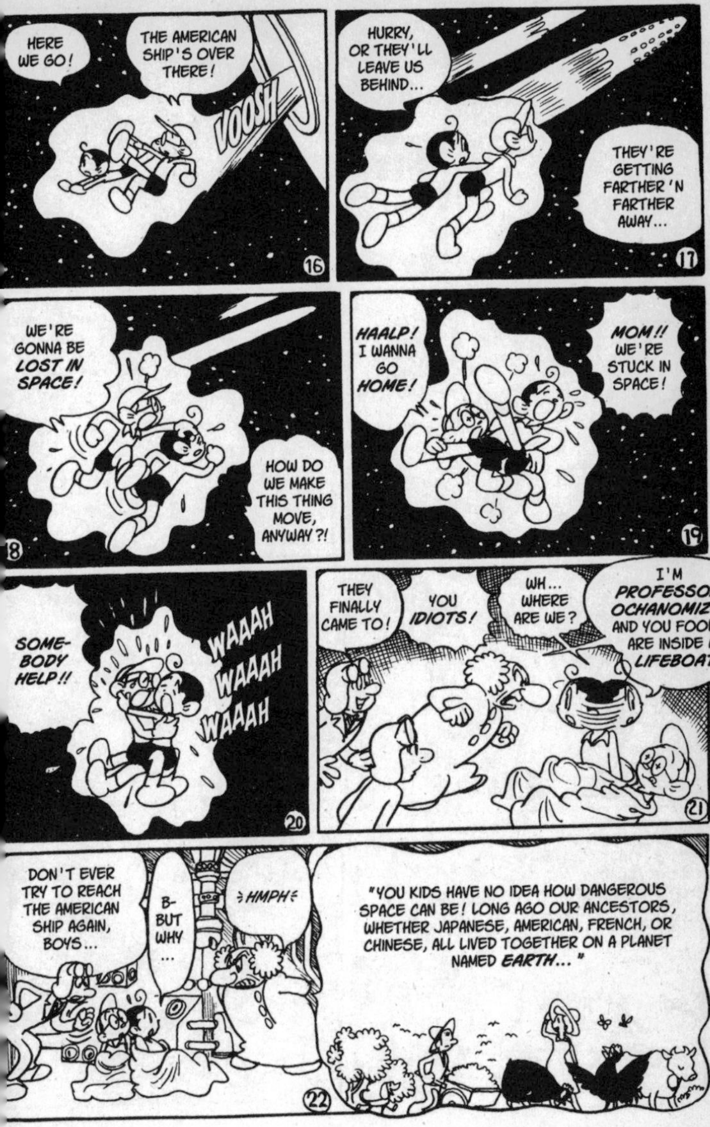
HERE WE GO!
THE AMERICAN SHIP'S OVER THERE!
VOOSH
HURRY, OR THEY'LL LEAVE US BEHIND...
THEY'RE GETTING FARTHER 'N FARTHER AWAY...
WE'RE GONNA BE LOST IN SPACE!
HOW DO WE MAKE THIS THING MOVE, ANYWAY?!
HAALP! I WANNA GO HOME!
MOM!! WE'RE STUCK IN SPACE!
SOMEBODY HELP!!
WAAAH WAAAH WAAAH
THEY FINALLY CAME TO!
YOU IDIOTS!
WH... WHERE ARE WE?
I'M PROFESSOR OCHANOMIZU, AND YOU FOOLS ARE INSIDE A LIFEBOAT!
DON'T EVER TRY TO REACH THE AMERICAN SHIP AGAIN, BOYS...
B-BUT WHY ...
HMPH
"YOU KIDS HAVE NO IDEA HOW DANGEROUS SPACE CAN BE! LONG AGO OUR ANCESTORS, WHETHER JAPANESE, AMERICAN, FRENCH, OR CHINESE, ALL LIVED TOGETHER ON A PLANET NAMED EARTH..."

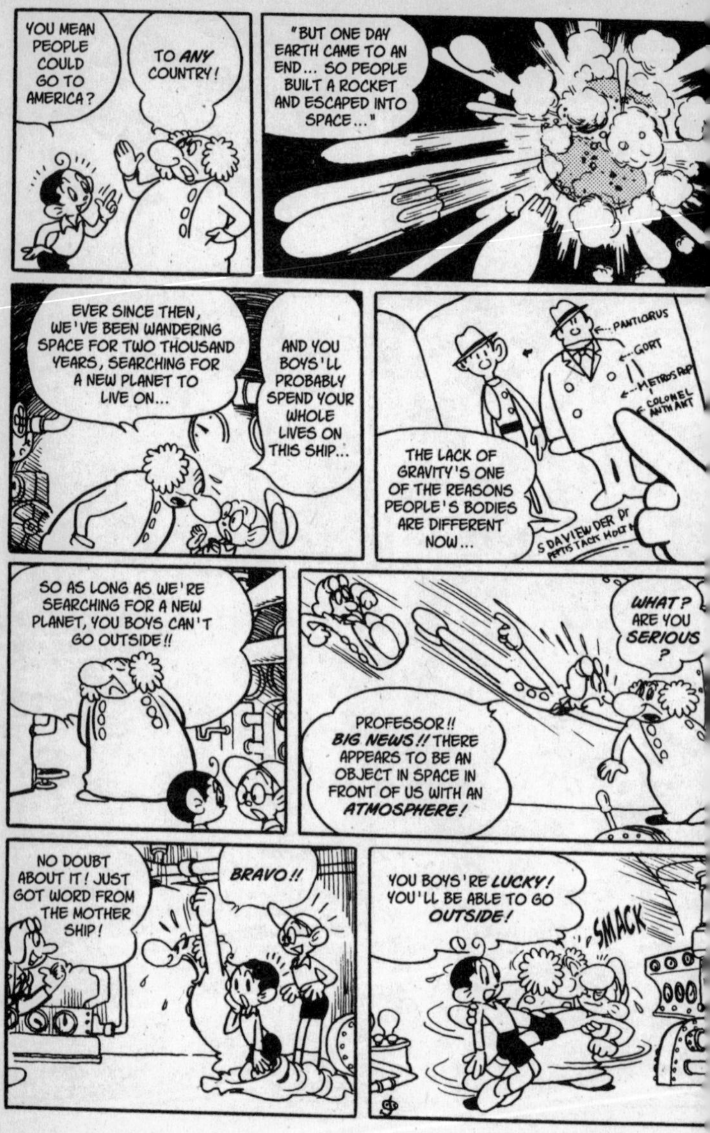
YOU MEAN PEOPLE COULD GO TO AMERICA?
TO *ANY* COUNTRY!
"BUT ONE DAY EARTH CAME TO AN END... SO PEOPLE BUILT A ROCKET AND ESCAPED INTO SPACE..."
EVER SINCE THEN, WE'VE BEEN WANDERING SPACE FOR TWO THOUSAND YEARS, SEARCHING FOR A NEW PLANET TO LIVE ON...
AND YOU BOYS'LL PROBABLY SPEND YOUR WHOLE LIVES ON THIS SHIP...
THE LACK OF GRAVITY'S ONE OF THE REASONS PEOPLE'S BODIES ARE DIFFERENT NOW...
SO AS LONG AS WE'RE SEARCHING FOR A NEW PLANET, YOU BOYS CAN'T GO OUTSIDE!!
WHAT? ARE YOU *SERIOUS*?
PROFESSOR!! *BIG NEWS!!* THERE APPEARS TO BE AN OBJECT IN SPACE IN FRONT OF US WITH AN *ATMOSPHERE!*
NO DOUBT ABOUT IT! JUST GOT WORD FROM THE MOTHER SHIP!
BRAVO!!
YOU BOYS'RE *LUCKY!* YOU'LL BE ABLE TO GO *OUTSIDE!*
SMACK

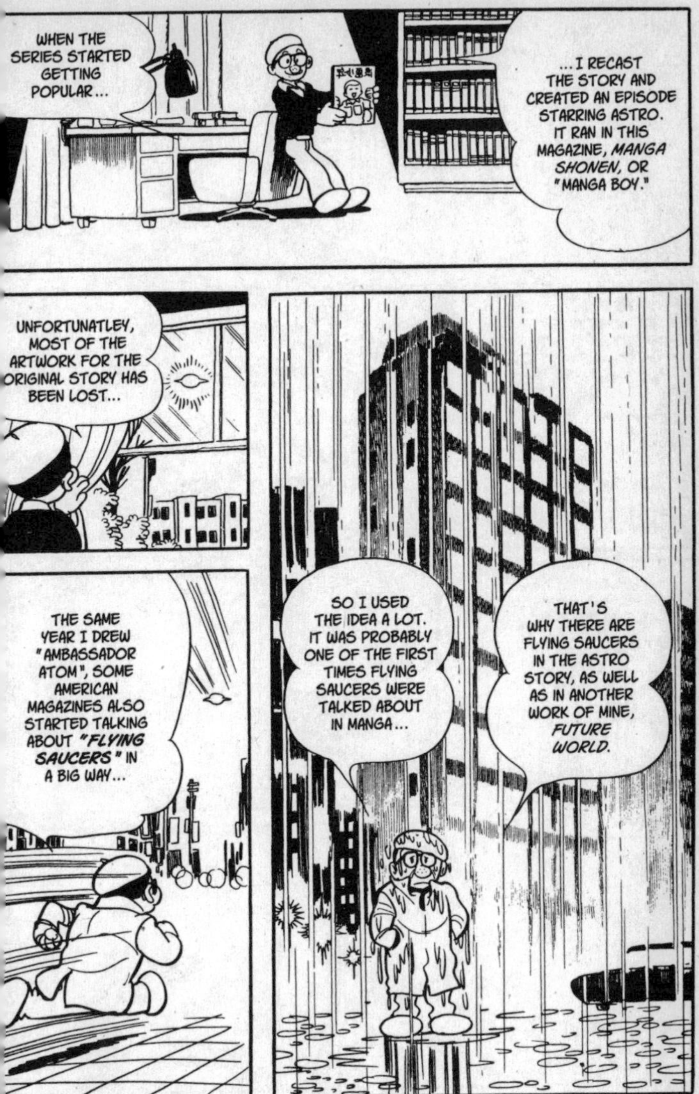
WHEN THE SERIES STARTED GETTING POPULAR...
...I RECAST THE STORY AND CREATED AN EPISODE STARRING ASTRO. IT RAN IN THIS MAGAZINE, *MANGA SHONEN*, OR "MANGA BOY."
UNFORTUNATLEY, MOST OF THE ARTWORK FOR THE ORIGINAL STORY HAS BEEN LOST...
THE SAME YEAR I DREW "AMBASSADOR ATOM", SOME AMERICAN MAGAZINES ALSO STARTED TALKING ABOUT *"FLYING SAUCERS"* IN A BIG WAY...
SO I USED THE IDEA A LOT. IT WAS PROBABLY ONE OF THE FIRST TIMES FLYING SAUCERS WERE TALKED ABOUT IN MANGA...
THAT'S WHY THERE ARE FLYING SAUCERS IN THE ASTRO STORY, AS WELL AS IN ANOTHER WORK OF MINE, *FUTURE WORLD*.

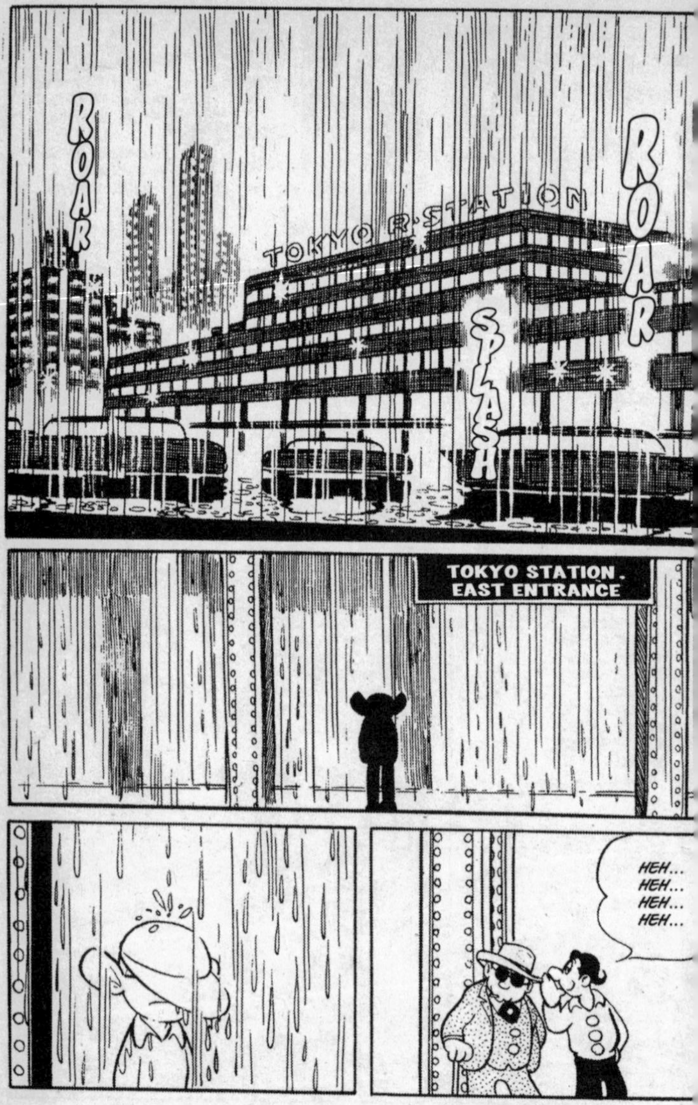
ROAR
TOKYO R STATION
ROAR
SPLASH
TOKYO STATION EAST ENTRANCE
HEH... HEH... HEH... HEH...

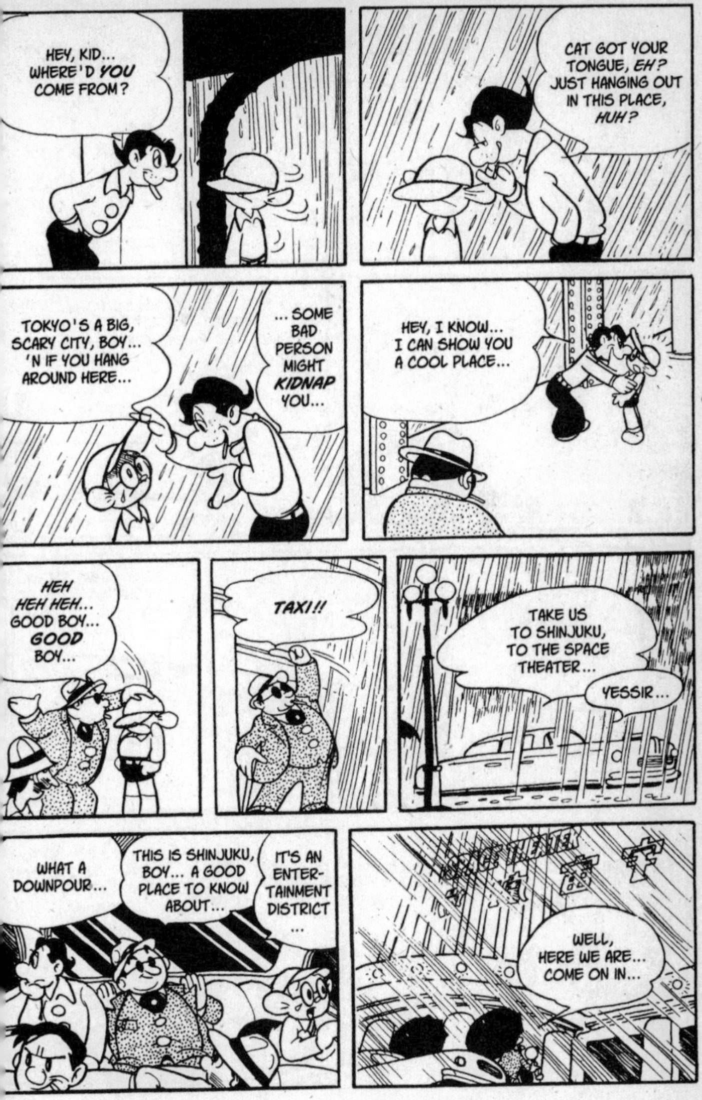
HEY, KID... WHERE'D YOU COME FROM?
CAT GOT YOUR TONGUE, EH? JUST HANGING OUT IN THIS PLACE, HUH?
TOKYO'S A BIG, SCARY CITY, BOY... 'N IF YOU HANG AROUND HERE...
... SOME BAD PERSON MIGHT KIDNAP YOU...
HEY, I KNOW... I CAN SHOW YOU A COOL PLACE...
HEH HEH HEH... GOOD BOY... GOOD BOY...
TAXI!!
TAKE US TO SHINJUKU, TO THE SPACE THEATER...
YESSIR...
WHAT A DOWNPOUR...
THIS IS SHINJUKU, BOY... A GOOD PLACE TO KNOW ABOUT...
IT'S AN ENTER-TAINMENT DISTRICT ...
WELL, HERE WE ARE... COME ON IN...

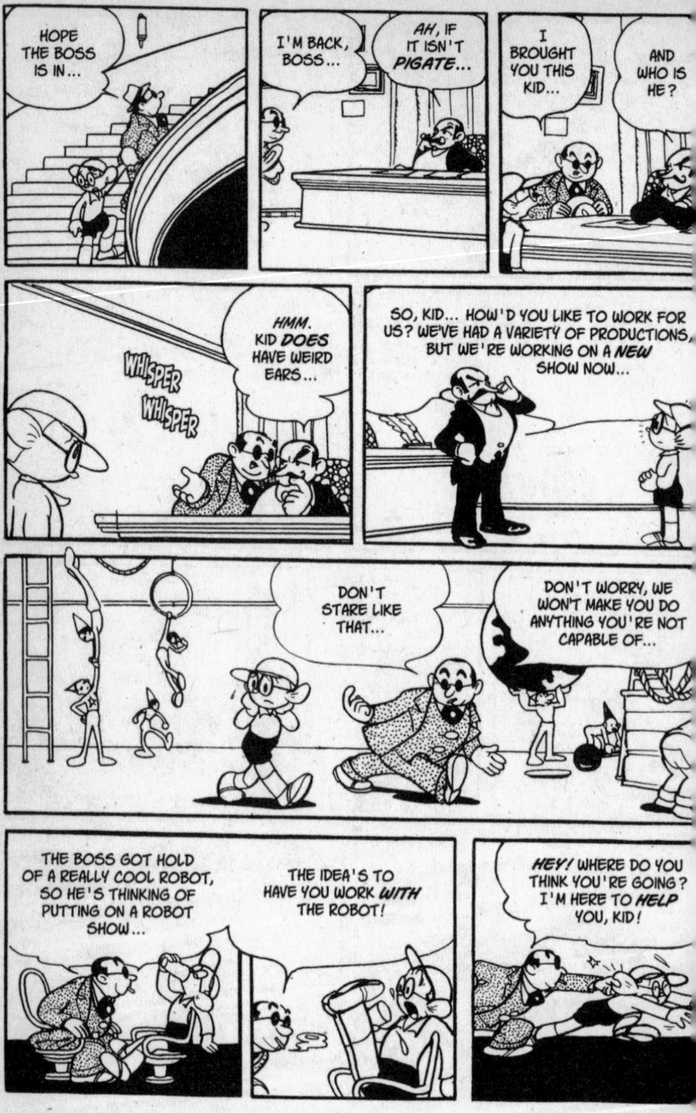
HOPE THE BOSS IS IN...
I'M BACK, BOSS...
AH, IF IT ISN'T PIGATE...
I BROUGHT YOU THIS KID...
AND WHO IS HE?
WHISPER
WHISPER
HMM. KID DOES HAVE WEIRD EARS...
SO, KID... HOW'D YOU LIKE TO WORK FOR US? WE'VE HAD A VARIETY OF PRODUCTIONS, BUT WE'RE WORKING ON A NEW SHOW NOW...
DON'T STARE LIKE THAT...
DON'T WORRY, WE WON'T MAKE YOU DO ANYTHING YOU'RE NOT CAPABLE OF...
THE BOSS GOT HOLD OF A REALLY COOL ROBOT, SO HE'S THINKING OF PUTTING ON A ROBOT SHOW...
THE IDEA'S TO HAVE YOU WORK WITH THE ROBOT!
HEY! WHERE DO YOU THINK YOU'RE GOING? I'M HERE TO HELP YOU, KID!

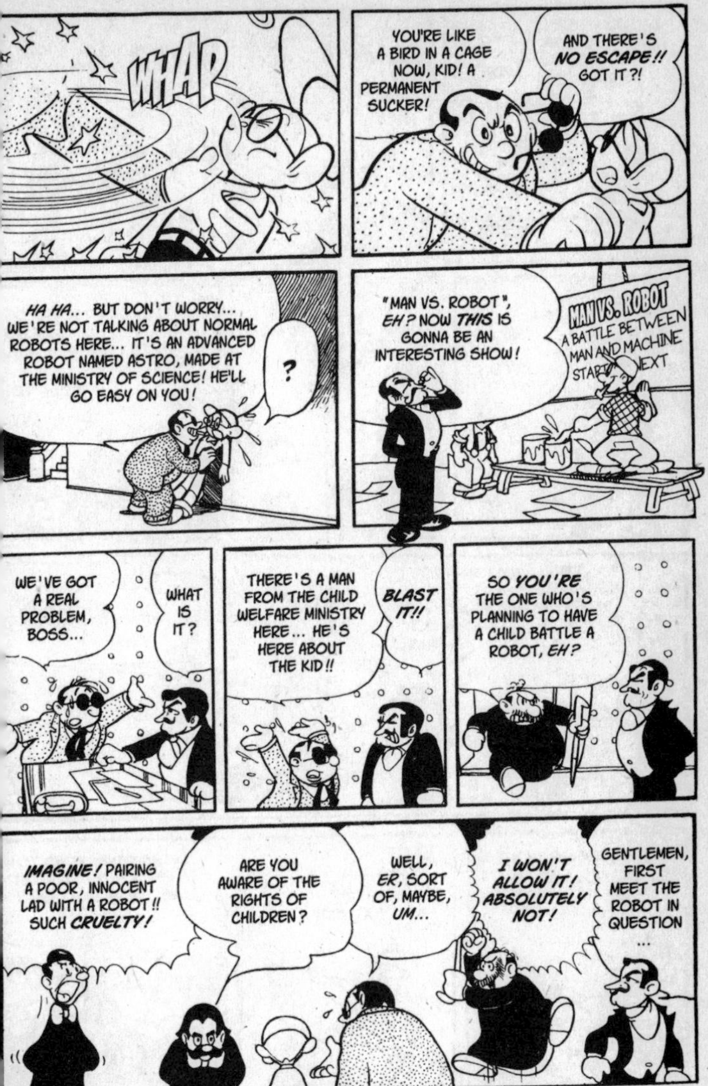
WHAP
YOU'RE LIKE A BIRD IN A CAGE NOW, KID! A PERMANENT SUCKER!
AND THERE'S NO ESCAPE!! GOT IT?!
HA HA... BUT DON'T WORRY... WE'RE NOT TALKING ABOUT NORMAL ROBOTS HERE... IT'S AN ADVANCED ROBOT NAMED ASTRO, MADE AT THE MINISTRY OF SCIENCE! HE'LL GO EASY ON YOU!
?
"MAN VS. ROBOT", EH? NOW THIS IS GONNA BE AN INTERESTING SHOW!
MAN VS. ROBOT
A BATTLE BETWEEN MAN AND MACHINE
WE'VE GOT A REAL PROBLEM, BOSS...
WHAT IS IT?
THERE'S A MAN FROM THE CHILD WELFARE MINISTRY HERE... HE'S HERE ABOUT THE KID!!
BLAST IT!!
SO YOU'RE THE ONE WHO'S PLANNING TO HAVE A CHILD BATTLE A ROBOT, EH?
IMAGINE! PAIRING A POOR, INNOCENT LAD WITH A ROBOT!! SUCH CRUELTY!
ARE YOU AWARE OF THE RIGHTS OF CHILDREN?
WELL, ER, SORT OF, MAYBE, UM...
I WON'T ALLOW IT! ABSOLUTELY NOT!
GENTLEMEN, FIRST MEET THE ROBOT IN QUESTION ...

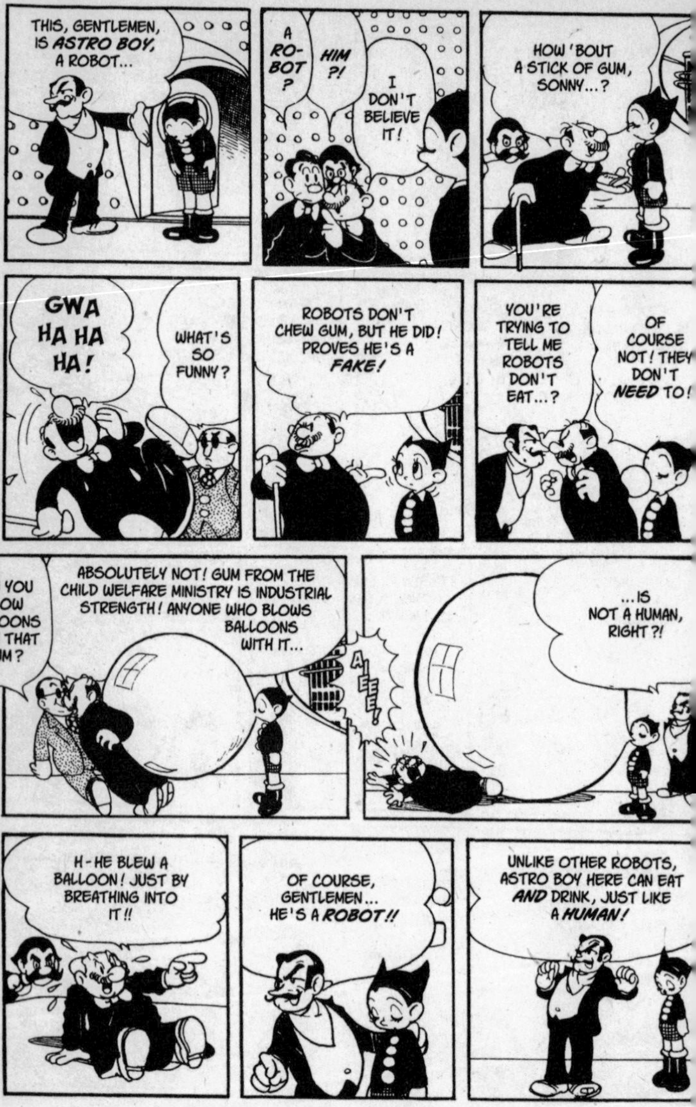

THIS, GENTLEMEN, IS ASTRO BOY, A ROBOT...
A RO-BOT?
HIM?!
I DON'T BELIEVE IT!
HOW 'BOUT A STICK OF GUM, SONNY...?
GWA HA HA HA!
WHAT'S SO FUNNY?
ROBOTS DON'T CHEW GUM, BUT HE DID! PROVES HE'S A FAKE!
YOU'RE TRYING TO TELL ME ROBOTS DON'T EAT...?
OF COURSE NOT! THEY DON'T NEED TO!
C'N YOU BLOW BALLOONS WITH THAT GUM?
ABSOLUTELY NOT! GUM FROM THE CHILD WELFARE MINISTRY IS INDUSTRIAL STRENGTH! ANYONE WHO BLOWS BALLOONS WITH IT...
AIEEE!
...IS NOT A HUMAN, RIGHT?!
H-HE BLEW A BALLOON! JUST BY BREATHING INTO IT!!
OF COURSE, GENTLEMEN... HE'S A ROBOT!!
UNLIKE OTHER ROBOTS, ASTRO BOY HERE CAN EAT AND DRINK, JUST LIKE A HUMAN!

ALLOW ME TO EXPLAIN, GENTLEMEN, ABOUT THIS ROBOT AND HOW HE CAME INTO MY POSSESSION...

ASTRO IS A *WORK OF ART*, CREATED AT THE MINISTRY OF SCIENCE BY *DR. TENMA*.

THAT, OVER THERE, IS THE ADVANCED FACTORY WHERE HE WAS MANUFACTURED!

DR. TENMA?! BUT ISN'T HE THE HEAD OF THE MINISTRY OF SCIENCE?

DR. TENMA:

BORN INTO A LONG LINE OF HORSE RADISH FARMERS, IN THE PARTICULARLY UNLUCKY YEAR OF THE HORSE, IN GUNMA ("HORSE HERD") PREFECTURE. REAL NAME IS TARO UMA ("HORSE"). GRADUATED FROM THE UNIVERSITY OF NERIMA ("WALKING HORSE"), AND THOUGH A COMPLETE DARK HORSE, THROUGH AN AMAZING DEMONSTRATION OF INTELLECTUAL HORSEPOWER ROSE TO BE THE HEAD OF THE MINISTRY OF SCIENCE -- IN AN AREA OF TOKYO KNOWN AS TAKADANOBABA, WHICH LOOSELY TRANSLATES INTO A "HIGH PASTURE FOR HORSES." AMONG THOSE WISHING TO UNSEAT HIM, HE IS KNOWN AS A REAL HORSE OF A DIFFERENT COLOR.

"THIS DR. TENMA HAD A SON OF HIS OWN, NAMED *TOBIO*..."

"... AND HE LOVED HIS SON *DEEPLY*..."

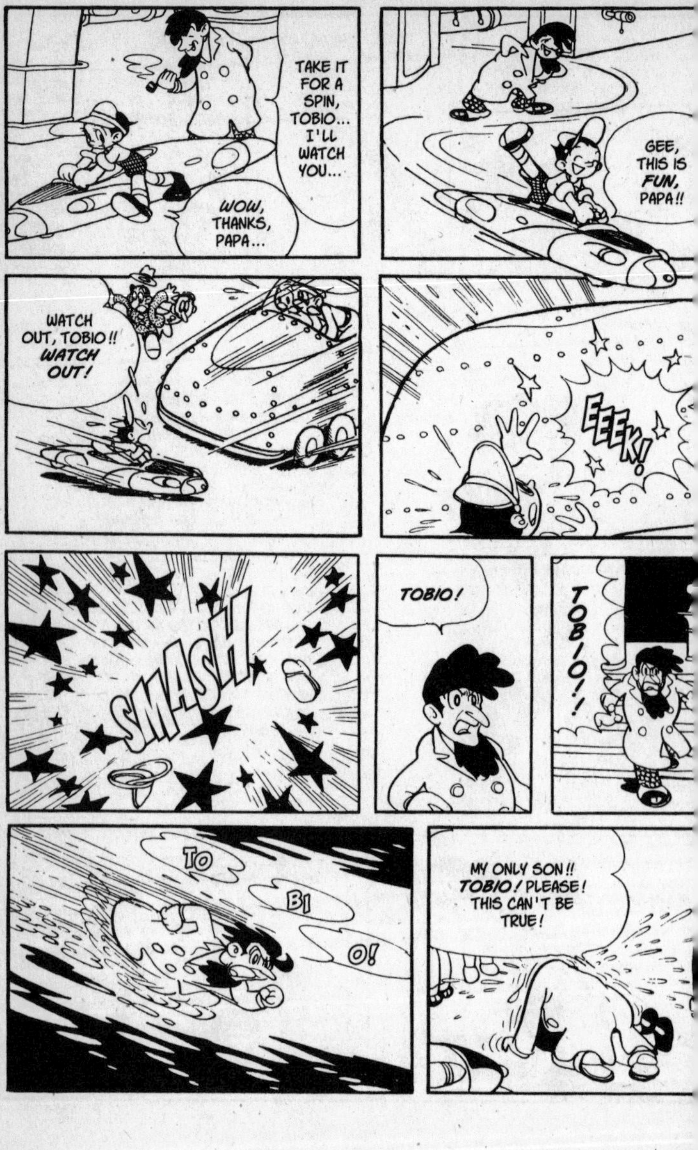
TAKE IT FOR A SPIN, TOBIO... I'LL WATCH YOU...
WOW, THANKS, PAPA...
GEE, THIS IS FUN, PAPA!!
WATCH OUT, TOBIO!! WATCH OUT!
EEEK!
SMASH
TOBIO!
TOBIO!!
TO
BI
O!
MY ONLY SON!! TOBIO! PLEASE! THIS CAN'T BE TRUE!

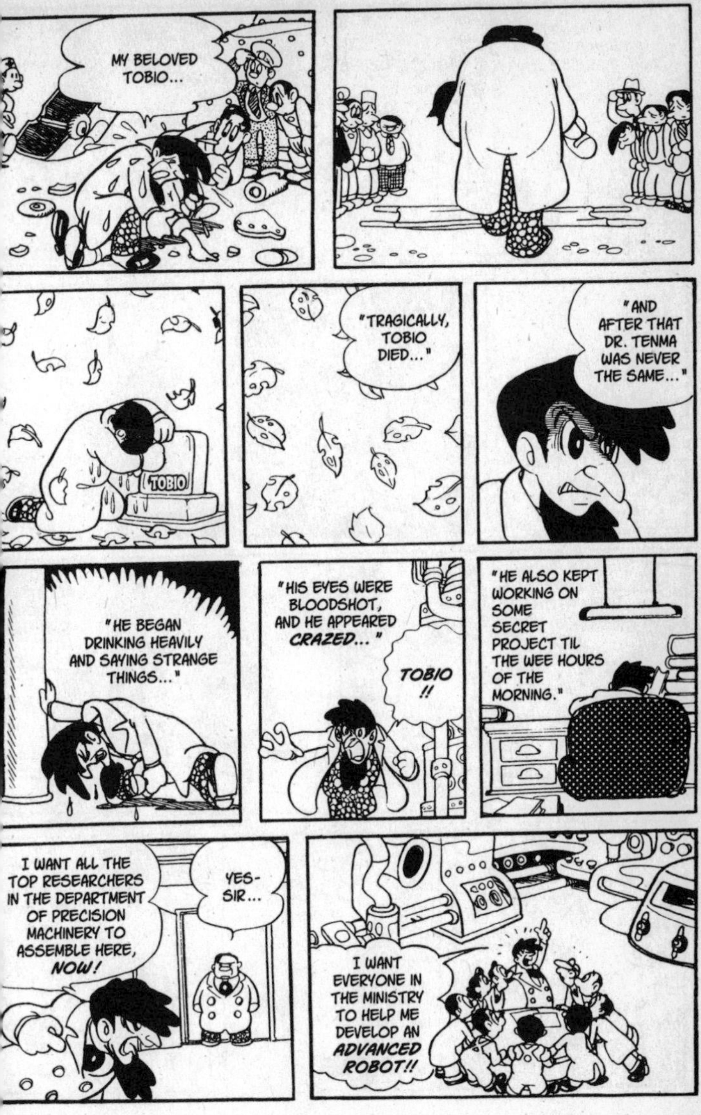
MY BELOVED TOBIO...
TOBIO
"TRAGICALLY, TOBIO DIED..."
"AND AFTER THAT DR. TENMA WAS NEVER THE SAME..."
"HE BEGAN DRINKING HEAVILY AND SAYING STRANGE THINGS..."
"HIS EYES WERE BLOODSHOT, AND HE APPEARED *CRAZED...*"
TOBIO !!
"HE ALSO KEPT WORKING ON SOME SECRET PROJECT TIL THE WEE HOURS OF THE MORNING."
I WANT ALL THE TOP RESEARCHERS IN THE DEPARTMENT OF PRECISION MACHINERY TO ASSEMBLE HERE, *NOW!*
YES-SIR...
I WANT EVERYONE IN THE MINISTRY TO HELP ME DEVELOP AN *ADVANCED ROBOT!!*

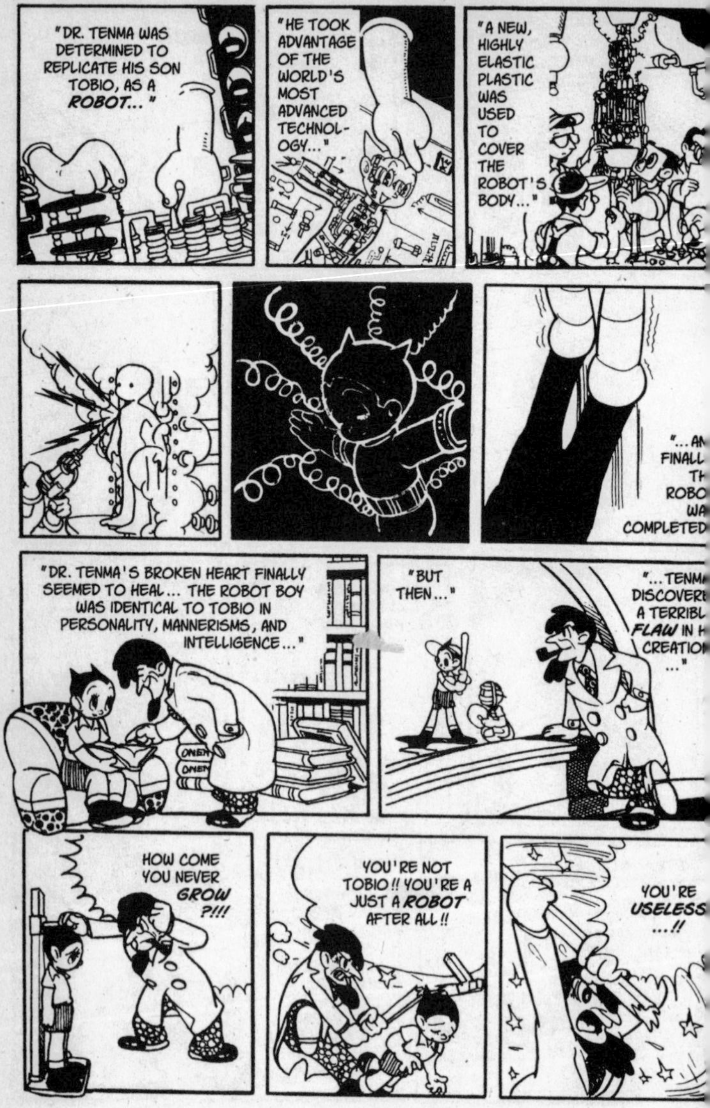
"DR. TENMA WAS DETERMINED TO REPLICATE HIS SON TOBIO, AS A *ROBOT*..."
"HE TOOK ADVANTAGE OF THE WORLD'S MOST ADVANCED TECHNOL-OGY..."
"A NEW, HIGHLY ELASTIC PLASTIC WAS USED TO COVER THE ROBOT'S BODY..."
"...AN FINALL TH ROBO WA COMPLETED
"DR. TENMA'S BROKEN HEART FINALLY SEEMED TO HEAL... THE ROBOT BOY WAS IDENTICAL TO TOBIO IN PERSONALITY, MANNERISMS, AND INTELLIGENCE..."
"BUT THEN..."
"...TENM DISCOVER A TERRIBL *FLAW* IN H CREATIO ..."
HOW COME YOU NEVER *GROW* ?!!!
YOU'RE NOT TOBIO!! YOU'RE A JUST A *ROBOT* AFTER ALL!!
YOU'RE *USELESS* ...!!

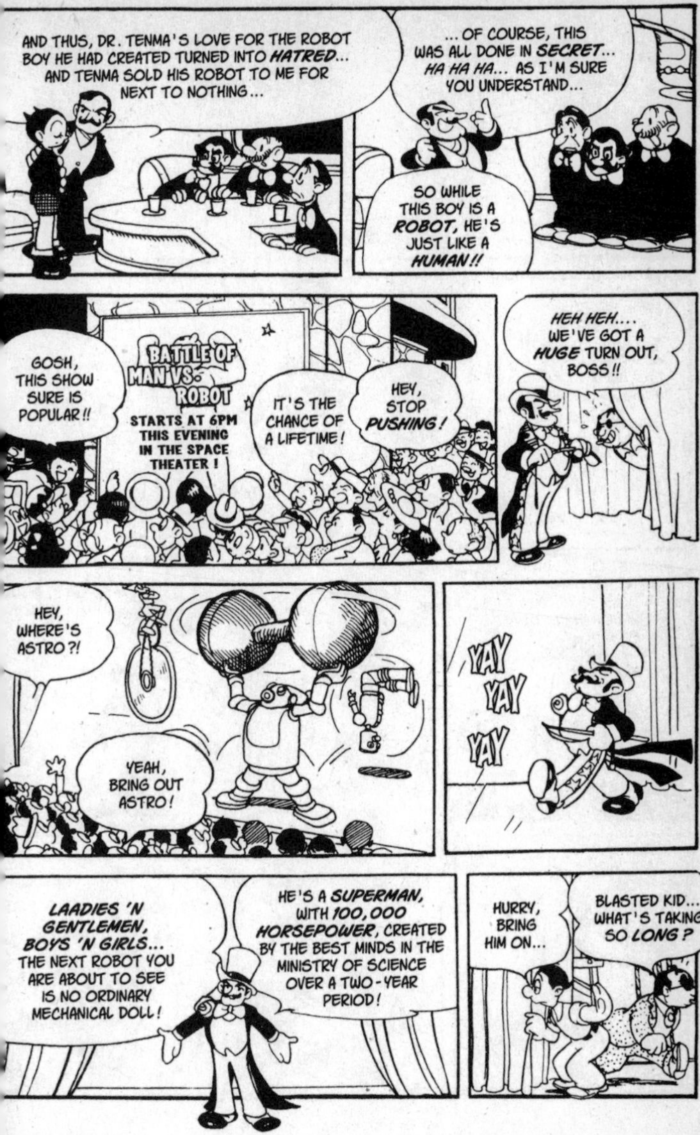
AND THUS, DR. TENMA'S LOVE FOR THE ROBOT BOY HE HAD CREATED TURNED INTO HATRED... AND TENMA SOLD HIS ROBOT TO ME FOR NEXT TO NOTHING...
... OF COURSE, THIS WAS ALL DONE IN SECRET... HA HA HA... AS I'M SURE YOU UNDERSTAND...
SO WHILE THIS BOY IS A ROBOT, HE'S JUST LIKE A HUMAN!!
GOSH, THIS SHOW SURE IS POPULAR!!
BATTLE OF MAN VS. ROBOT
STARTS AT 6PM THIS EVENING IN THE SPACE THEATER!
IT'S THE CHANCE OF A LIFETIME!
HEY, STOP PUSHING!
HEH HEH.... WE'VE GOT A HUGE TURN OUT, BOSS!!
HEY, WHERE'S ASTRO?!
YEAH, BRING OUT ASTRO!
YAY
YAY
YAY
LAADIES 'N GENTLEMEN, BOYS 'N GIRLS... THE NEXT ROBOT YOU ARE ABOUT TO SEE IS NO ORDINARY MECHANICAL DOLL!
HE'S A SUPERMAN, WITH 100,000 HORSEPOWER, CREATED BY THE BEST MINDS IN THE MINISTRY OF SCIENCE OVER A TWO-YEAR PERIOD!
HURRY, BRING HIM ON...
BLASTED KID... WHAT'S TAKING SO LONG?

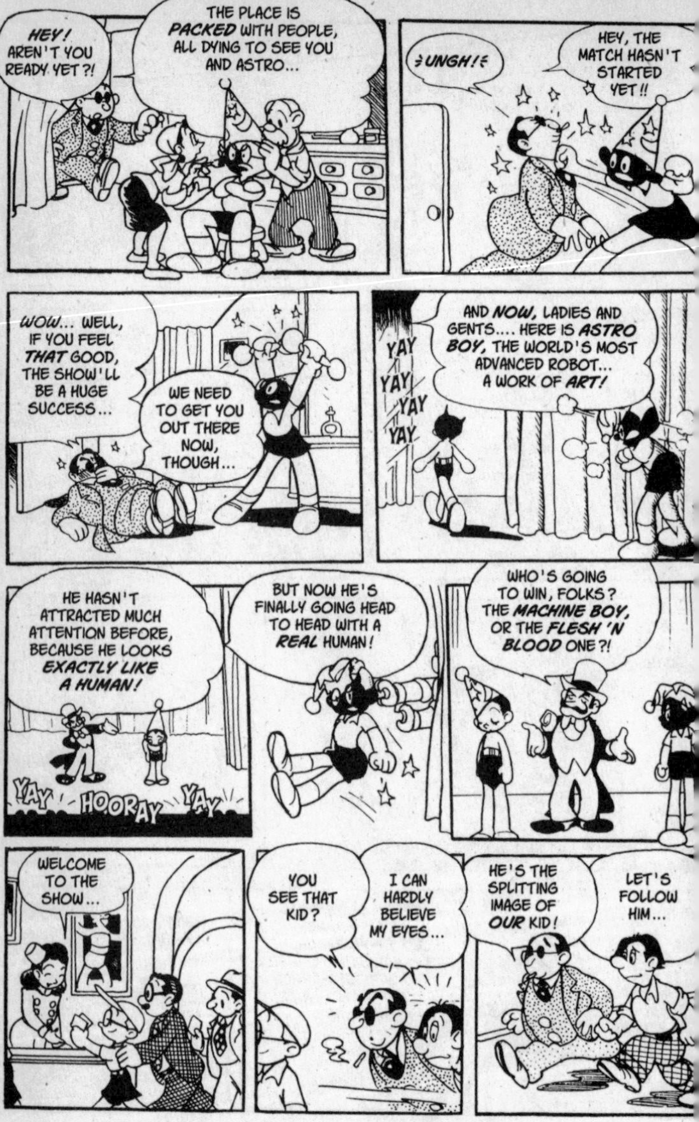
HEY! AREN'T YOU READY YET?!
THE PLACE IS PACKED WITH PEOPLE, ALL DYING TO SEE YOU AND ASTRO...
UNGH!
HEY, THE MATCH HASN'T STARTED YET!!
WOW... WELL, IF YOU FEEL THAT GOOD, THE SHOW'LL BE A HUGE SUCCESS...
WE NEED TO GET YOU OUT THERE NOW, THOUGH...
YAY YAY YAY YAY
AND NOW, LADIES AND GENTS.... HERE IS ASTRO BOY, THE WORLD'S MOST ADVANCED ROBOT... A WORK OF ART!
HE HASN'T ATTRACTED MUCH ATTENTION BEFORE, BECAUSE HE LOOKS EXACTLY LIKE A HUMAN!
YAY HOORAY YAY
BUT NOW HE'S FINALLY GOING HEAD TO HEAD WITH A REAL HUMAN!
WHO'S GOING TO WIN, FOLKS? THE MACHINE BOY, OR THE FLESH 'N BLOOD ONE?!
WELCOME TO THE SHOW...
YOU SEE THAT KID?
I CAN HARDLY BELIEVE MY EYES...
HE'S THE SPLITTING IMAGE OF OUR KID!
LET'S FOLLOW HIM...

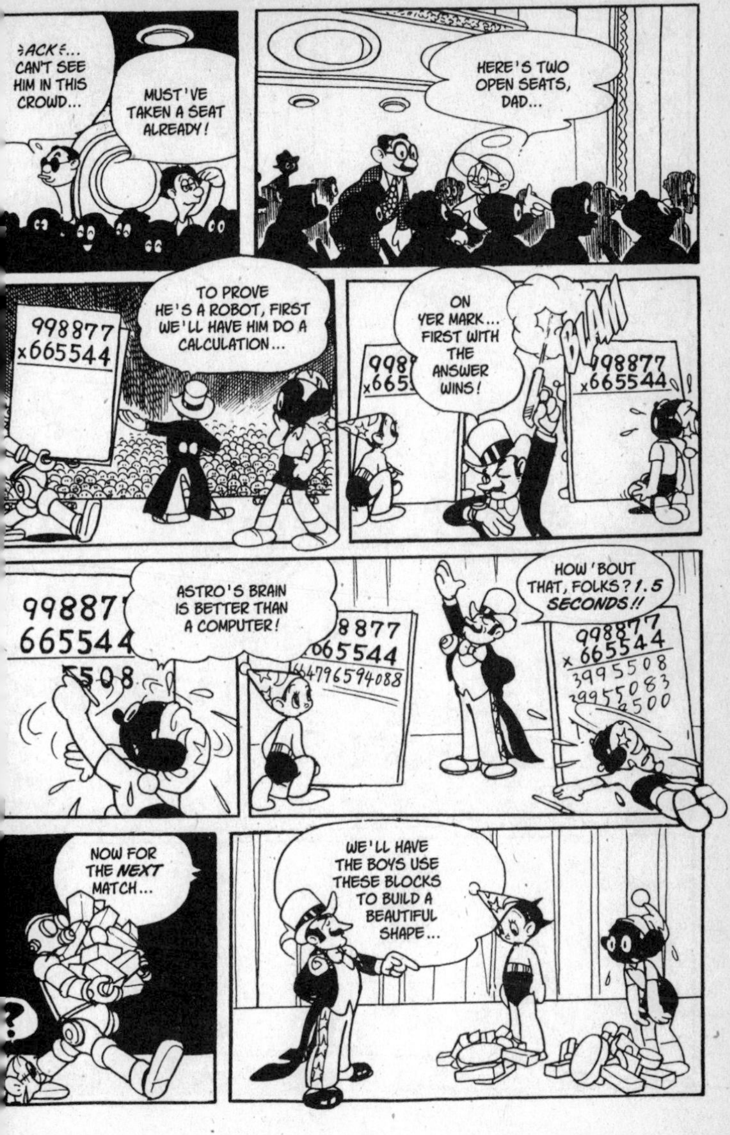

ACK... CAN'T SEE HIM IN THIS CROWD...
MUST'VE TAKEN A SEAT ALREADY!
HERE'S TWO OPEN SEATS, DAD...
998877
x665544
TO PROVE HE'S A ROBOT, FIRST WE'LL HAVE HIM DO A CALCULATION...
ON YER MARK... FIRST WITH THE ANSWER WINS!
BLAM
998877
x665544
ASTRO'S BRAIN IS BETTER THAN A COMPUTER!
HOW 'BOUT THAT, FOLKS? *1.5 SECONDS!!*
NOW FOR THE *NEXT* MATCH...
WE'LL HAVE THE BOYS USE THESE BLOCKS TO BUILD A BEAUTIFUL SHAPE...

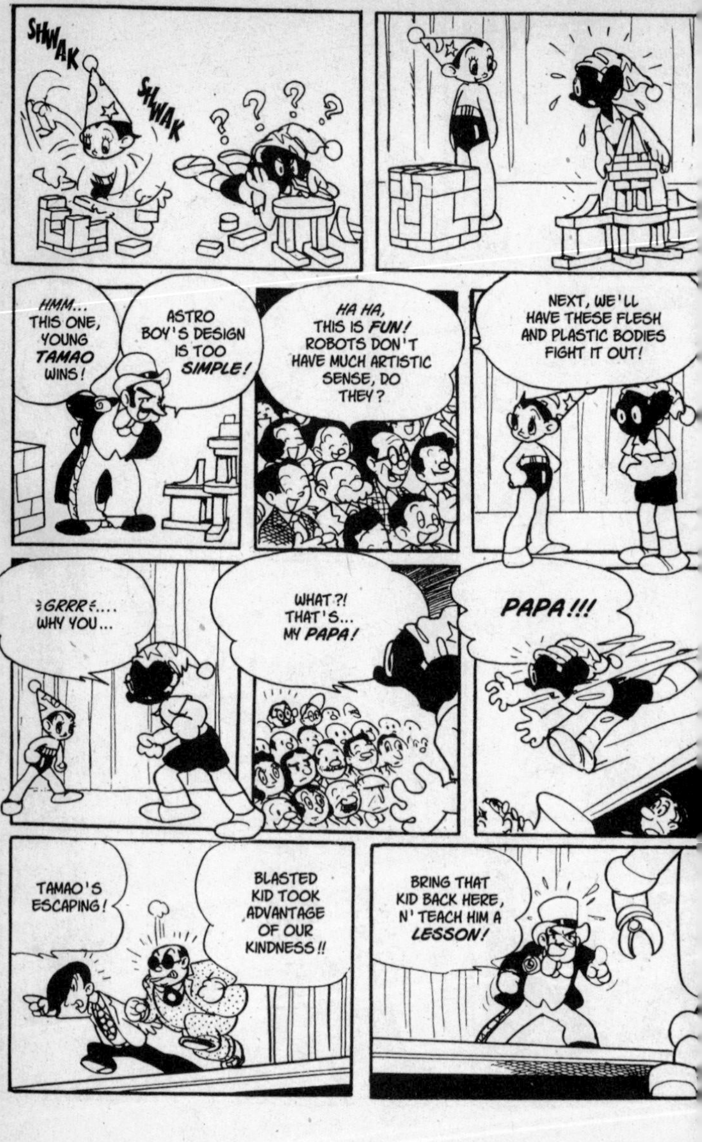
SHWAK
SHWAK
HMM... THIS ONE, YOUNG TAMAO WINS!
ASTRO BOY'S DESIGN IS TOO SIMPLE!
HA HA, THIS IS FUN! ROBOTS DON'T HAVE MUCH ARTISTIC SENSE, DO THEY?
NEXT, WE'LL HAVE THESE FLESH AND PLASTIC BODIES FIGHT IT OUT!
GRRR.... WHY YOU...
WHAT?! THAT'S... MY PAPA!
PAPA!!!
TAMAO'S ESCAPING!
BLASTED KID TOOK ADVANTAGE OF OUR KINDNESS!!
BRING THAT KID BACK HERE, N' TEACH HIM A LESSON!

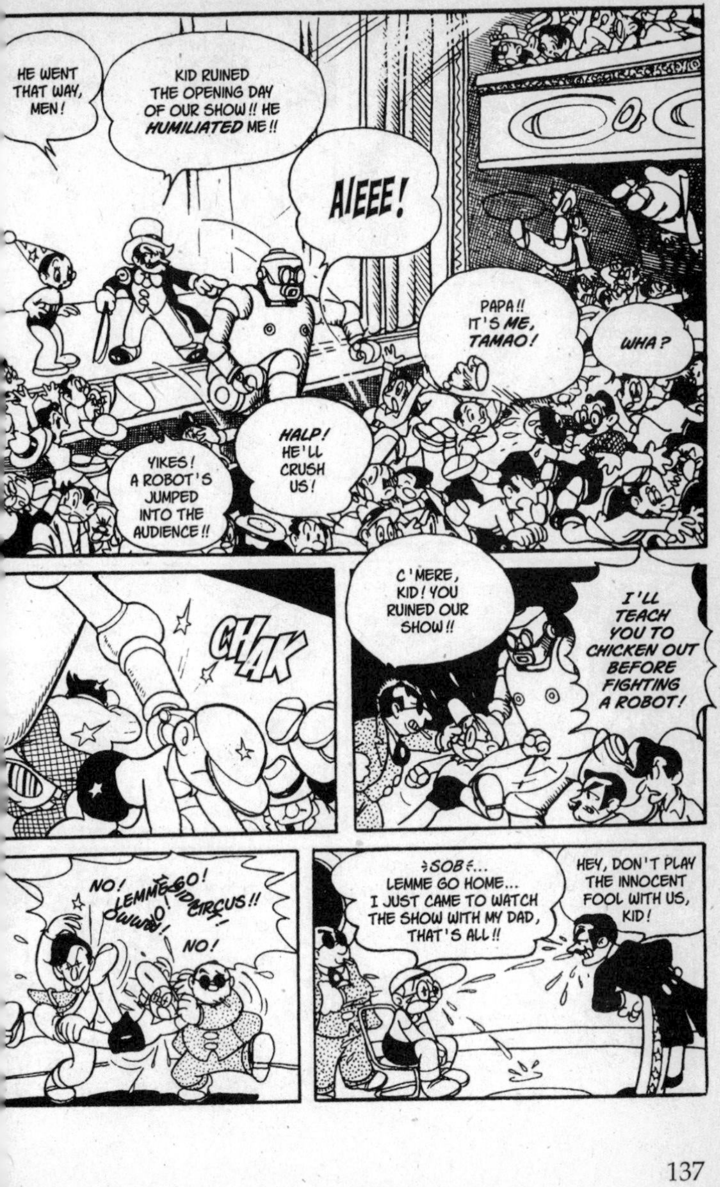
HE WENT THAT WAY, MEN!
KID RUINED THE OPENING DAY OF OUR SHOW!! HE *HUMILIATED* ME!!
AIEEE!
PAPA!! IT'S *ME, TAMAO!*
WHA?
YIKES! A ROBOT'S JUMPED INTO THE AUDIENCE!!
HALP! HE'LL CRUSH US!
CHAK
C'MERE, KID! YOU RUINED OUR SHOW!!
I'LL TEACH YOU TO CHICKEN OUT BEFORE FIGHTING A ROBOT!
NO!
LEMME GO!
STUPID CIRCUS!!
OWWW!
NO!
≯SOB≮... LEMME GO HOME... I JUST CAME TO WATCH THE SHOW WITH MY DAD, THAT'S ALL!!
HEY, DON'T PLAY THE INNOCENT FOOL WITH US, KID!

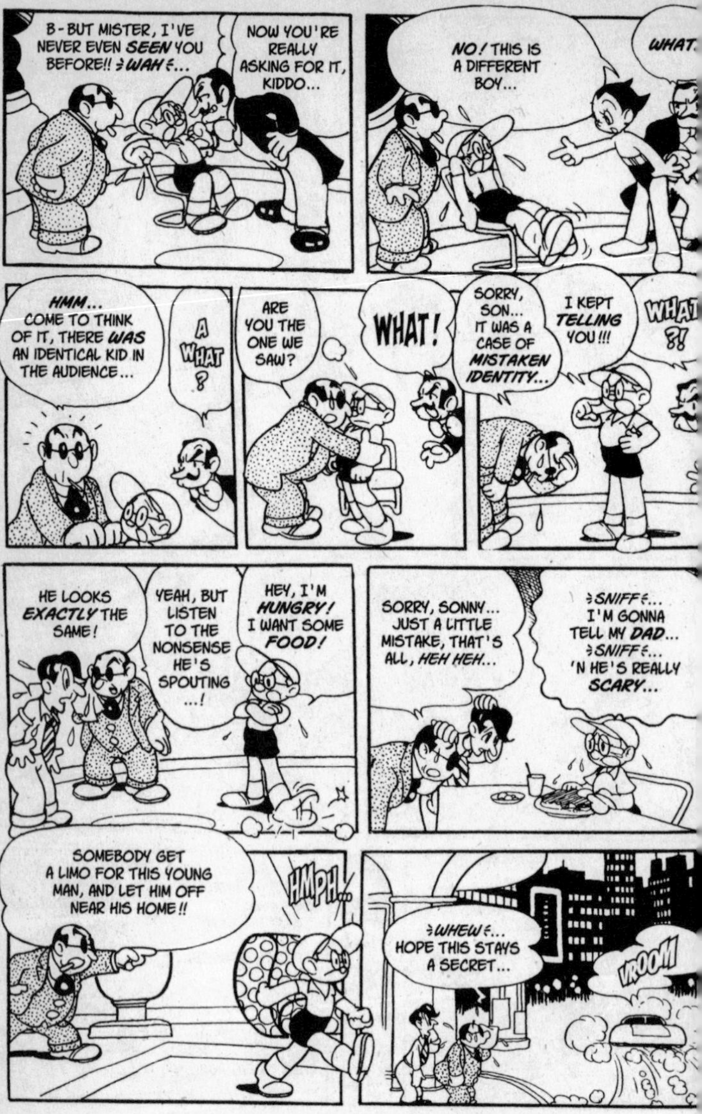

B-BUT MISTER, I'VE NEVER EVEN SEEN YOU BEFORE!! ⋟WAH⋞...
NOW YOU'RE REALLY ASKING FOR IT, KIDDO...
NO! THIS IS A DIFFERENT BOY...
WHAT.
HMM... COME TO THINK OF IT, THERE WAS AN IDENTICAL KID IN THE AUDIENCE...
A WHAT ?
ARE YOU THE ONE WE SAW?
WHAT!
SORRY, SON... IT WAS A CASE OF MISTAKEN IDENTITY...
I KEPT TELLING YOU!!!
WHAT ?!
HE LOOKS EXACTLY THE SAME!
YEAH, BUT LISTEN TO THE NONSENSE HE'S SPOUTING ...!
HEY, I'M HUNGRY! I WANT SOME FOOD!
SORRY, SONNY... JUST A LITTLE MISTAKE, THAT'S ALL, HEH HEH...
⋟SNIFF⋞... I'M GONNA TELL MY DAD... ⋟SNIFF⋞... 'N HE'S REALLY SCARY...
SOMEBODY GET A LIMO FOR THIS YOUNG MAN, AND LET HIM OFF NEAR HIS HOME!!
HMPH...
⋟WHEW⋞... HOPE THIS STAYS A SECRET...
VROOM

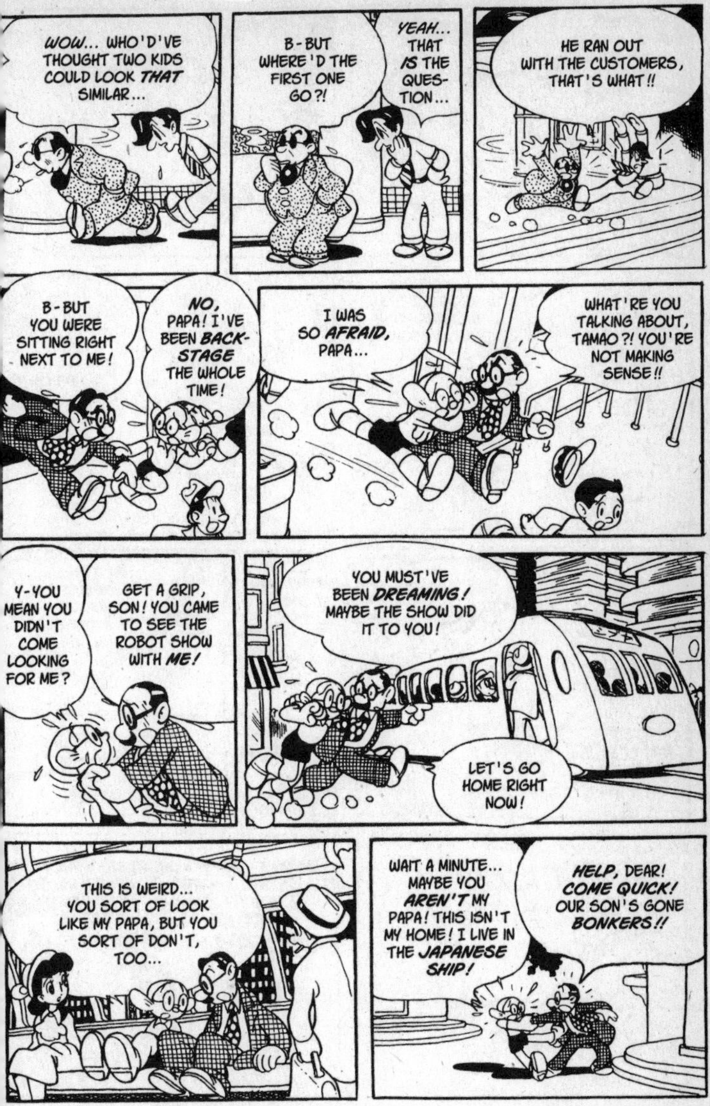
WOW... WHO'D'VE THOUGHT TWO KIDS COULD LOOK THAT SIMILAR...
B-BUT WHERE'D THE FIRST ONE GO?!
YEAH... THAT IS THE QUES-TION...
HE RAN OUT WITH THE CUSTOMERS, THAT'S WHAT!!
B-BUT YOU WERE SITTING RIGHT NEXT TO ME!
NO, PAPA! I'VE BEEN BACK-STAGE THE WHOLE TIME!
I WAS SO AFRAID, PAPA...
WHAT'RE YOU TALKING ABOUT, TAMAO?! YOU'RE NOT MAKING SENSE!!
Y-YOU MEAN YOU DIDN'T COME LOOKING FOR ME?
GET A GRIP, SON! YOU CAME TO SEE THE ROBOT SHOW WITH ME!
YOU MUST'VE BEEN DREAMING! MAYBE THE SHOW DID IT TO YOU!
LET'S GO HOME RIGHT NOW!
THIS IS WEIRD... YOU SORT OF LOOK LIKE MY PAPA, BUT YOU SORT OF DON'T, TOO...
WAIT A MINUTE... MAYBE YOU AREN'T MY PAPA! THIS ISN'T MY HOME! I LIVE IN THE JAPANESE SHIP!
HELP, DEAR! COME QUICK! OUR SON'S GONE BONKERS!!

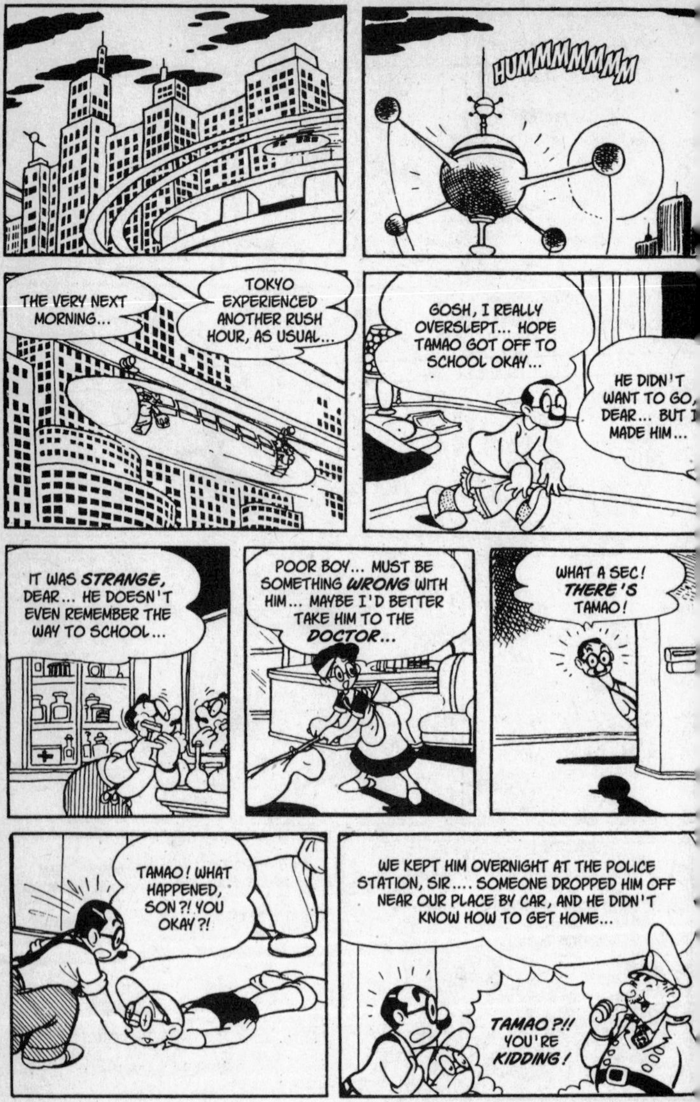
HUMMMMMMMM
THE VERY NEXT MORNING...
TOKYO EXPERIENCED ANOTHER RUSH HOUR, AS USUAL...
GOSH, I REALLY OVERSLEPT... HOPE TAMAO GOT OFF TO SCHOOL OKAY...
HE DIDN'T WANT TO GO, DEAR... BUT I MADE HIM...
IT WAS STRANGE, DEAR... HE DOESN'T EVEN REMEMBER THE WAY TO SCHOOL...
POOR BOY... MUST BE SOMETHING WRONG WITH HIM... MAYBE I'D BETTER TAKE HIM TO THE DOCTOR...
WHAT A SEC! THERE'S TAMAO!
TAMAO! WHAT HAPPENED, SON?! YOU OKAY?!
WE KEPT HIM OVERNIGHT AT THE POLICE STATION, SIR.... SOMEONE DROPPED HIM OFF NEAR OUR PLACE BY CAR, AND HE DIDN'T KNOW HOW TO GET HOME...
TAMAO?!! YOU'RE KIDDING!

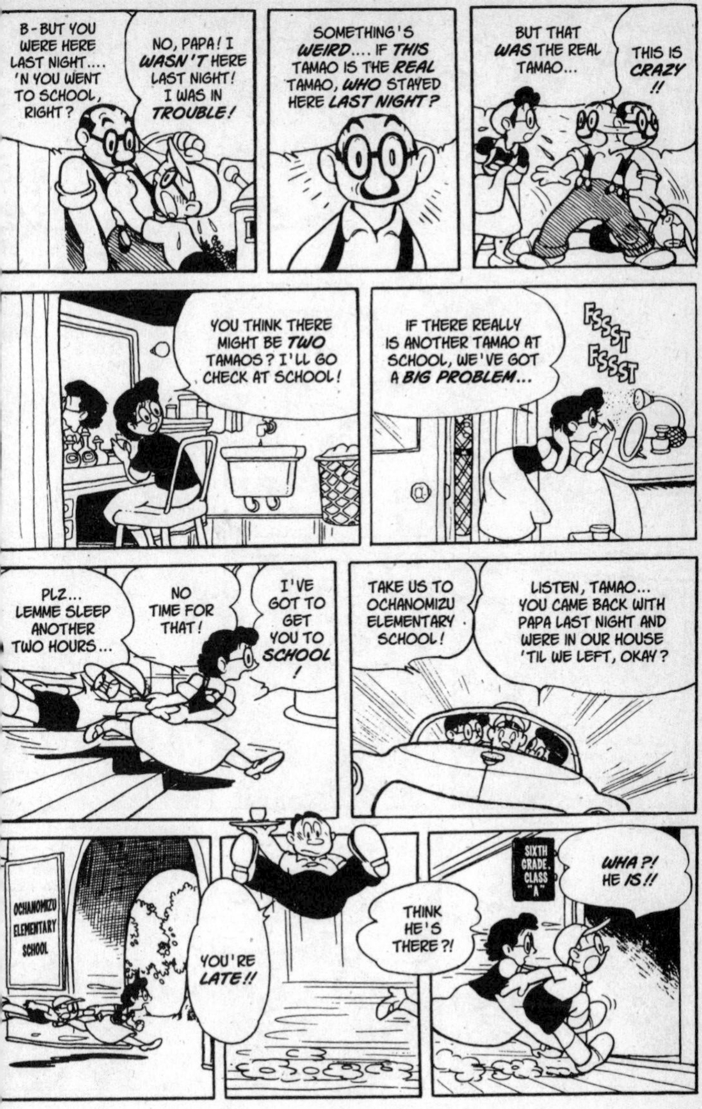

B-BUT YOU WERE HERE LAST NIGHT.... 'N YOU WENT TO SCHOOL, RIGHT?
NO, PAPA! I *WASN'T* HERE LAST NIGHT! I WAS IN *TROUBLE!*
SOMETHING'S *WEIRD*.... IF *THIS* TAMAO IS THE *REAL* TAMAO, *WHO* STAYED HERE *LAST NIGHT?*
BUT THAT *WAS* THE REAL TAMAO...
THIS IS *CRAZY* !!
YOU THINK THERE MIGHT BE *TWO* TAMAOS? I'LL GO CHECK AT SCHOOL!
IF THERE REALLY IS ANOTHER TAMAO AT SCHOOL, WE'VE GOT A *BIG PROBLEM...*
FSSST
FSSST
PLZ... LEMME SLEEP ANOTHER TWO HOURS...
NO TIME FOR THAT!
I'VE GOT TO GET YOU TO *SCHOOL* !
TAKE US TO OCHANOMIZU ELEMENTARY SCHOOL!
LISTEN, TAMAO... YOU CAME BACK WITH PAPA LAST NIGHT AND WERE IN OUR HOUSE 'TIL WE LEFT, OKAY?
OCHANOMIZU ELEMENTARY SCHOOL
YOU'RE *LATE!!*
SIXTH GRADE. CLASS "A"
THINK HE'S THERE?!
WHA?! HE *IS!!*

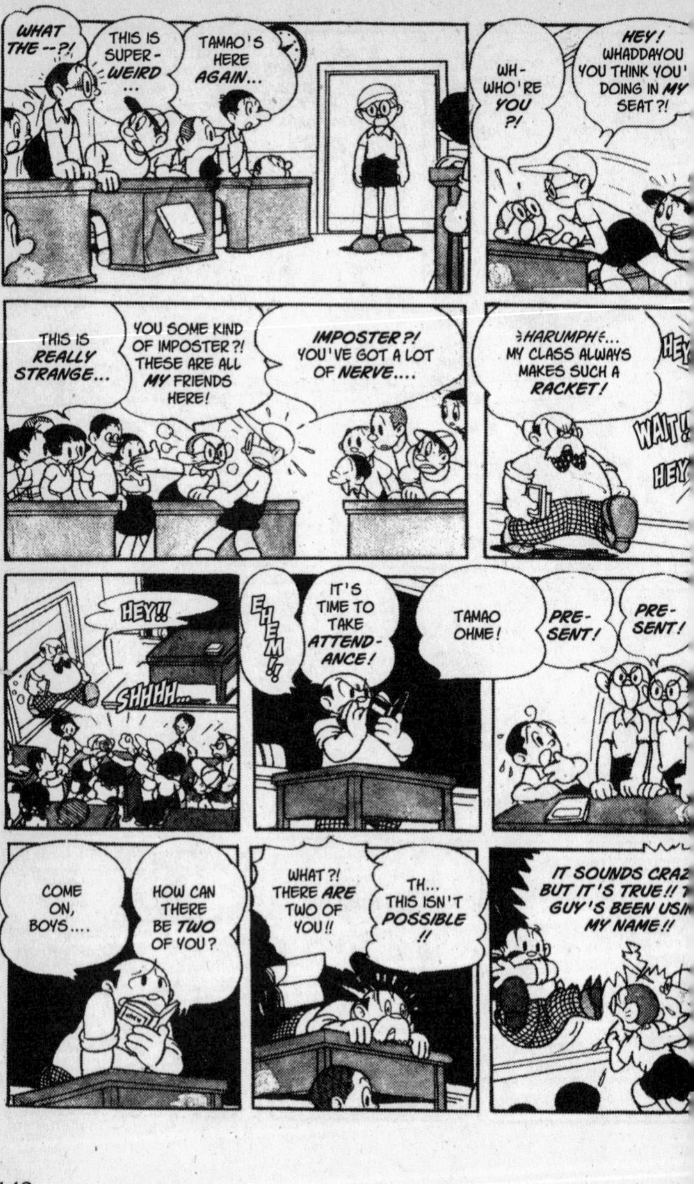

WHAT THE --?!
THIS IS SUPER-WEIRD ...
TAMAO'S HERE AGAIN...
WH-WHO'RE YOU ?!
HEY! WHADDAYOU YOU THINK YOU' DOING IN MY SEAT ?!
THIS IS REALLY STRANGE...
YOU SOME KIND OF IMPOSTER ?! THESE ARE ALL MY FRIENDS HERE!
IMPOSTER ?! YOU'VE GOT A LOT OF NERVE....
HARUMPH... MY CLASS ALWAYS MAKES SUCH A RACKET!
HEY
WAIT!!
HEY
HEY!!
SHHHH...
EHEM!!
IT'S TIME TO TAKE ATTENDANCE!
TAMAO OHME!
PRE-SENT!
PRE-SENT!
COME ON, BOYS....
HOW CAN THERE BE TWO OF YOU?
WHAT ?! THERE ARE TWO OF YOU!!
TH... THIS ISN'T POSSIBLE !!
IT SOUNDS CRAZ BUT IT'S TRUE!! T GUY'S BEEN USIN MY NAME!!

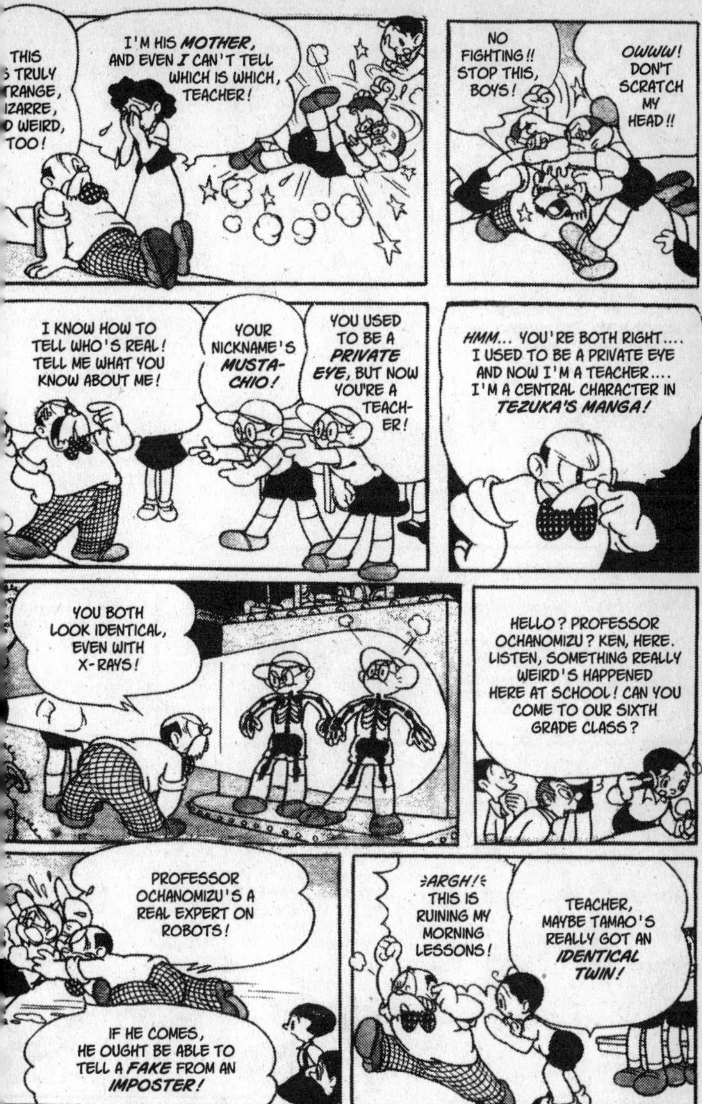
THIS S TRULY TRANGE, IZARRE, D WEIRD, TOO!
I'M HIS **MOTHER**, AND EVEN **I** CAN'T TELL WHICH IS WHICH, TEACHER!
NO FIGHTING!! STOP THIS, BOYS!
OWWW! DON'T SCRATCH MY HEAD!!
I KNOW HOW TO TELL WHO'S REAL! TELL ME WHAT YOU KNOW ABOUT ME!
YOUR NICKNAME'S **MUSTA-CHIO!**
YOU USED TO BE A **PRIVATE EYE**, BUT NOW YOU'RE A TEACH-ER!
HMM... YOU'RE BOTH RIGHT.... I USED TO BE A PRIVATE EYE AND NOW I'M A TEACHER.... I'M A CENTRAL CHARACTER IN **TEZUKA'S MANGA!**
YOU BOTH LOOK IDENTICAL, EVEN WITH X-RAYS!
HELLO? PROFESSOR OCHANOMIZU? KEN, HERE. LISTEN, SOMETHING REALLY WEIRD'S HAPPENED HERE AT SCHOOL! CAN YOU COME TO OUR SIXTH GRADE CLASS?
PROFESSOR OCHANOMIZU'S A REAL EXPERT ON ROBOTS!
IF HE COMES, HE OUGHT BE ABLE TO TELL A **FAKE** FROM AN **IMPOSTER!**
ARGH! THIS IS RUINING MY MORNING LESSONS!
TEACHER, MAYBE TAMAO'S REALLY GOT AN **IDENTICAL TWIN!**

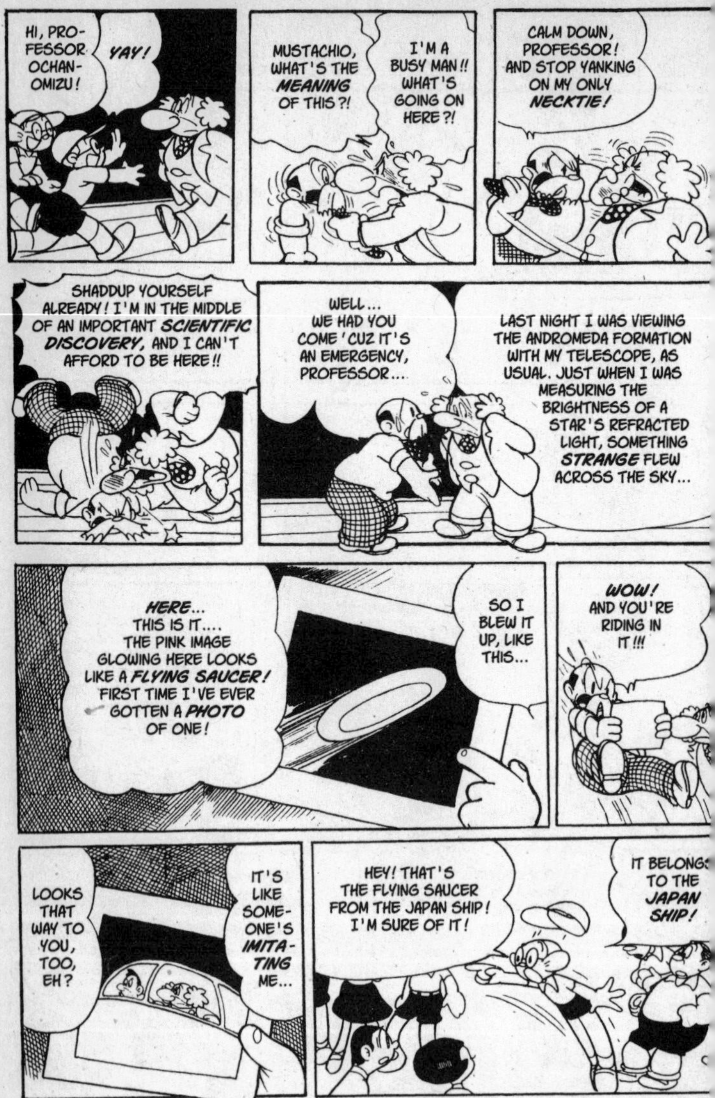
HI, PRO-FESSOR OCHAN-OMIZU!
YAY!
MUSTACHIO, WHAT'S THE MEANING OF THIS?!
I'M A BUSY MAN!! WHAT'S GOING ON HERE?!
CALM DOWN, PROFESSOR! AND STOP YANKING ON MY ONLY NECKTIE!
SHADDUP YOURSELF ALREADY! I'M IN THE MIDDLE OF AN IMPORTANT SCIENTIFIC DISCOVERY, AND I CAN'T AFFORD TO BE HERE!!
WELL... WE HAD YOU COME 'CUZ IT'S AN EMERGENCY, PROFESSOR....
LAST NIGHT I WAS VIEWING THE ANDROMEDA FORMATION WITH MY TELESCOPE, AS USUAL. JUST WHEN I WAS MEASURING THE BRIGHTNESS OF A STAR'S REFRACTED LIGHT, SOMETHING STRANGE FLEW ACROSS THE SKY...
HERE... THIS IS IT.... THE PINK IMAGE GLOWING HERE LOOKS LIKE A FLYING SAUCER! FIRST TIME I'VE EVER GOTTEN A PHOTO OF ONE!
SO I BLEW IT UP, LIKE THIS...
WOW! AND YOU'RE RIDING IN IT!!!
LOOKS THAT WAY TO YOU, TOO, EH?
IT'S LIKE SOME-ONE'S IMITA-TING ME...
HEY! THAT'S THE FLYING SAUCER FROM THE JAPAN SHIP! I'M SURE OF IT!
IT BELONGS TO THE JAPAN SHIP!

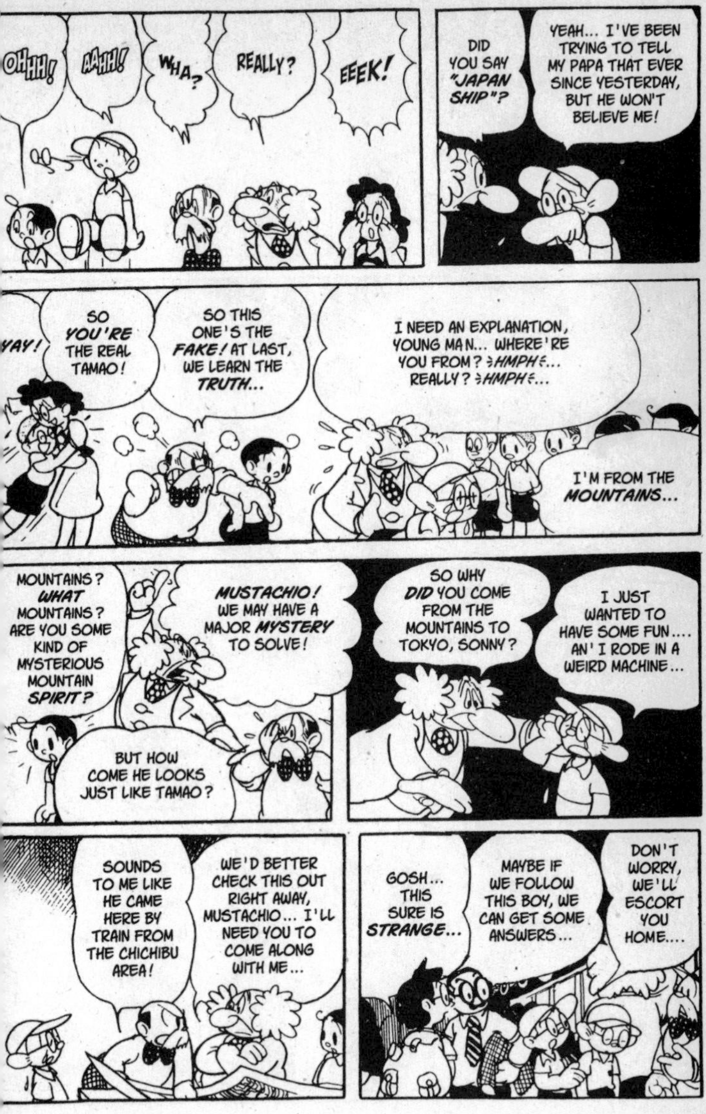
OHHH!
AAHH!
WHA?
REALLY?
EEEK!
DID YOU SAY "JAPAN SHIP"?
YEAH... I'VE BEEN TRYING TO TELL MY PAPA THAT EVER SINCE YESTERDAY, BUT HE WON'T BELIEVE ME!
YAY!
SO YOU'RE THE REAL TAMAO!
SO THIS ONE'S THE FAKE! AT LAST, WE LEARN THE TRUTH...
I NEED AN EXPLANATION, YOUNG MAN... WHERE'RE YOU FROM? ≥HMPH≤... REALLY? ≥HMPH≤...
I'M FROM THE MOUNTAINS...
MOUNTAINS? WHAT MOUNTAINS? ARE YOU SOME KIND OF MYSTERIOUS MOUNTAIN SPIRIT?
MUSTACHIO! WE MAY HAVE A MAJOR MYSTERY TO SOLVE!
BUT HOW COME HE LOOKS JUST LIKE TAMAO?
SO WHY DID YOU COME FROM THE MOUNTAINS TO TOKYO, SONNY?
I JUST WANTED TO HAVE SOME FUN.... AN' I RODE IN A WEIRD MACHINE...
SOUNDS TO ME LIKE HE CAME HERE BY TRAIN FROM THE CHICHIBU AREA!
WE'D BETTER CHECK THIS OUT RIGHT AWAY, MUSTACHIO... I'LL NEED YOU TO COME ALONG WITH ME...
GOSH... THIS SURE IS STRANGE...
MAYBE IF WE FOLLOW THIS BOY, WE CAN GET SOME ANSWERS...
DON'T WORRY, WE'LL ESCORT YOU HOME....

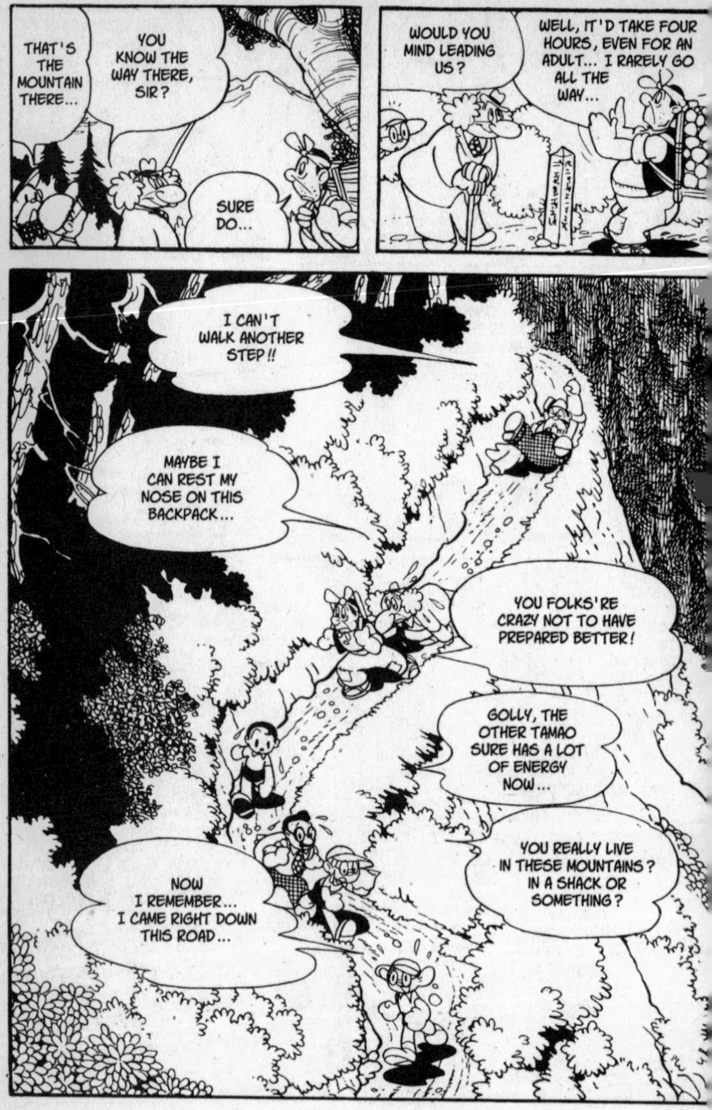
THAT'S THE MOUNTAIN THERE...
YOU KNOW THE WAY THERE, SIR?
SURE DO...
WOULD YOU MIND LEADING US?
WELL, IT'D TAKE FOUR HOURS, EVEN FOR AN ADULT... I RARELY GO ALL THE WAY...
I CAN'T WALK ANOTHER STEP!!
MAYBE I CAN REST MY NOSE ON THIS BACKPACK...
YOU FOLKS'RE CRAZY NOT TO HAVE PREPARED BETTER!
GOLLY, THE OTHER TAMAO SURE HAS A LOT OF ENERGY NOW...
NOW I REMEMBER... I CAME RIGHT DOWN THIS ROAD...
YOU REALLY LIVE IN THESE MOUNTAINS? IN A SHACK OR SOMETHING?

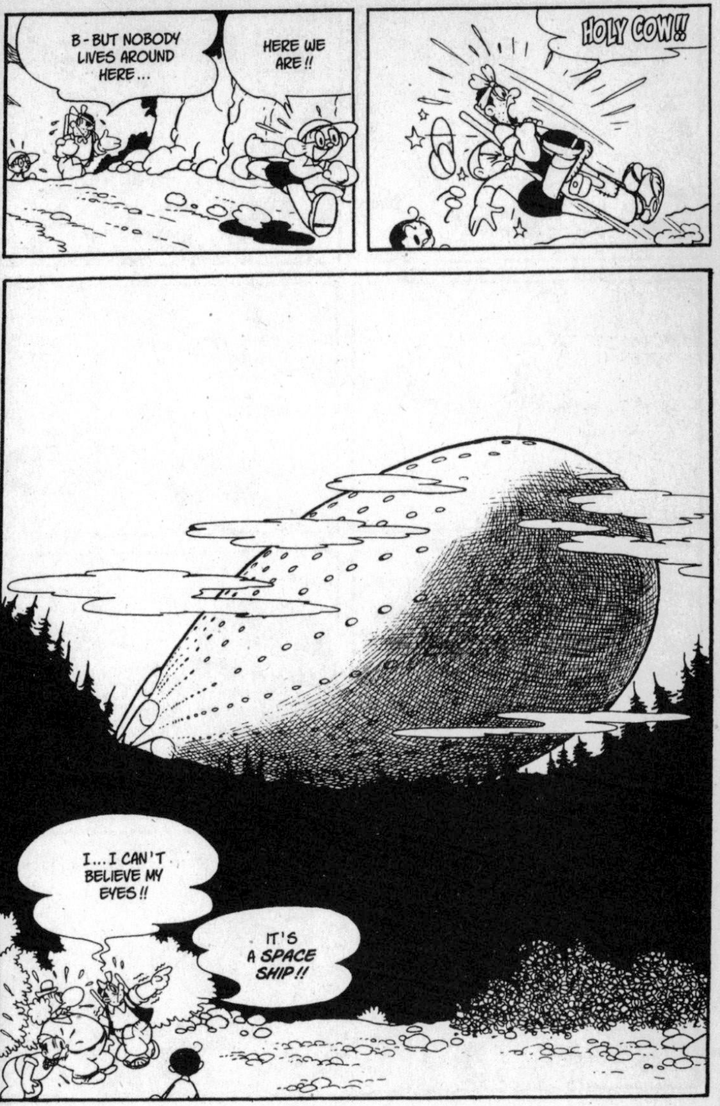
B-BUT NOBODY LIVES AROUND HERE...
HERE WE ARE!!
HOLY COW!!
I...I CAN'T BELIEVE MY EYES!!
IT'S A SPACE SHIP!!

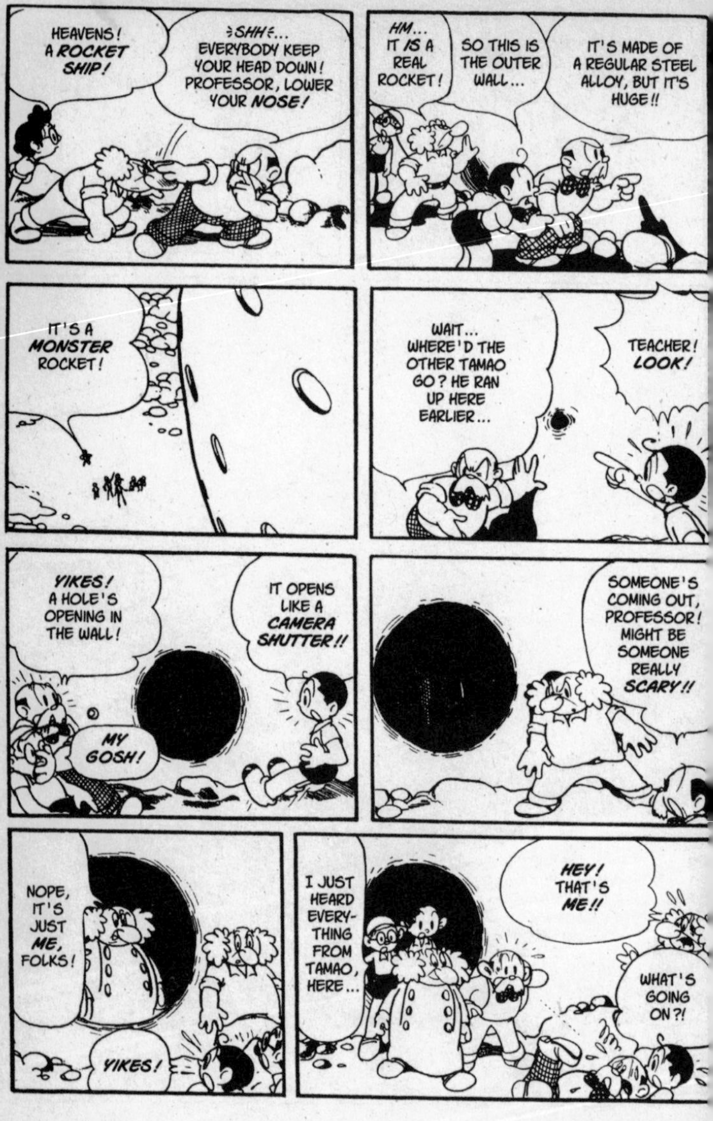
HEAVENS! A ROCKET SHIP!
SHH... EVERYBODY KEEP YOUR HEAD DOWN! PROFESSOR, LOWER YOUR NOSE!
HM... IT IS A REAL ROCKET!
SO THIS IS THE OUTER WALL...
IT'S MADE OF A REGULAR STEEL ALLOY, BUT IT'S HUGE!!
IT'S A MONSTER ROCKET!
WAIT... WHERE'D THE OTHER TAMAO GO? HE RAN UP HERE EARLIER...
TEACHER! LOOK!
YIKES! A HOLE'S OPENING IN THE WALL!
IT OPENS LIKE A CAMERA SHUTTER!!
MY GOSH!
SOMEONE'S COMING OUT, PROFESSOR! MIGHT BE SOMEONE REALLY SCARY!!
NOPE, IT'S JUST ME, FOLKS!
YIKES!
I JUST HEARD EVERY-THING FROM TAMAO, HERE...
HEY! THAT'S ME!!
WHAT'S GOING ON?!

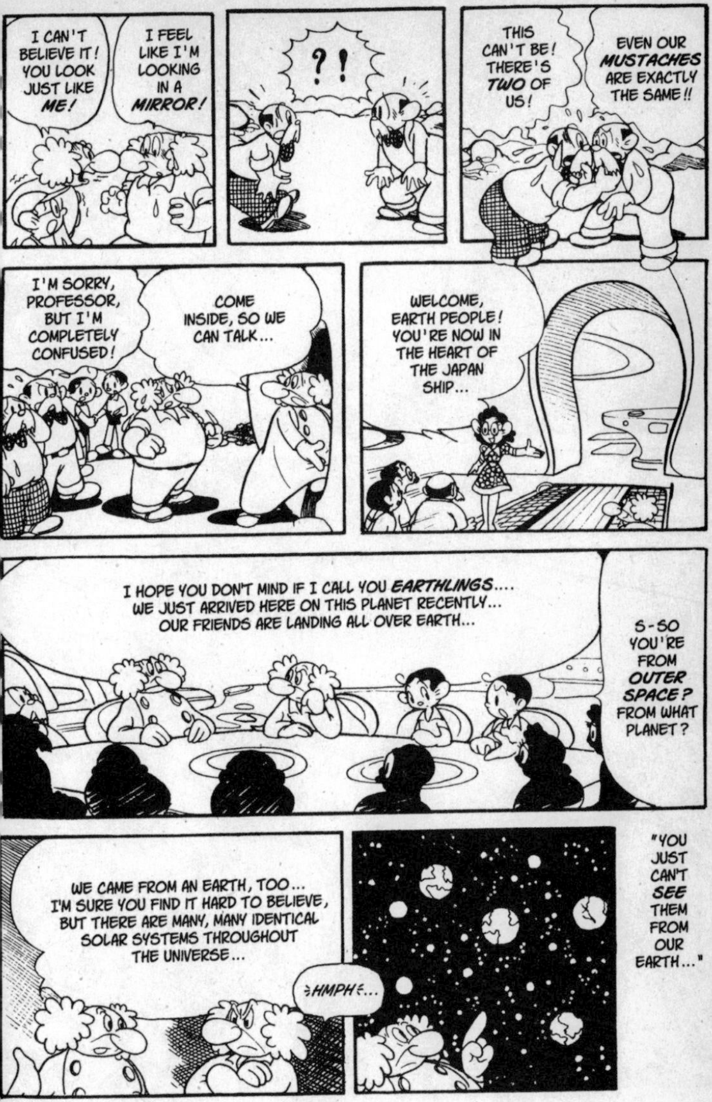
I CAN'T BELIEVE IT! YOU LOOK JUST LIKE ME!
I FEEL LIKE I'M LOOKING IN A MIRROR!
? !
THIS CAN'T BE! THERE'S TWO OF US!
EVEN OUR MUSTACHES ARE EXACTLY THE SAME!!
I'M SORRY, PROFESSOR, BUT I'M COMPLETELY CONFUSED!
COME INSIDE, SO WE CAN TALK...
WELCOME, EARTH PEOPLE! YOU'RE NOW IN THE HEART OF THE JAPAN SHIP...
I HOPE YOU DON'T MIND IF I CALL YOU EARTHLINGS.... WE JUST ARRIVED HERE ON THIS PLANET RECENTLY... OUR FRIENDS ARE LANDING ALL OVER EARTH...
S-SO YOU'RE FROM OUTER SPACE? FROM WHAT PLANET?
WE CAME FROM AN EARTH, TOO... I'M SURE YOU FIND IT HARD TO BELIEVE, BUT THERE ARE MANY, MANY IDENTICAL SOLAR SYSTEMS THROUGHOUT THE UNIVERSE...
HMPH...
"YOU JUST CAN'T SEE THEM FROM OUR EARTH..."

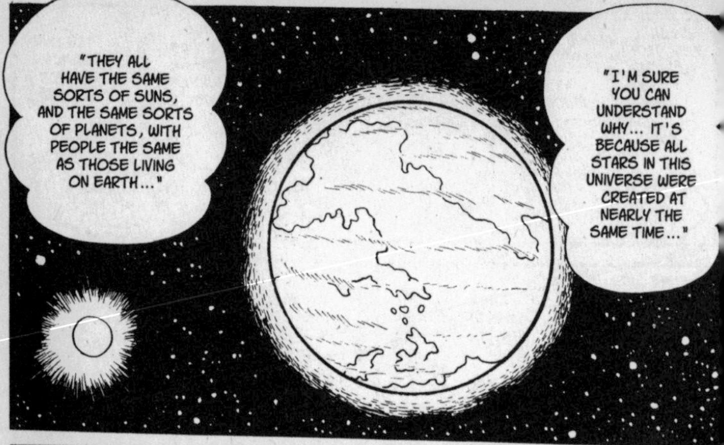
"THEY ALL HAVE THE SAME SORTS OF SUNS, AND THE SAME SORTS OF PLANETS, WITH PEOPLE THE SAME AS THOSE LIVING ON EARTH..."
"I'M SURE YOU CAN UNDERSTAND WHY... IT'S BECAUSE ALL STARS IN THIS UNIVERSE WERE CREATED AT NEARLY THE SAME TIME..."
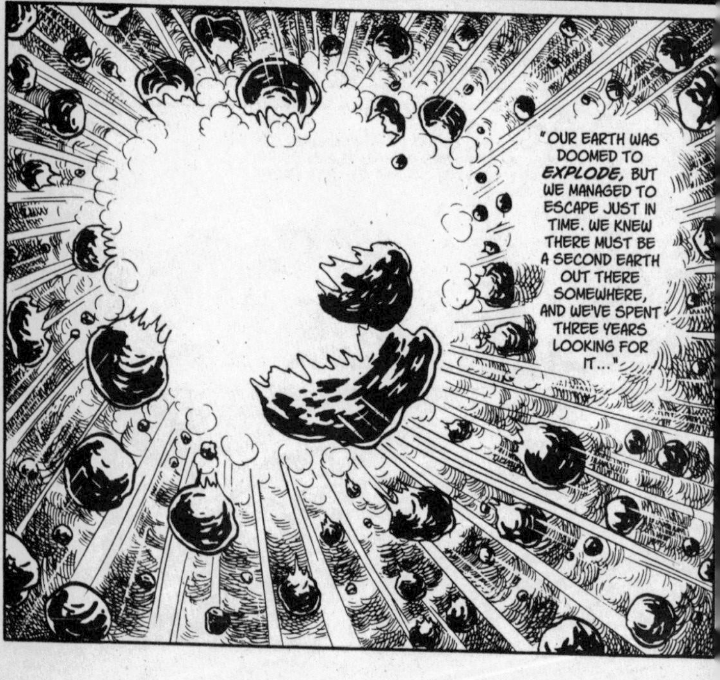
"OUR EARTH WAS DOOMED TO *EXPLODE,* BUT WE MANAGED TO ESCAPE JUST IN TIME. WE KNEW THERE MUST BE A SECOND EARTH OUT THERE SOMEWHERE, AND WE'VE SPENT THREE YEARS LOOKING FOR IT..."

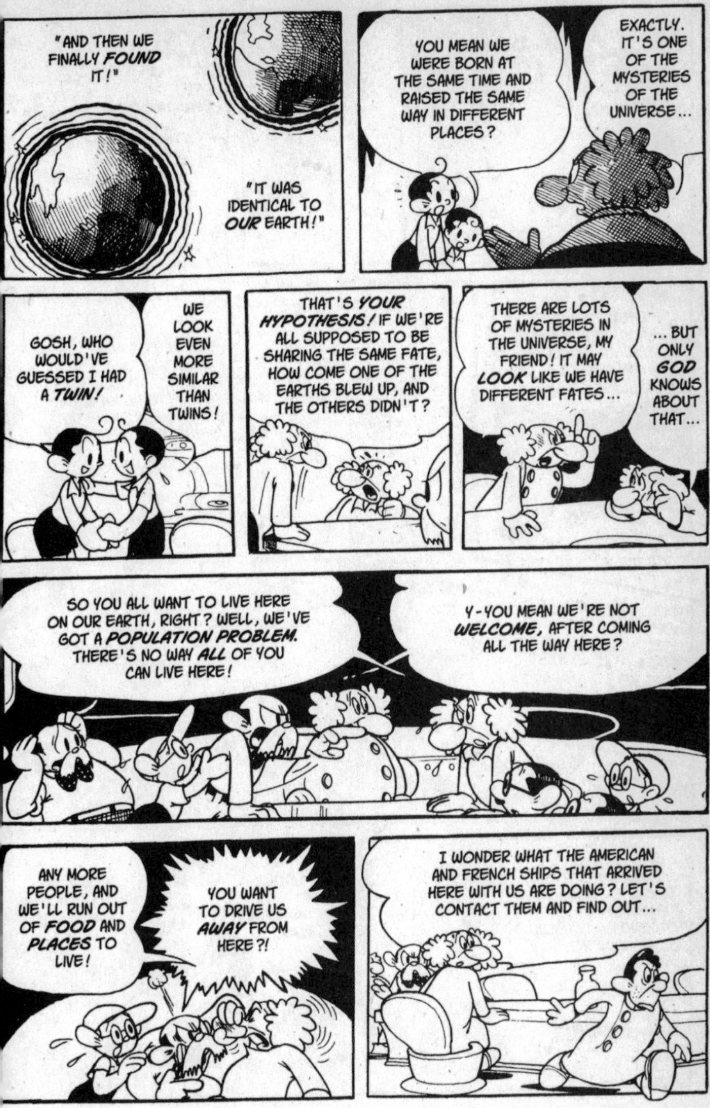
"AND THEN WE FINALLY *FOUND* IT!"
"IT WAS IDENTICAL TO *OUR* EARTH!"
YOU MEAN WE WERE BORN AT THE SAME TIME AND RAISED THE SAME WAY IN DIFFERENT PLACES?
EXACTLY. IT'S ONE OF THE MYSTERIES OF THE UNIVERSE...
GOSH, WHO WOULD'VE GUESSED I HAD A *TWIN!*
WE LOOK EVEN MORE SIMILAR THAN TWINS!
THAT'S *YOUR HYPOTHESIS!* IF WE'RE ALL SUPPOSED TO BE SHARING THE SAME FATE, HOW COME ONE OF THE EARTHS BLEW UP, AND THE OTHERS DIDN'T?
THERE ARE LOTS OF MYSTERIES IN THE UNIVERSE, MY FRIEND! IT MAY *LOOK* LIKE WE HAVE DIFFERENT FATES...
...BUT ONLY *GOD* KNOWS ABOUT THAT...
SO YOU ALL WANT TO LIVE HERE ON OUR EARTH, RIGHT? WELL, WE'VE GOT A *POPULATION PROBLEM.* THERE'S NO WAY *ALL* OF YOU CAN LIVE HERE!
Y-YOU MEAN WE'RE NOT *WELCOME,* AFTER COMING ALL THE WAY HERE?
ANY MORE PEOPLE, AND WE'LL RUN OUT OF *FOOD* AND *PLACES* TO LIVE!
YOU WANT TO DRIVE US *AWAY* FROM HERE?!
I WONDER WHAT THE AMERICAN AND FRENCH SHIPS THAT ARRIVED HERE WITH US ARE DOING? LET'S CONTACT THEM AND FIND OUT...

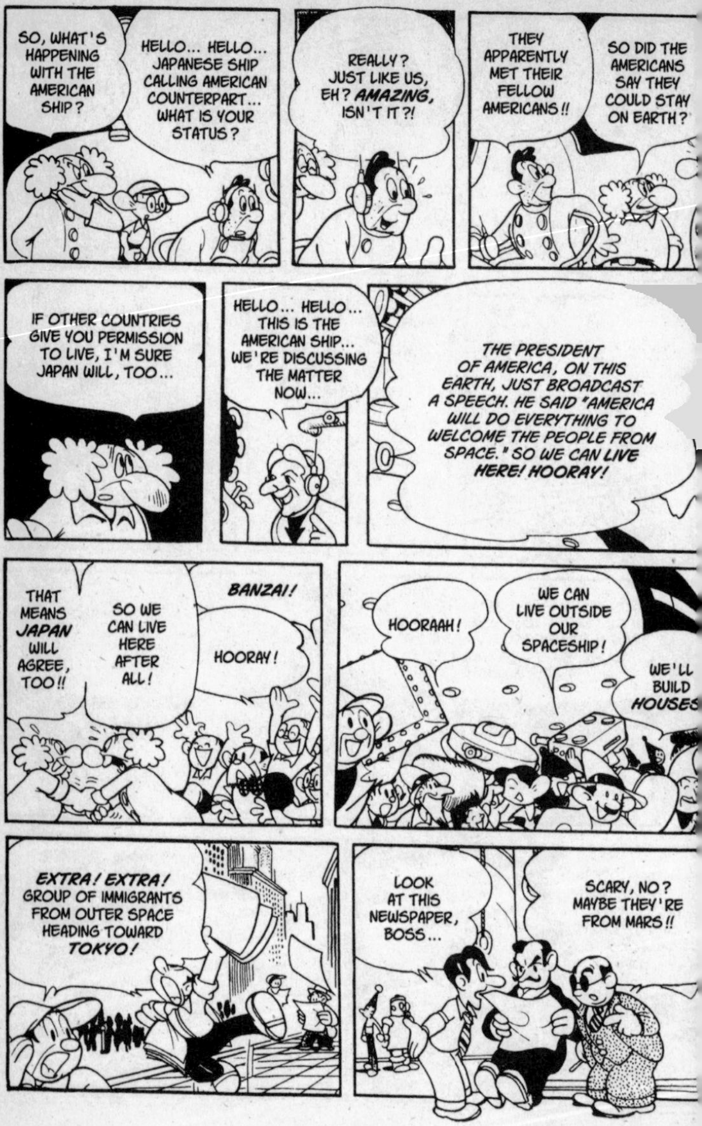
SO, WHAT'S HAPPENING WITH THE AMERICAN SHIP?
HELLO... HELLO... JAPANESE SHIP CALLING AMERICAN COUNTERPART... WHAT IS YOUR STATUS?
REALLY? JUST LIKE US, EH? AMAZING, ISN'T IT?!
THEY APPARENTLY MET THEIR FELLOW AMERICANS!!
SO DID THE AMERICANS SAY THEY COULD STAY ON EARTH?
IF OTHER COUNTRIES GIVE YOU PERMISSION TO LIVE, I'M SURE JAPAN WILL, TOO...
HELLO... HELLO... THIS IS THE AMERICAN SHIP... WE'RE DISCUSSING THE MATTER NOW...
THE PRESIDENT OF AMERICA, ON THIS EARTH, JUST BROADCAST A SPEECH. HE SAID "AMERICA WILL DO EVERYTHING TO WELCOME THE PEOPLE FROM SPACE." SO WE CAN LIVE HERE! HOORAY!
THAT MEANS JAPAN WILL AGREE, TOO!!
SO WE CAN LIVE HERE AFTER ALL!
BANZAI!
HOORAY!
HOORAAH!
WE CAN LIVE OUTSIDE OUR SPACESHIP!
WE'LL BUILD HOUSES
EXTRA! EXTRA! GROUP OF IMMIGRANTS FROM OUTER SPACE HEADING TOWARD TOKYO!
LOOK AT THIS NEWSPAPER, BOSS...
SCARY, NO? MAYBE THEY'RE FROM MARS!!

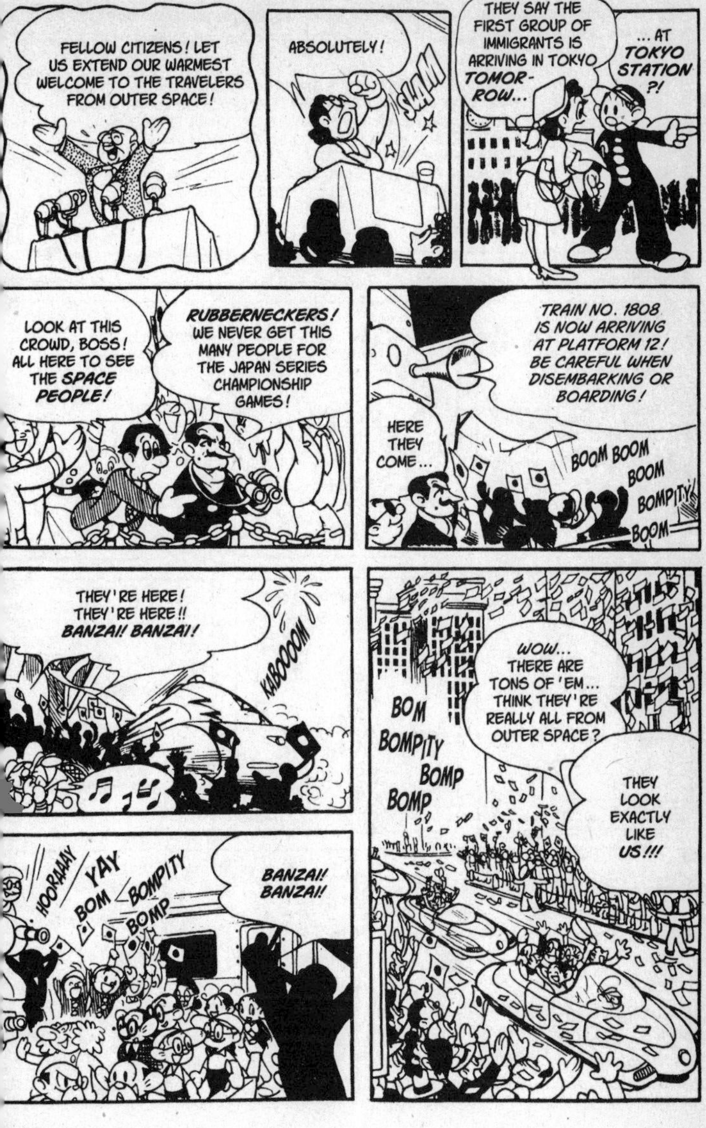
FELLOW CITIZENS! LET US EXTEND OUR WARMEST WELCOME TO THE TRAVELERS FROM OUTER SPACE!
ABSOLUTELY!
SLAM
THEY SAY THE FIRST GROUP OF IMMIGRANTS IS ARRIVING IN TOKYO TOMORROW...
... AT TOKYO STATION ?!
LOOK AT THIS CROWD, BOSS! ALL HERE TO SEE THE SPACE PEOPLE!
RUBBERNECKERS! WE NEVER GET THIS MANY PEOPLE FOR THE JAPAN SERIES CHAMPIONSHIP GAMES!
TRAIN NO. 1808 IS NOW ARRIVING AT PLATFORM 12! BE CAREFUL WHEN DISEMBARKING OR BOARDING!
HERE THEY COME...
BOOM BOOM
BOOM
BOMPITY
BOOM
THEY'RE HERE! THEY'RE HERE!! BANZAI! BANZAI!
KABOOOOM
HOORAAAY
YAY
BOM
BOMPITY
BOMP
BANZAI! BANZAI!
WOW... THERE ARE TONS OF 'EM... THINK THEY'RE REALLY ALL FROM OUTER SPACE?
BOM
BOMPITY
BOMP
BOMP
THEY LOOK EXACTLY LIKE US!!!

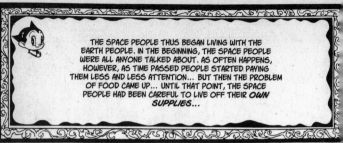

THE SPACE PEOPLE THUS BEGAN LIVING WITH THE EARTH PEOPLE. IN THE BEGINNING, THE SPACE PEOPLE WERE ALL ANYONE TALKED ABOUT. AS OFTEN HAPPENS, HOWEVER, AS TIME PASSED PEOPLE STARTED PAYING THEM LESS AND LESS ATTENTION... BUT THEN THE PROBLEM OF FOOD CAME UP... UNTIL THAT POINT, THE SPACE PEOPLE HAD BEEN CAREFUL TO LIVE OFF THEIR *OWN SUPPLIES*...

BLAM

HEY! YOU THREW MY AIM OFF!!

B-BUT WHY'RE YOU *KILLING* THEM?

WHY?

TO HAVE SOMETHING TO *EAT*, THAT'S WHY!

BUT I FEEL SORRY FOR THE BIRDS...

WHAT'RE WE HUMANS S'POSED TO EAT, THEN?!

YIKES!!

YOU'RE BEING SO *CRUEL!*

KNOCK IT OFF, WILL YOU? SO WHAT'RE YOU *SPACE GUYS* EATING, ANYWAY?

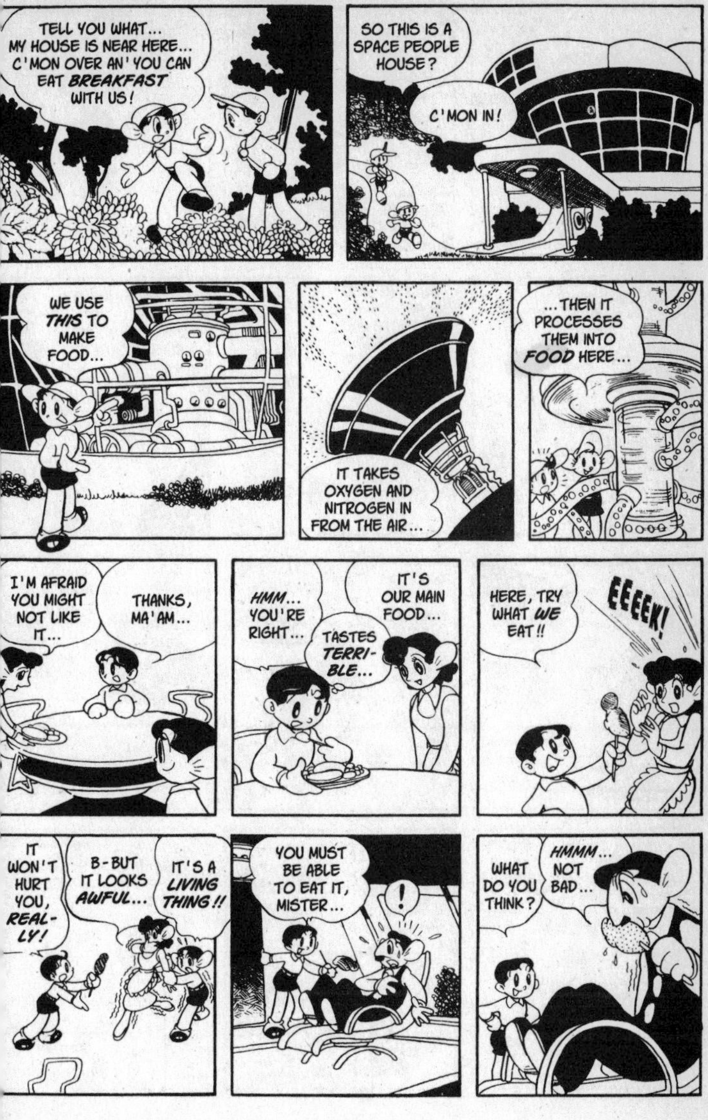
TELL YOU WHAT... MY HOUSE IS NEAR HERE... C'MON OVER AN' YOU CAN EAT BREAKFAST WITH US!
SO THIS IS A SPACE PEOPLE HOUSE?
C'MON IN!
WE USE THIS TO MAKE FOOD...
IT TAKES OXYGEN AND NITROGEN IN FROM THE AIR...
...THEN IT PROCESSES THEM INTO FOOD HERE...
I'M AFRAID YOU MIGHT NOT LIKE IT...
THANKS, MA'AM...
HMM... YOU'RE RIGHT...
IT'S OUR MAIN FOOD...
TASTES TERRIBLE...
HERE, TRY WHAT WE EAT!!
EEEEK!
IT WON'T HURT YOU, REALLY!
B-BUT IT LOOKS AWFUL...
IT'S A LIVING THING!!
YOU MUST BE ABLE TO EAT IT, MISTER...
!
WHAT DO YOU THINK?
HMMM... NOT BAD...

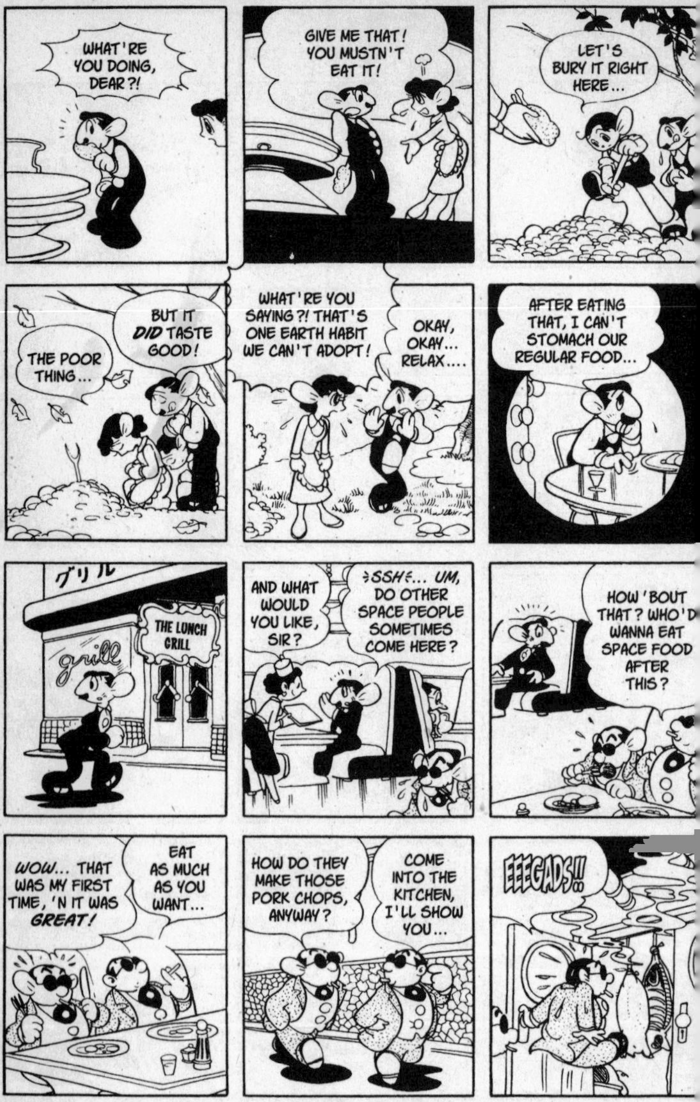
WHAT'RE YOU DOING, DEAR?!
GIVE ME THAT! YOU MUSTN'T EAT IT!
LET'S BURY IT RIGHT HERE...
THE POOR THING...
BUT IT DID TASTE GOOD!
WHAT'RE YOU SAYING?! THAT'S ONE EARTH HABIT WE CAN'T ADOPT!
OKAY, OKAY... RELAX....
AFTER EATING THAT, I CAN'T STOMACH OUR REGULAR FOOD...
グリル
THE LUNCH GRILL
grill
AND WHAT WOULD YOU LIKE, SIR?
SSH... UM, DO OTHER SPACE PEOPLE SOMETIMES COME HERE?
HOW 'BOUT THAT? WHO'D WANNA EAT SPACE FOOD AFTER THIS?
WOW... THAT WAS MY FIRST TIME, 'N IT WAS GREAT!
EAT AS MUCH AS YOU WANT...
HOW DO THEY MAKE THOSE PORK CHOPS, ANYWAY?
COME INTO THE KITCHEN, I'LL SHOW YOU...
EEEGADS!!

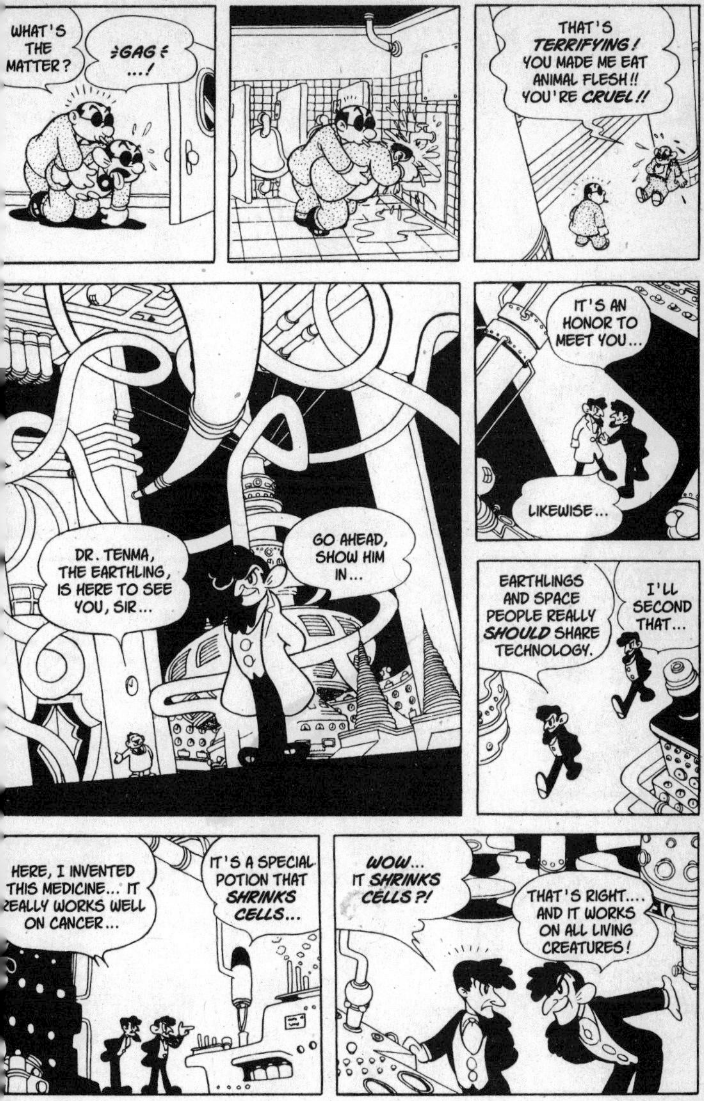
WHAT'S THE MATTER?
≷GAG≶ ...!
THAT'S TERRIFYING! YOU MADE ME EAT ANIMAL FLESH!! YOU'RE CRUEL!!
DR. TENMA, THE EARTHLING, IS HERE TO SEE YOU, SIR...
GO AHEAD, SHOW HIM IN...
IT'S AN HONOR TO MEET YOU...
LIKEWISE...
EARTHLINGS AND SPACE PEOPLE REALLY SHOULD SHARE TECHNOLOGY.
I'LL SECOND THAT...
HERE, I INVENTED THIS MEDICINE... IT REALLY WORKS WELL ON CANCER...
IT'S A SPECIAL POTION THAT SHRINKS CELLS...
WOW... IT SHRINKS CELLS?!
THAT'S RIGHT.... AND IT WORKS ON ALL LIVING CREATURES!

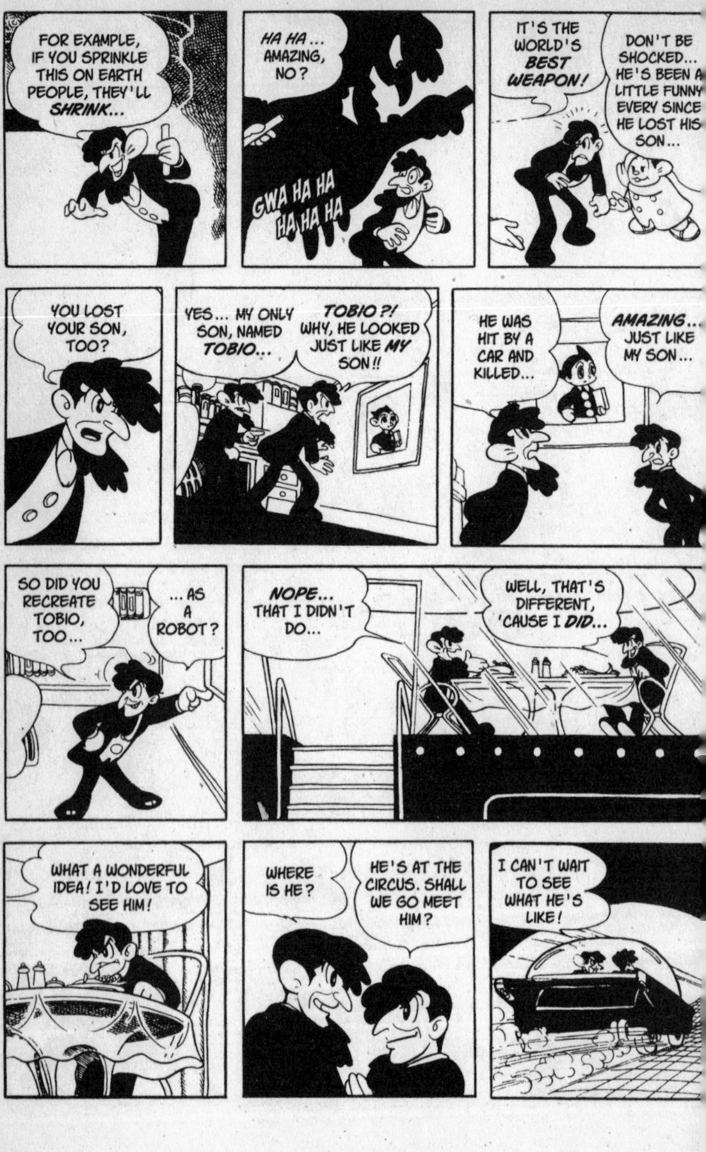
FOR EXAMPLE, IF YOU SPRINKLE THIS ON EARTH PEOPLE, THEY'LL *SHRINK*...
HA HA... AMAZING, NO?
GWA HA HA HA HA HA
IT'S THE WORLD'S *BEST WEAPON!*
DON'T BE SHOCKED... HE'S BEEN A LITTLE FUNNY EVERY SINCE HE LOST HIS SON...
YOU LOST YOUR SON, TOO?
YES... MY ONLY SON, NAMED *TOBIO*...
TOBIO?! WHY, HE LOOKED JUST LIKE *MY* SON!!
HE WAS HIT BY A CAR AND KILLED...
AMAZING... JUST LIKE MY SON...
SO DID YOU RECREATE TOBIO, TOO...
... AS A ROBOT?
NOPE... THAT I DIDN'T DO...
WELL, THAT'S DIFFERENT, 'CAUSE I *DID*...
WHAT A WONDERFUL IDEA! I'D LOVE TO SEE HIM!
WHERE IS HE?
HE'S AT THE CIRCUS. SHALL WE GO MEET HIM?
I CAN'T WAIT TO SEE WHAT HE'S LIKE!

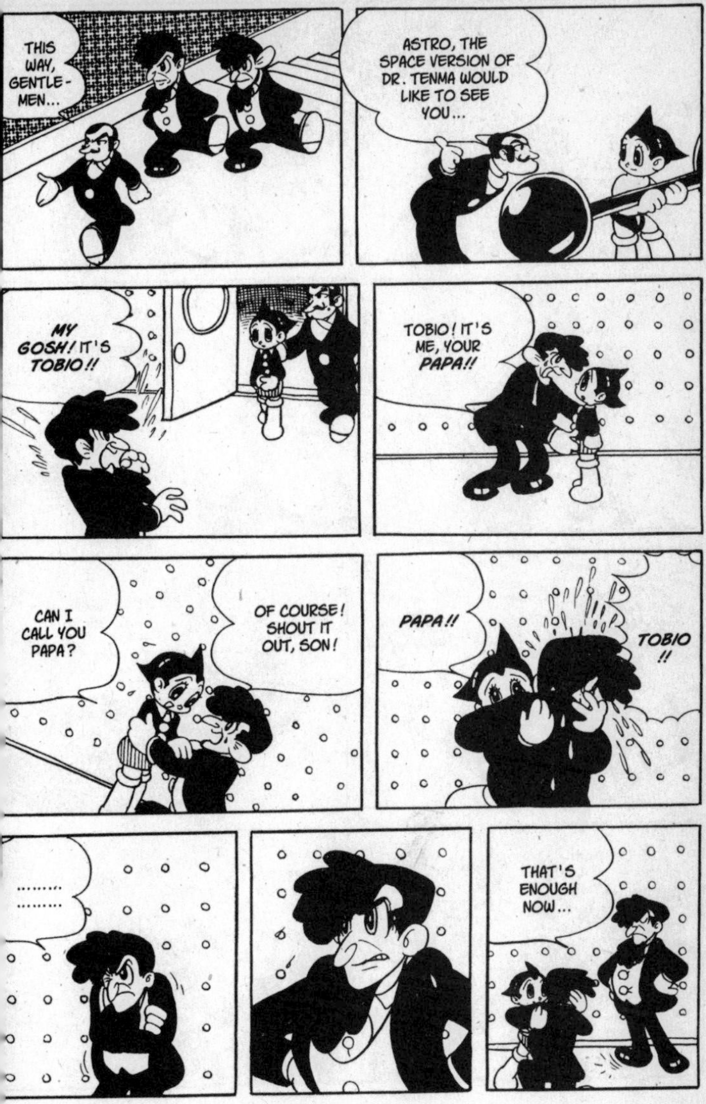
THIS WAY, GENTLE-MEN...
ASTRO, THE SPACE VERSION OF DR. TENMA WOULD LIKE TO SEE YOU...
MY GOSH! IT'S TOBIO!!
TOBIO! IT'S ME, YOUR PAPA!!
CAN I CALL YOU PAPA?
OF COURSE! SHOUT IT OUT, SON!
PAPA!!
TOBIO !!
....
....
THAT'S ENOUGH NOW...

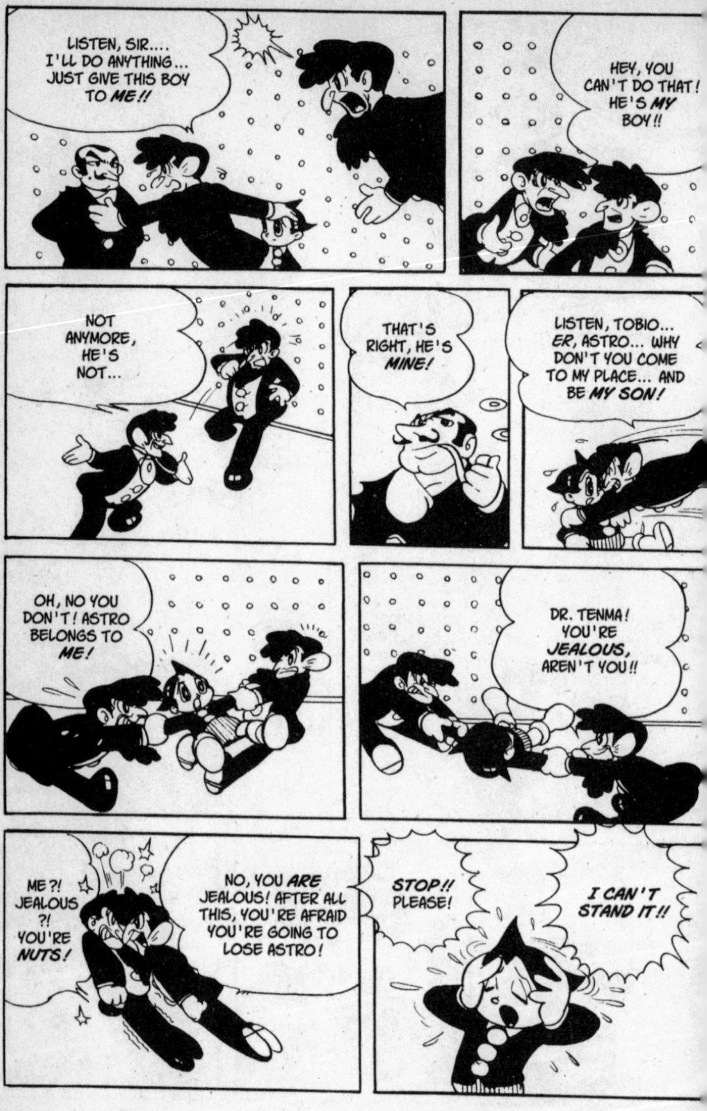
LISTEN, SIR.... I'LL DO ANYTHING... JUST GIVE THIS BOY TO ME!!
HEY, YOU CAN'T DO THAT! HE'S MY BOY!!
NOT ANYMORE, HE'S NOT...
THAT'S RIGHT, HE'S MINE!
LISTEN, TOBIO... ER, ASTRO... WHY DON'T YOU COME TO MY PLACE... AND BE MY SON!
OH, NO YOU DON'T! ASTRO BELONGS TO ME!
DR. TENMA! YOU'RE JEALOUS, AREN'T YOU!!
ME?! JEALOUS?! YOU'RE NUTS!
NO, YOU ARE JEALOUS! AFTER ALL THIS, YOU'RE AFRAID YOU'RE GOING TO LOSE ASTRO!
STOP!! PLEASE!
I CAN'T STAND IT!!

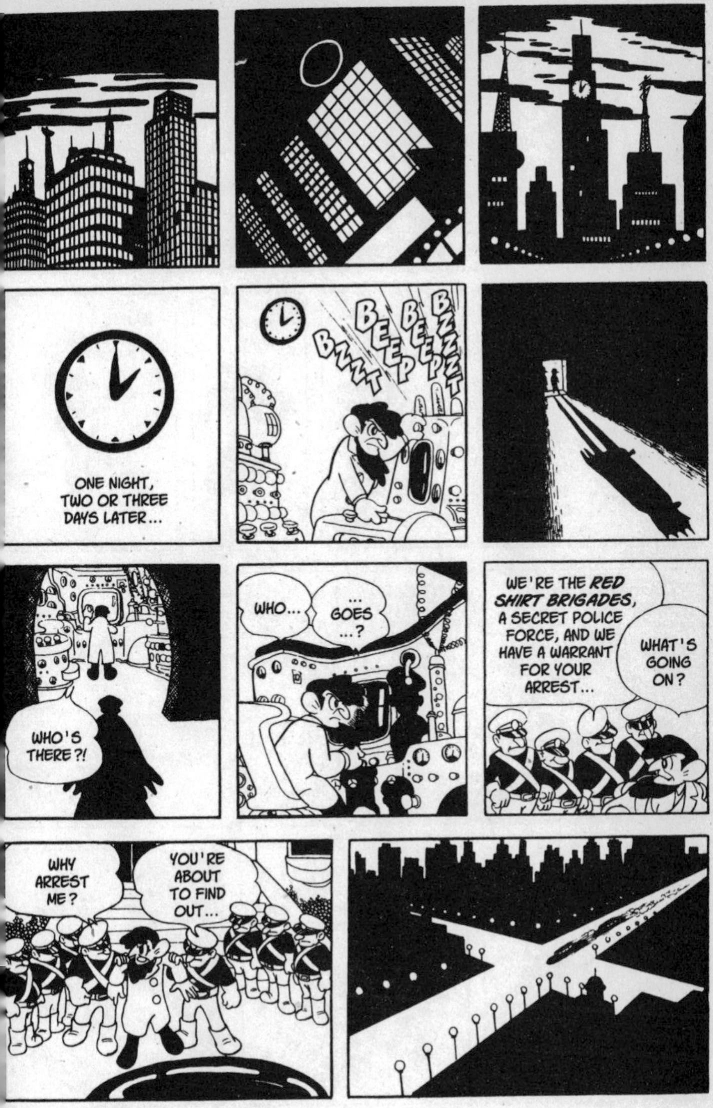
ONE NIGHT, TWO OR THREE DAYS LATER...
BZZZT
BEEEP
BEEEP
BZZZZT
WHO'S THERE?!
WHO...
... GOES ...?
WE'RE THE RED SHIRT BRIGADES, A SECRET POLICE FORCE, AND WE HAVE A WARRANT FOR YOUR ARREST...
WHAT'S GOING ON?
WHY ARREST ME?
YOU'RE ABOUT TO FIND OUT...

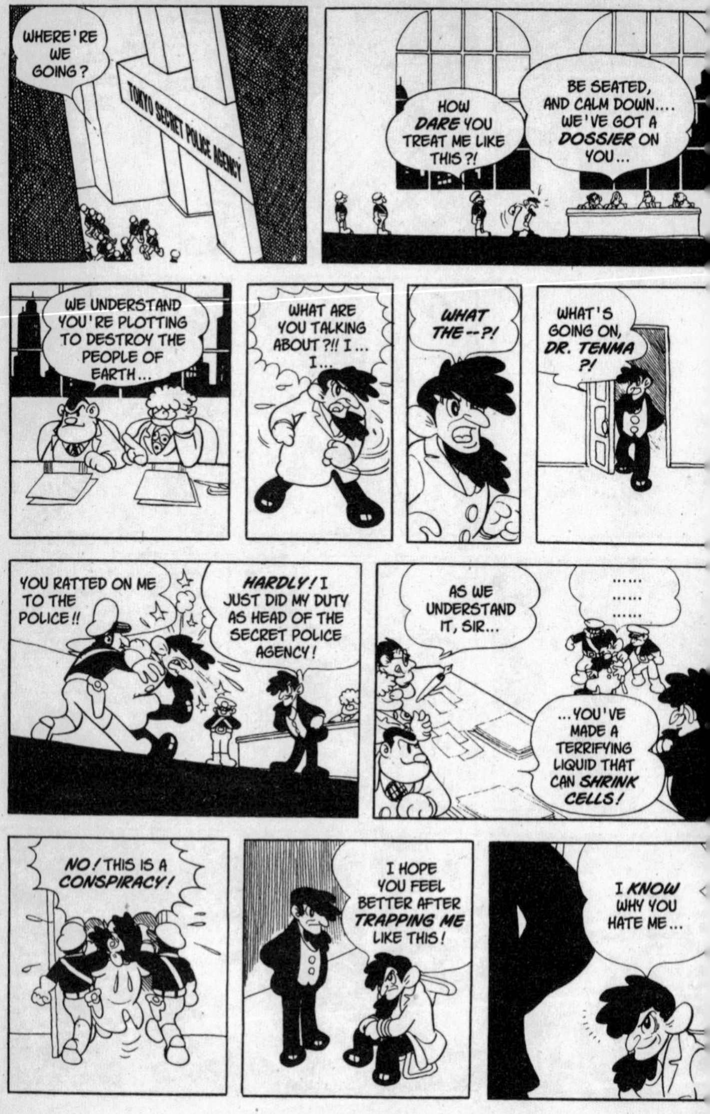
WHERE'RE WE GOING?
TOKYO SECRET POLICE AGENCY
HOW DARE YOU TREAT ME LIKE THIS?!
BE SEATED, AND CALM DOWN.... WE'VE GOT A DOSSIER ON YOU...
WE UNDERSTAND YOU'RE PLOTTING TO DESTROY THE PEOPLE OF EARTH...
WHAT ARE YOU TALKING ABOUT?!! I... I...
WHAT THE--?!
WHAT'S GOING ON, DR. TENMA?!
YOU RATTED ON ME TO THE POLICE!!
HARDLY! I JUST DID MY DUTY AS HEAD OF THE SECRET POLICE AGENCY!
AS WE UNDERSTAND IT, SIR...
....
...YOU'VE MADE A TERRIFYING LIQUID THAT CAN SHRINK CELLS!
NO! THIS IS A CONSPIRACY!
I HOPE YOU FEEL BETTER AFTER TRAPPING ME LIKE THIS!
I KNOW WHY YOU HATE ME...

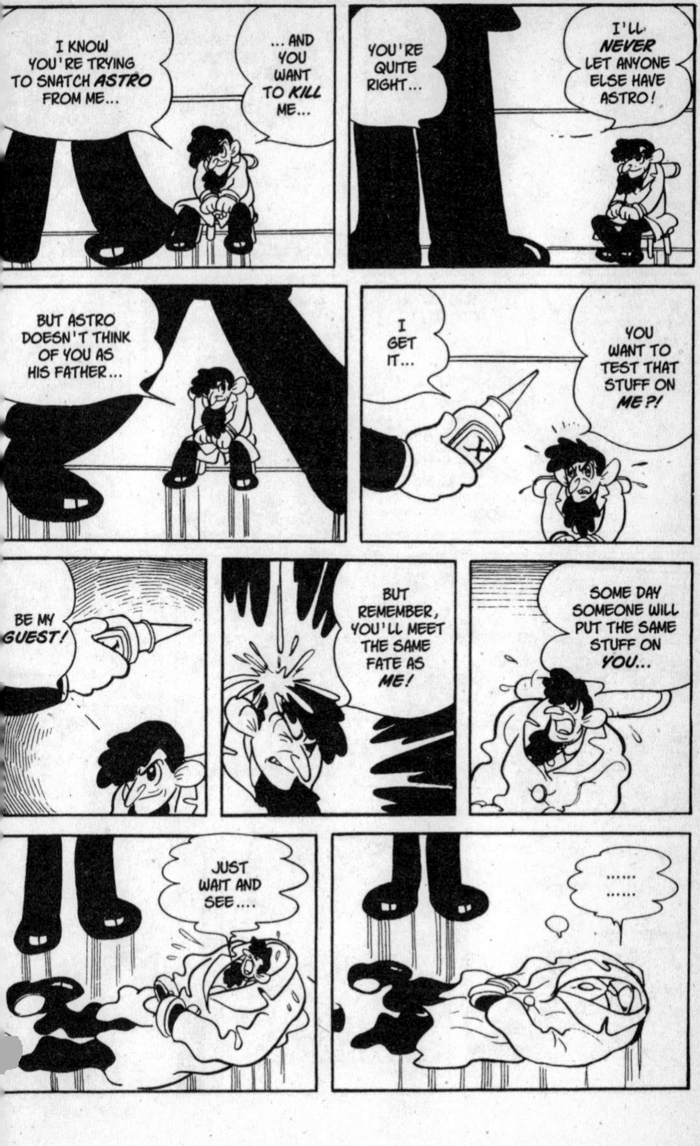
I KNOW YOU'RE TRYING TO SNATCH ASTRO FROM ME...
... AND YOU WANT TO KILL ME...
YOU'RE QUITE RIGHT...
I'LL NEVER LET ANYONE ELSE HAVE ASTRO!
BUT ASTRO DOESN'T THINK OF YOU AS HIS FATHER...
I GET IT...
YOU WANT TO TEST THAT STUFF ON ME?!
BE MY GUEST!
BUT REMEMBER, YOU'LL MEET THE SAME FATE AS ME!
SOME DAY SOMEONE WILL PUT THE SAME STUFF ON YOU...
JUST WAIT AND SEE....
......
......

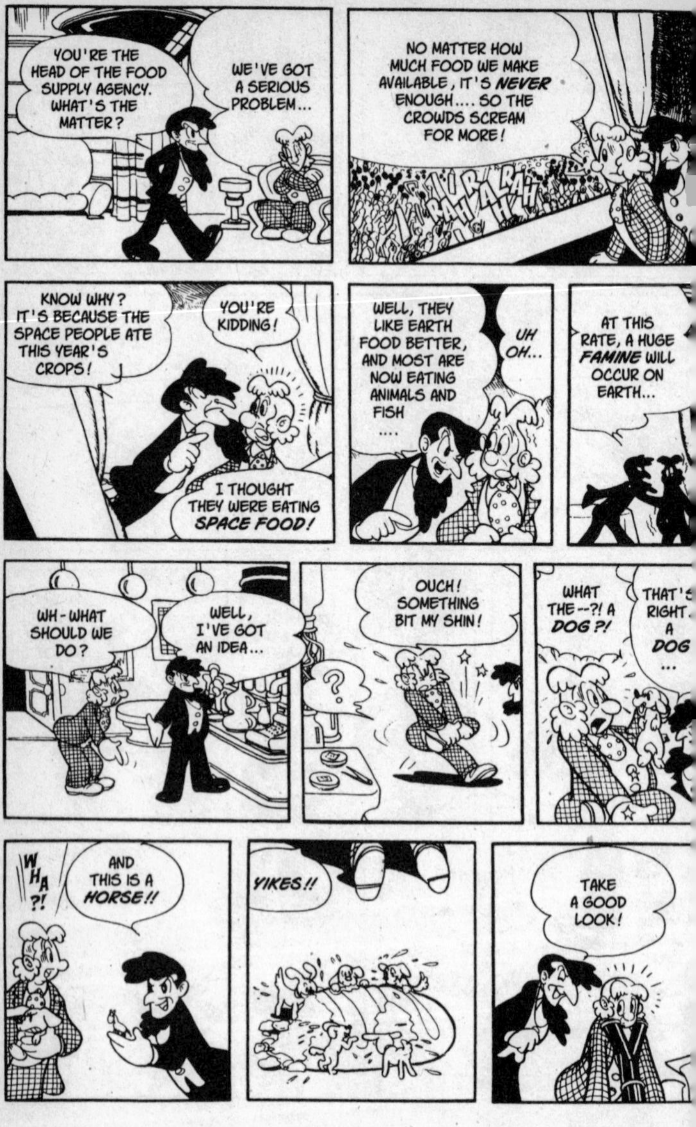
YOU'RE THE HEAD OF THE FOOD SUPPLY AGENCY. WHAT'S THE MATTER?
WE'VE GOT A SERIOUS PROBLEM...
NO MATTER HOW MUCH FOOD WE MAKE AVAILABLE, IT'S *NEVER* ENOUGH.... SO THE CROWDS SCREAM FOR MORE!
KNOW WHY? IT'S BECAUSE THE SPACE PEOPLE ATE THIS YEAR'S CROPS!
YOU'RE KIDDING!
I THOUGHT THEY WERE EATING *SPACE FOOD!*
WELL, THEY LIKE EARTH FOOD BETTER, AND MOST ARE NOW EATING ANIMALS AND FISH ....
UH OH...
AT THIS RATE, A HUGE *FAMINE* WILL OCCUR ON EARTH...
WH-WHAT SHOULD WE DO?
WELL, I'VE GOT AN IDEA...
?
OUCH! SOMETHING BIT MY SHIN!
WHAT THE--?! A *DOG?!*
THAT'S RIGHT. A *DOG* ...
WHA ?!
AND THIS IS A *HORSE!!*
YIKES!!
TAKE A GOOD LOOK!

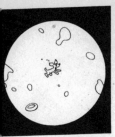

WH-WHAT'S GOING ON!

I USED *SHRINKING LIQUID!*

YOU USED A DRUG?!

RIGHT. IT MAKES THINGS *SMALLER!*

AND YOU KNOW WHAT?! IF YOU MAKE THINGS SMALLER, THEY *EAT LESS...*

B-BUT WHAT'RE YOU GOING TO MAKE SMALLER?!

THE SPACE PEOPLE! ALL OF 'EM!

BONK

YIKES!

IS WHAT YOU JUST SAID TRUE, DR. TENMA?

ASTRO! WHAT'RE YOU DOING HERE?

YOU SAID YOU'RE GONNA MAKE THE SPACE PEOPLE SMALLER, ... RIGHT?

HA HA... AND IT'S NONE OF YOUR BUSINESS...

ASTRO BOY...

B..BUT IT'S *NOT RIGHT!* YOU'VE GOTTA *STOP!*

IT'S A *BAD THING!* A *TERRIBLE* THING!!

DON'T WORRY ABOUT THIS, ASTRO... JUST BE MY *SON* AGAIN, OKAY?

NO!!

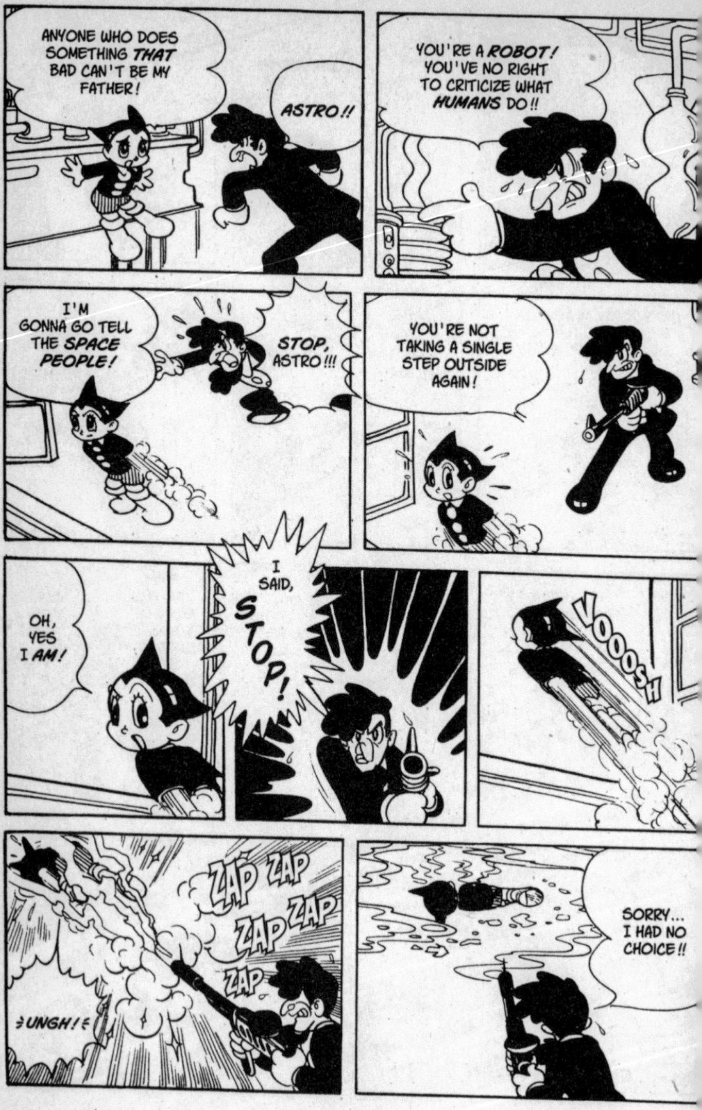
ANYONE WHO DOES SOMETHING THAT BAD CAN'T BE MY FATHER!
ASTRO!!
YOU'RE A ROBOT! YOU'VE NO RIGHT TO CRITICIZE WHAT HUMANS DO!!
I'M GONNA GO TELL THE SPACE PEOPLE!
STOP, ASTRO!!!
YOU'RE NOT TAKING A SINGLE STEP OUTSIDE AGAIN!
OH, YES I AM!
I SAID, STOP!
VOOOOSH
ZAP ZAP ZAP ZAP ZAP
UNGH!
SORRY... I HAD NO CHOICE!!

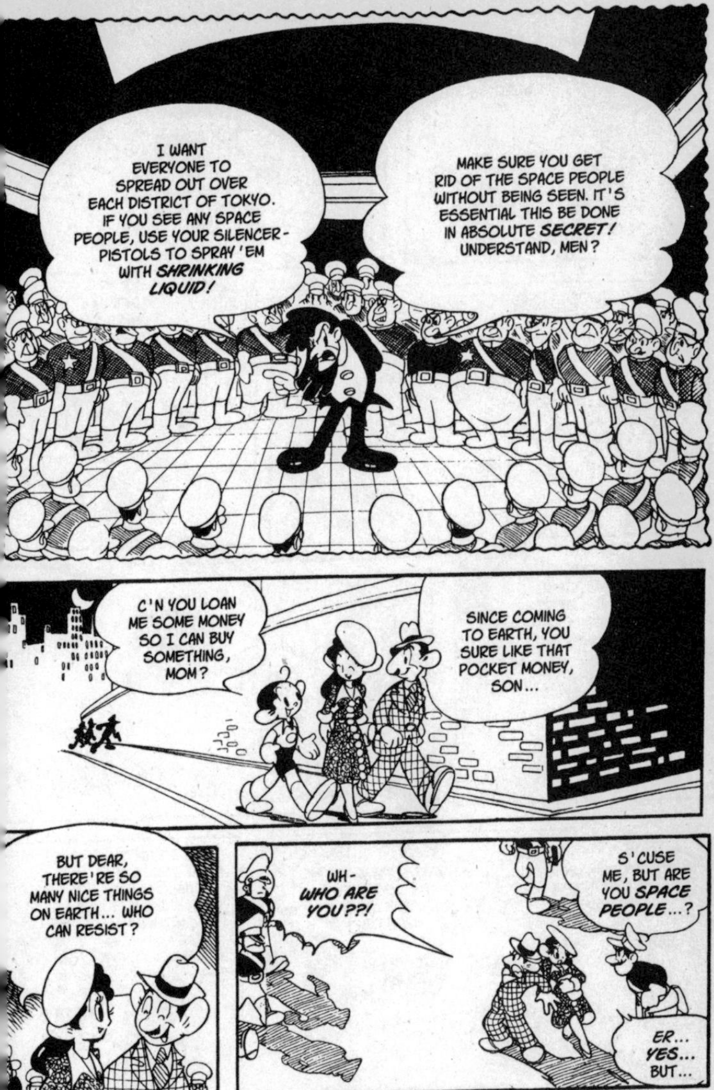
I WANT EVERYONE TO SPREAD OUT OVER EACH DISTRICT OF TOKYO. IF YOU SEE ANY SPACE PEOPLE, USE YOUR SILENCER-PISTOLS TO SPRAY 'EM WITH SHRINKING LIQUID!
MAKE SURE YOU GET RID OF THE SPACE PEOPLE WITHOUT BEING SEEN. IT'S ESSENTIAL THIS BE DONE IN ABSOLUTE SECRET! UNDERSTAND, MEN?
C'N YOU LOAN ME SOME MONEY SO I CAN BUY SOMETHING, MOM?
SINCE COMING TO EARTH, YOU SURE LIKE THAT POCKET MONEY, SON...
BUT DEAR, THERE'RE SO MANY NICE THINGS ON EARTH... WHO CAN RESIST?
WH- WHO ARE YOU??!
S'CUSE ME, BUT ARE YOU SPACE PEOPLE...?
ER... YES... BUT...

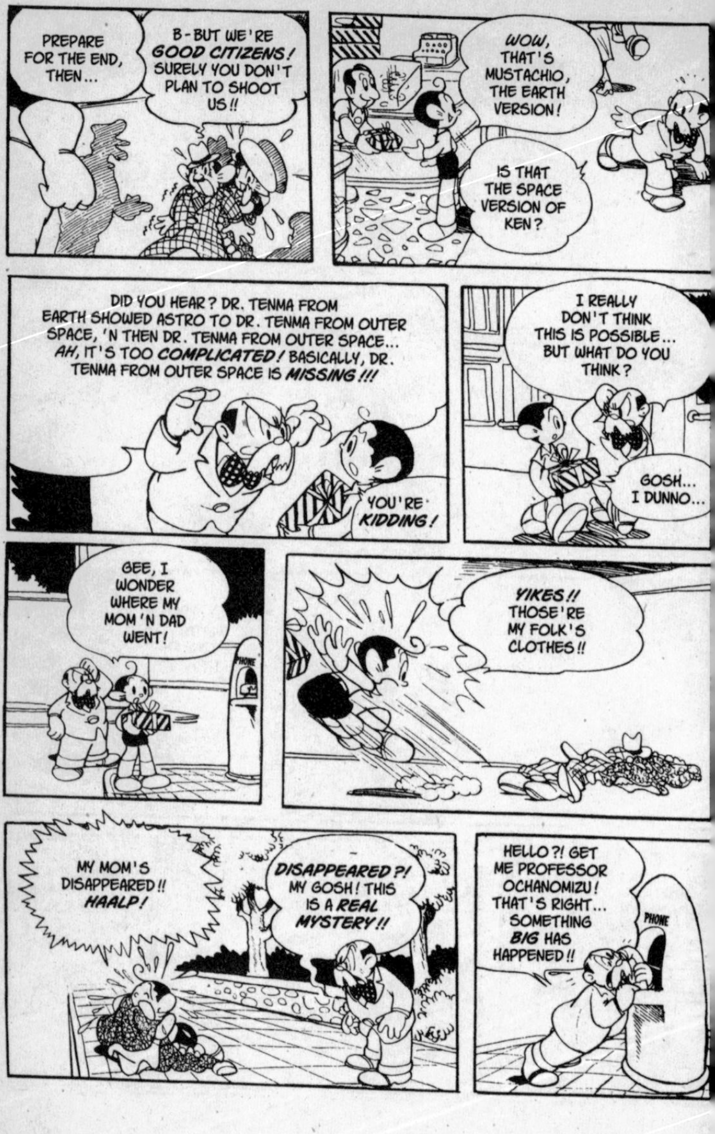
PREPARE FOR THE END, THEN...
B-BUT WE'RE GOOD CITIZENS! SURELY YOU DON'T PLAN TO SHOOT US!!
WOW, THAT'S MUSTACHIO, THE EARTH VERSION!
IS THAT THE SPACE VERSION OF KEN?
DID YOU HEAR? DR. TENMA FROM EARTH SHOWED ASTRO TO DR. TENMA FROM OUTER SPACE, 'N THEN DR. TENMA FROM OUTER SPACE... AH, IT'S TOO COMPLICATED! BASICALLY, DR. TENMA FROM OUTER SPACE IS MISSING!!!
YOU'RE KIDDING!
I REALLY DON'T THINK THIS IS POSSIBLE... BUT WHAT DO YOU THINK?
GOSH... I DUNNO...
GEE, I WONDER WHERE MY MOM 'N DAD WENT!
PHONE
YIKES!! THOSE'RE MY FOLK'S CLOTHES!!
MY MOM'S DISAPPEARED!! HAALP!
DISAPPEARED?! MY GOSH! THIS IS A REAL MYSTERY!!
HELLO?! GET ME PROFESSOR OCHANOMIZU! THAT'S RIGHT... SOMETHING BIG HAS HAPPENED!!
PHONE

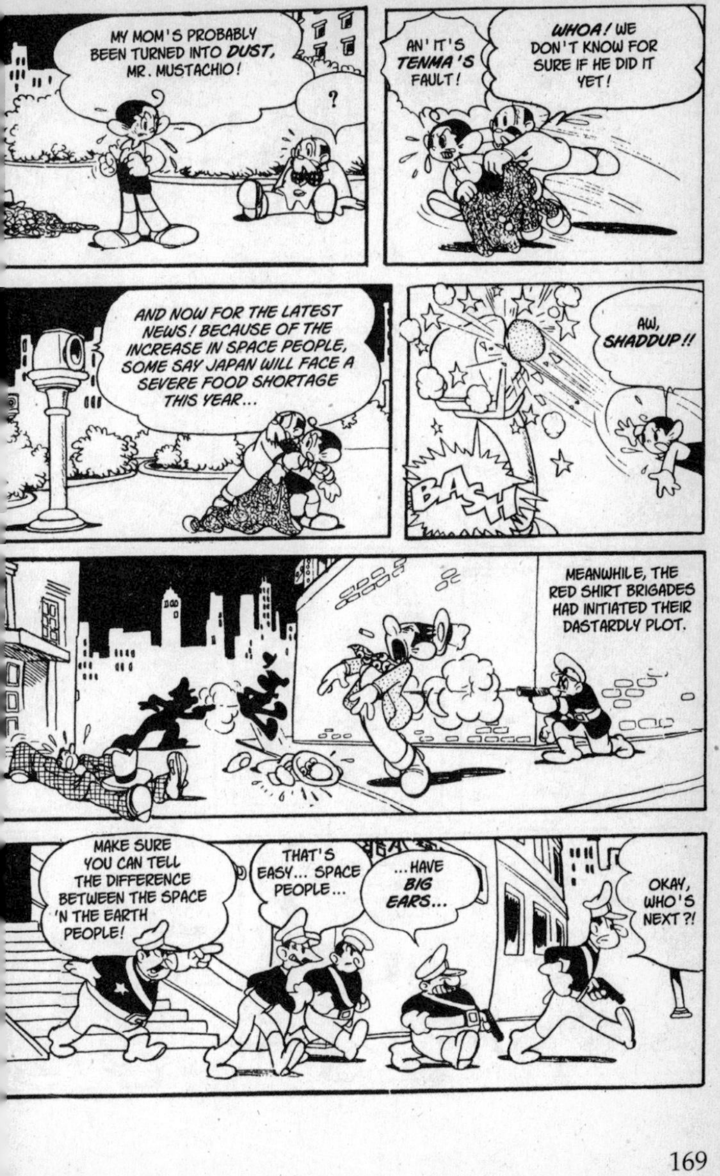
MY MOM'S PROBABLY BEEN TURNED INTO DUST, MR. MUSTACHIO!
?
AN' IT'S TENMA'S FAULT!
WHOA! WE DON'T KNOW FOR SURE IF HE DID IT YET!
AND NOW FOR THE LATEST NEWS! BECAUSE OF THE INCREASE IN SPACE PEOPLE, SOME SAY JAPAN WILL FACE A SEVERE FOOD SHORTAGE THIS YEAR...
AW, SHADDUP!!
BASH
MEANWHILE, THE RED SHIRT BRIGADES HAD INITIATED THEIR DASTARDLY PLOT.
MAKE SURE YOU CAN TELL THE DIFFERENCE BETWEEN THE SPACE 'N THE EARTH PEOPLE!
THAT'S EASY... SPACE PEOPLE...
...HAVE BIG EARS...
OKAY, WHO'S NEXT?!

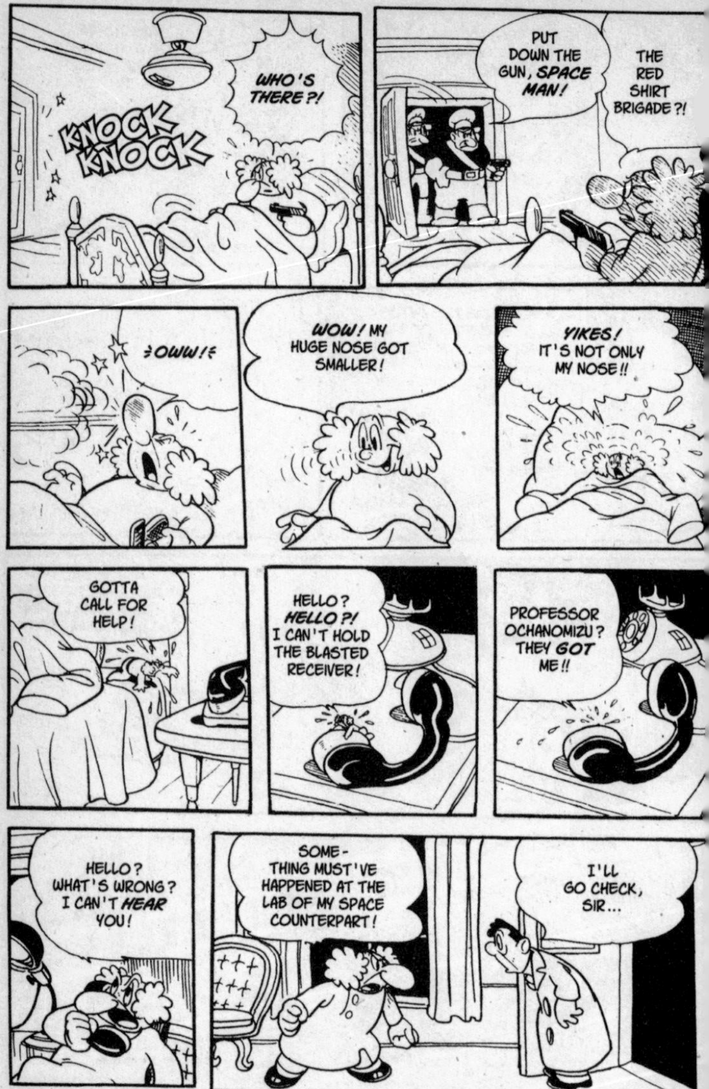
KNOCK KNOCK
WHO'S THERE?!
PUT DOWN THE GUN, SPACE MAN!
THE RED SHIRT BRIGADE?!
OWW!
WOW! MY HUGE NOSE GOT SMALLER!
YIKES! IT'S NOT ONLY MY NOSE!!
GOTTA CALL FOR HELP!
HELLO? HELLO?! I CAN'T HOLD THE BLASTED RECEIVER!
PROFESSOR OCHANOMIZU? THEY GOT ME!!
HELLO? WHAT'S WRONG? I CAN'T HEAR YOU!
SOME-THING MUST'VE HAPPENED AT THE LAB OF MY SPACE COUNTERPART!
I'LL GO CHECK, SIR...

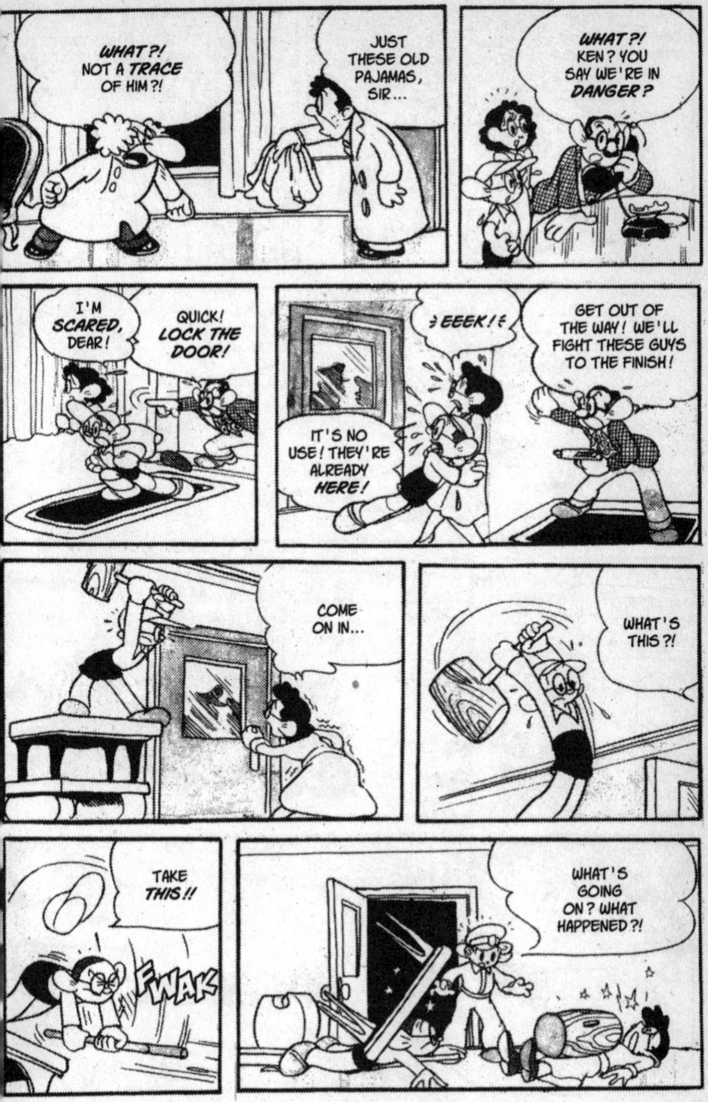
WHAT?! NOT A TRACE OF HIM?!
JUST THESE OLD PAJAMAS, SIR...
WHAT?! KEN? YOU SAY WE'RE IN DANGER?
I'M SCARED, DEAR!
QUICK! LOCK THE DOOR!
EEEK!
GET OUT OF THE WAY! WE'LL FIGHT THESE GUYS TO THE FINISH!
IT'S NO USE! THEY'RE ALREADY HERE!
COME ON IN...
WHAT'S THIS?!
TAKE THIS!!
FWAK
WHAT'S GOING ON? WHAT HAPPENED?!

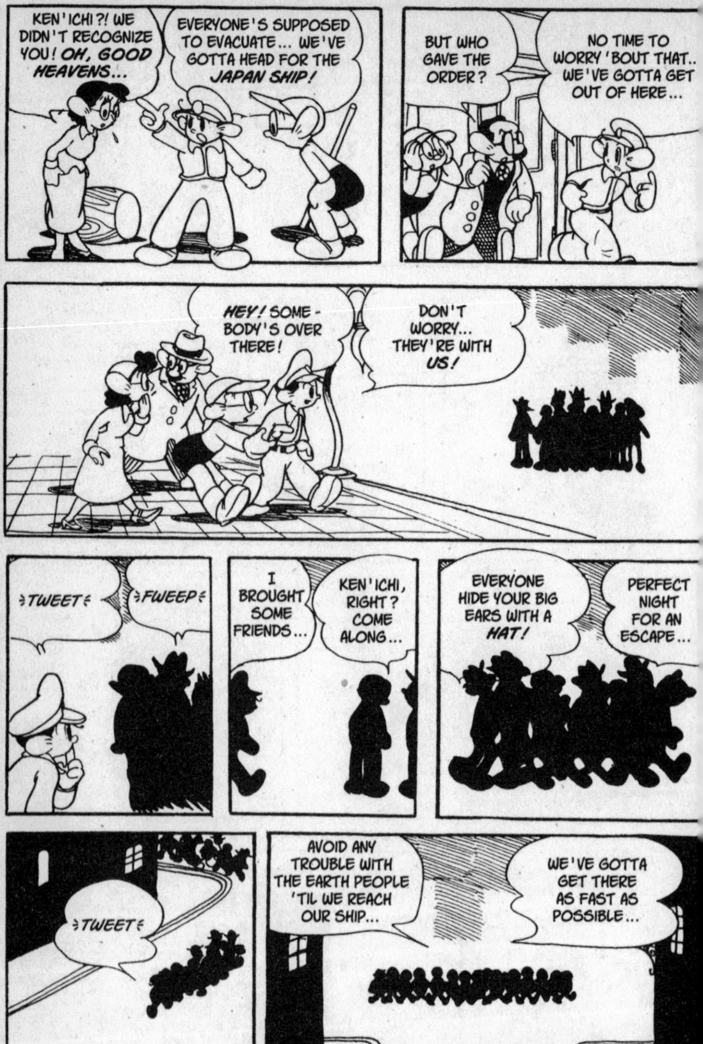
KEN'ICHI?! WE DIDN'T RECOGNIZE YOU! OH, GOOD HEAVENS...
EVERYONE'S SUPPOSED TO EVACUATE... WE'VE GOTTA HEAD FOR THE JAPAN SHIP!
BUT WHO GAVE THE ORDER?
NO TIME TO WORRY 'BOUT THAT.. WE'VE GOTTA GET OUT OF HERE...
HEY! SOME-BODY'S OVER THERE!
DON'T WORRY... THEY'RE WITH US!
TWEET
FWEEP
I BROUGHT SOME FRIENDS...
KEN'ICHI, RIGHT? COME ALONG...
EVERYONE HIDE YOUR BIG EARS WITH A HAT!
PERFECT NIGHT FOR AN ESCAPE...
TWEET
AVOID ANY TROUBLE WITH THE EARTH PEOPLE 'TIL WE REACH OUR SHIP...
WE'VE GOTTA GET THERE AS FAST AS POSSIBLE...

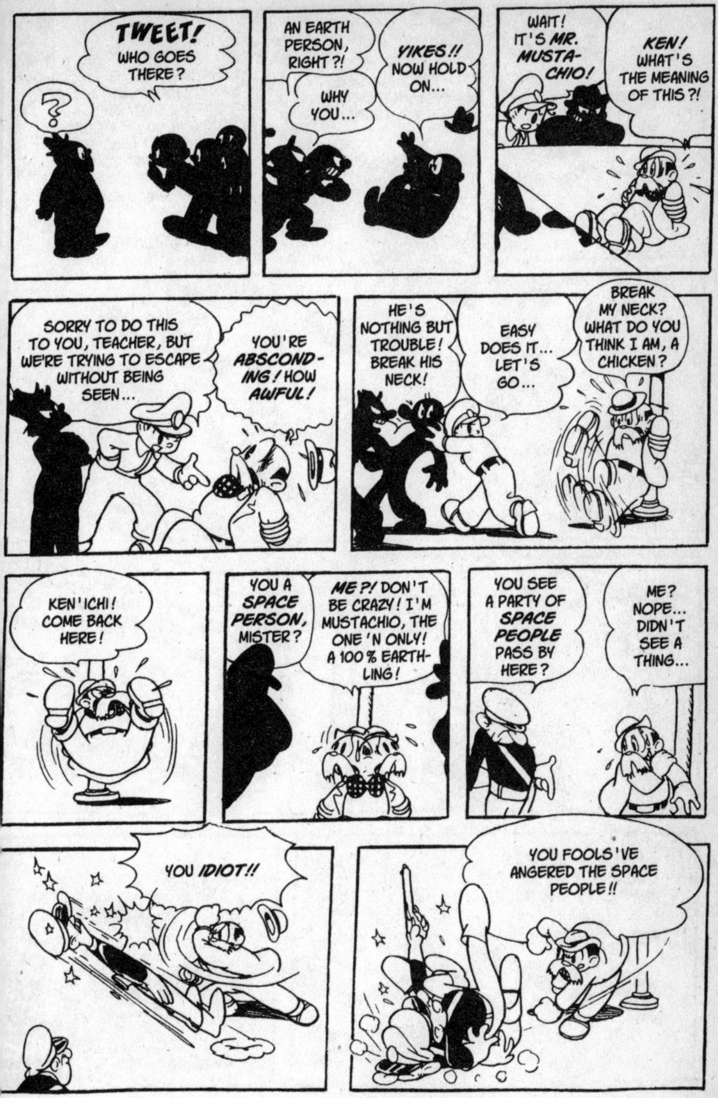
TWEET! WHO GOES THERE?
?
AN EARTH PERSON, RIGHT?!
WHY YOU...
YIKES!! NOW HOLD ON...
WAIT! IT'S MR. MUSTA-CHIO!
KEN! WHAT'S THE MEANING OF THIS?!
SORRY TO DO THIS TO YOU, TEACHER, BUT WE'RE TRYING TO ESCAPE WITHOUT BEING SEEN...
YOU'RE ABSCOND-ING! HOW AWFUL!
HE'S NOTHING BUT TROUBLE! BREAK HIS NECK!
EASY DOES IT... LET'S GO...
BREAK MY NECK? WHAT DO YOU THINK I AM, A CHICKEN?
KEN'ICHI! COME BACK HERE!
YOU A SPACE PERSON, MISTER?
ME?! DON'T BE CRAZY! I'M MUSTACHIO, THE ONE 'N ONLY! A 100% EARTH-LING!
YOU SEE A PARTY OF SPACE PEOPLE PASS BY HERE?
ME? NOPE... DIDN'T SEE A THING...
YOU IDIOT!!
YOU FOOLS'VE ANGERED THE SPACE PEOPLE!!

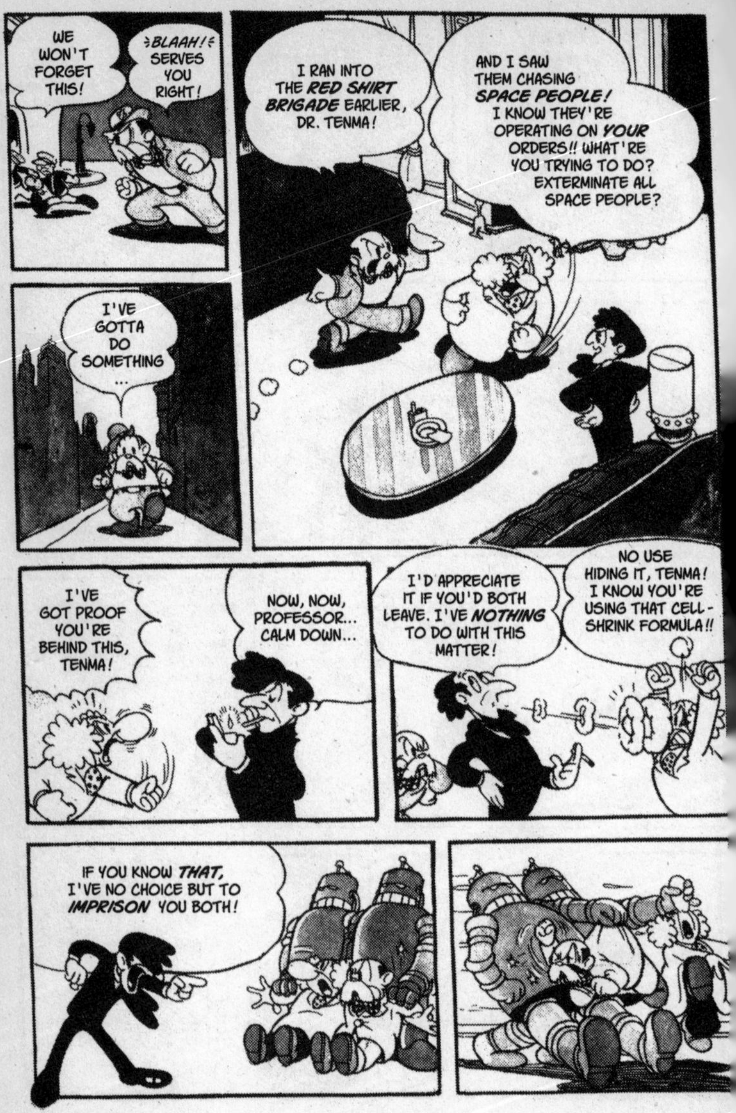
WE WON'T FORGET THIS!
BLAAH! SERVES YOU RIGHT!
I RAN INTO THE RED SHIRT BRIGADE EARLIER, DR. TENMA!
AND I SAW THEM CHASING SPACE PEOPLE! I KNOW THEY'RE OPERATING ON YOUR ORDERS!! WHAT'RE YOU TRYING TO DO? EXTERMINATE ALL SPACE PEOPLE?
I'VE GOTTA DO SOMETHING ...
I'VE GOT PROOF YOU'RE BEHIND THIS, TENMA!
NOW, NOW, PROFESSOR... CALM DOWN...
I'D APPRECIATE IT IF YOU'D BOTH LEAVE. I'VE NOTHING TO DO WITH THIS MATTER!
NO USE HIDING IT, TENMA! I KNOW YOU'RE USING THAT CELL-SHRINK FORMULA!!
IF YOU KNOW THAT, I'VE NO CHOICE BUT TO IMPRISON YOU BOTH!

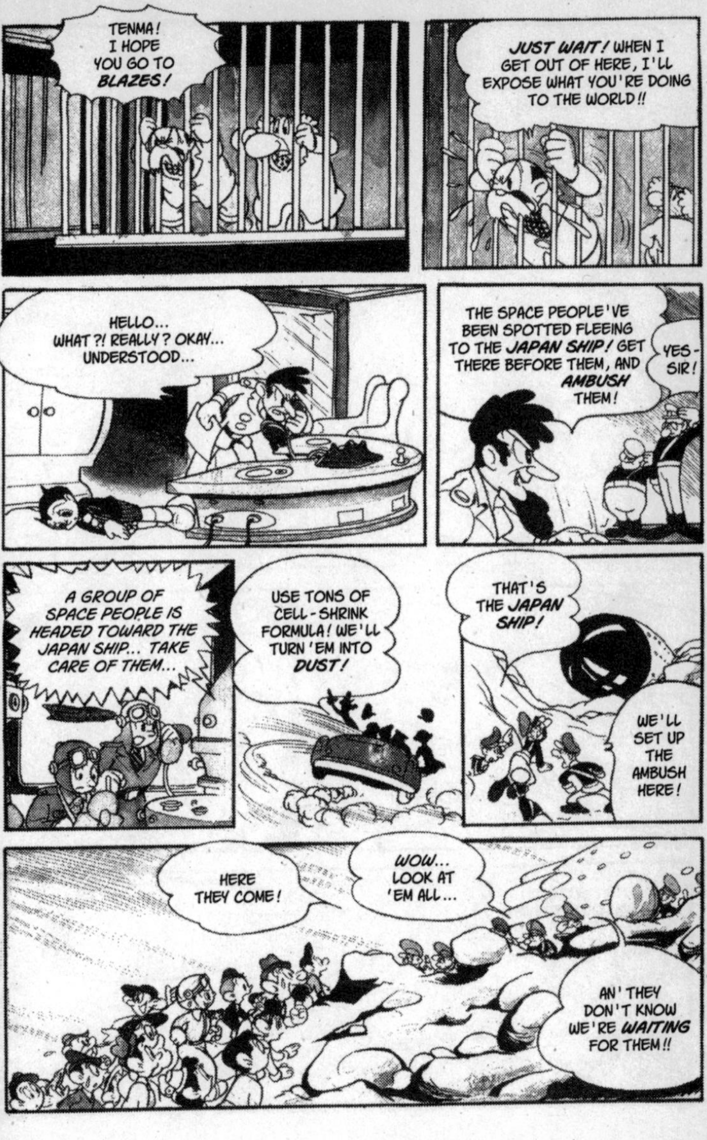
TENMA! I HOPE YOU GO TO BLAZES!
JUST WAIT! WHEN I GET OUT OF HERE, I'LL EXPOSE WHAT YOU'RE DOING TO THE WORLD!!
HELLO... WHAT?! REALLY? OKAY... UNDERSTOOD...
THE SPACE PEOPLE'VE BEEN SPOTTED FLEEING TO THE JAPAN SHIP! GET THERE BEFORE THEM, AND AMBUSH THEM!
YES-SIR!
A GROUP OF SPACE PEOPLE IS HEADED TOWARD THE JAPAN SHIP... TAKE CARE OF THEM...
USE TONS OF CELL-SHRINK FORMULA! WE'LL TURN 'EM INTO DUST!
THAT'S THE JAPAN SHIP!
WE'LL SET UP THE AMBUSH HERE!
HERE THEY COME!
WOW... LOOK AT 'EM ALL...
AN' THEY DON'T KNOW WE'RE WAITING FOR THEM!!

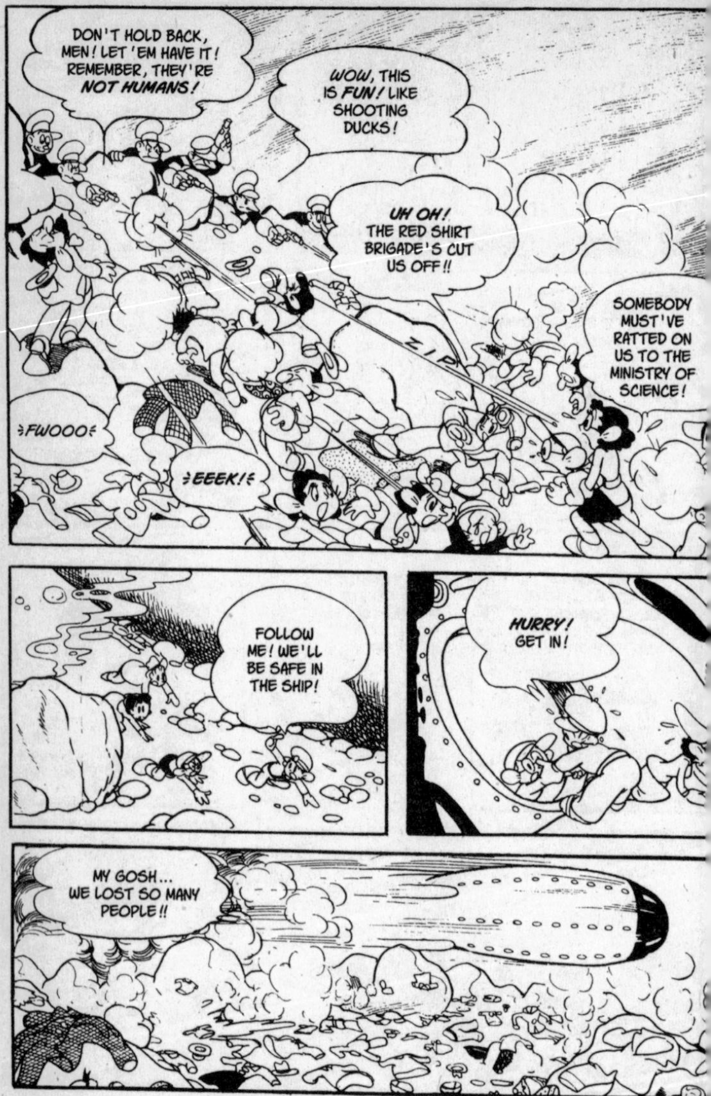
DON'T HOLD BACK, MEN! LET 'EM HAVE IT! REMEMBER, THEY'RE NOT HUMANS!
WOW, THIS IS FUN! LIKE SHOOTING DUCKS!
UH OH! THE RED SHIRT BRIGADE'S CUT US OFF!!
ZIP
SOMEBODY MUST'VE RATTED ON US TO THE MINISTRY OF SCIENCE!
FWOOO
EEEK!
FOLLOW ME! WE'LL BE SAFE IN THE SHIP!
HURRY! GET IN!
MY GOSH... WE LOST SO MANY PEOPLE!!

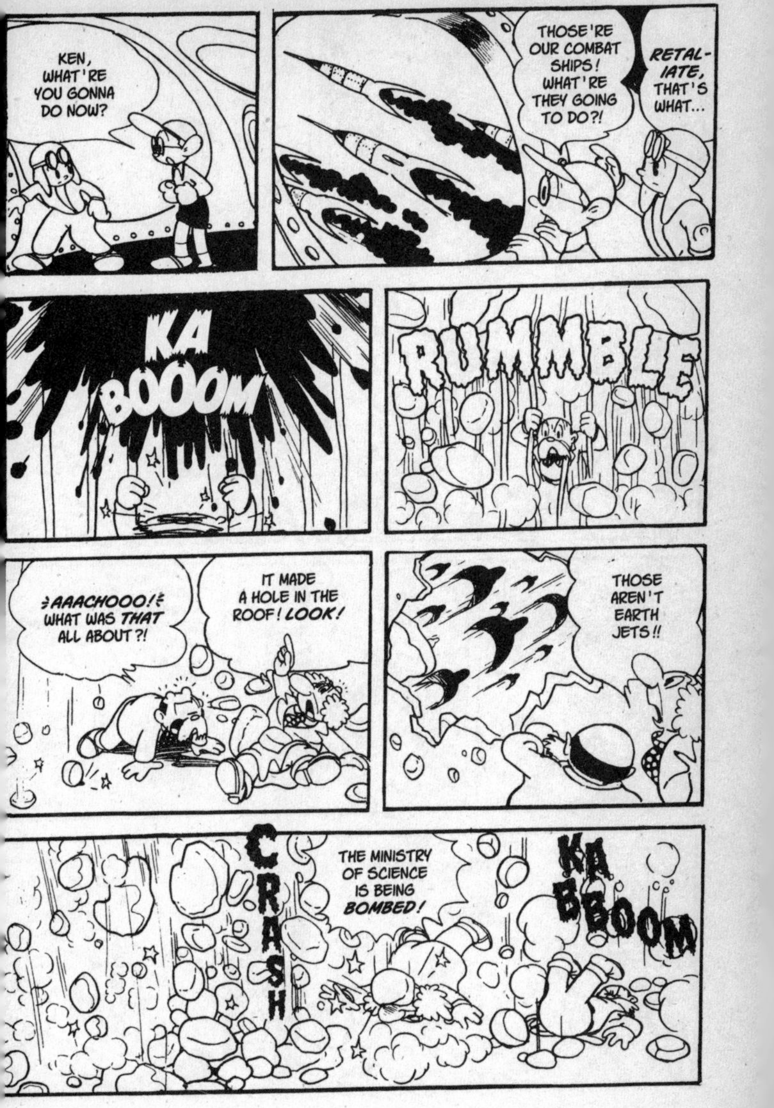
KEN, WHAT'RE YOU GONNA DO NOW?
THOSE'RE OUR COMBAT SHIPS! WHAT'RE THEY GOING TO DO?!
RETAL-IATE, THAT'S WHAT...
KA BOOOM
RUMMBLE
AAACHOOO! WHAT WAS THAT ALL ABOUT?!
IT MADE A HOLE IN THE ROOF! LOOK!
THOSE AREN'T EARTH JETS!!
CRASH
THE MINISTRY OF SCIENCE IS BEING BOMBED!
KA BBOOM

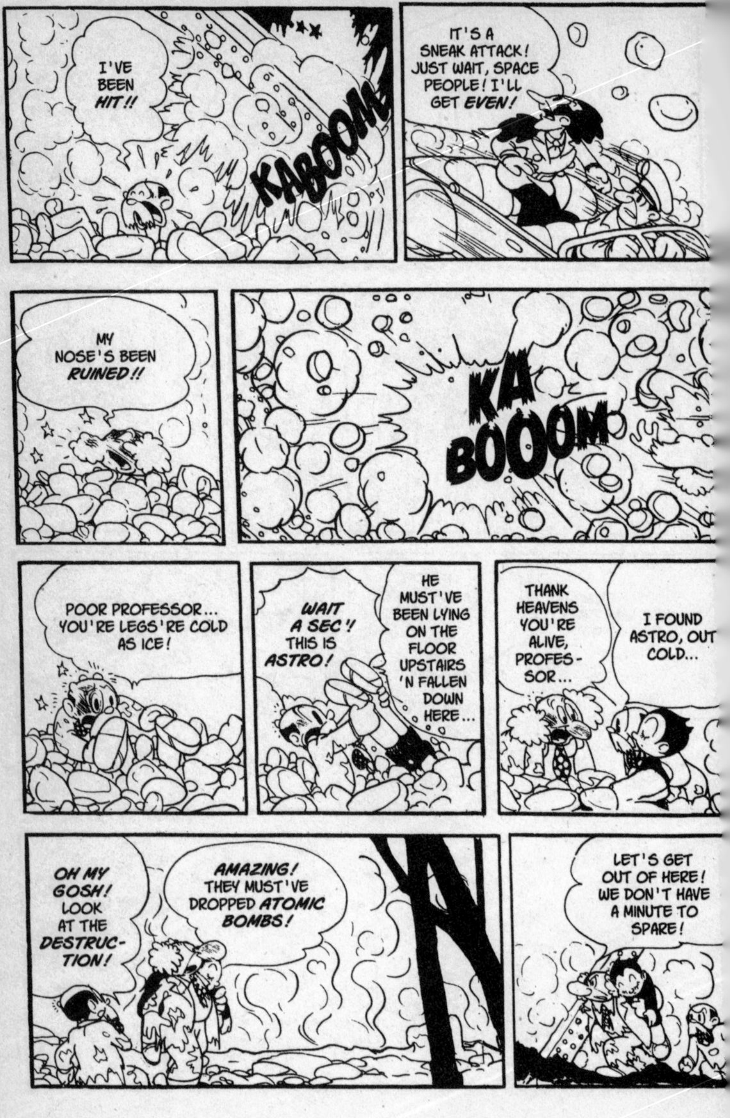
I'VE BEEN HIT!!
KABOOM
IT'S A SNEAK ATTACK! JUST WAIT, SPACE PEOPLE! I'LL GET EVEN!
MY NOSE'S BEEN RUINED!!
KA BOOOM
POOR PROFESSOR... YOU'RE LEGS'RE COLD AS ICE!
WAIT A SEC'! THIS IS ASTRO!
HE MUST'VE BEEN LYING ON THE FLOOR UPSTAIRS 'N FALLEN DOWN HERE...
THANK HEAVENS YOU'RE ALIVE, PROFES-SOR...
I FOUND ASTRO, OUT COLD...
OH MY GOSH! LOOK AT THE DESTRUC-TION!
AMAZING! THEY MUST'VE DROPPED ATOMIC BOMBS!
LET'S GET OUT OF HERE! WE DON'T HAVE A MINUTE TO SPARE!

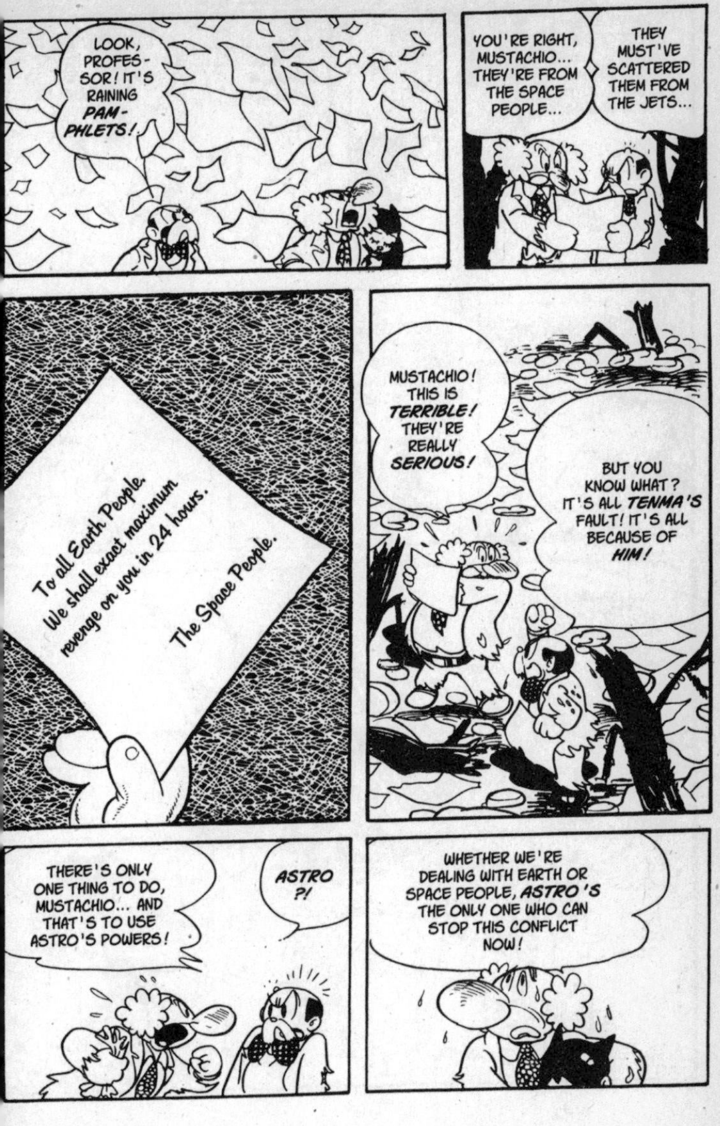
LOOK, PROFES-SOR! IT'S RAINING PAM-PHLETS!
YOU'RE RIGHT, MUSTACHIO... THEY'RE FROM THE SPACE PEOPLE...
THEY MUST'VE SCATTERED THEM FROM THE JETS...
To all Earth People.
We shall exact maximum revenge on you in 24 hours.
The Space People.
MUSTACHIO! THIS IS TERRIBLE! THEY'RE REALLY SERIOUS!
BUT YOU KNOW WHAT? IT'S ALL TENMA'S FAULT! IT'S ALL BECAUSE OF HIM!
THERE'S ONLY ONE THING TO DO, MUSTACHIO... AND THAT'S TO USE ASTRO'S POWERS!
ASTRO?!
WHETHER WE'RE DEALING WITH EARTH OR SPACE PEOPLE, ASTRO'S THE ONLY ONE WHO CAN STOP THIS CONFLICT NOW!

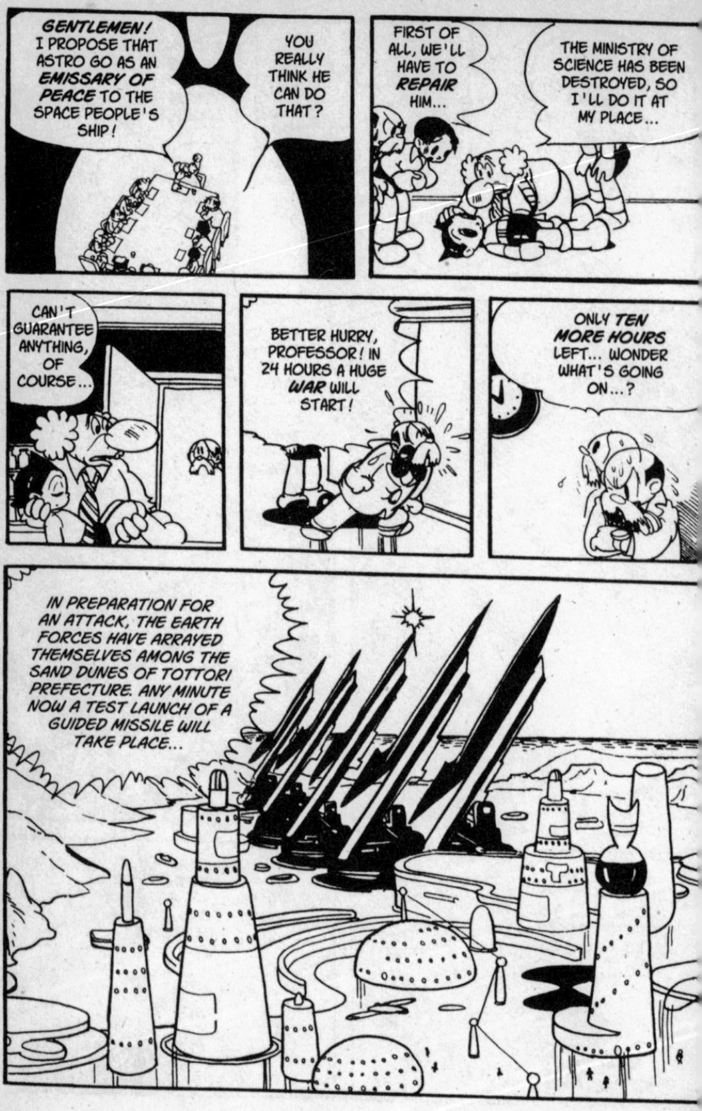
GENTLEMEN! I PROPOSE THAT ASTRO GO AS AN EMISSARY OF PEACE TO THE SPACE PEOPLE'S SHIP!
YOU REALLY THINK HE CAN DO THAT?
FIRST OF ALL, WE'LL HAVE TO REPAIR HIM...
THE MINISTRY OF SCIENCE HAS BEEN DESTROYED, SO I'LL DO IT AT MY PLACE...
CAN'T GUARANTEE ANYTHING, OF COURSE...
BETTER HURRY, PROFESSOR! IN 24 HOURS A HUGE WAR WILL START!
ONLY TEN MORE HOURS LEFT... WONDER WHAT'S GOING ON...?
IN PREPARATION FOR AN ATTACK, THE EARTH FORCES HAVE ARRAYED THEMSELVES AMONG THE SAND DUNES OF TOTTORI PREFECTURE. ANY MINUTE NOW A TEST LAUNCH OF A GUIDED MISSILE WILL TAKE PLACE...

ONLY *FIVE MORE HOURS* LEFT, PROFESSOR!!

WHA?!

MY GOSH! IT'S *ASTRO BOY!!!*

OKAY, ASTRO! GO TO THE SPACE SHIP AND EXPLAIN TO THE PEOPLE WHAT WE ON EARTH *REALLY* BELIEVE!

YESSIR!

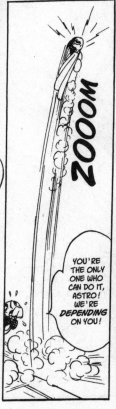

ZOOOM

YOU'RE THE ONLY ONE WHO CAN DO IT, ASTRO! WE'RE *DEPENDING* ON YOU!

RUMBLE CRACKLE RUMBLE

LIGHTNING AND THUNDER....

FLASH

...CAN'T STOP *ME!*

181

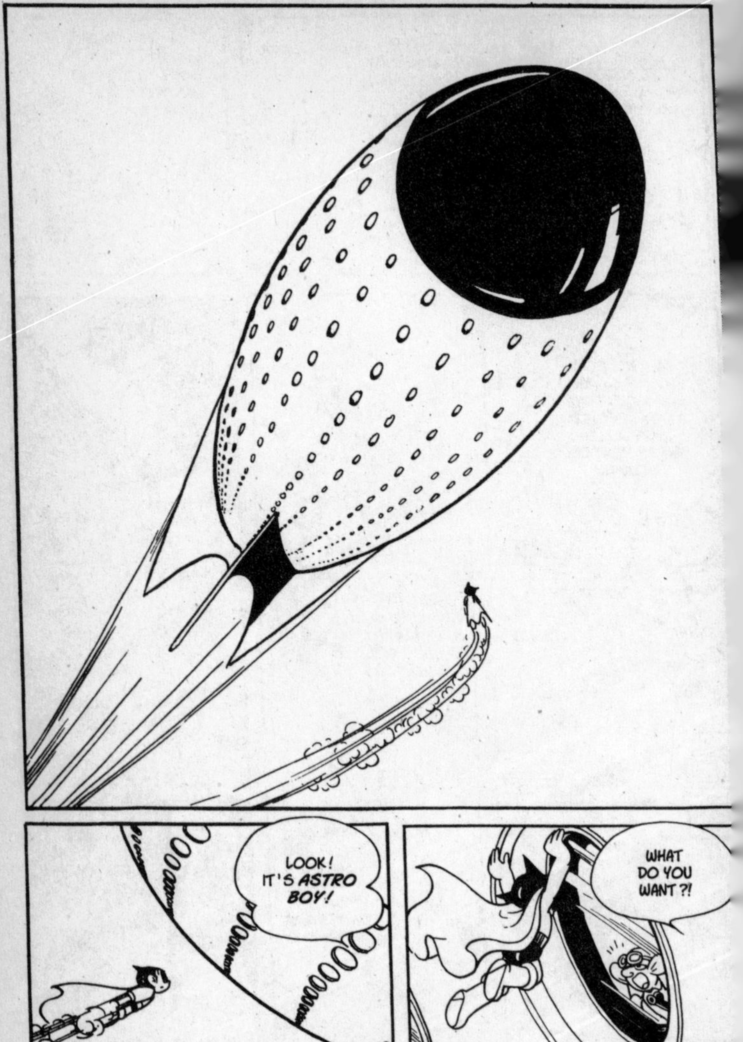
LOOK! IT'S ASTRO BOY!
WHAT DO YOU WANT?!

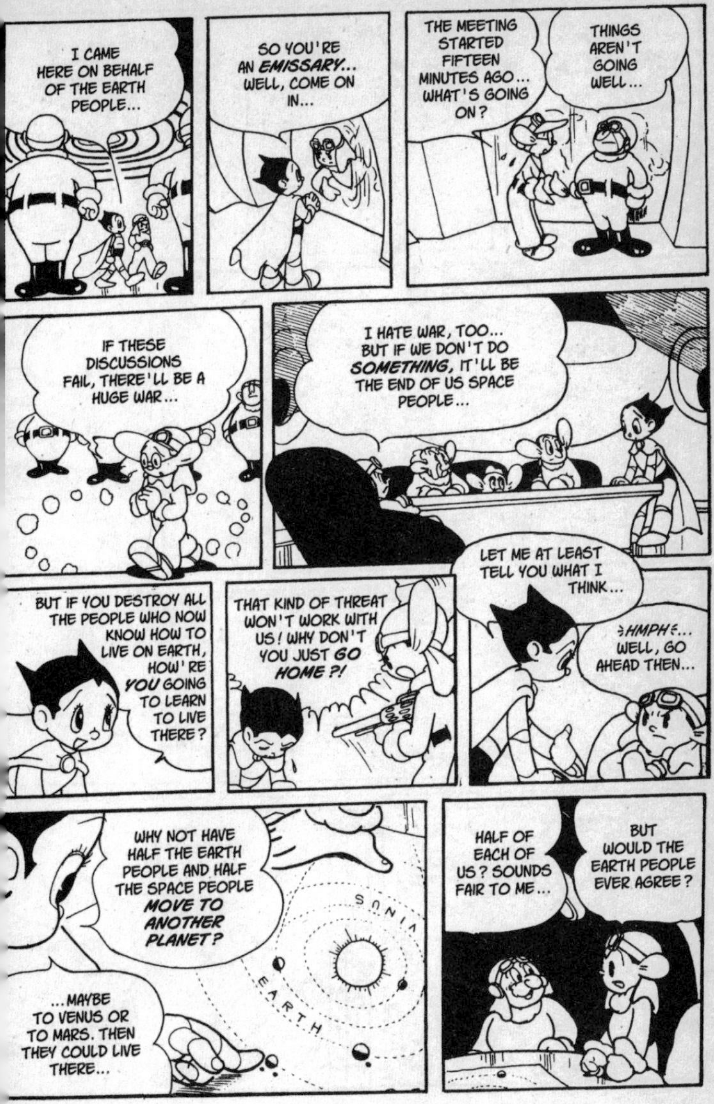
I CAME HERE ON BEHALF OF THE EARTH PEOPLE...
SO YOU'RE AN ***EMISSARY...*** WELL, COME ON IN...
THE MEETING STARTED FIFTEEN MINUTES AGO... WHAT'S GOING ON?
THINGS AREN'T GOING WELL...
IF THESE DISCUSSIONS FAIL, THERE'LL BE A HUGE WAR...
I HATE WAR, TOO... BUT IF WE DON'T DO ***SOMETHING,*** IT'LL BE THE END OF US SPACE PEOPLE...
BUT IF YOU DESTROY ALL THE PEOPLE WHO NOW KNOW HOW TO LIVE ON EARTH, HOW'RE ***YOU*** GOING TO LEARN TO LIVE THERE?
THAT KIND OF THREAT WON'T WORK WITH US! WHY DON'T YOU JUST ***GO HOME?!***
LET ME AT LEAST TELL YOU WHAT I THINK...
HMPH... WELL, GO AHEAD THEN...
WHY NOT HAVE HALF THE EARTH PEOPLE AND HALF THE SPACE PEOPLE ***MOVE TO ANOTHER PLANET?***
VENUS
EARTH
...MAYBE TO VENUS OR TO MARS. THEN THEY COULD LIVE THERE...
HALF OF EACH OF US? SOUNDS FAIR TO ME...
BUT WOULD THE EARTH PEOPLE EVER AGREE?

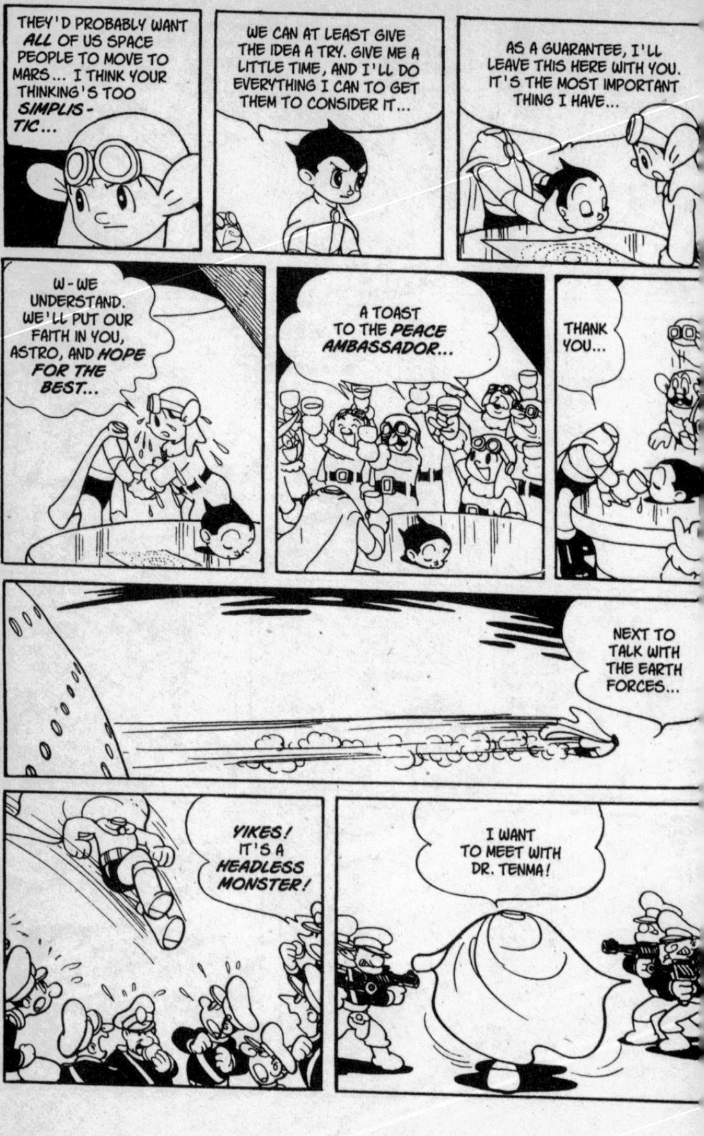
THEY'D PROBABLY WANT ALL OF US SPACE PEOPLE TO MOVE TO MARS... I THINK YOUR THINKING'S TOO SIMPLISTIC...
WE CAN AT LEAST GIVE THE IDEA A TRY. GIVE ME A LITTLE TIME, AND I'LL DO EVERYTHING I CAN TO GET THEM TO CONSIDER IT...
AS A GUARANTEE, I'LL LEAVE THIS HERE WITH YOU. IT'S THE MOST IMPORTANT THING I HAVE...
W-WE UNDERSTAND. WE'LL PUT OUR FAITH IN YOU, ASTRO, AND HOPE FOR THE BEST...
A TOAST TO THE PEACE AMBASSADOR...
THANK YOU...
NEXT TO TALK WITH THE EARTH FORCES...
YIKES! IT'S A HEADLESS MONSTER!
I WANT TO MEET WITH DR. TENMA!

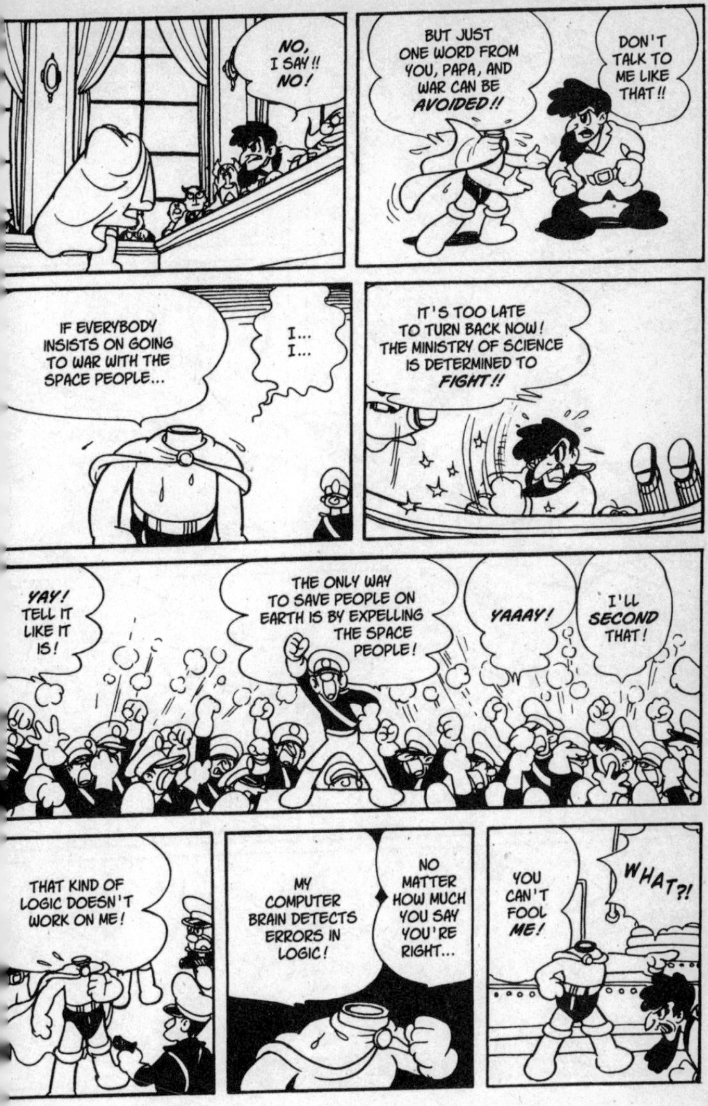
NO, I SAY!! NO!
BUT JUST ONE WORD FROM YOU, PAPA, AND WAR CAN BE AVOIDED!!
DON'T TALK TO ME LIKE THAT!!
IF EVERYBODY INSISTS ON GOING TO WAR WITH THE SPACE PEOPLE...
I... I...
IT'S TOO LATE TO TURN BACK NOW! THE MINISTRY OF SCIENCE IS DETERMINED TO FIGHT!!
YAY! TELL IT LIKE IT IS!
THE ONLY WAY TO SAVE PEOPLE ON EARTH IS BY EXPELLING THE SPACE PEOPLE!
YAAAY!
I'LL SECOND THAT!
THAT KIND OF LOGIC DOESN'T WORK ON ME!
MY COMPUTER BRAIN DETECTS ERRORS IN LOGIC!
NO MATTER HOW MUCH YOU SAY YOU'RE RIGHT...
YOU CAN'T FOOL ME!
WHAT?!

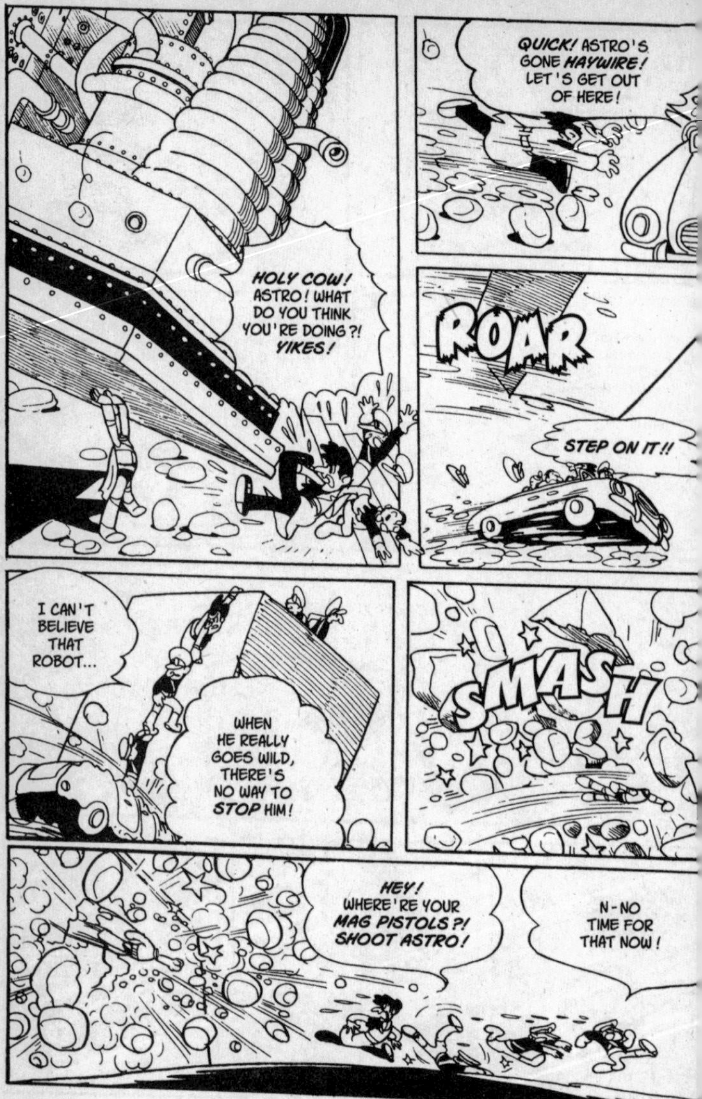
HOLY COW! ASTRO! WHAT DO YOU THINK YOU'RE DOING?! YIKES!
QUICK! ASTRO'S GONE HAYWIRE! LET'S GET OUT OF HERE!
ROAR
STEP ON IT!!
I CAN'T BELIEVE THAT ROBOT...
WHEN HE REALLY GOES WILD, THERE'S NO WAY TO STOP HIM!
SMASH
HEY! WHERE'RE YOUR MAG PISTOLS?! SHOOT ASTRO!
N-NO TIME FOR THAT NOW!

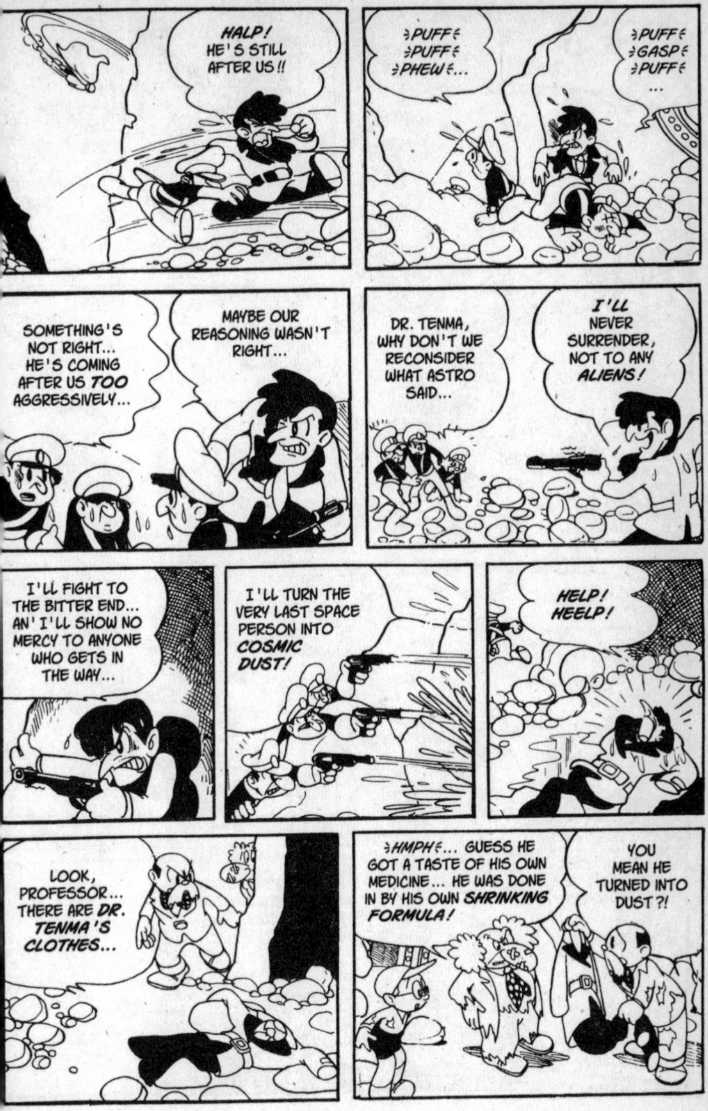
HALP!
HE'S STILL AFTER US!!
≯PUFF≮ ≯PUFF≮ ≯PHEW≮...
≯PUFF≮ ≯GASP≮ ≯PUFF≮ ...
SOMETHING'S NOT RIGHT... HE'S COMING AFTER US TOO AGGRESSIVELY...
MAYBE OUR REASONING WASN'T RIGHT...
DR. TENMA, WHY DON'T WE RECONSIDER WHAT ASTRO SAID...
I'LL NEVER SURRENDER, NOT TO ANY ALIENS!
I'LL FIGHT TO THE BITTER END... AN' I'LL SHOW NO MERCY TO ANYONE WHO GETS IN THE WAY...
I'LL TURN THE VERY LAST SPACE PERSON INTO COSMIC DUST!
HELP! HEELP!
LOOK, PROFESSOR... THERE ARE DR. TENMA'S CLOTHES...
≯HMPH≮... GUESS HE GOT A TASTE OF HIS OWN MEDICINE... HE WAS DONE IN BY HIS OWN SHRINKING FORMULA!
YOU MEAN HE TURNED INTO DUST?!

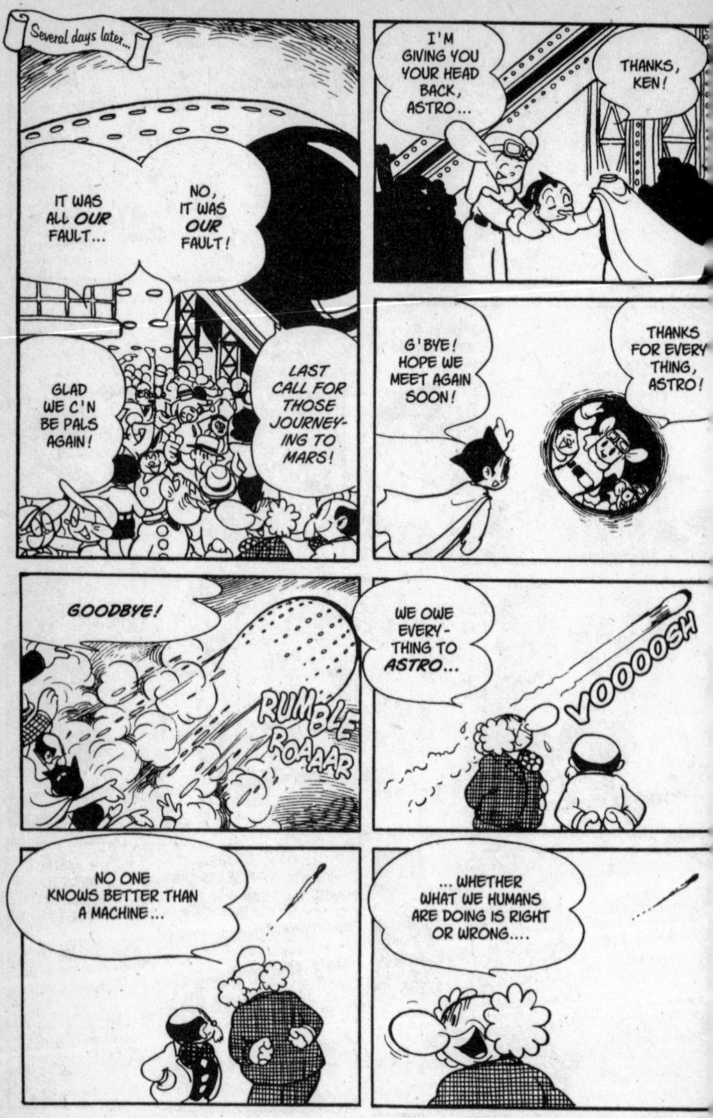
Several days later...
IT WAS ALL OUR FAULT...
NO, IT WAS OUR FAULT!
GLAD WE C'N BE PALS AGAIN!
LAST CALL FOR THOSE JOURNEYING TO MARS!
I'M GIVING YOU YOUR HEAD BACK, ASTRO...
THANKS, KEN!
G'BYE! HOPE WE MEET AGAIN SOON!
THANKS FOR EVERY THING, ASTRO!
GOODBYE!
RUMBLE
ROAAAR
WE OWE EVERY-THING TO ASTRO...
VOOOOSH
NO ONE KNOWS BETTER THAN A MACHINE...
... WHETHER WHAT WE HUMANS ARE DOING IS RIGHT OR WRONG....

GAS PEOPLE

First serialized from April to October 1952 in *Shonen* magazine.

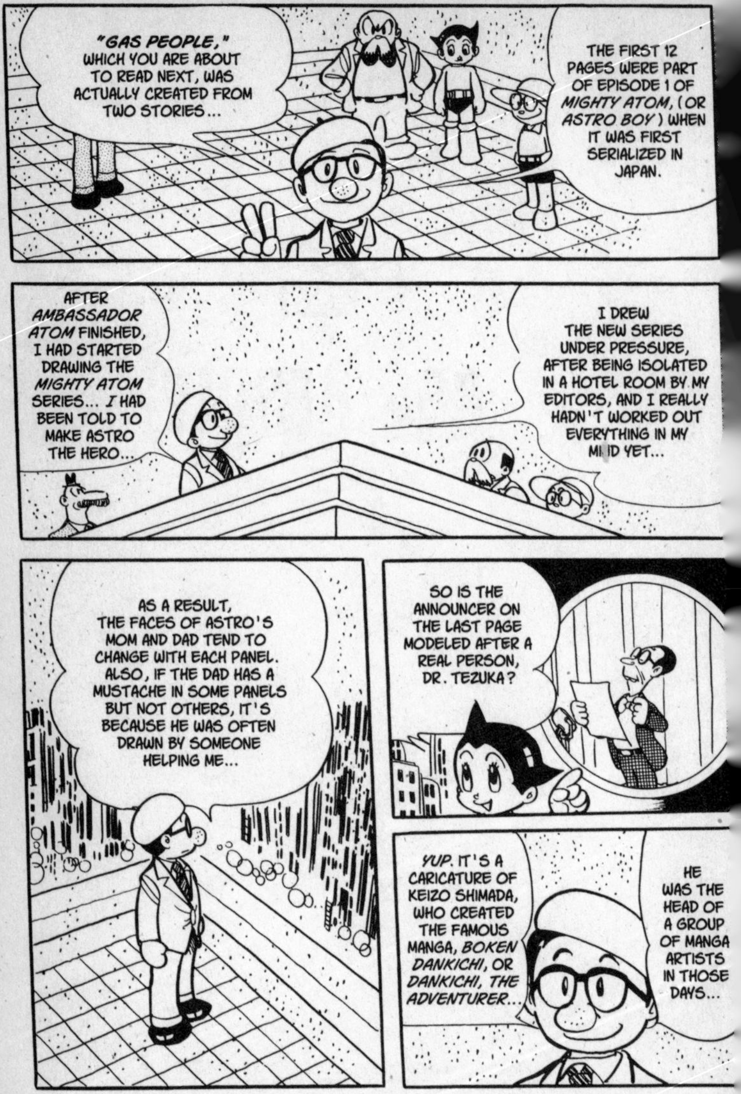
"GAS PEOPLE," WHICH YOU ARE ABOUT TO READ NEXT, WAS ACTUALLY CREATED FROM TWO STORIES...
THE FIRST 12 PAGES WERE PART OF EPISODE 1 OF MIGHTY ATOM, (OR ASTRO BOY) WHEN IT WAS FIRST SERIALIZED IN JAPAN.
AFTER AMBASSADOR ATOM FINISHED, I HAD STARTED DRAWING THE MIGHTY ATOM SERIES... I HAD BEEN TOLD TO MAKE ASTRO THE HERO...
I DREW THE NEW SERIES UNDER PRESSURE, AFTER BEING ISOLATED IN A HOTEL ROOM BY MY EDITORS, AND I REALLY HADN'T WORKED OUT EVERYTHING IN MY MIND YET...
AS A RESULT, THE FACES OF ASTRO'S MOM AND DAD TEND TO CHANGE WITH EACH PANEL. ALSO, IF THE DAD HAS A MUSTACHE IN SOME PANELS BUT NOT OTHERS, IT'S BECAUSE HE WAS OFTEN DRAWN BY SOMEONE HELPING ME...
SO IS THE ANNOUNCER ON THE LAST PAGE MODELED AFTER A REAL PERSON, DR. TEZUKA?
YUP. IT'S A CARICATURE OF KEIZO SHIMADA, WHO CREATED THE FAMOUS MANGA, BOKEN DANKICHI, OR DANKICHI, THE ADVENTURER...
HE WAS THE HEAD OF A GROUP OF MANGA ARTISTS IN THOSE DAYS...

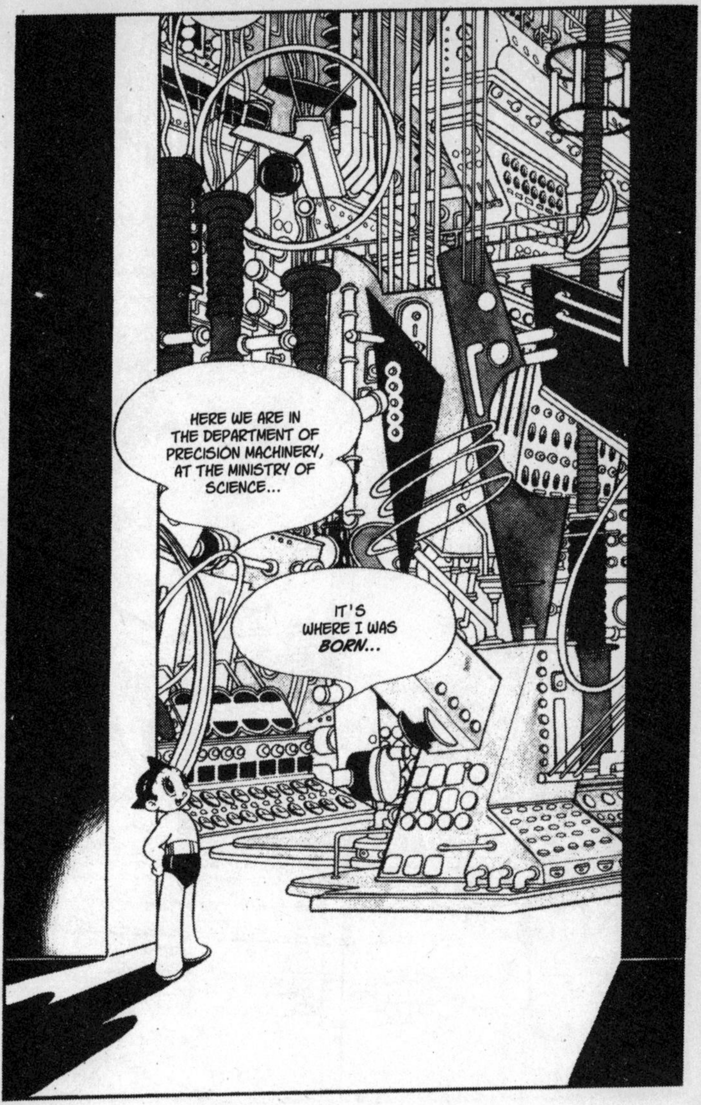
HERE WE ARE IN THE DEPARTMENT OF PRECISION MACHINERY, AT THE MINISTRY OF SCIENCE...
IT'S WHERE I WAS *BORN...*

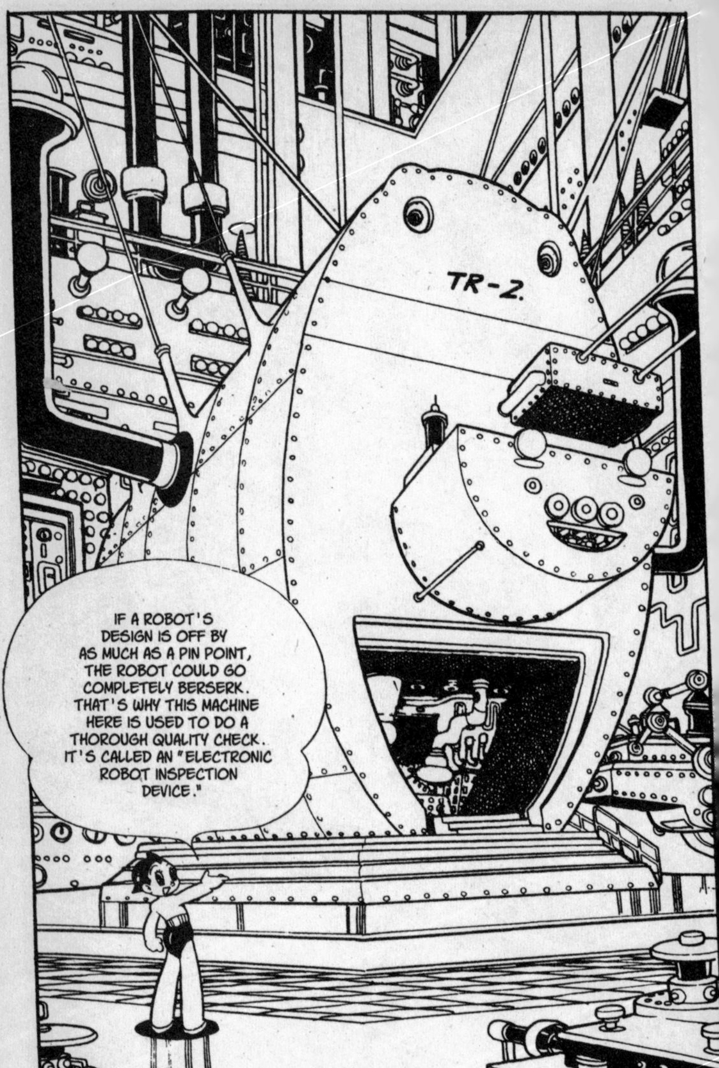
TR-2.
IF A ROBOT'S DESIGN IS OFF BY AS MUCH AS A PIN POINT, THE ROBOT COULD GO COMPLETELY BERSERK. THAT'S WHY THIS MACHINE HERE IS USED TO DO A THOROUGH QUALITY CHECK. IT'S CALLED AN "ELECTRONIC ROBOT INSPECTION DEVICE."

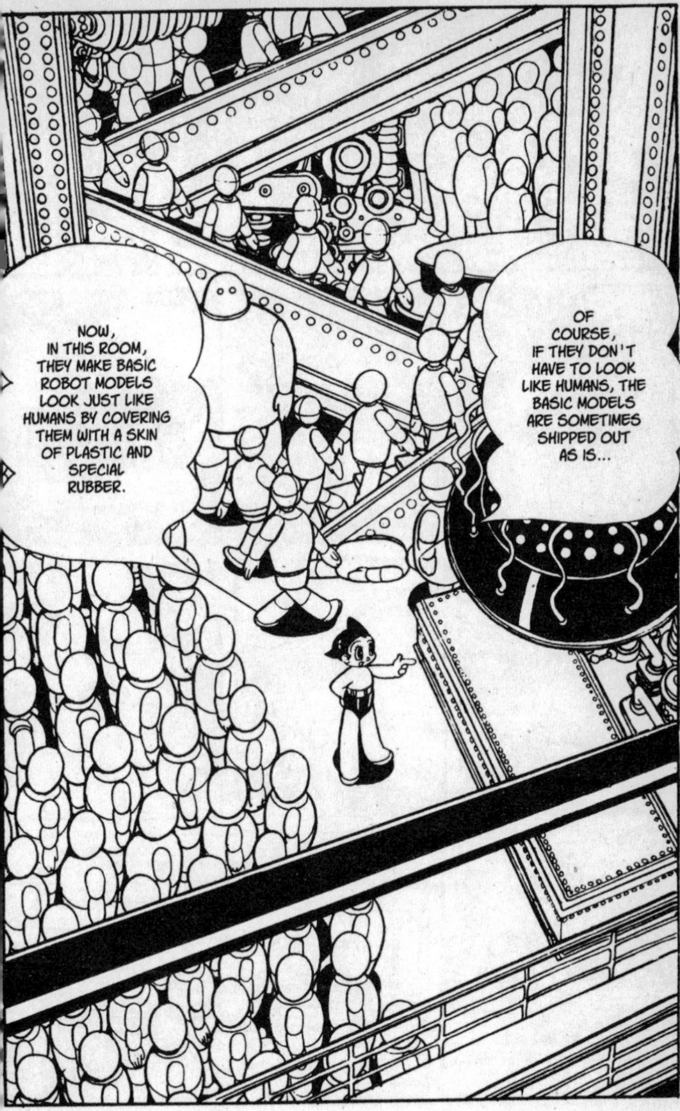
NOW, IN THIS ROOM, THEY MAKE BASIC ROBOT MODELS LOOK JUST LIKE HUMANS BY COVERING THEM WITH A SKIN OF PLASTIC AND SPECIAL RUBBER.
OF COURSE, IF THEY DON'T HAVE TO LOOK LIKE HUMANS, THE BASIC MODELS ARE SOMETIMES SHIPPED OUT AS IS...

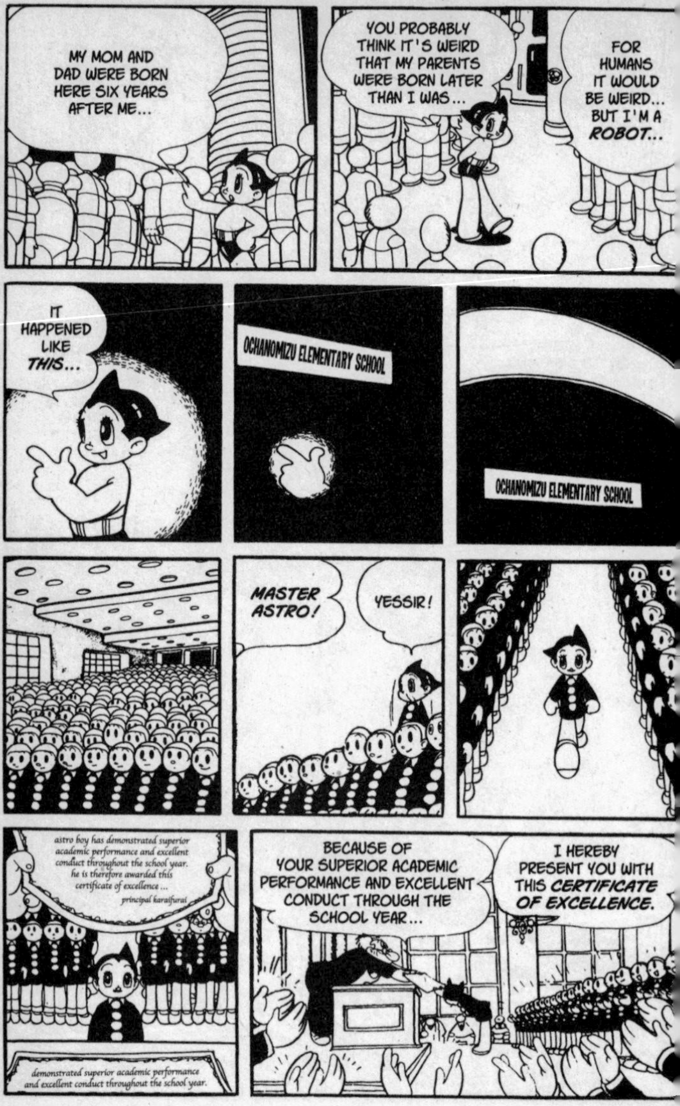
MY MOM AND DAD WERE BORN HERE SIX YEARS AFTER ME...
YOU PROBABLY THINK IT'S WEIRD THAT MY PARENTS WERE BORN LATER THAN I WAS...
FOR HUMANS IT WOULD BE WEIRD... BUT I'M A ROBOT...
IT HAPPENED LIKE THIS...
OCHANOMIZU ELEMENTARY SCHOOL
OCHANOMIZU ELEMENTARY SCHOOL
MASTER ASTRO!
YESSIR!
astro boy has demonstrated superior academic performance and excellent conduct throughout the school year. he is therefore awarded this certificate of excellence ...
principal karaifurai
demonstrated superior academic performance and excellent conduct throughout the school year.
BECAUSE OF YOUR SUPERIOR ACADEMIC PERFORMANCE AND EXCELLENT CONDUCT THROUGH THE SCHOOL YEAR...
I HEREBY PRESENT YOU WITH THIS CERTIFICATE OF EXCELLENCE.

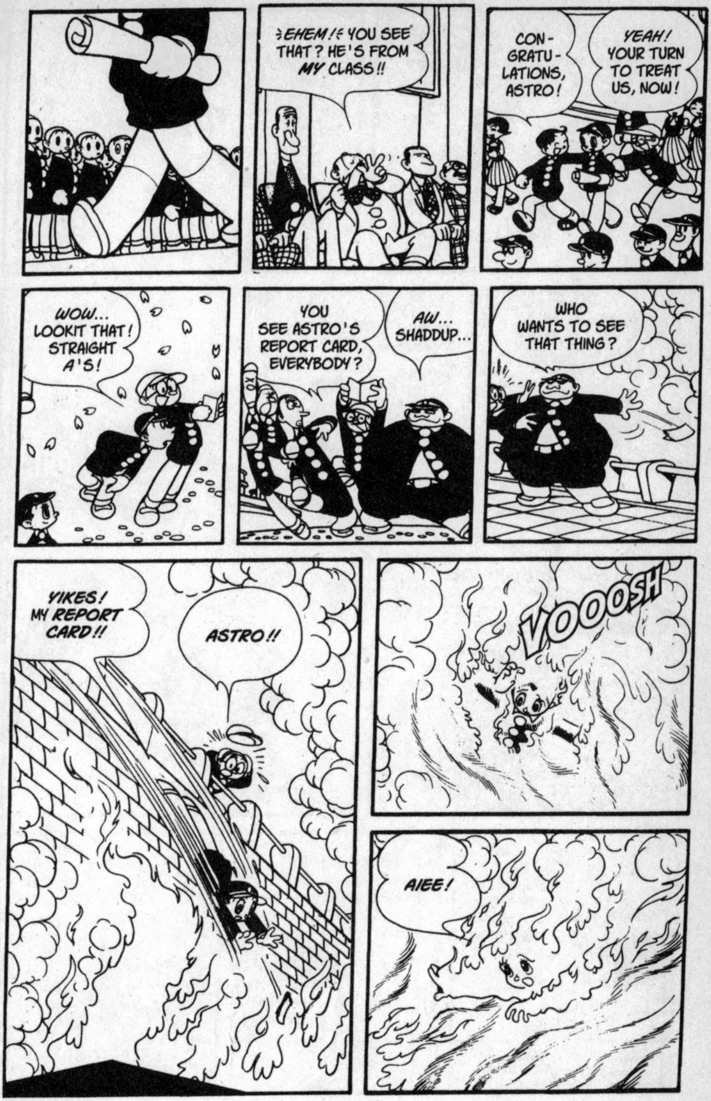
EHEM! YOU SEE THAT? HE'S FROM MY CLASS!!
CON-GRATU-LATIONS, ASTRO!
YEAH! YOUR TURN TO TREAT US, NOW!
WOW... LOOKIT THAT! STRAIGHT A'S!
YOU SEE ASTRO'S REPORT CARD, EVERYBODY?
AW... SHADDUP...
WHO WANTS TO SEE THAT THING?
YIKES! MY REPORT CARD!!
ASTRO!!
VOOOSH
AIEE!

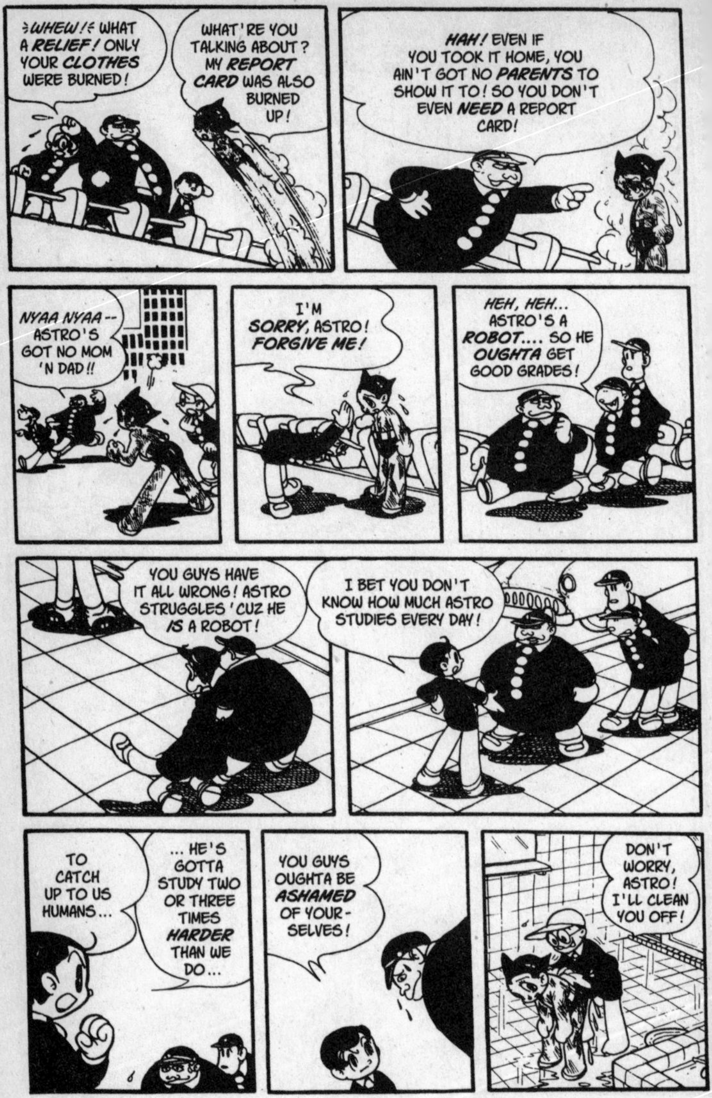

WHEW! WHAT A RELIEF! ONLY YOUR CLOTHES WERE BURNED!
WHAT'RE YOU TALKING ABOUT? MY REPORT CARD WAS ALSO BURNED UP!
HAH! EVEN IF YOU TOOK IT HOME, YOU AIN'T GOT NO PARENTS TO SHOW IT TO! SO YOU DON'T EVEN NEED A REPORT CARD!
NYAA NYAA -- ASTRO'S GOT NO MOM 'N DAD!!
I'M SORRY, ASTRO! FORGIVE ME!
HEH, HEH... ASTRO'S A ROBOT.... SO HE OUGHTA GET GOOD GRADES!
YOU GUYS HAVE IT ALL WRONG! ASTRO STRUGGLES 'CUZ HE IS A ROBOT!
I BET YOU DON'T KNOW HOW MUCH ASTRO STUDIES EVERY DAY!
TO CATCH UP TO US HUMANS...
... HE'S GOTTA STUDY TWO OR THREE TIMES HARDER THAN WE DO...
YOU GUYS OUGHTA BE ASHAMED OF YOUR-SELVES!
DON'T WORRY, ASTRO! I'LL CLEAN YOU OFF!

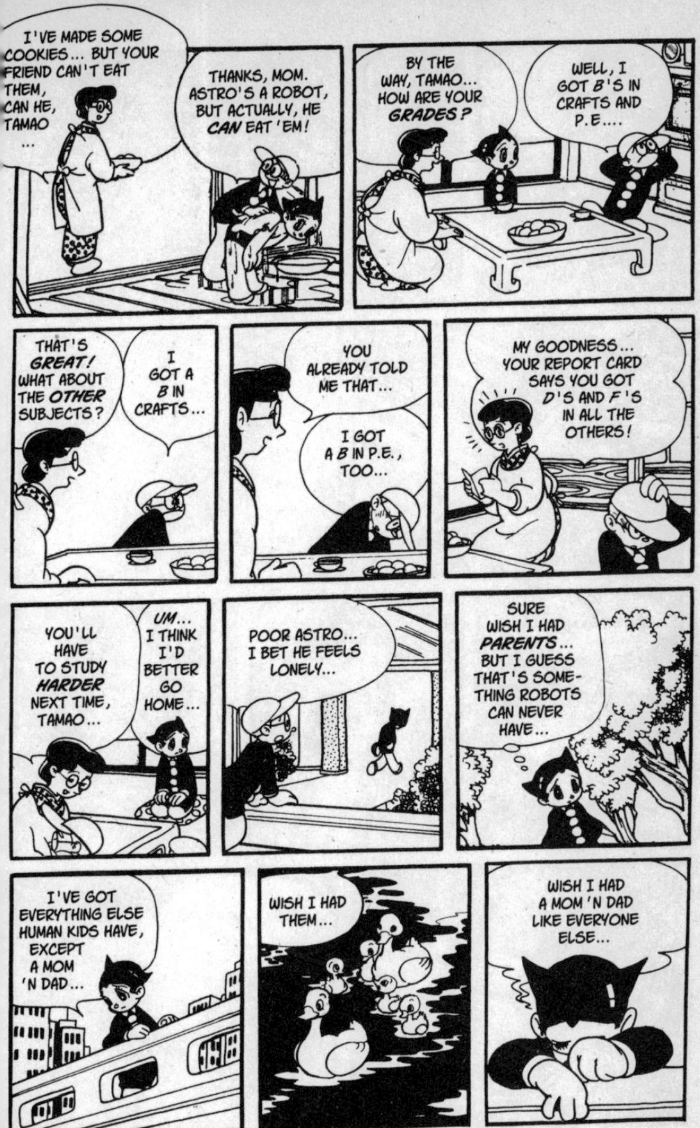
I'VE MADE SOME COOKIES... BUT YOUR FRIEND CAN'T EAT THEM, CAN HE, TAMAO ...
THANKS, MOM. ASTRO'S A ROBOT, BUT ACTUALLY, HE CAN EAT 'EM!
BY THE WAY, TAMAO... HOW ARE YOUR GRADES?
WELL, I GOT B'S IN CRAFTS AND P.E....
THAT'S GREAT! WHAT ABOUT THE OTHER SUBJECTS?
I GOT A B IN CRAFTS...
YOU ALREADY TOLD ME THAT...
I GOT A B IN P.E., TOO...
MY GOODNESS... YOUR REPORT CARD SAYS YOU GOT D'S AND F'S IN ALL THE OTHERS!
YOU'LL HAVE TO STUDY HARDER NEXT TIME, TAMAO...
UM... I THINK I'D BETTER GO HOME...
POOR ASTRO... I BET HE FEELS LONELY...
SURE WISH I HAD PARENTS... BUT I GUESS THAT'S SOMETHING ROBOTS CAN NEVER HAVE...
I'VE GOT EVERYTHING ELSE HUMAN KIDS HAVE, EXCEPT A MOM 'N DAD...
WISH I HAD THEM...
WISH I HAD A MOM 'N DAD LIKE EVERYONE ELSE...

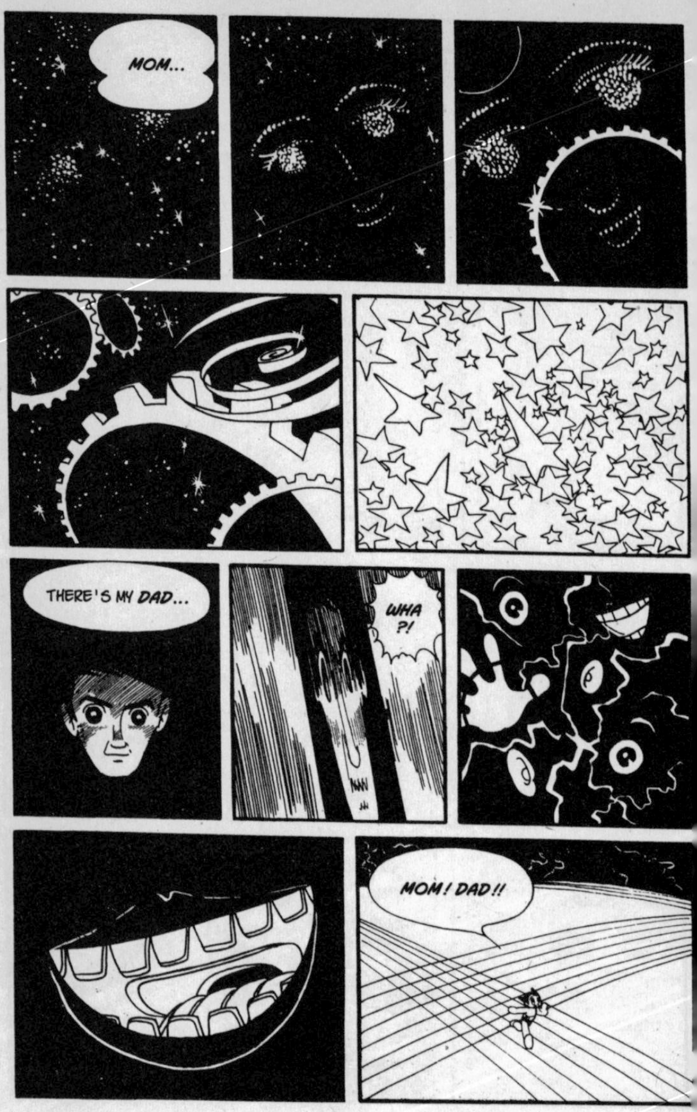
MOM...
THERE'S MY DAD...
WHA ?!
MOM! DAD!!

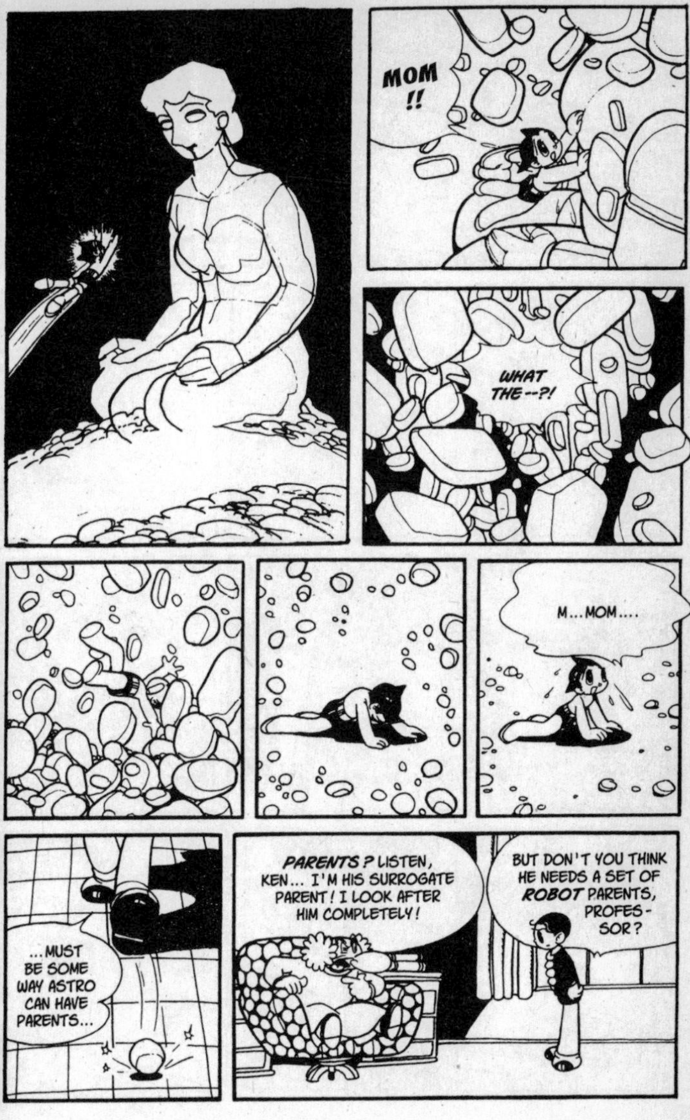
MOM !!
WHAT THE--?!
M...MOM....
...MUST BE SOME WAY ASTRO CAN HAVE PARENTS...
PARENTS? LISTEN, KEN... I'M HIS SURROGATE PARENT! I LOOK AFTER HIM COMPLETELY!
BUT DON'T YOU THINK HE NEEDS A SET OF ROBOT PARENTS, PROFES-SOR?

GOSH, KEN... I NEVER THOUGHT OF THAT! LET'S GO FIND HIM A PAIR!

WELL, PROFESSOR... I'VE HAD LOTS OF REQUESTS FOR *ROBOTS*, BUT NEVER FOR *ROBOT PARENTS*...

NOW'S YOUR CHANCE TO SHOW WHAT YOU CAN DO! I WANT A GREAT MOM AND DAD FOR ASTRO!

OKAY, THEN... PICK A FACE FROM AMONG THESE!

WHAT ?! NOBODY WANTS PARENTS THAT LOOK LIKE *IDIOTS!!*

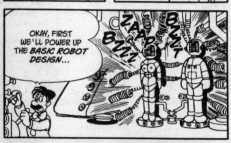

OKAY, FIRST WE'LL POWER UP THE *BASIC ROBOT DESIGN*...

ZAAP BZZZ BZZT BZZZ

THEN WE APPLY A *PLASTIC SKIN*...

NOW FOR THE *FACE!*

HE'S FINALLY TAKING SHAPE...

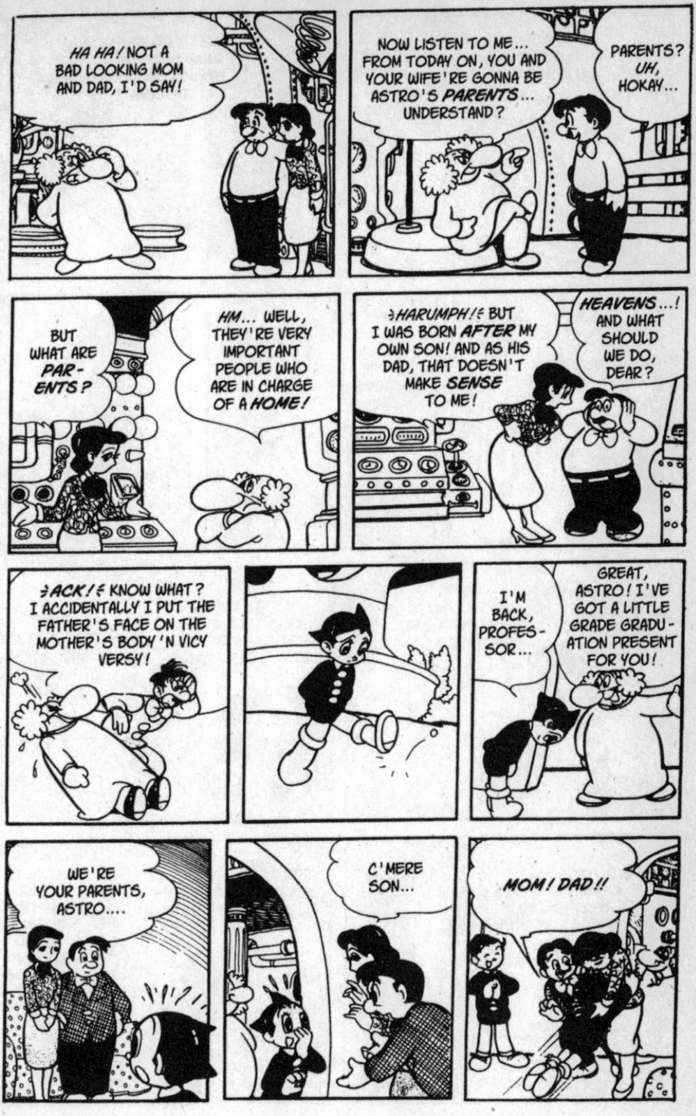
HA HA! NOT A BAD LOOKING MOM AND DAD, I'D SAY!
NOW LISTEN TO ME... FROM TODAY ON, YOU AND YOUR WIFE'RE GONNA BE ASTRO'S PARENTS... UNDERSTAND?
PARENTS? UH, HOKAY...
BUT WHAT ARE PAR-ENTS?
HM... WELL, THEY'RE VERY IMPORTANT PEOPLE WHO ARE IN CHARGE OF A HOME!
HARUMPH! BUT I WAS BORN AFTER MY OWN SON! AND AS HIS DAD, THAT DOESN'T MAKE SENSE TO ME!
HEAVENS...! AND WHAT SHOULD WE DO, DEAR?
ACK! KNOW WHAT? I ACCIDENTALLY I PUT THE FATHER'S FACE ON THE MOTHER'S BODY 'N VICY VERSY!
I'M BACK, PROFES-SOR...
GREAT, ASTRO! I'VE GOT A LITTLE GRADE GRADU-ATION PRESENT FOR YOU!
WE'RE YOUR PARENTS, ASTRO....
C'MERE SON...
MOM! DAD!!

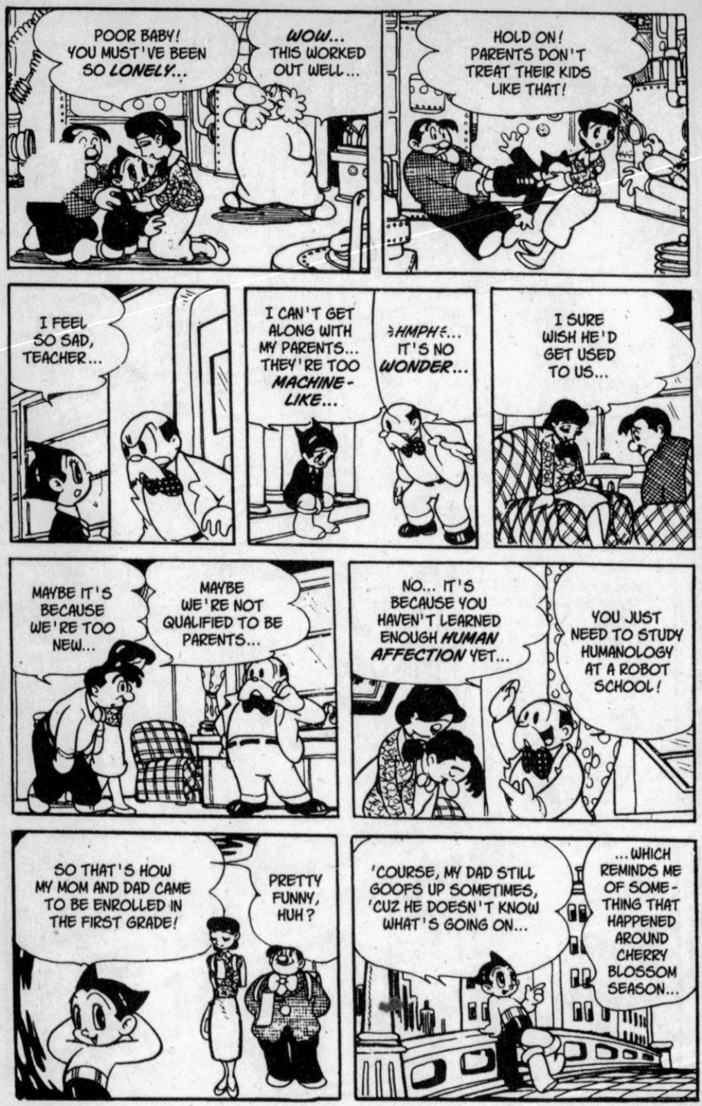
POOR BABY! YOU MUST'VE BEEN SO *LONELY*...
WOW... THIS WORKED OUT WELL...
HOLD ON! PARENTS DON'T TREAT THEIR KIDS LIKE THAT!
I FEEL SO SAD, TEACHER...
I CAN'T GET ALONG WITH MY PARENTS... THEY'RE TOO *MACHINE-LIKE*...
HMPH... IT'S NO *WONDER*...
I SURE WISH HE'D GET USED TO US...
MAYBE IT'S BECAUSE WE'RE TOO NEW...
MAYBE WE'RE NOT QUALIFIED TO BE PARENTS...
NO... IT'S BECAUSE YOU HAVEN'T LEARNED ENOUGH *HUMAN AFFECTION* YET...
YOU JUST NEED TO STUDY HUMANOLOGY AT A ROBOT SCHOOL!
SO THAT'S HOW MY MOM AND DAD CAME TO BE ENROLLED IN THE FIRST GRADE!
PRETTY FUNNY, HUH?
'COURSE, MY DAD STILL GOOFS UP SOMETIMES, 'CUZ HE DOESN'T KNOW WHAT'S GOING ON...
...WHICH REMINDS ME OF SOME-THING THAT HAPPENED AROUND CHERRY BLOSSOM SEASON...

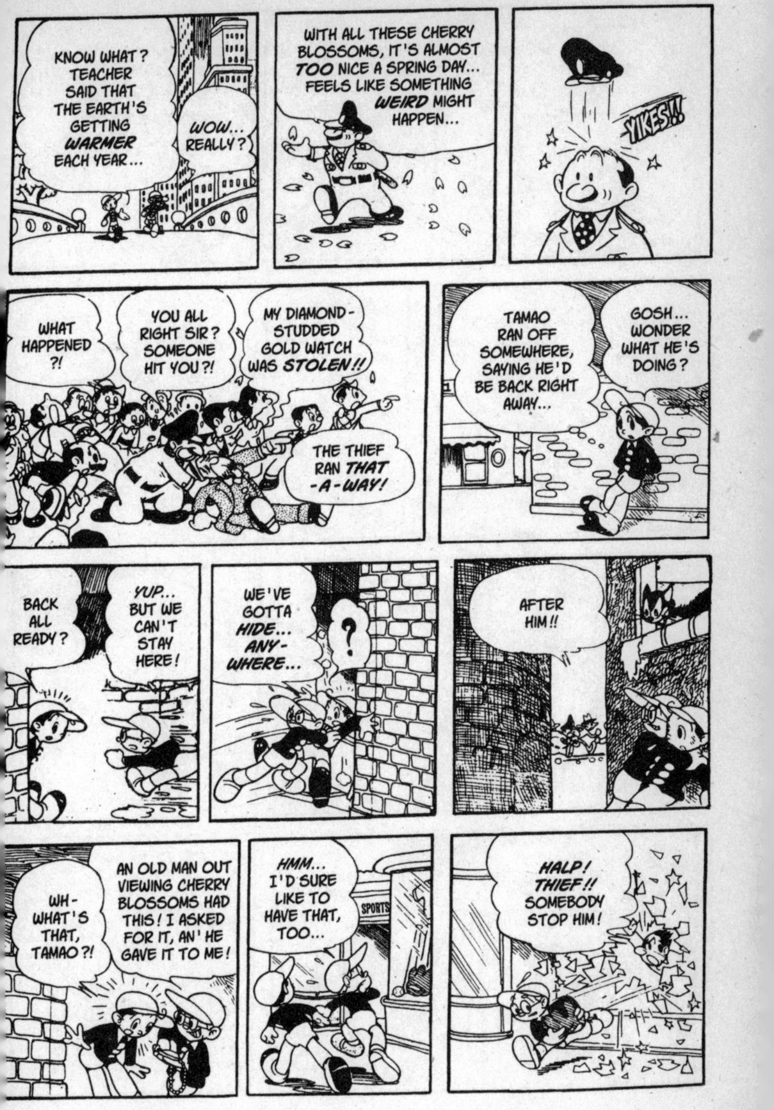
KNOW WHAT? TEACHER SAID THAT THE EARTH'S GETTING WARMER EACH YEAR...
WOW... REALLY?
WITH ALL THESE CHERRY BLOSSOMS, IT'S ALMOST TOO NICE A SPRING DAY... FEELS LIKE SOMETHING WEIRD MIGHT HAPPEN...
YIKES!!
WHAT HAPPENED?!
YOU ALL RIGHT SIR? SOMEONE HIT YOU?!
MY DIAMOND-STUDDED GOLD WATCH WAS STOLEN!!
THE THIEF RAN THAT-A-WAY!
TAMAO RAN OFF SOMEWHERE, SAYING HE'D BE BACK RIGHT AWAY...
GOSH... WONDER WHAT HE'S DOING?
BACK ALL READY?
YUP... BUT WE CAN'T STAY HERE!
WE'VE GOTTA HIDE... ANY-WHERE...
?
AFTER HIM!!
WH-WHAT'S THAT, TAMAO?!
AN OLD MAN OUT VIEWING CHERRY BLOSSOMS HAD THIS! I ASKED FOR IT, AN' HE GAVE IT TO ME!
HMM... I'D SURE LIKE TO HAVE THAT, TOO...
SPORTS
HALP! THIEF!! SOMEBODY STOP HIM!

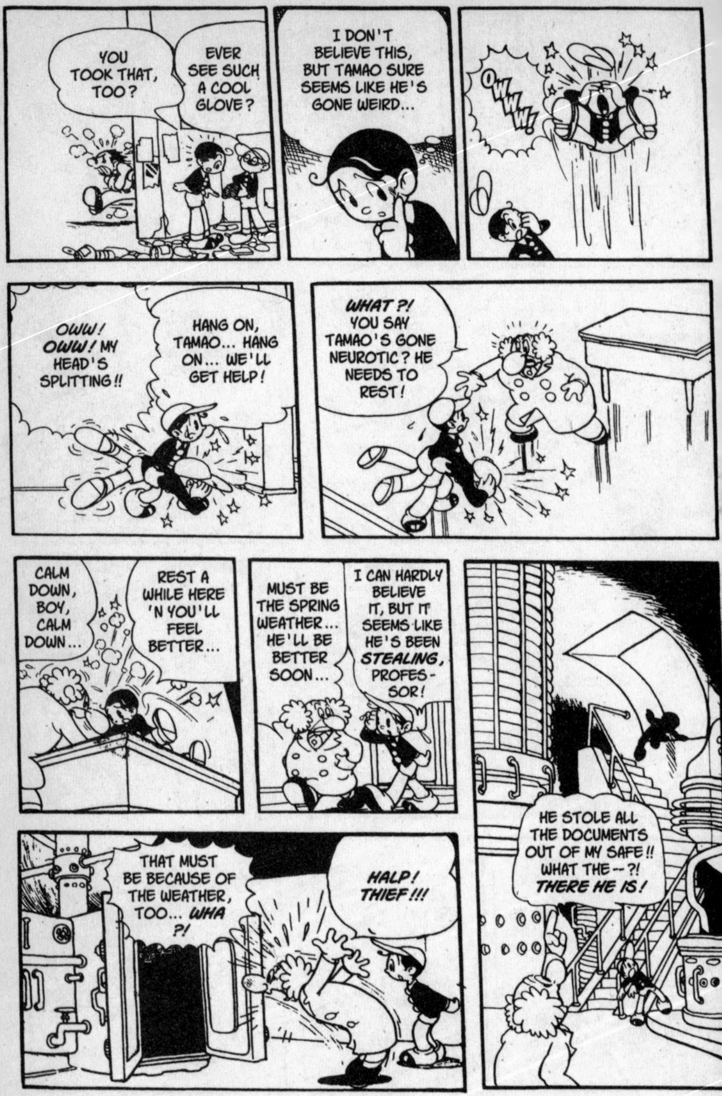
YOU TOOK THAT, TOO?
EVER SEE SUCH A COOL GLOVE?
I DON'T BELIEVE THIS, BUT TAMAO SURE SEEMS LIKE HE'S GONE WEIRD...
OWWW!
OWW! OWW! MY HEAD'S SPLITTING!!
HANG ON, TAMAO... HANG ON... WE'LL GET HELP!
WHAT?! YOU SAY TAMAO'S GONE NEUROTIC? HE NEEDS TO REST!
CALM DOWN, BOY, CALM DOWN...
REST A WHILE HERE 'N YOU'LL FEEL BETTER...
MUST BE THE SPRING WEATHER... HE'LL BE BETTER SOON...
I CAN HARDLY BELIEVE IT, BUT IT SEEMS LIKE HE'S BEEN STEALING, PROFES-SOR!
THAT MUST BE BECAUSE OF THE WEATHER, TOO... WHA?!
HALP! THIEF!!!
HE STOLE ALL THE DOCUMENTS OUT OF MY SAFE!! WHAT THE--?! THERE HE IS!

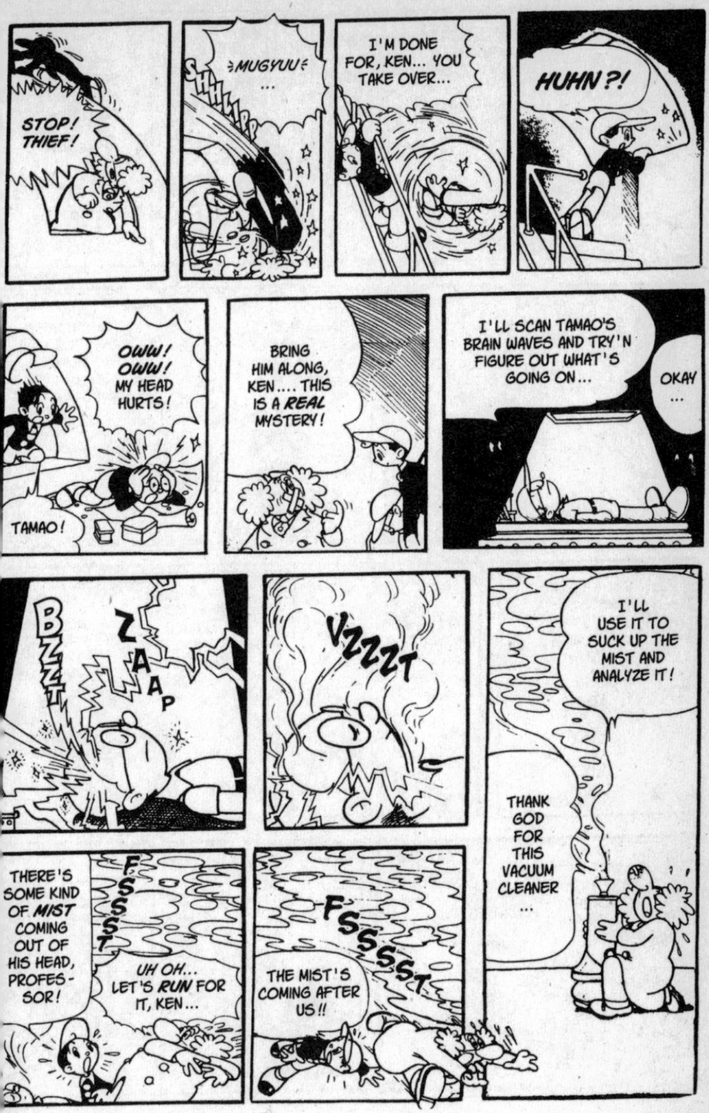
STOP! THIEF!
SHHLIPP
MUGYUU ...
I'M DONE FOR, KEN... YOU TAKE OVER...
HUHN?!
OWW! OWW! MY HEAD HURTS!
TAMAO!
BRING HIM ALONG, KEN.... THIS IS A *REAL* MYSTERY!
I'LL SCAN TAMAO'S BRAIN WAVES AND TRY'N FIGURE OUT WHAT'S GOING ON...
OKAY ...
BZZZT
ZAAAP
VZZZZT
THERE'S SOME KIND OF *MIST* COMING OUT OF HIS HEAD, PROFES-SOR!
FSSST
UH OH... LET'S *RUN* FOR IT, KEN...
FSSSSST
THE MIST'S COMING AFTER US!!
I'LL USE IT TO SUCK UP THE MIST AND ANALYZE IT!
THANK GOD FOR THIS VACUUM CLEANER ...

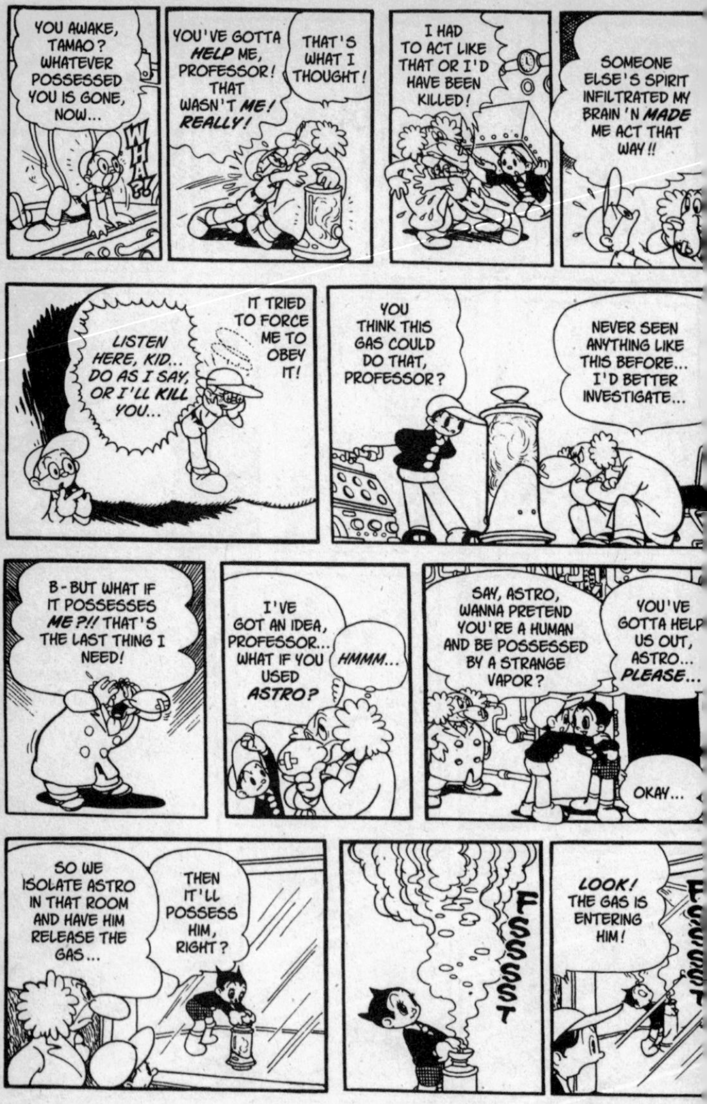
YOU AWAKE, TAMAO? WHATEVER POSSESSED YOU IS GONE, NOW...
WHA?!
YOU'VE GOTTA HELP ME, PROFESSOR! THAT WASN'T ME! REALLY!
THAT'S WHAT I THOUGHT!
I HAD TO ACT LIKE THAT OR I'D HAVE BEEN KILLED!
SOMEONE ELSE'S SPIRIT INFILTRATED MY BRAIN 'N MADE ME ACT THAT WAY!!
LISTEN HERE, KID... DO AS I SAY, OR I'LL KILL YOU...
IT TRIED TO FORCE ME TO OBEY IT!
YOU THINK THIS GAS COULD DO THAT, PROFESSOR?
NEVER SEEN ANYTHING LIKE THIS BEFORE... I'D BETTER INVESTIGATE...
B-BUT WHAT IF IT POSSESSES ME?!! THAT'S THE LAST THING I NEED!
I'VE GOT AN IDEA, PROFESSOR... WHAT IF YOU USED ASTRO?
HMMM...
SAY, ASTRO, WANNA PRETEND YOU'RE A HUMAN AND BE POSSESSED BY A STRANGE VAPOR?
YOU'VE GOTTA HELP US OUT, ASTRO... PLEASE...
OKAY...
SO WE ISOLATE ASTRO IN THAT ROOM AND HAVE HIM RELEASE THE GAS...
THEN IT'LL POSSESS HIM, RIGHT?
FSSSST
LOOK! THE GAS IS ENTERING HIM!
FSSSST

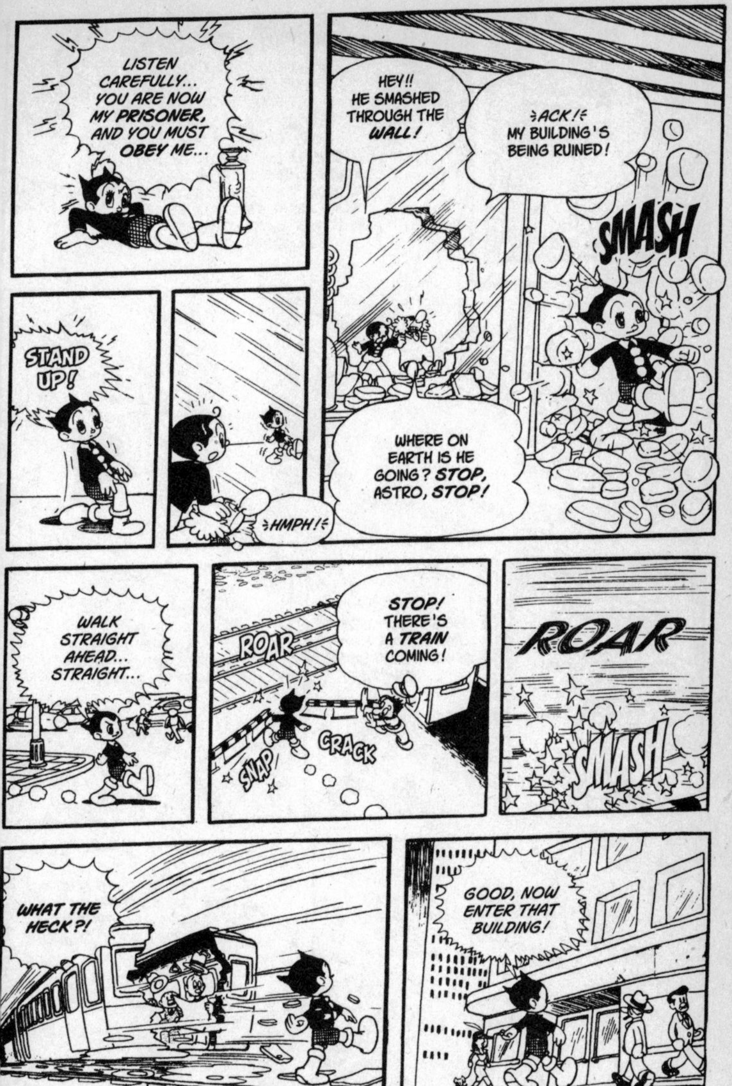

LISTEN CAREFULLY... YOU ARE NOW MY PRISONER, AND YOU MUST OBEY ME...
STAND UP!
HMPH!
HEY!! HE SMASHED THROUGH THE WALL!
ACK! MY BUILDING'S BEING RUINED!
SMASH
WHERE ON EARTH IS HE GOING? STOP, ASTRO, STOP!
WALK STRAIGHT AHEAD... STRAIGHT...
ROAR
STOP! THERE'S A TRAIN COMING!
SNAP
CRACK
ROAR
SMASH
WHAT THE HECK?!
GOOD, NOW ENTER THAT BUILDING!

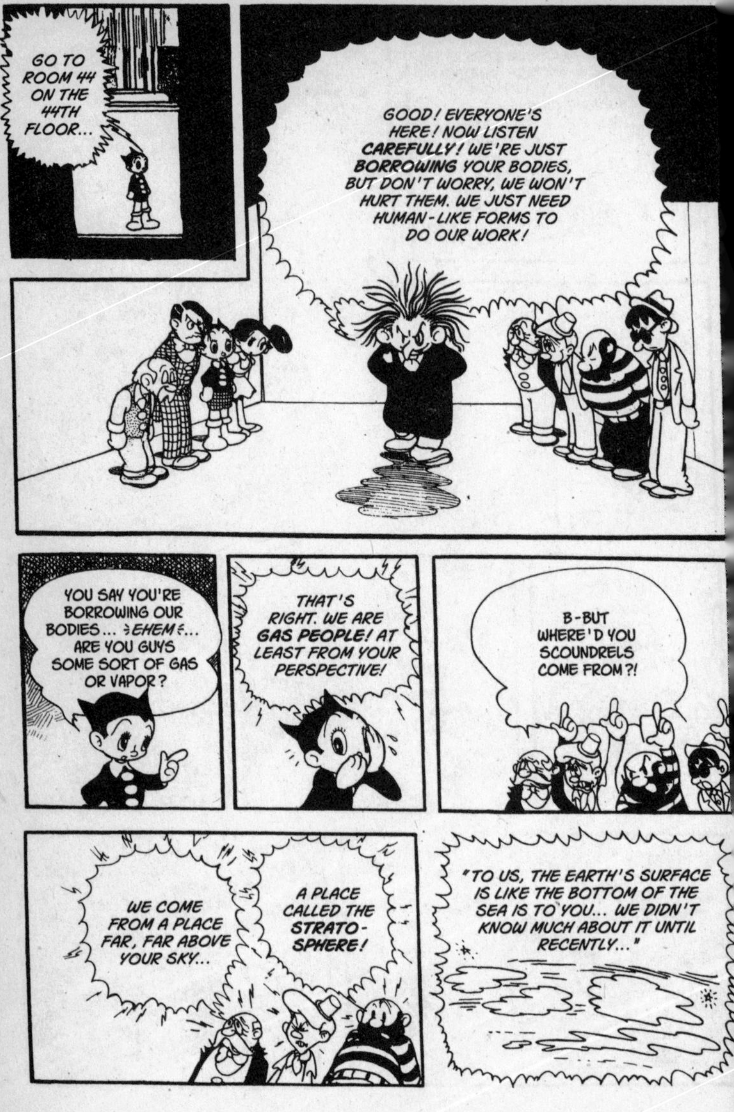
GO TO ROOM 44 ON THE 44TH FLOOR...
GOOD! EVERYONE'S HERE! NOW LISTEN CAREFULLY! WE'RE JUST BORROWING YOUR BODIES, BUT DON'T WORRY, WE WON'T HURT THEM. WE JUST NEED HUMAN-LIKE FORMS TO DO OUR WORK!
YOU SAY YOU'RE BORROWING OUR BODIES... ≷EHEM≶... ARE YOU GUYS SOME SORT OF GAS OR VAPOR?
THAT'S RIGHT. WE ARE GAS PEOPLE! AT LEAST FROM YOUR PERSPECTIVE!
B-BUT WHERE'D YOU SCOUNDRELS COME FROM?!
WE COME FROM A PLACE FAR, FAR ABOVE YOUR SKY...
A PLACE CALLED THE STRATO-SPHERE!
"TO US, THE EARTH'S SURFACE IS LIKE THE BOTTOM OF THE SEA IS TO YOU... WE DIDN'T KNOW MUCH ABOUT IT UNTIL RECENTLY..."

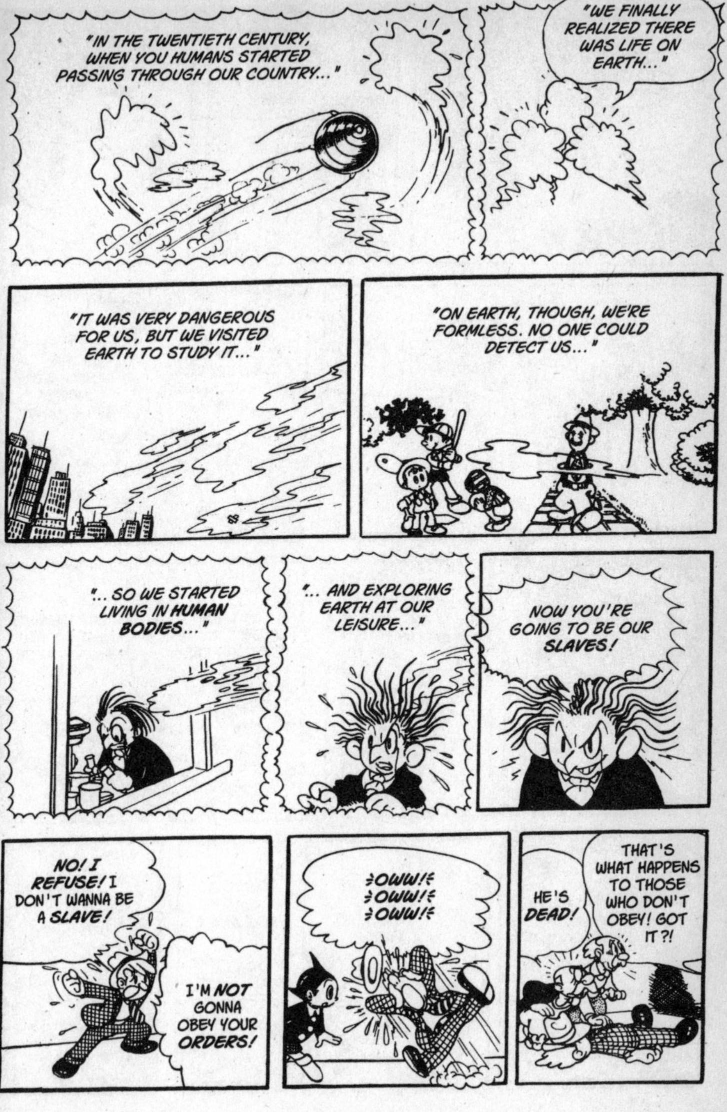
"IN THE TWENTIETH CENTURY, WHEN YOU HUMANS STARTED PASSING THROUGH OUR COUNTRY..."
"WE FINALLY REALIZED THERE WAS LIFE ON EARTH..."
"IT WAS VERY DANGEROUS FOR US, BUT WE VISITED EARTH TO STUDY IT..."
"ON EARTH, THOUGH, WE'RE FORMLESS. NO ONE COULD DETECT US..."
"... SO WE STARTED LIVING IN **HUMAN BODIES**..."
"... AND EXPLORING EARTH AT OUR LEISURE..."
NOW YOU'RE GOING TO BE OUR **SLAVES!**
NO! I REFUSE! I DON'T WANNA BE A **SLAVE!**
I'M **NOT** GONNA OBEY YOUR **ORDERS!**
OWW!! OWW!! OWW!!
HE'S **DEAD!**
THAT'S WHAT HAPPENS TO THOSE WHO DON'T OBEY! GOT IT?!

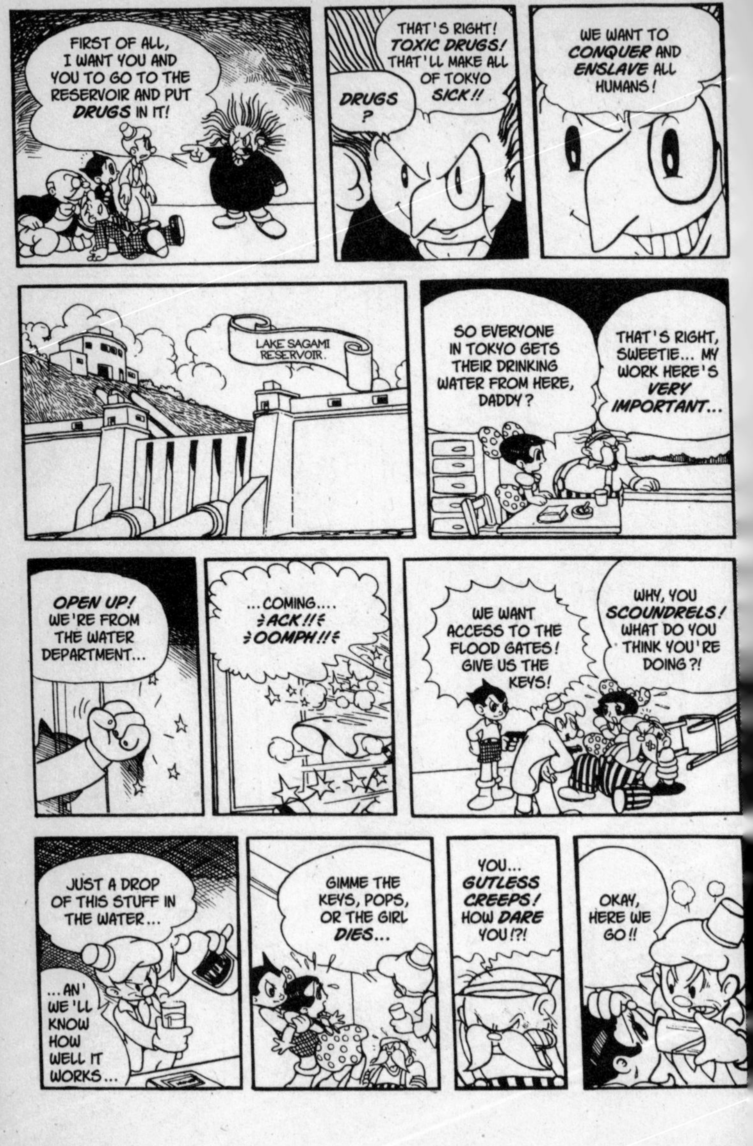
FIRST OF ALL, I WANT YOU AND YOU TO GO TO THE RESERVOIR AND PUT DRUGS IN IT!
DRUGS?
THAT'S RIGHT! TOXIC DRUGS! THAT'LL MAKE ALL OF TOKYO SICK!!
WE WANT TO CONQUER AND ENSLAVE ALL HUMANS!
LAKE SAGAMI RESERVOIR.
SO EVERYONE IN TOKYO GETS THEIR DRINKING WATER FROM HERE, DADDY?
THAT'S RIGHT, SWEETIE... MY WORK HERE'S VERY IMPORTANT...
OPEN UP! WE'RE FROM THE WATER DEPARTMENT...
...COMING....
ACK!!
OOMPH!!
WE WANT ACCESS TO THE FLOOD GATES! GIVE US THE KEYS!
WHY, YOU SCOUNDRELS! WHAT DO YOU THINK YOU'RE DOING?!
JUST A DROP OF THIS STUFF IN THE WATER...
...AN' WE'LL KNOW HOW WELL IT WORKS...
GIMME THE KEYS, POPS, OR THE GIRL DIES...
YOU... GUTLESS CREEPS! HOW DARE YOU!?!
OKAY, HERE WE GO!!

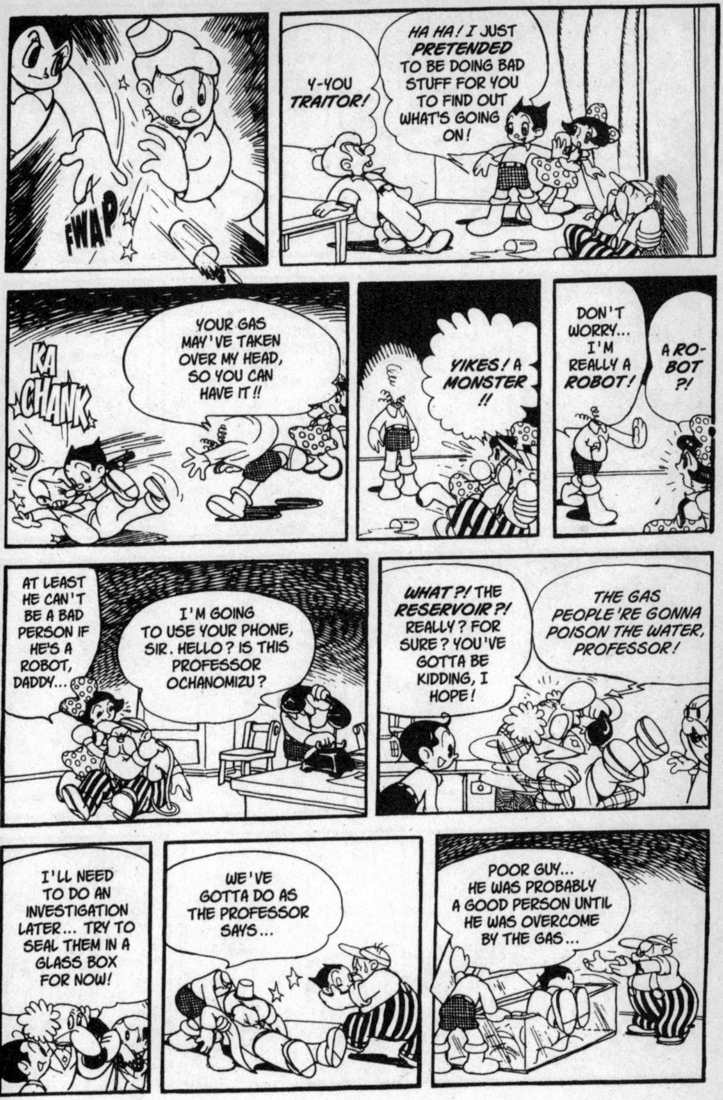
FWAP
Y-YOU TRAITOR!
HA HA! I JUST PRETENDED TO BE DOING BAD STUFF FOR YOU TO FIND OUT WHAT'S GOING ON!
KA CHANK
YOUR GAS MAY'VE TAKEN OVER MY HEAD, SO YOU CAN HAVE IT!!
YIKES! A MONSTER!!
DON'T WORRY... I'M REALLY A ROBOT!
A RO-BOT?!
AT LEAST HE CAN'T BE A BAD PERSON IF HE'S A ROBOT, DADDY...
I'M GOING TO USE YOUR PHONE, SIR. HELLO? IS THIS PROFESSOR OCHANOMIZU?
WHAT?! THE RESERVOIR?! REALLY? FOR SURE? YOU'VE GOTTA BE KIDDING, I HOPE!
THE GAS PEOPLE'RE GONNA POISON THE WATER, PROFESSOR!
I'LL NEED TO DO AN INVESTIGATION LATER... TRY TO SEAL THEM IN A GLASS BOX FOR NOW!
WE'VE GOTTA DO AS THE PROFESSOR SAYS...
POOR GUY... HE WAS PROBABLY A GOOD PERSON UNTIL HE WAS OVERCOME BY THE GAS...

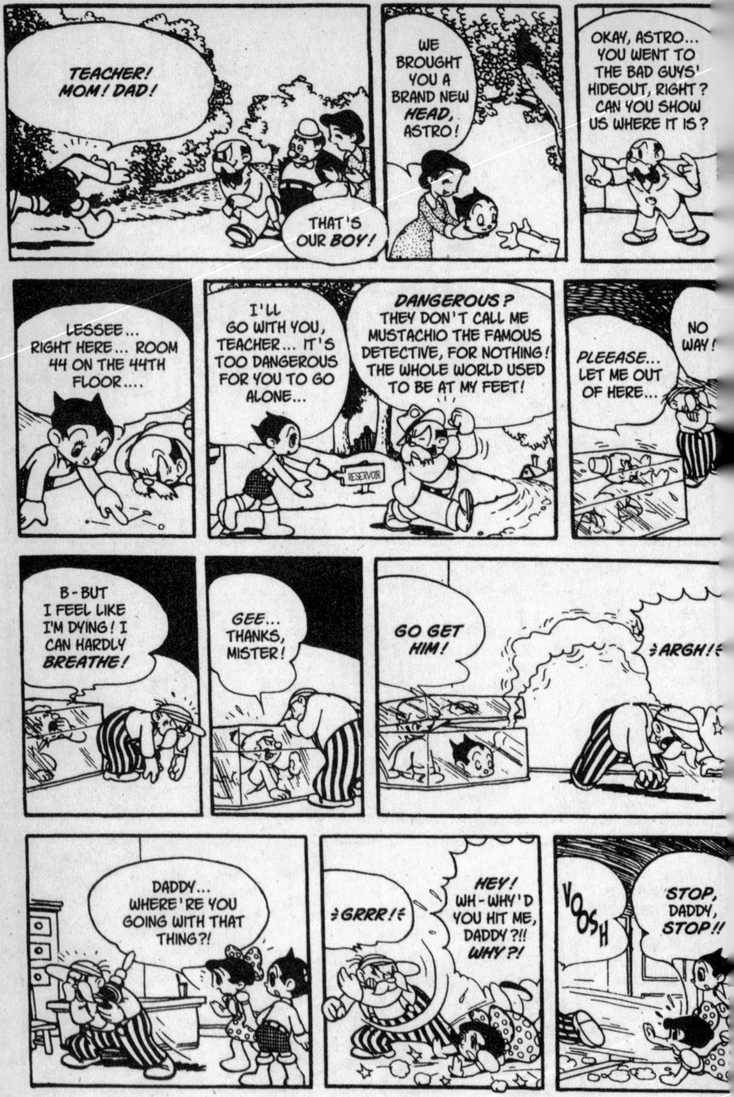

TEACHER! MOM! DAD!
THAT'S OUR BOY!
WE BROUGHT YOU A BRAND NEW HEAD, ASTRO!
OKAY, ASTRO... YOU WENT TO THE BAD GUYS' HIDEOUT, RIGHT? CAN YOU SHOW US WHERE IT IS?
LESSEE... RIGHT HERE... ROOM 44 ON THE 44TH FLOOR....
I'LL GO WITH YOU, TEACHER... IT'S TOO DANGEROUS FOR YOU TO GO ALONE...
RESERVOIR
DANGEROUS? THEY DON'T CALL ME MUSTACHIO THE FAMOUS DETECTIVE, FOR NOTHING! THE WHOLE WORLD USED TO BE AT MY FEET!
PLEEASE... LET ME OUT OF HERE...
NO WAY!
B-BUT I FEEL LIKE I'M DYING! I CAN HARDLY BREATHE!
GEE... THANKS, MISTER!
GO GET HIM!
ARGH!
DADDY... WHERE'RE YOU GOING WITH THAT THING?!
GRRR!
HEY! WH-WHY'D YOU HIT ME, DADDY?!! WHY?!
VOOSH
STOP, DADDY, STOP!!

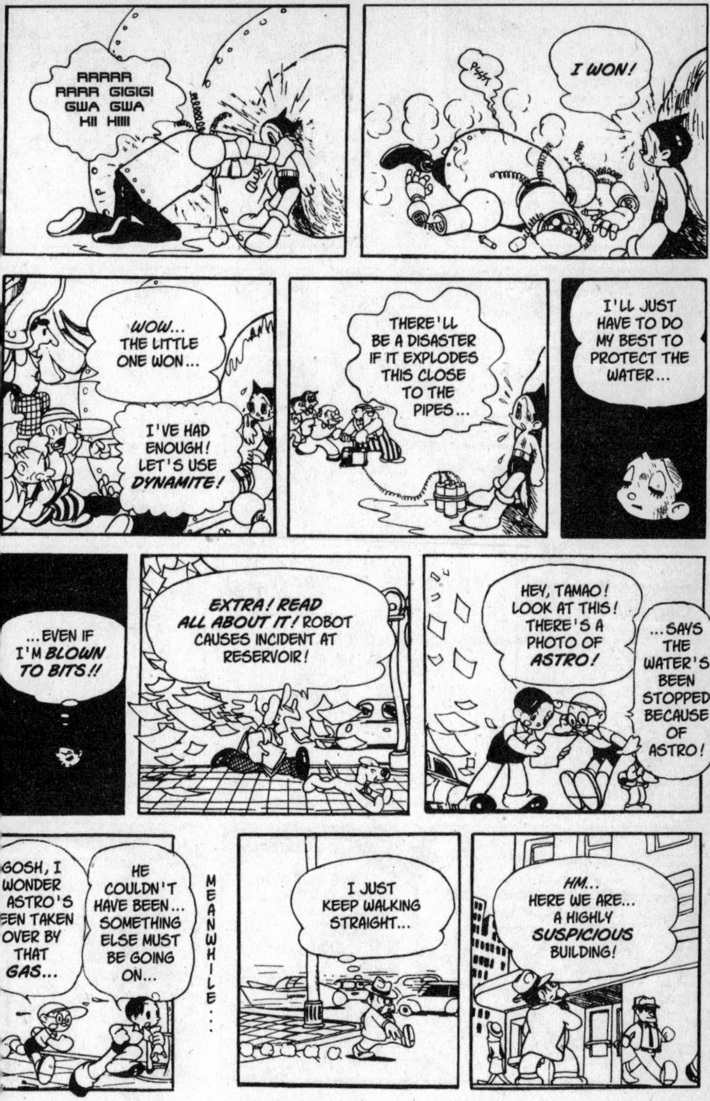
RRRRR
RRRR GIGIGI
GWA GWA
HII HIIII
PSSST
I WON!
WOW... THE LITTLE ONE WON...
I'VE HAD ENOUGH! LET'S USE DYNAMITE!
THERE'LL BE A DISASTER IF IT EXPLODES THIS CLOSE TO THE PIPES...
I'LL JUST HAVE TO DO MY BEST TO PROTECT THE WATER...
...EVEN IF I'M BLOWN TO BITS!!
EXTRA! READ ALL ABOUT IT! ROBOT CAUSES INCIDENT AT RESERVOIR!
HEY, TAMAO! LOOK AT THIS! THERE'S A PHOTO OF ASTRO!
...SAYS THE WATER'S BEEN STOPPED BECAUSE OF ASTRO!
GOSH, I WONDER ASTRO'S EEN TAKEN OVER BY THAT GAS...
HE COULDN'T HAVE BEEN... SOMETHING ELSE MUST BE GOING ON...
MEANWHILE...
I JUST KEEP WALKING STRAIGHT...
HM... HERE WE ARE... A HIGHLY SUSPICIOUS BUILDING!

⋝HMPH.. R.R. PHARMA-CEUTICALS... FANCY IN NAME, ONLY...

PHARMACEUTICALS

LOOKS LIKE THE SAME DRUG I SAW AT THE RESERVOIR!

WELL, WELL... A VISITOR! _PLEASE DO COME IN!_

I'D LIKE TO BUY A CERTAIN BLUE DRUG... I'VE HEARD YOU MAKE IT HERE...

_AH,_ YOU MEAN _METHYLENE BLUE,_ PERHAPS!

NO... SOME-THING SLIGHTLY MORE _TOXIC!_

MAYBE YOU MEAN _CARBONYL METROXIN?_

NO! THAT'S IT THERE!

THAT'S NOT FOR SALE!

BUT _THIS_ IS WHAT I WANT!

I SAID IT'S _NOT FOR SALE!_ GIVE IT _BACK!_

WHAT THE —?!

RATTLE RATTLE CLANK

YOU'RE NOT LEAVING NOW!

ALL RIGHT, MR. MUSTACHIO! WHERE'D YOU HEAR ABOUT THAT BLUE DRUG, EH? IT'S TIME TO _FESS UP!_

TIME FOR _YOU_ TO CONFESS, I'D SAY! I BET YOU'RE _POSSESSED_ BY THAT GAS!

YOU ALREADY KNOW TOO MUCH FOR ME TO LET YOU LIVE, MUSTACHIO...

216

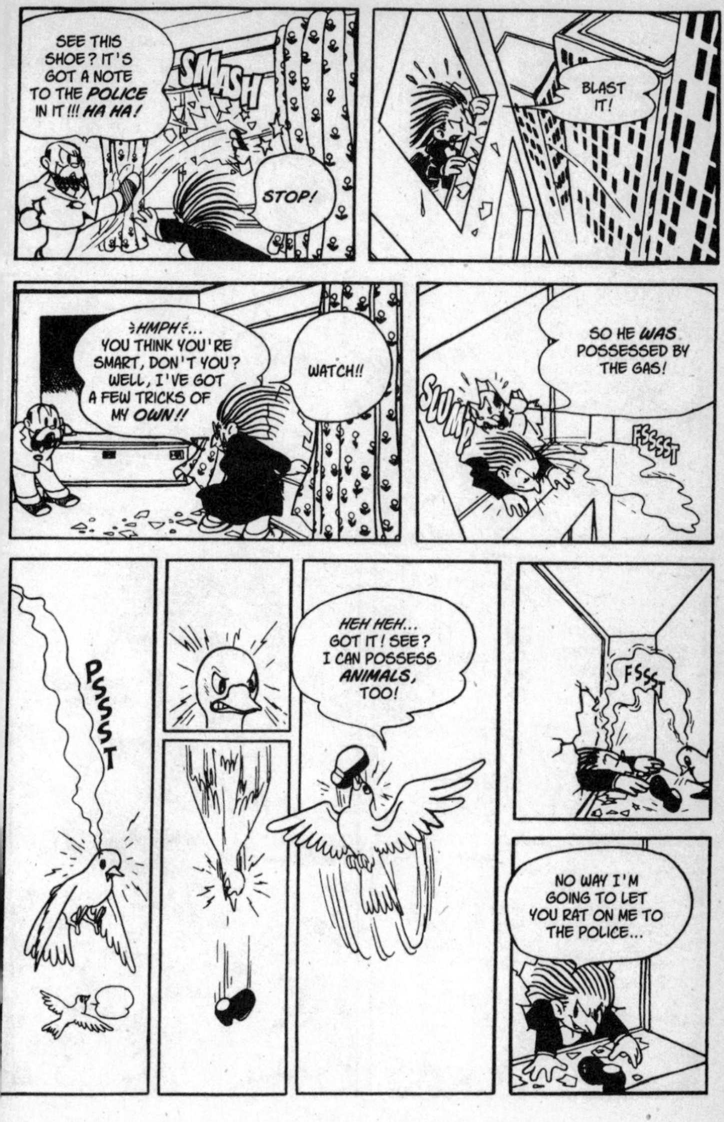

SEE THIS SHOE? IT'S GOT A NOTE TO THE *POLICE* IN IT!!! *HA HA!*
SMASH
STOP!
BLAST IT!
≯HMPH≮... YOU THINK YOU'RE SMART, DON'T YOU? WELL, I'VE GOT A FEW TRICKS OF MY *OWN!!*
WATCH!!
SLUMP
SO HE *WAS* POSSESSED BY THE GAS!
FSSSST
PSSST
HEH HEH... GOT IT! SEE? I CAN POSSESS *ANIMALS,* TOO!
FSSST
NO WAY I'M GOING TO LET YOU RAT ON ME TO THE POLICE...

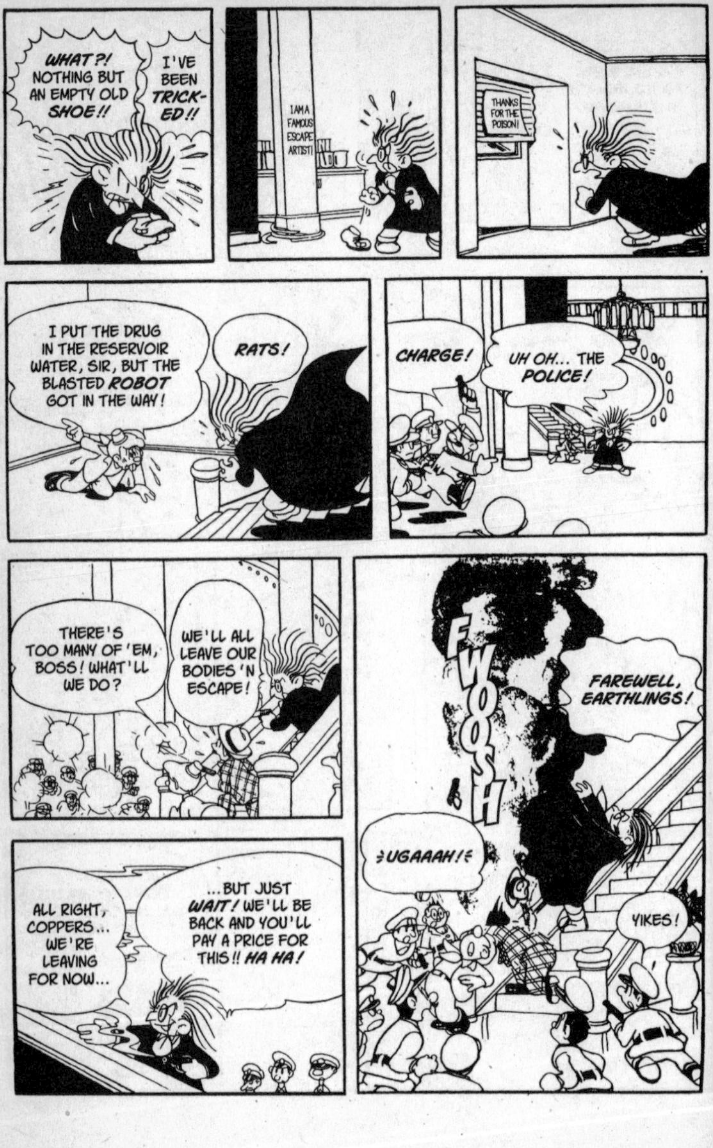
WHAT?! NOTHING BUT AN EMPTY OLD SHOE!!
I'VE BEEN TRICKED!!
I AM A FAMOUS ESCAPE ARTIST!
THANKS FOR THE POISON!
I PUT THE DRUG IN THE RESERVOIR WATER, SIR, BUT THE BLASTED ROBOT GOT IN THE WAY!
RATS!
CHARGE!
UH OH... THE POLICE!
THERE'S TOO MANY OF 'EM, BOSS! WHAT'LL WE DO?
WE'LL ALL LEAVE OUR BODIES 'N ESCAPE!
ALL RIGHT, COPPERS... WE'RE LEAVING FOR NOW...
...BUT JUST WAIT! WE'LL BE BACK AND YOU'LL PAY A PRICE FOR THIS!! HA HA!
FWOOSH
FAREWELL, EARTHLINGS!
UGAAAH!
YIKES!

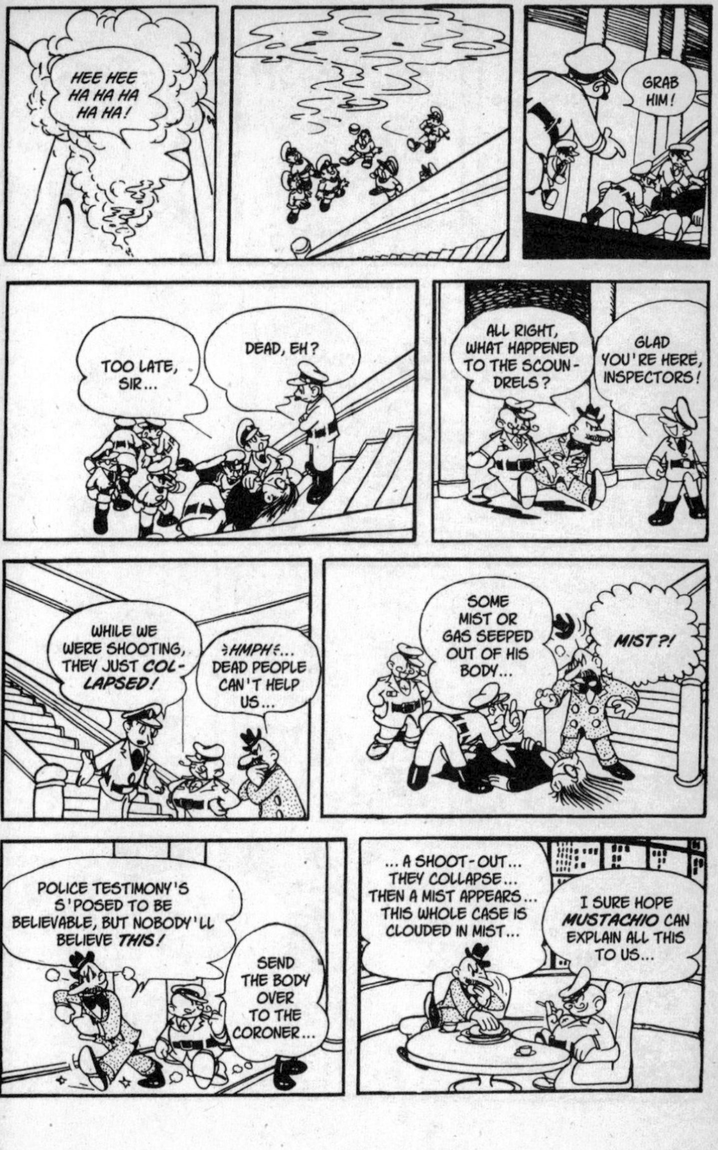
HEE HEE HA HA HA HA HA!
GRAB HIM!
TOO LATE, SIR...
DEAD, EH?
ALL RIGHT, WHAT HAPPENED TO THE SCOUNDRELS?
GLAD YOU'RE HERE, INSPECTORS!
WHILE WE WERE SHOOTING, THEY JUST COLLAPSED!
HMPH... DEAD PEOPLE CAN'T HELP US...
SOME MIST OR GAS SEEPED OUT OF HIS BODY...
MIST?!
POLICE TESTIMONY'S S'POSED TO BE BELIEVABLE, BUT NOBODY'LL BELIEVE THIS!
SEND THE BODY OVER TO THE CORONER...
... A SHOOT-OUT... THEY COLLAPSE... THEN A MIST APPEARS... THIS WHOLE CASE IS CLOUDED IN MIST...
I SURE HOPE MUSTACHIO CAN EXPLAIN ALL THIS TO US...

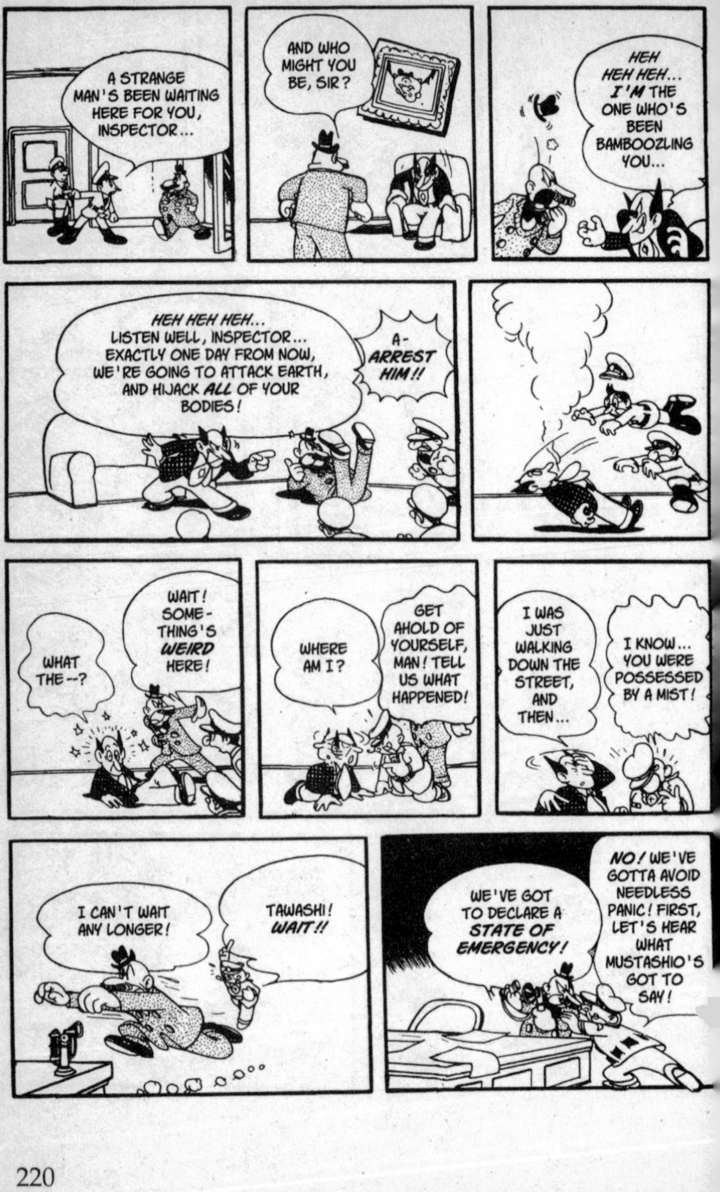
A STRANGE MAN'S BEEN WAITING HERE FOR YOU, INSPECTOR...
AND WHO MIGHT YOU BE, SIR?
HEH HEH HEH... *I'M* THE ONE WHO'S BEEN BAMBOOZLING YOU...
HEH HEH HEH... LISTEN WELL, INSPECTOR... EXACTLY ONE DAY FROM NOW, WE'RE GOING TO ATTACK EARTH, AND HIJACK *ALL* OF YOUR BODIES!
A- *ARREST HIM!!*
WHAT THE--?
WAIT! SOME-THING'S *WEIRD* HERE!
WHERE AM I?
GET AHOLD OF YOURSELF, MAN! TELL US WHAT HAPPENED!
I WAS JUST WALKING DOWN THE STREET, AND THEN...
I KNOW... YOU WERE POSSESSED BY A MIST!
I CAN'T WAIT ANY LONGER!
TAWASHI! *WAIT!!*
WE'VE GOT TO DECLARE A *STATE OF EMERGENCY!*
NO! WE'VE GOTTA AVOID NEEDLESS PANIC! FIRST, LET'S HEAR WHAT MUSTASHIO'S GOT TO SAY!

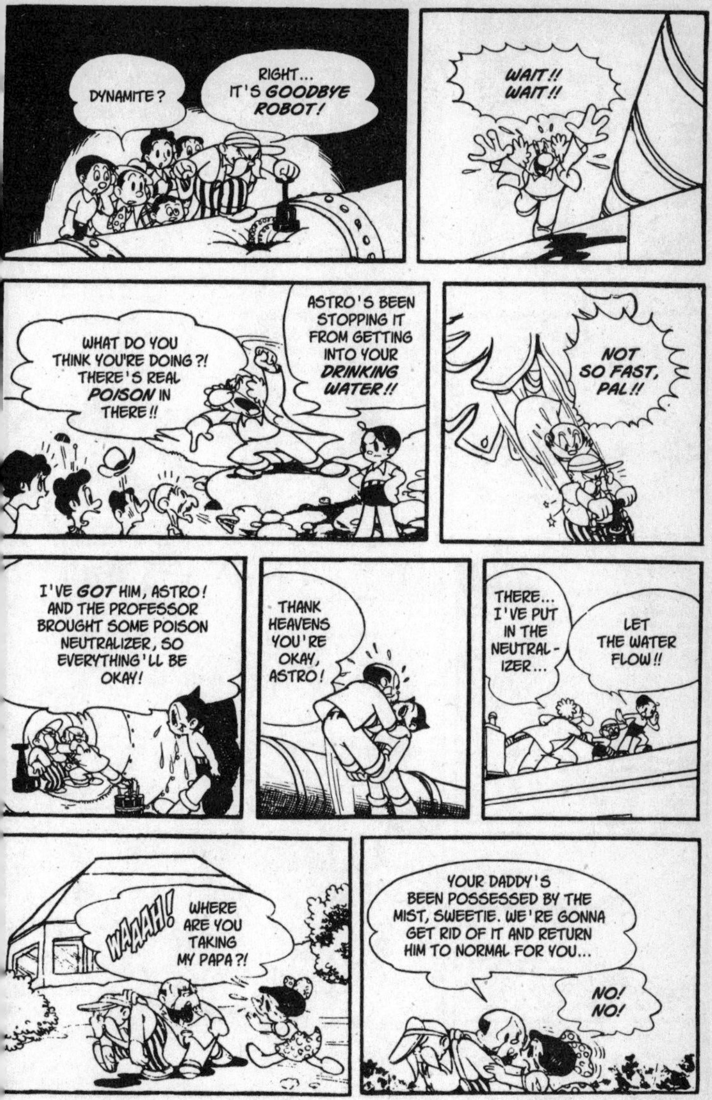
DYNAMITE?
RIGHT... IT'S GOODBYE ROBOT!
WAIT!! WAIT!!
WHAT DO YOU THINK YOU'RE DOING?! THERE'S REAL POISON IN THERE!!
ASTRO'S BEEN STOPPING IT FROM GETTING INTO YOUR DRINKING WATER!!
NOT SO FAST, PAL!!
I'VE GOT HIM, ASTRO! AND THE PROFESSOR BROUGHT SOME POISON NEUTRALIZER, SO EVERYTHING'LL BE OKAY!
THANK HEAVENS YOU'RE OKAY, ASTRO!
THERE... I'VE PUT IN THE NEUTRAL-IZER...
LET THE WATER FLOW!!
WAAAH!
WHERE ARE YOU TAKING MY PAPA?!
YOUR DADDY'S BEEN POSSESSED BY THE MIST, SWEETIE. WE'RE GONNA GET RID OF IT AND RETURN HIM TO NORMAL FOR YOU...
NO! NO!

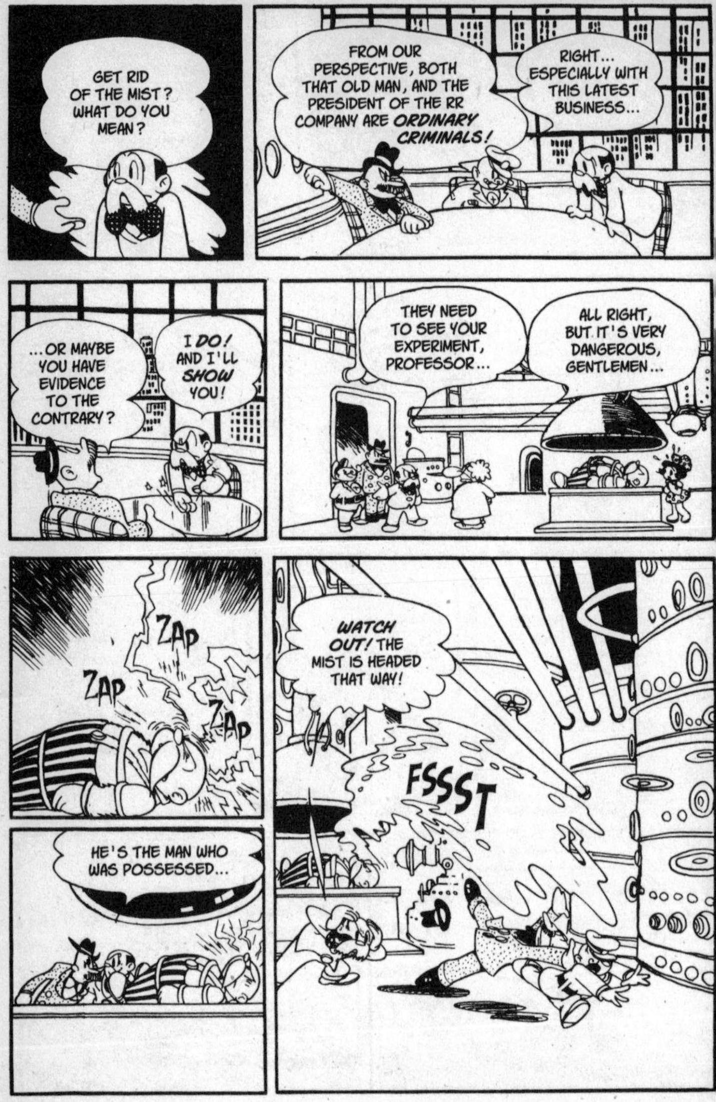
GET RID OF THE MIST? WHAT DO YOU MEAN?
FROM OUR PERSPECTIVE, BOTH THAT OLD MAN, AND THE PRESIDENT OF THE RR COMPANY ARE ORDINARY CRIMINALS!
RIGHT... ESPECIALLY WITH THIS LATEST BUSINESS...
...OR MAYBE YOU HAVE EVIDENCE TO THE CONTRARY?
I DO! AND I'LL SHOW YOU!
THEY NEED TO SEE YOUR EXPERIMENT, PROFESSOR...
ALL RIGHT, BUT IT'S VERY DANGEROUS, GENTLEMEN...
ZAP
ZAP
ZAP
HE'S THE MAN WHO WAS POSSESSED...
WATCH OUT! THE MIST IS HEADED THAT WAY!
FSSST

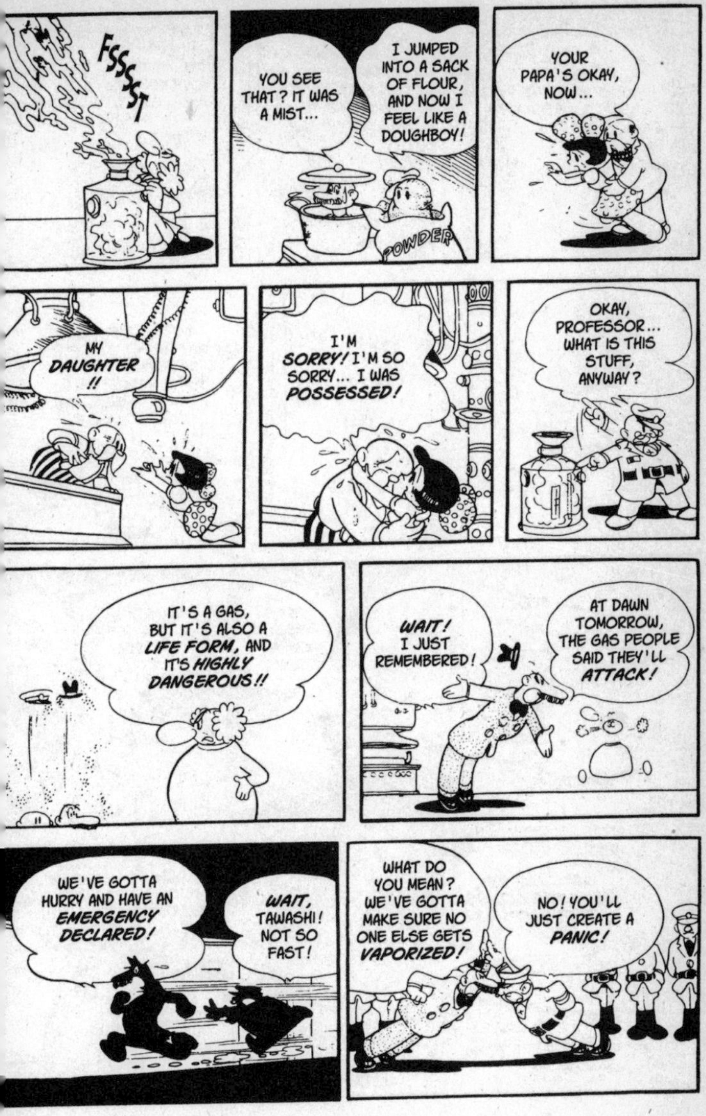
FSSSST
YOU SEE THAT? IT WAS A MIST...
I JUMPED INTO A SACK OF FLOUR, AND NOW I FEEL LIKE A DOUGHBOY!
POWDER
YOUR PAPA'S OKAY, NOW...
MY DAUGHTER !!
I'M SORRY! I'M SO SORRY... I WAS POSSESSED!
OKAY, PROFESSOR... WHAT IS THIS STUFF, ANYWAY?
IT'S A GAS, BUT IT'S ALSO A LIFE FORM, AND IT'S HIGHLY DANGEROUS!!
WAIT! I JUST REMEMBERED!
AT DAWN TOMORROW, THE GAS PEOPLE SAID THEY'LL ATTACK!
WE'VE GOTTA HURRY AND HAVE AN EMERGENCY DECLARED!
WAIT, TAWASHI! NOT SO FAST!
WHAT DO YOU MEAN? WE'VE GOTTA MAKE SURE NO ONE ELSE GETS VAPORIZED!
NO! YOU'LL JUST CREATE A PANIC!

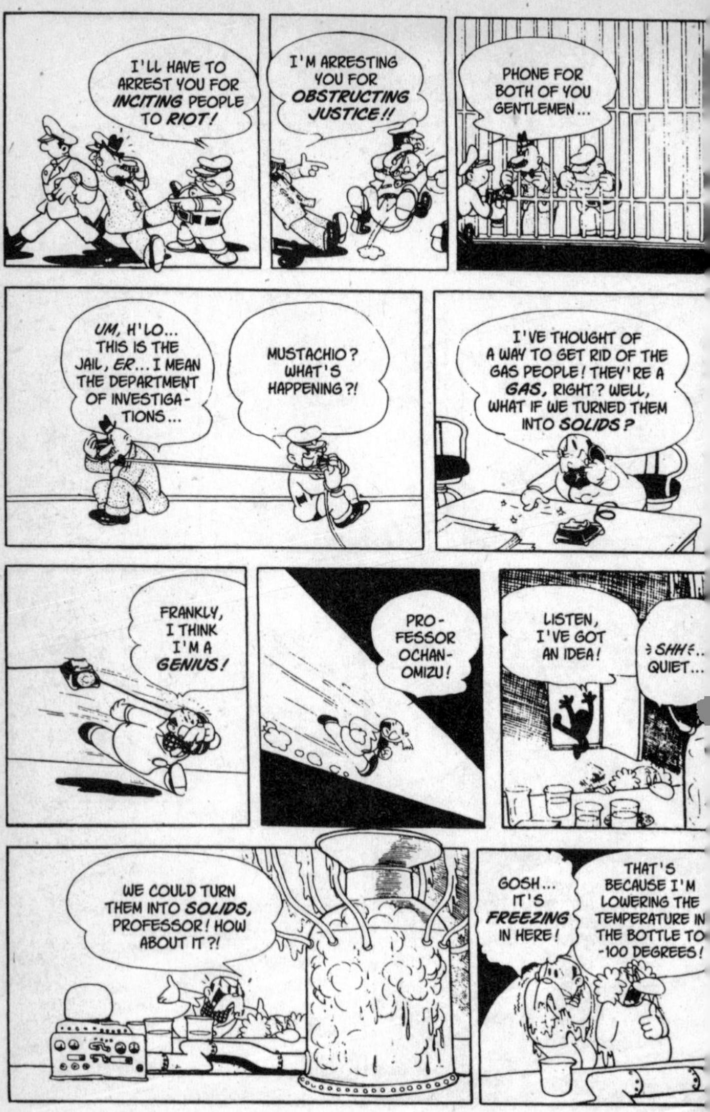
I'LL HAVE TO ARREST YOU FOR *INCITING* PEOPLE TO *RIOT!*
I'M ARRESTING YOU FOR *OBSTRUCTING JUSTICE!!*
PHONE FOR BOTH OF YOU GENTLEMEN...
UM, H'LO... THIS IS THE JAIL, *ER*... I MEAN THE DEPARTMENT OF INVESTIGA-TIONS...
MUSTACHIO? WHAT'S HAPPENING?!
I'VE THOUGHT OF A WAY TO GET RID OF THE GAS PEOPLE! THEY'RE A *GAS,* RIGHT? WELL, WHAT IF WE TURNED THEM INTO *SOLIDS?*
FRANKLY, I THINK I'M A *GENIUS!*
PRO-FESSOR OCHAN-OMIZU!
LISTEN, I'VE GOT AN IDEA!
SHH.. QUIET...
WE COULD TURN THEM INTO *SOLIDS,* PROFESSOR! HOW ABOUT IT?!
GOSH... IT'S *FREEZING* IN HERE!
THAT'S BECAUSE I'M LOWERING THE TEMPERATURE IN THE BOTTLE TO -100 DEGREES!

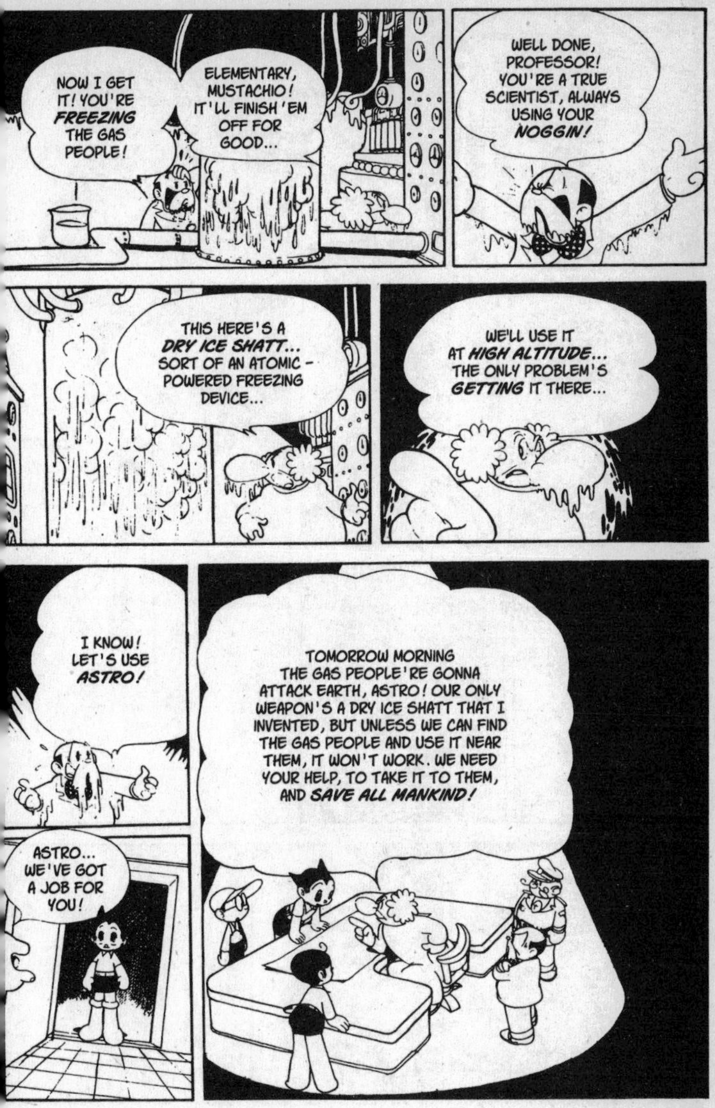
NOW I GET IT! YOU'RE FREEZING THE GAS PEOPLE!
ELEMENTARY, MUSTACHIO! IT'LL FINISH 'EM OFF FOR GOOD...
WELL DONE, PROFESSOR! YOU'RE A TRUE SCIENTIST, ALWAYS USING YOUR NOGGIN!
THIS HERE'S A DRY ICE SHATT... SORT OF AN ATOMIC-POWERED FREEZING DEVICE...
WE'LL USE IT AT HIGH ALTITUDE... THE ONLY PROBLEM'S GETTING IT THERE...
I KNOW! LET'S USE ASTRO!
ASTRO... WE'VE GOT A JOB FOR YOU!
TOMORROW MORNING THE GAS PEOPLE'RE GONNA ATTACK EARTH, ASTRO! OUR ONLY WEAPON'S A DRY ICE SHATT THAT I INVENTED, BUT UNLESS WE CAN FIND THE GAS PEOPLE AND USE IT NEAR THEM, IT WON'T WORK. WE NEED YOUR HELP, TO TAKE IT TO THEM, AND SAVE ALL MANKIND!

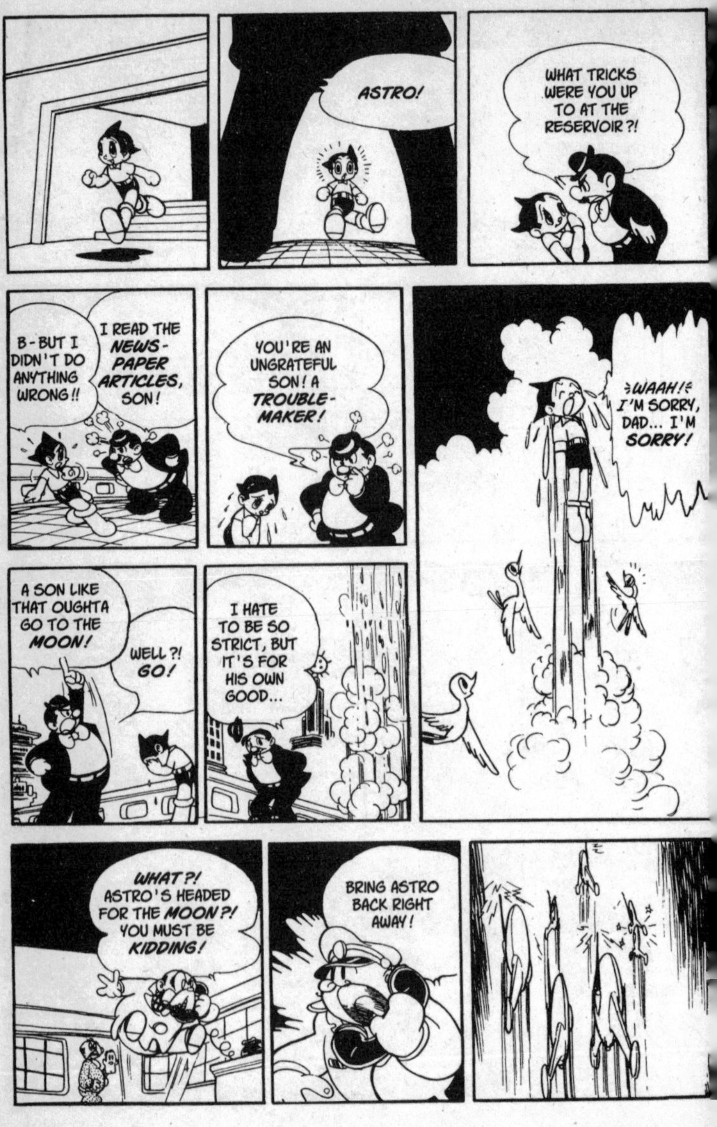
ASTRO!
WHAT TRICKS WERE YOU UP TO AT THE RESERVOIR?!
B-BUT I DIDN'T DO ANYTHING WRONG!!
I READ THE NEWS-PAPER ARTICLES, SON!
YOU'RE AN UNGRATEFUL SON! A TROUBLE-MAKER!
WAAH! I'M SORRY, DAD... I'M SORRY!
A SON LIKE THAT OUGHTA GO TO THE MOON!
WELL?! GO!
I HATE TO BE SO STRICT, BUT IT'S FOR HIS OWN GOOD...
WHAT?! ASTRO'S HEADED FOR THE MOON?! YOU MUST BE KIDDING!
BRING ASTRO BACK RIGHT AWAY!

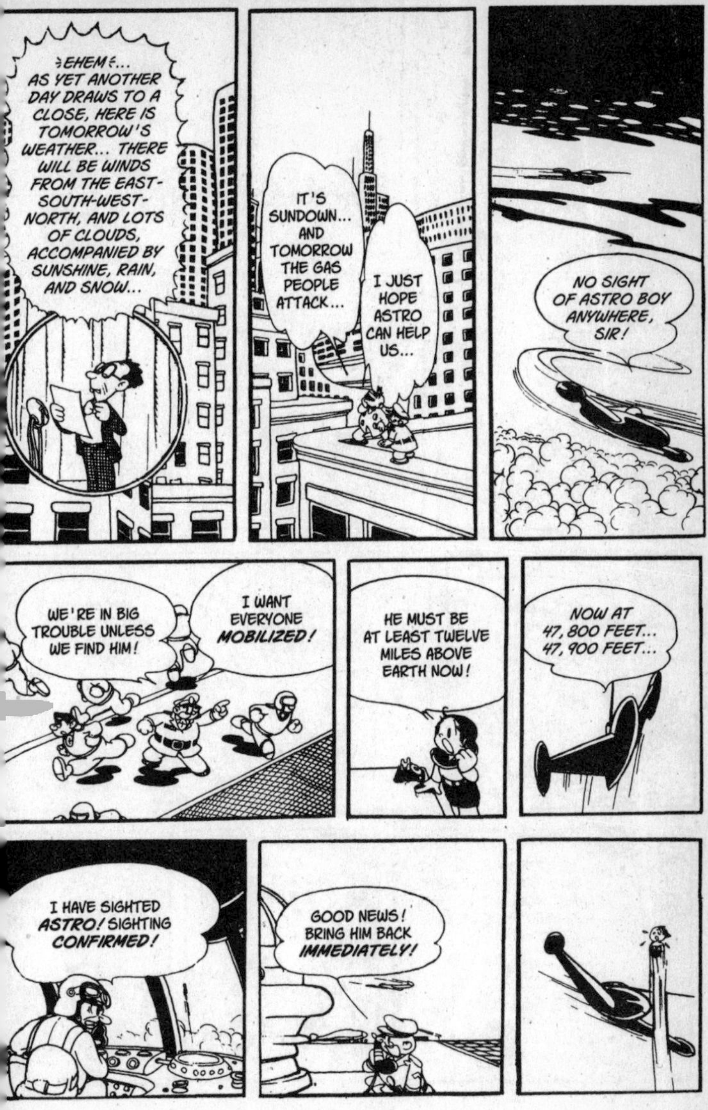

EHEM... AS YET ANOTHER DAY DRAWS TO A CLOSE, HERE IS TOMORROW'S WEATHER... THERE WILL BE WINDS FROM THE EAST-SOUTH-WEST-NORTH, AND LOTS OF CLOUDS, ACCOMPANIED BY SUNSHINE, RAIN, AND SNOW...
IT'S SUNDOWN... AND TOMORROW THE GAS PEOPLE ATTACK...
I JUST HOPE ASTRO CAN HELP US...
NO SIGHT OF ASTRO BOY ANYWHERE, SIR!
WE'RE IN BIG TROUBLE UNLESS WE FIND HIM!
I WANT EVERYONE MOBILIZED!
HE MUST BE AT LEAST TWELVE MILES ABOVE EARTH NOW!
NOW AT 47,800 FEET... 47,900 FEET...
I HAVE SIGHTED ASTRO! SIGHTING CONFIRMED!
GOOD NEWS! BRING HIM BACK IMMEDIATELY!

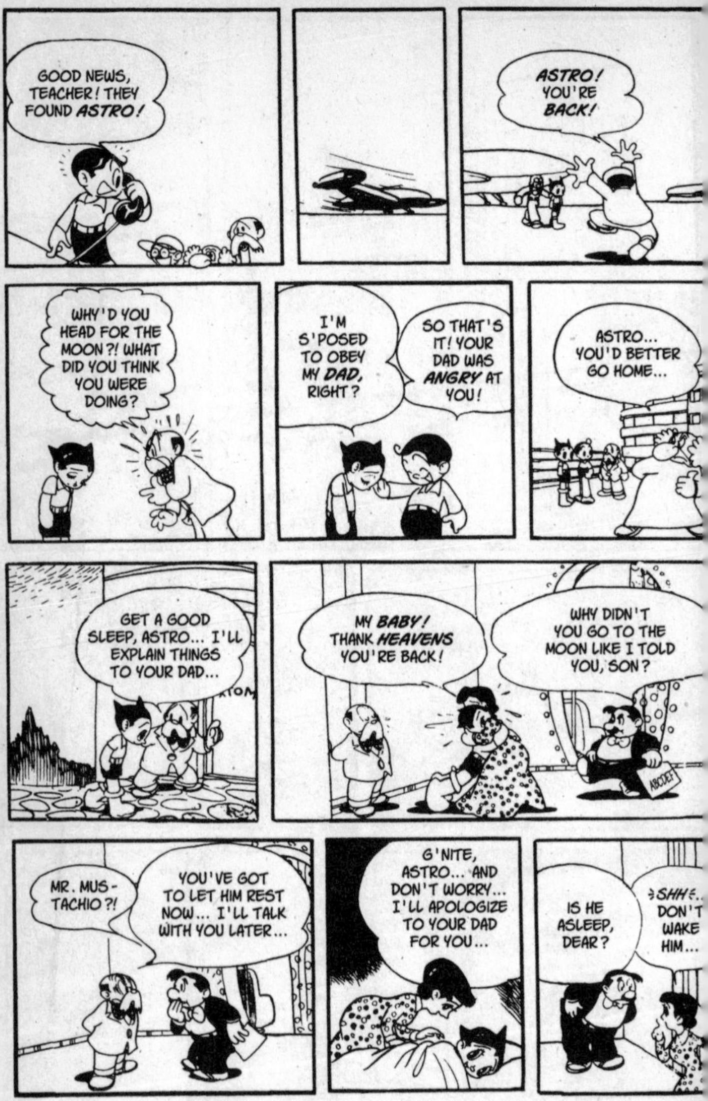
GOOD NEWS, TEACHER! THEY FOUND ASTRO!
ASTRO! YOU'RE BACK!
WHY'D YOU HEAD FOR THE MOON?! WHAT DID YOU THINK YOU WERE DOING?
I'M S'POSED TO OBEY MY DAD, RIGHT?
SO THAT'S IT! YOUR DAD WAS ANGRY AT YOU!
ASTRO... YOU'D BETTER GO HOME...
GET A GOOD SLEEP, ASTRO... I'LL EXPLAIN THINGS TO YOUR DAD...
ATOM
MY BABY! THANK HEAVENS YOU'RE BACK!
WHY DIDN'T YOU GO TO THE MOON LIKE I TOLD YOU, SON?
ABCDEF
MR. MUS-TACHIO?!
YOU'VE GOT TO LET HIM REST NOW... I'LL TALK WITH YOU LATER...
G'NITE, ASTRO... AND DON'T WORRY... I'LL APOLOGIZE TO YOUR DAD FOR YOU...
IS HE ASLEEP, DEAR?
SHH... DON'T WAKE HIM...

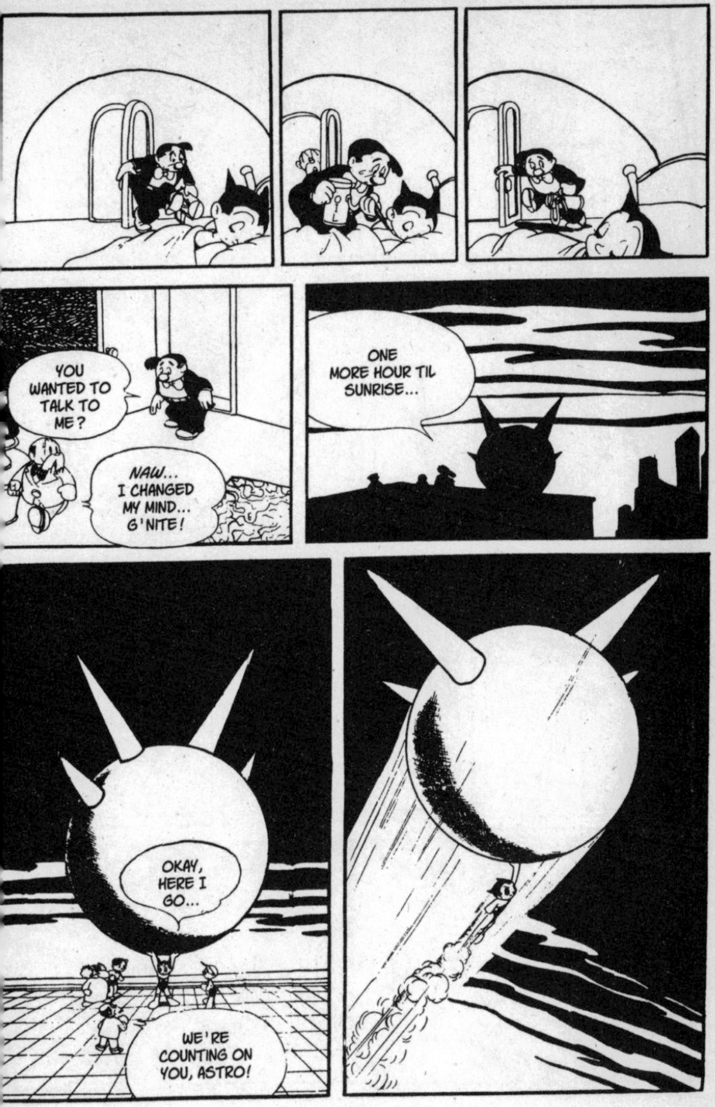
YOU WANTED TO TALK TO ME?
NAW... I CHANGED MY MIND... G'NITE!
ONE MORE HOUR TIL SUNRISE...
OKAY, HERE I GO...
WE'RE COUNTING ON YOU, ASTRO!

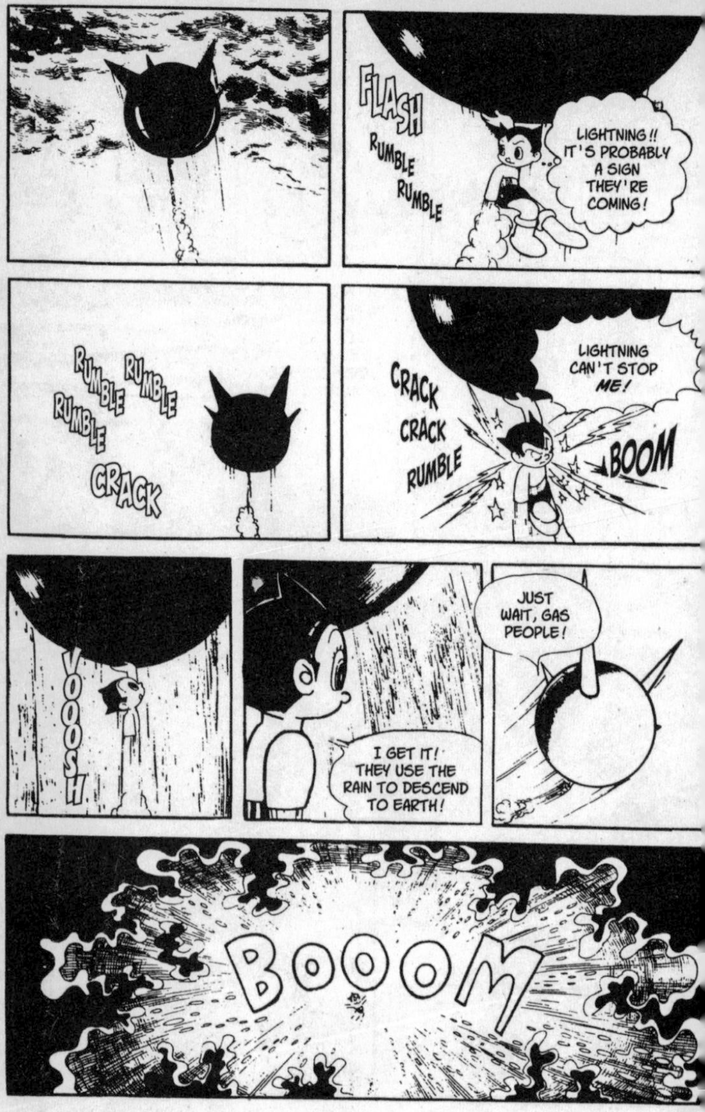
FLASH
RUMBLE
RUMBLE
LIGHTNING!! IT'S PROBABLY A SIGN THEY'RE COMING!
RUMBLE
RUMBLE
RUMBLE
CRACK
LIGHTNING CAN'T STOP ME!
CRACK
CRACK
RUMBLE
BOOM
VOOOSH
I GET IT! THEY USE THE RAIN TO DESCEND TO EARTH!
JUST WAIT, GAS PEOPLE!
BOOOM

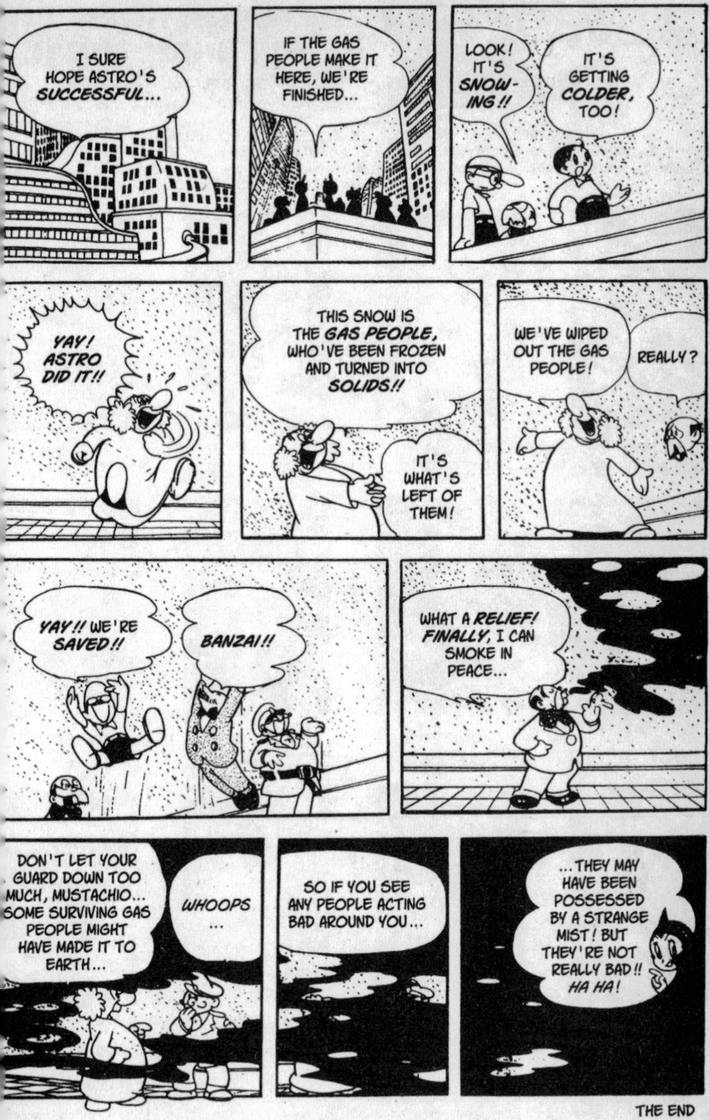

I SURE HOPE ASTRO'S SUCCESSFUL...
IF THE GAS PEOPLE MAKE IT HERE, WE'RE FINISHED...
LOOK! IT'S SNOW-ING!!
IT'S GETTING COLDER, TOO!
YAY! ASTRO DID IT!!
THIS SNOW IS THE GAS PEOPLE, WHO'VE BEEN FROZEN AND TURNED INTO SOLIDS!!
IT'S WHAT'S LEFT OF THEM!
WE'VE WIPED OUT THE GAS PEOPLE!
REALLY?
YAY!! WE'RE SAVED!!
BANZAI!!
WHAT A RELIEF! FINALLY, I CAN SMOKE IN PEACE...
DON'T LET YOUR GUARD DOWN TOO MUCH, MUSTACHIO... SOME SURVIVING GAS PEOPLE MIGHT HAVE MADE IT TO EARTH...
WHOOPS ...
SO IF YOU SEE ANY PEOPLE ACTING BAD AROUND YOU...
...THEY MAY HAVE BEEN POSSESSED BY A STRANGE MIST! BUT THEY'RE NOT REALLY BAD!! HA HA!

THE END

Osamu Tezuka's Original

ASTRO BOY®

JET-POWERED! SUPER-STRONG
EVIL-ROBOT-BASHING!
ALIEN-INVASION-SMASHING!

Each volume retails for $9.95!
New volumes available every month!

Volume 1
1-56971-676-5

Volume 2
1-56971-677-3

Volume 3
1-56971-678-1

Volume 4
1-56971-679-

Volume 5
1-56971-680-3

Volume 6
1-56971-681-1

Volume 7
1-56971-790-7

Volume 8
1-56971-791-

Volume 9
1-56971-792-3

Volume 10
1-56971-793-1

Volume 11
1-56971-812-1

Volume 12
1-56971-813-